Victorian Keats and Romantic Carlyle

The Fusions and Confusions of Literary Periods

Edited by C.C. Barfoot

Amsterdam - Atlanta, GA
1999

ISBN 90-420-0588-2 (bound)

Cover design: Hendrik van Delft

Printed in The Netherlands

CONTENTS

INTRODUCTION: VICTORIAN KEATS AND ROMANTIC CARLYLE

For the most part, *Victorian Keats and Romantic Carlyle* derives from the Ninth Leiden October Conference, the idea for which originated in a few lines of a poem I had written many years before, itself based on a earlier lecture. The larger area with which the 1995 conference was concerned becomes clearer if one considers the text of the whole poem, entitled "Victoria's Beards":

> Sometime in the mid-nineteenth century
> men grew beards again, after two hundred beardless years
> in polite society, in the plush decades
> after the Great Exhibition and in tribute
> to the men besieging Sevastopol (who
> also brought smoking back into fashion,
> according to Trevelyan).
>
> Who was the first great poet
> since Donne to wear a beard? Browning
> or Tennyson?
> Undoubtedly their beards were different
> from the trim silk-hosed Elizabethan
> variety. Yet can anyone
> imagine Keats or Shelley or Byron
> with a beard and a pipe, who
> did not even live to ride on the railway?
> Though Carlyle did
> — grow a beard, smoke a pipe (a churchwarden),
> ride on a railway train to survive
> his exact contemporary, Keats (b. 1795), to become
> an eminent Victorian, a Victorian sage
> with a beard.
>
> Victorian beards did not distinguish poets
> from bankers or officers or engine-drivers or kings.
> Certainly beards after forty did not make
> Dickens or Tennyson appear more stable
> or less dis-eased; while Browning was as bluff and hearty

before the beard as after (although he forgot what
Sordello ever meant). Carlyle's prose
was wild and shaggy before his whiskers showed it.

Nevertheless
beards would not have caught on
had they not manifested an otherwise hidden image
of Victorian society: Victorians
had to have their beards as
Americans their crewcuts.

The Sage beard was neither jaunty
nor satanic (derived neither from paintbrush
nor man-about-town). It was a solemn beard, a grave
beard, a beard to add thirty years to your age, a beard
to rumble in, to frighten little children in,
for little children to hop in, for birds to nest in,
for earwigs to bore in, spiders spin in.
A beard to hide behind, a patriarchal beard. A married
beard (who could have gone courting in such a beard?). A
beard of masculine independence, of ancient biblical vigour
promising immortality to middle age, threatening
eternity to women. The beard
of an earnest man desiring
to be taken seriously, a man with
a stake in society and a share in the nation's
prosperity.

The beard is a mark of gravity
in a man whose decisions are far-reaching, dutiful,
burdensome and responsible,
touching men and places throughout the globe
landing each morning on his plate with *The Times*,
the "thunderer", concerning the franchise, education,
hygiene, his investments, poverty, prostitution, involving
black men, brown men, yellow men, and wee-
men, Russians, Prussians, Turks, Indians, Moslems,
convicts and babus, etc., etc.
and including anxieties
about vestments and altar
candles, opium,
evolution
& God.

The beard was necessary
in a perplexed society to mutter
solemn imprecations in, to utter dire

warnings from, a place in which to let the voice lose its
bewildered self. The beard was a portable growlery
for men who knew they could change the world, if others
would believe them, with railways and lathes and looms,
alter the face of the earth, now
that Nobodaddy had gone missing
down his white fissioning beard — a poetic suspicion
confirmed by the gay science in 1882 (Nietzsche's
Die fröhliche Wissenschaft) which announced
God was dead (although for some years
the Poor Law commissioners had let him out on Sundays
from the workhouse, like Old Nandy).

Victoria's beards were swords and drawbridges.
A beard was a flag and a vizor, a mask of
patriarch and wildman, showing the
father to hide the child. Making
a man uneasy about whether
his words answer to his appearance
and win respect unearned by the eyes
above, behind the bearded front. A
man's conscience is troubled
to vindicate the mystery
and allure of his beard. A man
might beard his way out of dilemmas, hold on
by his beard, parachute
with his beard, trim his beard
with and to the locomotive of progress.

The Tsar and his cousin,
the King, kept their beards; Franz Josef
went down with his beard, while the Kaiser
was smooth-chopped.
All other
beards too were shaven off
in time for the Great War.

One of the several questions prompting this poem, and it is a question that remains to tease us still, is what defines a period, a cultural period or a literary period? Styles of language, styles of art, styles of dress, of grooming, of decorum? Long hair, short hair, long skirts or mini-skirts, wigs or beards: what have these literally superficial features of style and fashion to do with behaviour and manners, social attitudes, or artistic and literary motives, themes, modes and forms?

Since 1995 was the bicentenary of the birth both of John Keats and Thomas Carlyle, two very different writers one rarely thinks of in any sort of combination, although brought together for the first time in my imagination in "Victoria's Beards", they became the focus of the conference, and hence of this book. As I suggested in the "Call for Papers" for the Conference it is difficult to think either of Carlyle as a young Romantic or of Keats as a Victorian Sage with a beard, but went on to propose that

> had Carlyle died prematurely (although not quite as prematurely as Keats) and had Keats lived to a ripe old age, might it have been that we would now be considering the Romantic Carlyle and the Victorian Keats? The bicentenary of the birth of these two important writers provides an occasion to consider the use and abuse, and the fusions and confusions, of period terms in literary history and in literary criticism. Does Carlyle represent literary Romanticism as typically as Keats? Does Keats's work give us any cause to believe that he might have developed into a Victorian poet? And do these terms "Romanticism" and "Victorian" have any useful literary historical and literary critical value? If so, what are the marks of the transition from one to the other? Or is the existence of such a transition an illusion?

As a result of this proposition an interesting range of papers and, subsequently, of essays came together, in some instances considering aspects of either Keats or Carlyle independently, or together, and on other occasions focusing on contemporaries of one or other or of both and exploring the effect of their literary and ideological relationships, and the often indefinable sense that we all have of different styles, manners and periods, as well as the awareness that we might all be equally deceived about such distinctive boundaries and definitions.

As with all of the publications stimulated by the Leiden October Conferences, there are many individuals to whom we are indebted — the original contributors of papers, as well as those who later agreed to write something for this volume, and those who ensured the smooth running of the original event — and also, as ever, the Leiden Faculty of Letters and KNAW (the Royal Dutch Academy of Sciences) who provided all the necessary financial support. I am grateful to Jacqueline Burrough for her assistance in the penultimate stages of the preparation of the book and in the compiling of the Index. One brief bibliographical note is in order: for references to Carlyle's works, wherever possible the appropriate volume of the Centenary Edition has been used (*The Works of Thomas Carlyle*, ed. H.D. Traill, Centenary Edition, 30 vols, London, 1896-99); however, for Keats's poetry, where relevant, references will be given to various of the equally trustworthy editions.

C.C. Barfoot

"HYPERION TO A SATYR": KEATS, CARLYLE, AND "THIS STRANGE DISEASE OF MODERN LIFE"

C.C. BARFOOT

Neither of the quotations in my title should require any identification;[1] but their use for this introduction possibly requires a justification. I believe that it is not quite too fanciful to propose that of these two brothers in letters, united only by the not very remarkable fact that they were born in the same year, 1795, Keats was the Hyperion who died at the "absurdly early age"[2] of twenty-five, and Carlyle the Satyr who survived into the even greater absurdity of 85 years of age. Actually the circumstance of their being born in the same year is made slightly more remarkable by the fact that their actual birth dates, Keats on 31 October and Carlyle on 4 December, and their death dates, Keats on 23 February, Carlyle on 4 February are also surprisingly close. They were not only born within five weeks of each other, but they also died within three weeks of each other — allowing, in the case of their deaths, for a small matter of sixty years between.

I am no astrologer and I am not going to consider the implications of these coincidences and concurrences in association with the stars and their ascendent planets, but let us dwell on the comparison between Hyperion and Satyr for a while longer before moving onto other themes.

"Hyperion to a Satyr"

Hyperion — "See what grace was seated on [his] brow" — though destined by custom and myth to be usurped and fall, a Titan

1. But should anyone be puzzled, they are to be found in *Hamlet* (I.ii.140), and in Matthew Arnold's "The Scholar-Gipsy", l. 203 (*The Poems of Matthew Arnold*, ed. Kenneth Allott, London, 1965, 342).

2. Sandra M. Gilbert and Susan Gubar in *The Madwoman in the Attic: The Woman Writer and the Nineteenth-Century Literary Imagination*, New Haven and London, 1979, 553.

overwhelmed by the new gods, in Keats's version was doomed to remain unfinished, and like the poet himself left incomplete, launched through time and space with an uncertain landing:

> Anon rushed by the bright Hyperion;
> His flaming robes streamed out beyond his heels,
> And gave a roar, as if of earthly fire,
> That scared away the meek ethereal hours
> And made their dove-wings tremble. On he flared .... [3]

Until fairly recently, Keats was usually considered to be the least politically conscious of the great Romantic poets,[4] but the epic myth that he was struggling with in 1818 and 1819 was a prescriptive myth of revolution, with parallels with the French Revolution, in which an *ancien régime* is superseded by a new. Yet the fact that Keats had already abandoned the project either in its original form or in its recast version before the onset of his fatal illness suggests that he was not happy with the revolutionary theme. It is even more likely that he had problems with the distribution of sympathy — Apollo was to represent the startling creative energies of the new gods, but he was born into his poetic destiny with pain and suffering as we see at the end of the first version of the poem:

> During the pain Mnemosyne upheld
> Her arms as one who prophesied. At length
> Apollo shrieked; — and lo! from all his limbs
> Celestial ....[5]

Hyperion, however, is the mature creative figure with whom in the unfinished text we are best acquainted and with whom we have the greatest empathy. Could it be that Keats felt the same? Was Keats a god or a Titan? Was he a Titan scripted to become a god, but for reasons both accidental and innate, failing? Could it be that his sympathies were essentially with the old regime? Could this be also understood politically

---

3. *The Fall of Hyperion*, II 56-61: the last lines of the unfinished poem (*The Poems of John Keats*, ed. Miriam Allott, London, 1970, 685.

4. However, Andrew Motion's recent biography has attempted to establish in a popular fashion the notion of Keats as someone with a resonant political conscience, an argument that has been stirring in academic circles for some time: see Andrew Motion, *Keats*, London, 1997, xxii-xxv, 455-56 and *passim*.

5. *Hyperion*, III 133-36 (*The Poems of John Keats*, 441).

— that being born of a generation in the midst of a failing French Revolution, he was bound to develop a scepticism or even an indifference to the claims of the revolutionaries? Therefore unlike Shelley or Byron, his nearest poetic contemporaries, he was unable to carry the revolutionary flag of the older Romantic generation? Poetically, one could make a case, for Keats having a great deal more in common, both in style and taste, with the poets of sensibility, the poets of that period immediately before Wordsworth and Coleridge, characterized by figures like Mary Robinson or Mary Tighe, than with the authors and consequences of *Lyrical Ballads*.

Keats, therefore, may be claimed as both a political and a poetical Hyperion. And what about his eminent and longer lived contemporary, Carlyle, who may unjustly or not be described as a satyr? The New Cambridge Shakespeare edition of *Hamlet* glosses "satyr" as "Grotesque creature, half-human but with the legs of a goat, attendant on Dionysus, and synonymous with lechery". Not much akin with Carlyle we might suppose, and if we were to assert it was, it must be a gross slander, especially if we recall the ribald speculation about Thomas Carlyle's impotence, and his supposedly unconsummated marriage.[6] Nevertheless, Carlyle's first biographer, James Anthony Froude, in a letter referring to the Carlyles said that "There is something *demonic* both in him and her which will never be adequately understood";[7] and Carlyle's prose might on occasions provoke us all to exclaim against its shaggy goatlike rhetoric, and its dithyrambic syntax and diction. Some of his later opinions about the state of the world in general, the condition of England and the situation of black people, in such essays as "The Nigger Question" (1849) and "Shooting Niagara: And After?" (1867), probably strike most of us today as worst than Bacchic or Dionysian, more than demonic even, and positively diabolic. Whereas Carlyle identified the evil of what he called *Swarmery* in the world about him, we might be more inclined to identify Carlyle's own state of mind as being more "inexpressibly delirious" than that world:

> Inexpressibly delirious seems to me, at present in my solitude, the puddle of Parliament and Public upon what it calls the

---

6. See John Stewart Collis, *The Carlyles*, London, 1971, 48-49, and Appendix, 179-82.

7. Letter to his sister-in-law, Mrs Kingsley, *c.* 20 October 1884, in Waldo Hilary Dunn's *James Anthony Froude*, Oxford, 1963, II, 497 (and see Gertrude Himmelfarb, *Victorian Minds: Essays on Nineteenth-Century Intellectuals*, London, 1968, 246).

> "Reform Measure;" that is to say, The calling in of new supplies of blockheadism, gullibility, bribeability, amenability to beer and balderdash, by way of amending the woes we have had from our previous supplies of that bad article. The intellect of a man who believes in the possibility of "improvement" by such a method is to me a finished-off and shut-up intellect, with which I would not argue: mere waste of wind between us to exchange words on that class of topics.

However, even then, Carlyle still has the power of prophecy, the vigour and the authority to shake our mild liberal persuasions (in the company of Carlyle, convictions we dare hardly avow):

> ... all the world assenting, and continually repeating and reverberating, there soon comes that singular phenomenon, which the Germans call *Schwärmerei* ("*enthusiasm*" is our poor Greek equivalent), which means simply "*Swarmery*," or the "Gathering of Men in Swarms," and what prodigies they are in the habit of doing and believing, when thrown into that miraculous condition .... the swarm once formed, finds itself impelled to action, as with one heart and mind. Singular, in the case of human swarms, with what perfection of unanimity and quasi-religious conviction the stupidest absurdities can be received as axioms of Euclid, nay, as articles of faith, which you are not only to believe, unless malignantly insane, but are (if you have any honour or morality) to push into practice, and without delay see *done*, if your soul would live! Divine commandment *to vote* ("Manhood Suffrage," — Horsehood, Doghood ditto not yet treated of); universal "glorious Liberty" (to Sons of the Devil in overwhelming majority, as would appear); count of Heads the God-appointed way in this Universe, all other ways Devil-appointed; in one brief word, which includes whatever of palpable incredibility and delirious absurdity, universally believed, can be uttered or imagined on these points, "the equality of men," any man equal to any other; Quashee Nigger to Socrates or Shakspeare; Judas Iscariot to Jesus Christ; — and Bedlam and Gehenna equal to the New Jerusalem, shall we say? If these things are taken up, not only as axioms of Euclid, but as articles of religion burning to be put into practice for the salvation of the world, — I think you must admit that *Swarmery* plays a wonderful part in the heads of poor Mankind; and that very considerable results are likely to follow from it in our day! ...[8]

---

8. "Shooting Niagara: And After?", in *The Works of Thomas Carlyle*, ed. H.D. Traill, Centenary Edition, 30 vols, London, 1896-99, XXX: *Critical and*

Living in our spasmodically "New Age" world, with our duty bound, not to say politically correct, inclination to embrace relative values and all manner of well-meaning protest movements, our own brand of enthusiastic axioms, our own style of *Swarmery*, we can see and even feel what he means. Watching active protests against the live export of animals on television (whatever the rights or wrongs of the issue), who can doubt that the rage of the Bacchantes can still be roused and raised. Is it Carlyle who is having a fit, or is it that location which so many politicians and commentators risibly insist on calling the "real world" that is in convulsions of passion and fury? It may just be that Carlyle's state of mind is indeed the condition of our world today.

These complex equivocal feelings about and charges against Carlyle are familiar, and are dealt with, on occasions directly but more often obliquely, by other contributors to this volume. What we can be more certain about is that the personalities and tastes of Keats and Carlyle seem antithetical. Keats, alas, did not live long enough to comment on Carlyle, and Carlyle's comments on Keats are meagre. This in itself may be significant, especially since Carlyle was friendly with Richard Monckton Milnes, responsible for the *Life, Letters, and Literary Remains, of John Keats*, published in two volumes in 1848. It is in Carlyle's reported response to Milnes that we have one of the clearest indications of his feelings about the poet:

> He [Carlyle] thought nothing of poetry. He had once tried to write in verse, and failed, but he did not realize that condescension towards poets was unbecoming on his part. He elected to overlook the fact that Tennyson was a poet and praised the man, but all lovers of Keats feel that Carlyle stained his own name by the *faux pas* he made. Milnes had written a book on Keats, and Carlyle described it as "an attempt to make us eat dead dog by exquisite currying and cooking", and declared that "the kind of man that Keats was gets ever more horrible to me. Force of hunger for pleasure of every kind, and want of all other force." Malice would have been preferable to that tone and that ignorance of the subject.[9]

Miscellaneous Essays, V, 9-10 and 3-4. "'Manhood Suffrage,' — Horsehood, Doghood ditto": presumably Carlyle would have included "Womanhood" amongst the "ditto".

9. Collis, 88.

Unfortunately Collis indicates no source for Carlyle's remarks provoked by Milnes' book; but to Milnes himself Carlyle is reported as saying: "Keats is a miserable creature, hungering after sweets which he can't get; going about saying, 'I'm so hungry; I should so like something pleasant!'." Some twenty years later, he was to say, "Keats wanted a world of treacle!".[10] In his early essay on Robert Burns, Carlyle had written:

> Poetry, except in such cases as that of Keats, where the whole consists in a weak-eyed maudlin sensibility, and a certain vague random tunefulness of nature, is no separate faculty, no organ which can be superadded to the rest, or disjoined from them; but rather the result of their general harmony and completion.[11]

Jane Welsh Carlyle in a letter to John Forster said, "Ah! I have read Keats! read the Eve of St Agnes! and — least said is soonest mended", which leads the editor of this particular volume of the letters of the Carlyles, Clyde de L. Ryals, to note that "JWC probably shared TC's scorn for Keats, who was little read till the publication of R.M. Milnes, *Life, Letters, and Literary Remains, of John Keats*, 2 vols. (1848)".[12] And as we have already seen Mr C did not think much of the value of Milnes' enterprise anyway.

There are a few other occasional references in Carlyle's letters indicating his awareness of Keats if not his approval: in a letter of 9 March 1821 to his brother, John Carlyle, there is a reference to his wasting "this whole blessed evening in reading poetry and stuff, while I should have been writing a substantial life of Necker", and a little later in the same letter he uses the phrase "waking dream", which leads the editor of the first volume of *The Collected Letters* to indicate a reference to line seventy-nine of Keats's "Ode to a Nightingale". This suggests that Carlyle might have been "wast[ing] this whole blessed evening" perusing Keats's 1820 volume. In a letter to his wife, 28

---

10. These two remarks come respectively from Wemyss Reid, *Life, Letters, and Friendships of R.M. Milnes*, London, 1890, I, 435 and *William Allingham's Diary* (1907), eds H. Allingham and D. Radford, London, 1967, 205 (both are cited in *Keats: The Critical Heritage*, ed. G.M. Matthews, London, 1971, 365).

11. "Burns" [1828], in *The Works of Thomas Carlyle*, XXVI: *Critical and Miscellaneous Essays*, I, 277-78.

12. Jane Welsh Carlyle, letter to John Forster, 19 January 1842, in *The Collected Letters of Thomas and Jane Welsh Carlyle*, Duke-Edinburgh edn, gen. ed. Charles Richard Sanders, Durham: NC, 1970 -, XIV, 17 and n.3.

February 1825, Carlyle refers to "people dying of Reviews", which may also be an allusion to Keats.[13]

So Mr and Mrs Satyr, the demonic Scottish couple of Cheyne Row, Chelsea, did not think much of Hyperion Keats, who in his turn presumably never knew of their existence. Now let us turn to the second part of my title.

"This strange disease of modern life"

Carlyle despised Keats as a weakling, as a writer wanting all force, and exhibiting only "a weak-eyed maudlin sensibility". Even as the most committed readers and students of Keats, we all know what he means, or at least why he should be provoked to say such things. The consumption and early death of the poet are only part of it. We know, as Carlyle himself could have known after the publication of Milnes' *Life, Letters, and Literary Remains*, had he had any initial sympathy and patience with the poet at all, that Keats was not all "sorrow/And leaden-eyed despairs"; we know something of the rougher, tougher determined Keats from his letters, as well as a great deal of the determination with which he strove to educate and strengthen himself as a poet. We are all familiar with how in his short career he strove to develop a more chaste and less luxuriant style.

But maybe Carlyle was one of those determined to take his cue from "The Ode to the Nightingale" with its expressive plaint about

> The weariness, the fever, and the fret
> Here, where men sit and hear each other groan;
> Where palsy shakes a few, sad, last gray hairs,
> Where youth grows pale, and spectre-thin, and dies ....

and unable or unwilling to see in the poem Keats own dramatization of his struggle with the temptations of evasion and escape either "on the viewless wings of poesy" or by means of "easeful death". Possibly reading back from the letters, and certainly enabled by them, we can see in many of Keats's greatest poems both the power of sensible impression and expression and his deliberate combat with an inclination to succumb to that power. As we know from a famous letter, Keats enjoyed the vigour and animation of dispute — "Though a quarrel in the streets is a thing to be hated, the energies displayed in it are fine; the commonest Man shows a grace in his quarrel" — and Keats shows in this same flight of confession and speculation a sympathy for even

13. *Ibid.*, I, 338 and n.4, and III, 288 and n.2.

misconceived notions, that suggests he would always have had more respect for Carlyle's opinionating than Carlyle for the poet: "By a superior being our reasoning[s] may take the same tone — though erroneous they may be fine —."[14]

Carlyle we know was only too alert to the sickness of the age, or what he was quick to condemn as the sickness of the age apparent in its increasing self-consciousness, notably expressed in "Characteristics" (1831):

> The healthy know not of their health, but only the sick: this is the Physician's Aphorism; and applicable in a far wider sense than he gives it. We may say, it holds no less in moral, intellectual, political, poetical, than in merely corporeal therapeutics ....
>
> In the Body ... the first condition of complete health is, that each organ perform its function unconsciously, unheeded; let but any organ announce its separate existence, were it even boastfully, and for pleasure, not for pain, then already has one of those unfortunate "false centres of sensibility" established itself, already is derangement there.[15]

One has very little difficulty in supposing that John Keats may well have been identified by Carlyle as a poet and a man exhibiting one of those "false centres of sensibility", the very embodiment of such an undesirable state of affairs, the very genius of unhealthy self-consciousness in a society:

> Never since the beginning of Time was there, that we hear and read of, so intensely self-conscious a Society. Our whole relations to the Universe and to our fellow-man have become an Inquiry, a Doubt; nothing will go on its own accord, and do its function quietly; but all things must be probed into, the whole working of man's world be anatomically studied.[16]

It would have hardly helped Keats's case that before he had devoted himself to the self-conscious anatomical probing of poetry he had been a medical student. No doubt Carlyle would have seen this as all one,

---

14. Letter to the George Keatses, 19 March 1819, in *The Letters of John Keats*, ed. Hyder Edward Rollins, 2 Vols, Cambridge: Mass., 1958, II, 80.

15. *The Works of Thomas Carlyle*, XXVIII: *Critical and Miscellaneous Essays*, III, 1.

16. *Ibid.*, 19.

since literature, too, has "its deep-seated, wide-spread maladies":

> Spontaneous devotedness to the object, being wholly possessed by the object, what we call Inspiration, has well-nigh ceased to appear in Literature. Which melodious Singer forgets that he is singing melodiously?

(One can hardly dodge the apparent reference to Keats and his nightingale here, and the envy of the poet for the creature of nature.)

> We have not the love of greatness, but the love of the love of greatness. Hence infinite Affectations, Distractions; in every case inevitable Error ....

And the candid Carlyle cannot leave his own literary niche out of the picture either:

> Nay, is not the diseased self-conscious state of Literature disclosed in this one fact, which lies so near us here, the prevalence of Reviewing! .... at the last Leipzig Fair, there was advertised a Review of Reviews. By and by it will be found that all Literature has become one boundless self-devouring Review.[17]

The early Carlyle is not all that different from the later Carlyle after all, and, we must admit unwillingly and uncomfortably, speaking as much to our age as to his own.

If we accept that Keats may have given a cue to Carlyle's analysis, or if that is not necessary since Carlyle was already there before he had the case of Keats and his work before him, may have given him, and certainly gives us, a palpable "sign of the times", Carlyle and Keats combined were later given a famously poetic transmutation in Matthew Arnold's "The Scholar-Gipsy":

> For early didst thou leave the world, with powers
> Fresh, undiverted to the world without,
> Firm to their mark, not spent on other things;
> Free from the sick fatigue, the languid doubt,
> Which much to have tried, in much been baffled, brings.

We know that Arnold is addressing that mythical or mythologized seventeenth-century student who dropped out of Oxford and joined the

---

17. *Ibid.*, 23, 23-24, and 24-25.

Gipsies, but for more than a moment one might suppose he was addressing Keats, whose stanza form and not a little of his diction and phraseology he seems to have hijacked. We know that Arnold was equivocal about the Romantics and both ambivalent and patronizing about Keats, but "The Scholar-Gipsy" almost seems to be positioned and to position us to contemplate and even admire a Keats who did not put up the fight that we see him involved in the Odes, particular in the "Ode to a Nightingale"; a Keats who did after all "leave the world unseen" and with the nightingale "fade away into the forest dim":

> O born in days when wits were fresh and clear,
> And life ran gaily as the sparkling Thames;
> Before this strange disease of modern life,
> With its sick hurry, its divided aims,
> Its heads o'ertaxed, its palsied hearts, was rife —
> Fly hence, our contact fear!
> Still fly, plunge deeper in the bowering wood![18]

Fusions and confusions

We are all aware that Arnold's attitude to Carlyle was as perplexed as his feelings towards Keats. Arnold had already labelled Carlyle a "moral desperado" in September 1849,[19] more that two months before the publication of the "Nigger Question" essay which was to shock so many of Carlyle's admirers. And in 1857 Arnold was to describe Carlyle as "part man — of genius — part fanatic — and part tomfool", and "two years later scornfully rejected 'that regular Carlylean strain which we all know by heart and which the clear-headed among us have so utter a contempt for'".[20] This is not the place to consider the complicated matter of Arnold's intellectual debt to Carlyle, which would no doubt start with a consideration of the relationship of the famous self-quotation with which Arnold begins "The Study of Poetry" (1880) with Carlyle's comparison of the relative vitality of religion and

---

18. "The Scholar-Gipsy", ll. 161-65, 201-205 (*The Poems of Matthew Arnold*, 339 and 342).

19. *Letters of Matthew Arnold to Arthur Hugh Clough*, ed. Howard Foster Lowry, London and New York, 1932, 111.

20. David J. DeLaura, "Carlyle and Arnold: The Religious Issue", in *Carlyle Past and Present*, eds K.J. Fielding and Rodger L. Tarr, London, 1976, 133.

literature in "Characteristics",[21] nor the history of his assimilations and rejections. But any superficial glance at the relationship between the two men's thought, taken in conjunction with their respective attitudes towards Keats, is enough to indicate the fusions and confusions that are involved in the transitions (if they indeed exist), in the transmutations (if they can be so described), in the responses and reactions (we can say no less) between Romanticism and Victorianism, of Romanticism and Victorianism, to and from Romanticism and Victorianism — those two very unequal "isms".

Take, for instance, the end of the second sentence of the first paragraph of "Characteristics", which I omitted. Having said that

> The healthy know not of their health, but only the sick: this is the Physician's Aphorism; and applicable in a far wider sense than he gives it. We may say, it holds no less in moral, intellectual, political, poetical, than in merely corporeal therapeutics ....

Carlyle goes on to say "that wherever, or in what shape soever, powers of the sort which can be named *vital* are at work, herein lies the test of their working right or working wrong". The key word, italicized in the original, is, of course, *vital*; one of the central concepts of Carlyle's diagnosis of and remedy for the sickly self-conscious "spirit of the age". As R.H. Super has noted Arnold seemed to make Keats's "early death a moral defect", and quotes from his essay on Heinrich Heine:

> Keats passionately gave himself up to a sensuous genius, to his faculty for interpreting nature;[22] and he died of consumption at twenty-five.

As we see in the following sentence, from his essay on Maurice de Guérin, Arnold implies something other than a fortuitous physical link or a casual syntactical connection between the nature of Keats's genius and the illness that killed him:

---

21. See *The Complete Prose Works of Matthew Arnold*, ed. R.H. Super, Ann Arbor: Mich., 1960-, IX, 161; *The Works of Thomas Carlyle*, XXVIII: *Critical and Miscellaneous Essays*, III, 23.

22. Cf. Carlyle's comments in "Characteristics" on "View-hunting", as one of the "infinite Affectations, Distractions" of the age (*The Works of Thomas Carlyle*, XXVIII: *Critical and Miscellaneous Essays*, III, 23-24).

> In him [Maurice de Guérin], as in Keats, ... the temperament, the talent itself, is deeply influenced by their mysterious malady; the temperament is *devouring*; it uses vital power too hard and too fast, paying the penalty in long hours of unutterable exhaustion and in premature death.[23]

With Arnold's use of "vital" here, there emerges an explicit association of the sapping in Keats of what Carlyle described as the "powers of the sort which can be named *vital*" and the peculiar aesthetic of his poetry. I use the word "peculiar" here to mean "particular or characteristic" deliberately to risk the ambiguity of being understood to signify "odd" or even "misguided", because "peculiar" in that sense is what often lies behind criticisms of Keats's poetry.

As Arnold said in a letter to Clough (in 1848 or 1849), "What harm he [Keats] has done in English Poetry". Arnold's analysis in this same letter seems very close to his identification of "this strange disease of modern life/ ... its sick hurry, its divided aims,/ Its heads o'ertaxed":

> As Browning is a man with a moderate gift passionately desiring movement and fulness, and obtaining but a confused multitudinousness, so Keats with a very high gift, is yet also consumed by this desire: and cannot produce the truly living and moving, as his conscience keeps telling him. They will not be patient neither understand that they must begin with an Idea of the world in order not to be prevailed over by the world's multitudinousness ....[24]

"The world's multitudinousness" seems to offer us another word to lay alongside Carlyle's alliterative trio of "mechanism, machines, materialism", as a condition of the modern (another word belonging to the same alliterative pack) world with which increasing self-consciousness is having to learn to cope.

Growing consciousness of the complexity of developed human societies created by the scientific and political revolutions, economic and industrial developments, the Encyclopaedists and the philosophical and the psychologist empiricists of the eighteenth century is both the

---

23. R.H. Super, "Arnold and Literary Criticism (ii)", in *Writers and Their Background: Matthew Arnold*, ed. Kenneth Allott, London, 1975, 172 n.2 (the passages from Arnold may be found in *The Complete Prose Works of Matthew Arnold*, III, 122 and 32).

24. *The Letters of Matthew Arnold to Arthur Hugh Clough*, 96 (quoted by R.H. Super in *The Complete Prose Works of Matthew Arnold*, IX, 392).

inspiration of Romanticism, and the provoker of Romantic reaction. Keats may be interpreted as a poet attempting to cope with the new world of sensibility and consciousness through an aesthetic of sensuality and beauty (with which towards the end of his very short life he may not have been satisfied); Carlyle, the other child of 1795, may be understood as a philosopher and historian trying to remove his and the world's contamination by this consciousness through abrasive and caustic rhetoric (which grew the more furious as the situation developed and refused to disappear); Arnold as an heir to both Keats and Carlyle and the condition they struggled with failed to resolve his own dilemmas both as a poet and a critic.

The Romantic crisis was not created by the Romantics but inherited by them, and the Victorians were equally unable either to dissolve the complex issues of Man and Nature, Man and God, Man and Woman, Man and Woman and Society, other Men and other Women and other Societies that the Romantic age had had to tackle, or to absolve themselves from those issues. Neither Nightingales, nor Scholar-Gipsies, nor a vitalist work-ethic were viable resolutions or solutions to the modern world, but in their various unsatisfactory, incomplete, tantalizing, infuriating and disappointing ways Keats, Carlyle and Arnold together all help to articulate and illuminate the life and conditions which we know only too well from our own direct experience at the end of the twentieth century.

KEATS AND THE SUBLIME

AVEEK SEN

In a letter to James Rice written on 24 March 1818, the day before he wrote his verse-epistle to John Hamilton Reynolds, Keats provides a pair of contrasting images by way of a provisional self-definition:

> What a happy thing it would be if we could settle our thoughts, make our minds up on any matter in five Minutes and remain content — that is to build a mental Cottage of feelings quiet and pleasant — to have a sort of Philosophical Back Garden, and cheerful holiday-keeping front one — but Alas! this never can be: for as the material cottager knows there are such places as france and Italy and the Andes and the Burning Mountains — so the spiritual Cottager has knowledge of the terra semi incognita of things unearthly; and cannot for his Life, keep in the check rein — .... I am obliged to run wild, being attracted by the Loadstone Concatenation.[1]

Keats is here juxtaposing two systems of imagery, each informed by a literary tradition. He presents the state of intellectual and philosophic complacence in terms of the eighteenth-century picturesque mode. The "spiritual Cottager" creates for himself a haven of cultivation and contemplation that transforms material securities through elegant labour into leisure and spiritual contentment. But outside the secure limits of this idyll lie the unfamiliar and perilous expanses of another landscape. In charting this imaginary terrain, Keats's imagery modulates to the language of the sublime. France, the land of the Napoleonic sublime, and Italy, associated with the sublimities of Raphael and Michelangelo, lead further beyond the achievements of European civilization into the obscure topographies of the New World.

1. *The Letters of John Keats*, ed. Hyder Edward Rollins, 2 vols, Cambridge: Mass., 1958, II, 254-55. All quotations from Keats's poems are from John Keats, *Complete Poems*, ed. Jack Stillinger, Cambridge: Mass, 1978.

Commentators have noted the influence of Buffon's *Natural History* and Robertson's *History of America* here,[2] but the presence of another important text behind this passage has hitherto remained unnoticed. In *The Spectator* No. 417 (28 June 1712), seventh in the series on "the pleasures of the imagination", Addison describes the distinct experiences of reading Homer, Virgil and Ovid in terms of the aesthetic categories of "Greatness", "Beauty" and "Novelty" defined earlier in No. 412:

> Reading the *Iliad* is like travelling through a country uninhabited, where the Fancy is entertained with a thousand Savage Prospects of vast Desarts, wide uncultivated Marshes, huge Forests, misshapen Rocks and Precipices. On the contrary, the *Aeneid* is like a well-ordered garden, where it is impossible to find out any Part unadorned, or to cast our Eyes on any Spot, that does not produce some beautiful Plant or Flower. But when we are in the *Metamorphosis* [*sic*], we are walking on enchanted Ground, and see nothing but Scenes of Magick lying round us.

The specifically literary implications of the Keats passage become clear when read alongside Addison's description, which goes on to associate Homer with the "Terrible" and "Sublime *Ideas*" in the reader's mind in a significant anticipation of Burke.[3] For Keats, these neoclassical modes of the "Great", the "Beautiful" and the "Strange" — derived from Addison, Burke and, perhaps, John Baillie are not only aesthetic or literary modes associated with reading particular authors or attempting certain genres of writing, but modes of cognition and experience. As inherited alternatives to choose from or move between they exist in difficult and uneasy relationships with one another; and Keats presents himself in an inevitable transition from the perceived limits and inadequacies of one mode into the daunting and hazardous, yet irresistible uncertainties and mysteries of the other.

This essay attempts to read Keats's verse-epistle of 25 March 1818 to John Hamilton Reynolds as a crucial moment in this transition. I will be considering Keats's engagements with the discourse of the sublime, in this poem, in relation to two areas of preoccupation that emerge from his correspondence with Reynolds. First, Keats and Reynolds were both inheritors of a British empiricist tradition which had, for them,

---

2. *Letters*, I, 255, and A.D. Atkinson, "Keats and Kamchatka", *Notes and Queries*, 4 (August 1951), 340-46.

3. *The Spectator*, ed. D.F. Bond, 4 vols, Oxford, 1965, III, 564-65.

disturbing implications for the life of the imagination. For Keats, an engagement with the sublime brought these implications in focus, and also made him explore critically another variant of the empiricist aesthetic — eighteenth-century associationism. Secondly, the idea of literary ambition acquires a particular urgency in the Keats-Reynolds correspondence. I will examine how the epistolary expression of this idea leads up to Keats's verse-letter and persists beyond its temporary resolutions into his mature poetry. I will be looking at the stylistic, figurative and allusive strategies employed by Keats and Reynolds in writing about it, and to the social material basis of this preoccupation in the case of two young poets trying to sustain their own sense of vocation in the face of domestic and professional demands and commitments.

For Keats and Reynolds, vocational anxieties were closely tied up with an urgent need to vindicate the reality and dignity of intellectual labour without undermining the creative potential and literary resonances of the states of idleness, indolence, luxury and melancholy. Recent work on the sublime by Frances Ferguson and Tom Furniss helps us to read Keats's epistle as a profoundly uneasy exploration of the implications of the sublime as derived from Addison, Baillie and Burke, and as embodied in the achievements of Milton and Wordsworth.[4] Specific forms and aspects of eighteenth-century poetry and aesthetics constituted a shared literary heritage for Keats and Reynolds, and I will also consider the manner in which Keats continually revalued this heritage in the light of his changing circumstances and convictions. What ensured Keats's survival as a poet was his ability to transform and even outgrow elements of this received neoclassicism in order to keep his poetry in vital contact with the "world of Circumstances", indeed to make the imagination's unceasing struggle with "a sense of real things" its abiding theme.

"Reliques of sensation": empiricism, associationism and the sublime

The great conversation poem that stands behind Keats's verse-epistle, and whose spirit haunts his letters to Reynolds, is Wordsworth's "Tintern Abbey". In a letter written a few weeks after the verse-epistle, Keats describes to Reynolds how the "dark passages" leading out of his

---

4. Frances Ferguson, "Legislating the Sublime", in *Studies in Eighteenth-Century British Art and Aesthetics*, ed. Ralph Cohen, Berkeley: CAL, 1985, 128-47, and *Solitude and the Sublime: Romanticism and the Aesthetics of Individuation*, London, 1992; Tom Furniss, *Edmund Burke's Aesthetic Ideology: Language, Gender, and Political Economy in Revolution*, Cambridge, 1993.

"Chamber of Maiden-Thought" merge with those that Wordsworth's "Genius is explorative of" in "Tintern Abbey".[5] However, the allusions to the poem in Keats's verse-epistle also express his instinctive unease with some of the implications of the Wordsworthian sublime. In Wordsworth's poem of grand consolations, the sense of the sublime, the tranquil restorations of memory and Dorothy's presence constitute the "abundant recompense" that enables the poet to look loss and perplexity in the face. Although anchored in his investment in a particular human relationship, the sublime empowers the poet to project a transcendent and universalizing vision which subsumes "the mind of man" into a "deeply interfused" universe of "all thinking things".[6] This idea of interfusion overcomes the perplexing discontinuities and divisions in the "self-experience"[7] of individual minds, as well as the sense of entrapment in "the dreary intercourse of daily life".

Keats's epistle records the failure of both these strategies of the sublime. Firstly, the letter fails to universalize the "moods" of an individual mind into the abstraction, "the mind of man". Secondly, Keats's poem avoids a transcendence of the quotidian, by which Wordsworth achieves a superior and creative solitariness amidst "the din of towns and cities" (ll. 25-26). Wordsworth's "din" becomes Keats's "jostle" — a word that suggests competitive struggle in an overpopulated environment and anticipates the vision of "eternal fierce destruction".[8] In that "world" — untransfigured by "elevated thoughts" and estranged from the sources of the sublime — the exquisite "fitting" of the "individual Mind" and the "external World" to each other, so joyously celebrated in the Prospectus to *The Excursion*, becomes a frustrating deadlock "shadow[ing] our own soul's daytime/In the dark

5. *Letters*, I, 281.

6. See "Tintern Abbey", ll. 85-101: all quotations from Wordsworth are from his *Poetical Works*, ed. Thomas Hutchinson, Oxford, 1969.

7. A Coleridgean compound. *The Collected Works of Samuel Taylor Coleridge*, eds Kathleen Coburn *et al.*, 16 vols, Princeton and London, 1971 - , VII: *Biographia Literaria*, eds James Engell and W. Jackson Bate (1983), ch. 7, I, 124.

8. See Blake's use of "jostling" in an epigram included in the series "English Encouragement of Art": "Great things are done when Men & Mountains meet/This is not Done by Jostling in the Street" (*The Complete Poetry and Prose of William Blake*, ed. David V. Erdman, New York, 1988, 511). For an important account of "the sense of psychic crowding" in Malthus and in some of his literary contemporaries constituting "a Romantic political economy", see Frances Ferguson, "Malthus, Godwin, Wordsworth, and the Spirit of Solitude", in her *Solitude and the Sublime*.

void of night". This "dark void" and the "Purgatory blind" recall Wordsworth's Miltonic image of the blind man whose eye is eternally denied the recollection of "beauteous forms". Keats's phrasing here also echoes Wordsworth's "living soul" (l. 46), but dislocates "soul" from Wordsworth's quasi-epiphanic context in order to associate it with what follows a few lines later: "darkness and ... the many shapes/Of joyless daylight" (ll. 51-52).

Keats's letter of 3 May 1818 to Reynolds dwells on Wordsworth's phrase "the burthen of the mystery",[9] and it is significant how Keats shifts the emphasis from the relieving of this burden by joy and vision, and chooses instead to ponder the nature of the burden itself. The phrase is echoed in the epistle's "mysterious tale" that renders its writer speechless, and the reading of which gives way to a vision "into the core/Of an eternal fierce destruction" that recalls with grim irony Wordsworth's "see[ing] into the life of things".

Keats's trope for this sombre revelation is "a sort of purgatory blind", a disabling and indeterminate terrain of eclipsed vision, a *dis*location experienced by the imagination as an unceasing conflict between transgression and confinement:

> ... Things cannot to the will
> Be settled, but they tease us out of thought.
> Or is it that imagination brought
> Beyond its proper bound, yet still confined, —
> Lost in a sort of purgatory blind,
> Cannot refer to any standard law
> Of either earth or heaven? ...
>
> (ll. 76-82)

What the imagination experiences here is the dichotomy inscribed within the etymology of the word "sublime":

> ... although the sublime gestures towards the infinite, its prefix — from the Latin *sub*, meaning "under, close to, up to, towards" — suggests that its effect depends upon a relation to the limen, the threshold or limit.

For the subject experiencing or confronting the sublime, this liminality implies an ambiguous and unstable position in relation to what Keats calls the "proper bound" — a confinement within it as well as a soaring

9. *Letters*, I, 227, 281.

beyond it. It is the simultaneity of these two states that constitutes the peculiar trauma of Keatsian purgatory, a loitering in thraldom that would find its most compelling narrative a year later in "La Belle Dame sans Merci".

Furniss traces this ambiguity in the discourse of the sublime back to Addison's *Spectator* essays and quotes a passage that is close to Keats's formulation:

> The mind of man naturally hates everything that looks like a restraint upon it, and is apt to fancy itself under a sort of confinement, when the sight is pent up in a narrow compass .... On the contrary, a spacious horizon is an image of liberty, where the eye has room to range abroad, to expatiate at large on the immensity of its views, and to lose itself amidst the variety of objects that offer themselves to its observation.[10]

In moving naturally from the "mind of man" to the eye, from intellectual to visual experience, Addison makes spectatorship not only a variety of, but an image for understanding the experience of the sublime.

Following the dominant empirical tradition of seventeenth-century philosophy, Addison's papers on "the pleasures of the imagination" begin with a celebration of sight:

> Our Sight is the most perfect and most delightful of all our Senses .... It is this sense which furnishes the Imagination with its Ideas; so that by the Pleasures of the Imagination or Fancy (which I shall use promiscuously) I here mean such as arise from visible Objects, either when we have them actually in our view, or when we call up their Ideas into our Minds by Paintings, Statues, Descriptions, or any the like Occasion.

He then goes on to distinguish between the two kinds of pleasure afforded by sight. The "Primary" pleasures "proceed from such Objects as are before our Eyes", and — more importantly for our discussion of Keats's poem — the "Secondary" pleasures "flow from the Ideas of visible Objects, when the Objects are not actually before the Eye, but are called up into our Memories, or formed into agreeable Visions of Things that are either Absent or Fictitious".[11] Keats offers Reynolds these secondary pleasures in his verse-epistle when he makes Claude's

10. Furniss, 23.

11. *The Spectator*, III, 535-37.

picture part of its "unconnected subject": "You know, I am sure, Claude's Enchanted Castle and I wish you may be pleased with my remembrance of it."[12] "Remembrance", recalling the importance of "memories" in Addison's definition, links the Claude ekphrasis with the series of fantastical and perverse images at the beginning of the poem: "shapes, and shadows and remembrances." The sleepless poet surrendering himself to the playfulness of memory and association is like a parody of Addison's "Man in a Dungeon ... capable of entertaining himself with Scenes and Landskips more beautiful than any that can be found in the whole Compass of Nature" with the help of his visual imagination.[13] But as this self-indulgence becomes increasingly ludic and extravagant, what starts surfacing in Keats's poem is an unease with the "lawlessness" inherent in this "complete lightheadedness".[14]

I deliberately invoke Coleridge here, because Keats would find in the *Biographia*'s chapters on Hartleyan associationism the fullest description of the creative activity represented in his poem. Coleridge's profound fear of "the phantasmal chaos of association"[15] uncontrolled by will or reason within the proper moral and theological framework is concomitant with the professed ideological mission of these chapters — the "emancipation" of the mind from "that despotism of the eye".[16] Addison's unmisgiving celebration of sight as well as Wordsworth and Coleridge's anti-empiricism become part of Keats's intellectual heritage. This results in a tension, within the poem, between a sensationist delight in images resulting in a frivolous pictorialism and the need to adopt a poetic voice that speaks of abstractions, rather than images, with greater moral and philosophical authority.

The aesthetics behind Keats's ekphrasis of Claude can also be understood in terms of some associationist theories of spectatorship. "There is nothing so pleasant as the association of ideas", wrote Reynolds, referring to his childhood reading, in an essay on *The Spectator* in *The Champion*;[17] and Keats, in his letters to Reynolds,

12. *Letters*, I, 263.

13. *The Spectator*, III, 537.

14. *Biographia Literaria*, ch. 6, II, 111-12.

15. *Ibid.*, II, 116.

16. *Ibid.*, I, 107.

17. *Selected Prose of John Hamilton Reynolds*, ed. L.M. Jones, Cambridge: Mass., 1966, 63.

frequently uses associationist language to describe his response to art and literature:

> This crossing a letter is not without its association — for chequer work leads us naturally to a Milkmaid, a Milkmaid to Hogarth Hogarth to Shakespeare Shakespear to Hazlitt — Hazlitt to Shakespeare and thus by merely pulling an apron string we set a pretty peal of Chimes at work ....[18]

The pleasure of allowing the memory to form whimsical connections between and within various orders of experience — literary, visual and sensual, is central to the associationism of Archibald Alison. His *Essays on the Nature and Principles of Taste* (1790) was reviewed by Francis Jeffrey in the *Edinburgh Review* in 1811 and ran into six editions by 1825.[19] In his "remembrance" of Claude, Keats invites Reynolds to share in what Alison calls "*individual* Associations", one of the several means enumerated by him, "by which the qualities of matter may be significant to us of the qualities of mind":

> ... when certain qualities or appearances of matter, are connected with our own private affections or remembrances; and when they give to these material qualities or appearances a character of interest which is solely the result of our own memory and affections.[20]

Both Alison and Jeffrey are particularly interested in the extent to which memory and affection, in determining our experience of art and nature, are themselves constituted by our reading. The world of imaginative associations that the educated modern spectator brings to aesthetic experience derives not only from ancient mythology and classical literature, but also from "the study of modern poetry". Alison's depiction of the reader's hybrid universe illuminates the process by which Keats transforms Claude's world of harmony and

---

18. *Letters*, I, 280, see also 246, 251, and II, 167.

19. The best historical surveys of associationism are in Elie Halevy, *The Growth of Philosophic Radicalism*, London, 1928, and Martin Kallich, *The Association of Ideas and Critical Theory in Eighteenth-Century England*, The Hague, 1970, especially 248 ff. on Alison's influence on nineteenth-century critical thought.

20. Archibald Alison, *Essays on the Nature and Principles of Taste*, 2 vols, 5th edn, Edinburgh, 1817, I, 419 and 422.

repose into an ominous and supernatural world of "faery" romance whose elements are drawn from contemporary Gothic. The "nature embellished and made sacred by the memory of Theocritus and Virgil, and Milton and Tasso" is also worked upon by "the awful forms of Gothic superstition, the wild and romantic imagery, which the turbulence of the middle ages, the Crusades, and the institution of chivalry ... have spread over every country of Europe" and which "arise to the imagination in every scene".[21] Keats's "poor herdsman", derived from Claude's figure of the banished Psyche sitting outside Cupid's castle, for instance, seems to have strayed out of Virgilian pastoral into a world of enchantment and fear:

> An echo of the sweet music doth create
> A fear in the poor herdsman who doth bring
> His beasts to trouble the enchanted spring:
> He tells of the sweet music and the spot
> To all his friends, and they believe him not.
>
> (ll. 62-66)

Keats's account of the castle's cumulative architecture also conforms accurately to associationist ideas of picturesque irregularity or incongruity, configured, once again, as a juxtaposition of classical and Gothic, and derived from the pictures of Claude Lorrain and Gaspar Poussin. Richard Payne Knight, in the section entitled "Association of Ideas" in *An Analytical Enquiry into the Principles of Taste*, recommends "that mixed style, which characterizes the buildings of Claude and the Poussins" as "the best style of architecture for irregular and picturesque houses":

> ... it is taken from models, which were built piece-meal, during many successive ages; and by several different nations, it is distinguished by no particular manner of execution, or class of ornaments; but admits of all promiscuously, from a plain wall or buttress, of the roughest masonry, to the most highly wrought Corinthian capital: and, in a style professedly miscellaneous, such contrasts may be employed to heighten the relish of beauty, without disturbing the enjoyment of it by any appearance of deceit or imposture.[22]

21. *Ibid.*, I, 64-65.

22. Richard Payne Knight, *An Analytical Inquiry into the Principles of Taste*, London, 1808, 225. On the idea of irregularity in picturesque architecture, see also *The Arrogant Connoisseur: Richard Payne Knight 1751-1824*, eds Michael Clarke

In the discourse of associationism, this architectural irregularity becomes analogous to the whimsicality of the associative imagination.[23] The associative faculty is also often seen as capable of self-delighting caprice and unrestrained inventiveness that could, in its apparent pointlessness, seem morally dubious, especially when contrasted with the teleological exertions of the sublime imagination. In Alison, "it is upon the vacant and the unemployed ... that the objects of taste make the strongest impression", because, in them, the associative imagination is the most "free and unembarrassed".[24] In contrast to the sublime, which, as I will show later, operates through conscious labour and strenuous exertion, association works best in a "powerless state of reverie"[25] that reduces music and poetry to forms of amusement and indulgence: "The seasons of care, grief, or of business, have other occupations, and ... produce a state of mind unfavourable to the indulgence of imagination."[26]

Keats's epistle starts and attempts to dwell initially in such an "unconnected" and "careless"[27] world of associationist reverie and ekphrasis. But this "wonted thread" of "things all disjointed" and the fantasy landscape that it leads to, remain restlessly aware of the "care, grief, or ... business" that Alison's state of reverie has succeeded in excluding. The peculiar tone of this Keatsian associationism is closer to Francis Jeffrey's engagement with the "compound and complicated nature" of the beauty that the association of ideas produces:

> ... this fluctuation of the imagination — this unsteadiness and the perpetual shifting in the particular objects of emotion, and to feel that there is nothing that is particularly appropriate to the form before us; and that the fancy wavers among an indistinct crowd of equal competitors ... presenting only dim and unbroken outlines, that fleet away in irregular succession.[28]

---

and Nicholas Penny, Manchester, 1982, 40-41, and Christopher Hussey, *The Picturesque: Studies in a Point of View*, London, 1967, 209-30.

23. On whimsicality in John Nash's architecture, see *Arrogant Connoisseur*, 45-46; and on irregularity as a characteristic of associative thought, see Alison, I, 76-77.

24. Alison, I, 10-11.

25. *Ibid.*, I, 59.

26. *Ibid.*, I, 11.

27. *Letters*, I, 265.

28. Francis Jeffrey's review of Alison's *Essays*, *Edinburgh Review*, XVIII/35 (May 1811), 28-29.

Jeffrey is aware of the radically unstable, pluralistic and, hence, egalitarian implications of Alison's notions of taste, in its emphasis on the individual's uniqueness as the subject of aesthetic experience, and in its tendency to challenge the unity and hegemony of the sublime.[29] Most significantly, his review ignores the Anglican piety and moralism that informs Alison's treatise, "the FINAL CAUSE of this constitution of our nature" that ultimately salvages Alison's aesthetics from "the phantasmal chaos of association"[30] in a redeeming telos.[31] In the absence of such an overarching theological framework, Jeffrey resorts to a curious double-standard of "two tastes":

> ... for those who labour for applause, the wisest course, perhaps, if it were only practicable, would be, to have two tastes, — one to enjoy, and one to work by, — one founded upon universal associations, according to which they finished those performances for which they challenged universal praise, — and another guided by all casual and individual associations, through which they looked fondly upon nature, and upon the objects of their secret admiration.[32]

Associationism, thus, opens up a chasm between the private and the public, the sensual and the consensual in aesthetic experience, separating the realm of neoclassical universals from the erotics of private enjoyment. Keats's verse-epistle articulates a similar division between the imagination's private modes of ludic self-indulgence and its more public commitments and aspirations. In this case, it is the act of epistolary communication that affirms the value of both sociability and solitariness as conditions that make poetry possible.

Misgivings regarding the centrality of the visual in the British empiricist tradition enter the discourse of the sublime in Part 5, Section V of Burke's *Philosophical Enquiry*, entitled "Examples that WORDS may affect without raising IMAGES". In this analysis of the manner in which poetic language affects the reader's passions, Burke dissociates the power of poetry from "the power of raising sensible images", thereby theorizing the effect of poetry in terms of sympathy rather than imitation: "The picturesque connection is not demanded; because no

---

29. *Ibid.*, 40-44.

30. *Biographia Literaria*, ch. 7, II, 116.

31. Alison, II, 423-47.

32. Jeffrey, 47.

real picture is formed; nor is the effect of the description at all the less upon this account." In terms of the binaries that structure Burke's discourse, picturesque description is aligned with the beautiful and the feminine, embodied in representations of Helen and Belphoebe, and is associated with Spenserian romance, whereas the sublimity of "ideas which present no distinct image to the mind" characterizes Miltonic epic.[33] Keats's position in relation to these binaries remains uncertain and uneasy in the poem. He too tries to sever the "picturesque connection", suddenly growing impatient with its facile and apparently unending play. Yet there is in him an ambivalence and unreadiness with the Wordsworthian-Miltonic imperative of the philosophical sublime — "the dread voice" of "a higher mood" that spurs the poet in "Lycidas" away from the "delights" of the pastoral towards "laborious days" and "Fame".[34] The post-empiricist imagination experiences its freedom from "the despotism of outward impression"[35] as a perplexing alienation from the world of actual sensations, figured in Keats's poem as blindness or a total absence of light.[36] If the "reliques of sensation"[37] are taken away from Addison's "Man in a Dungeon", he is left in darkness and confinement.

This sense of a claustrophobic solipsism ("shadow our own soul's daytime/In the dark void of night") as a possible terminus of empiricism is perhaps most memorably articulated by David Hume in *A Treatise of Human Nature*:

> Now since nothing is ever present to the mind but perception, and since all ideas are derived from something antecedently present to the mind; it follows, that 'tis impossible for us so much as to conceive or form an idea of any thing specifically different from ideas and impressions. Let us fix our attention out of ourselves as much as possible: Let us chace our imagination

33. Edmund Burke, *A Philosophical Enquiry into the Origin of our Ideas of the Sublime and Beautiful*, ed. Adam Phillips, Oxford, 1990, 156-61.

34. All quotations from Milton are from *The Poems of John Milton*, eds John Carey and Alastair Fowler, London, 1968.

35. *Biographia Literaria*, ch. 6, II, 111.

36. See also *The Spectator*, III, 546-47 for Addison's description of "the State of the Soul after its first Separation, in respect of the Images it will receive from Matter". Stillinger cites this passage as a possible literary source of "La Belle Dame sans Merci" in his edition of Keats's poems, 464.

37. *Biographia Literaria*, ch. 6, II, 113.

> to the heavens, or to the utmost limits of the universe; we never really advance a step beyond ourselves, nor can conceive any kind of existence, but those perceptions, which have appear'd in that narrow compass. This is the universe of the imagination, nor have we any idea but what is there produc'd.[38]

The terms in which the imagination, in Hume, experiences the bounds of its own universe, are strikingly similar to Keats's description of the imagination in the verse-epistle, suspended vertiginously between confinement and potential infinitude.

Spectator No. 420 discusses, among other things, "The *Bounds* and *Defects* of the Imagination. Whether these Defects are *Essential* to the Imagination."[39] Its opening paragraph also helps us to understand the role played by empiricism in Keats's ambivalent response to the sublime in this poem, especially his desire to establish a closer and more creative relationship between imaginative activity and things "of material sublime":[40]

> As the Writers in Poetry and Fiction borrow their several Materials from outward Objects, and join them together at their own Pleasure, there are others who are obliged to follow Nature more closely, and to take entire Scenes out of her. Such are Historians, natural Philosophers, Travellers, Geographers, and, in a Word, all who describe visible Objects of a real Existence.[41]

Addison is here extending the purview of imaginative writing beyond poetry and fiction to include historical, scientific and philosophical knowledge. These can also bring pleasure to the reader, and more importantly, provide the imagination with sublime objects or ideas for contemplation, thereby opening up an infinitude of imaginative and epistemological possibilities while being securely anchored to the empirical world.

It is interesting to note that the kinds of writing enumerated here — history, natural philosophy (especially astronomy), travel-literature, geography — constitute a significant part of Keats's reading from his

38. David Hume, *A Treatise of Human Nature*, ed. L.A. Selby-Bigge, Oxford, 1978, 67-68.

39. *The Spectator*, III, 582.

40. "To J.H. Reynolds", ll. 67-71.

41. *Ibid.*, III, 574.

early schooldays up to his adult life.[42] The programme of self-education that Keats envisions for himself reflects his conviction of the relevance and usefulness of such fields of knowledge for a young poet with Miltonic aspirations. "Every department of knowledge", he writes to Reynolds on 3 May 1818, "we see excellent and calculated towards a great whole"; and he goes on to apply this certainty to his favourite Wordsworthian theme, although deriving his recompense from a source very different from Wordsworth's:

> An extensive knowledge is very needful to thinking people — it takes away the heat and fever; and helps, by widening speculation, to ease the Burden of the Mystery: a thing I begin to understand a little, and which weighed upon you in the most gloomy and true sentence in your Letter.[43]

"Extensive knowledge" and "widening speculation" echo Addison's images of spatial expansion: "... there are none who more gratifie and enlarge the Imagination, than the Authors of the new Philosophy .... Nothing is more pleasant to the Fancy, than to enlarge itself ...."[44] For Keats, the imagination, cut loose from the realm of "visible Objects with a real Existence", experiences this infinite space "with all [the] horror of a bare shoulderd Creature" "falling continually ten thousand fathoms deep and being blown up again without wings", like Milton's Satan plumbing the "vast vacuity" between hell and heaven.[45]

In Addison, the sublime, even when opening up possibilities of liberation, remains a means for the reinstatement of limits, making us aware of "the proper Limits, as well as the Defectiveness, of our Imagination; how it is confined to a very small Quantity of Space, and immediately stopt in its Operations, when it endeavours to take in any thing that is very great, or very little". It is at such moments that the imagination needs the assuring presence of the empirical world:

---

42. On Keats's interest in these subjects, see Robert Gittings, *John Keats*, Penguin, 1979, 44 and *passim*; Charles Cowden Clarke, "Recollections of John Keats", in Charles and Mary Cowden Clarke, *Recollections of Writers*, New York, 1878; Douglas Bush, "Notes on Keats's Reading", *PMLA*, 50 (1935), 785-806; A.D. Atkinson, "Keats and Kamchatka"; *Letters*, II, 100.

43. *Letters*, I, 277.

44. *The Spectator*, III, 574-75.

45. *Paradise Lost*, II, 926-38.

> The Understanding, indeed, opens an infinite Space on every Side of us, but the Imagination, after a few faint Efforts, is immediately at a Stand, and finds her self swallowed up in the Immensity of the Void that surrounds it: Our Reason can pursue a Particle of Matter through an infinite variety of Divisions, but the Fancy soon loses sight of it, and feels in it self a kind of Chasm, that wants to be filled with Matter of a more sensible Bulk.[46]

Addison's unanxious acceptance of the "proper Limits" of the imagination becomes, in Hume, a disenchanted and sceptical vision of an inescapably circumscribed universe. Keats's verse-epistle ranges through the entire spectrum of attitudes between these two positions. Moving from a semi-delirious bodying forth of random "shapes, and shadows, and remembrances", the imagination passes through a nightmarish sense of deadlock with the empirical world, in order to rest, rather wearily, in a natural prospect. The immediate presence of this prospect is registered empirically through a willed regression into superceded modes of innocence — the gathering of "young spring-leaves, and flowers gay/Of periwinkle and wild strawberry".[47]

"The end and aim of Poesy": ambition, labour and the sublime

In *Sleep and Poetry* (1817), Keats's first expression of a troubled commitment to poetry uses the discourse of the sublime to represent the individual's confrontation with the magnitude of his poetic ambition:

> ... yet there ever rolls
> A vast idea before me, and I glean
> Therefrom my liberty: thence too I've seen
> The end and aim of Poesy.
>
> (ll. 290-93)

"The end and aim of Poesy" is a recurrent preoccupation in the Keats-Reynolds correspondence, and a consideration of the idiom in which it is articulated illuminates the general context of ideas, imagery and allusions in which Keats engages with the sublimity of this "vast idea" in his verse-epistle. In a letter to Reynolds, written on 18 April 1817 from the Isle of Wight, Keats attempts to convey the feel of the nervous and restless days by the sea before beginning *Endymion*:

---

46. *The Spectator*, III, 576.

47. "To J.H. Reynolds", ll. 100-101.

> I find that I cannot exist without poetry — without eternal poetry — the whole of it — I began with a little, but habit has made me a Leviathan — I had become all in a Tremble from not having written anything of late — the Sonnet over leaf ["On the Sea"] did me some good. I slept the better last night for it — this Morning, however, I am nearly as bad again — Just now I opened Spencer, and the first lines I saw were these. —
>
> "The noble Heart that harbours vertuous thought
> And is with Child of glorious great intent,
> Can never rest, until it forth have brought
> Th' eternal Brood of Glory excellent —"[48]

Keats is positing here a complex relationship between poetry and his existence, locating the personal implications of this relationship within a larger vision of society and of literature. When he declares that he "cannot *exist* without poetry" (my emphasis), he is not only conveying the intensity of his immersion in poetry, but also articulating, with a combination of heightened excitement and a sense of doom, his awareness that poetry has become for him the only means of subsistence, of physical and material, and not just intellectual or emotional, sustenance. As his livelihood, poetry is inevitably implicated in a Hobbesian world of competition, self-preservation and acquisitiveness rather than being an alternative sphere of escape and deliverance. His image of the Leviathan, by condensing Milton and Hobbes, becomes a telling figure of the ambitious poet engaged endlessly and obsessively in the consumption and production of literary capital in a competitive cultural marketplace. The capital, in his case, is "eternal poetry"; and Keats's prose obscures, at this point, any distinction between reading and writing, between the consumption and production of eternal poetry. Milton's leviathan, we recall, "draws in, and at his trunk spouts out a sea".[49] From the reader's point of view, literature is an inexhaustible resource, a realm of gold that does not diminish on plundering, providing capital for unlimited investment without the risk of impoverishment.

For the aspiring poet, however, this consoling and empowering idea of eternal poetry becomes an intimidating standard of sublime achievement, associated with a more hostile and much less egalitarian economy, within which Milton himself figures as a "gormandizer",

48. *Letters*, I, 133-34.

49. *Paradise Lost*, VII, 415.

devouring the world's intellectual resources.[50] Just the day before he wrote his verse-epistle to Reynolds, Keats asks James Rice, on a devilish whim, "Did Milton do more good or harm to the world?", and goes on to consider the possibility of Milton having monopolized the "certain portion of intellect ... spun forth into the thin Air for the Brains of Man to prey upon":

> That which is contained in the Pacific and lie in the hollow of the Caspian — that which was in Milton's head could not find Room in Charles the seconds — he like a Moon attracted Intellect to its flow — it has not ebbed yet — but has left the shore pebble all bare — I mean all Bucks Authors of Hengist and Castlereaghs of the present day — who without Milton's Gormandizing might have been all wise Men ....[51]

"Gormandizing" conflates, with deliberate and brilliant indecorum, the figure of the Puritan poet with the "surfeit-swelled" body of Falstaff being asked to "Leave gormandizing" by his "Royal Hal".[52] However, this Shakespearean allusion works within a Shandean context that is crucial for our purposes. When Tristram finally gets to write "The Author's Preface" in the third volume of Sterne's novel, it turns out to be a political economy of how "the great gifts and endowments both of wit and judgment" are distributed among humankind:

> ... of these heavenly emanations of *wit* and *judgment*, which I have so bountifully wished both for your worships and myself, — there is but a certain *quantum* stored up for us all, for the use and behoof of the whole race of mankind; and such small *modicums* of 'em are only set forth into this wide world, circulating here and there in one by corner or another, — and in such narrow streams, and at such prodigious intervals from each other, that one would wonder how it holds out, or would be sufficient for the wants and emergencies of so many great states, and populous empires.[53]

---

50. *Letters*, I, 255.

51. *Ibid.*, I, 225.

52. William Shakespeare, *The Second Part of King Henry IV*, ed. A.R. Humphreys, London, 1966, V.v.47-54.

53. Laurence Sterne, *The Life and Opinions of Tristram Shandy, Gentleman*, ed. Ian Campbell Ross, Oxford, 1983, 155.

The Shakespearean usage and Tristram's sense of overcrowding and competition, together with the self-parodic, obsessive fretfulness with which it is expressed ("*a jocis ad seria, a seriis vicissim ad jocos transire*"[54]) "dovetails" in Keats's writing to articulate a persistent anxiety regarding the implications of Milton's achievements for his own literary aspirations.[55]

The obverse of the inexhaustible resources of literature is an unappeasable hunger for imaginative experience through poetry, figured as the "starv'd lips" of the knight's dream in "La Belle Dame sans Merci". The doubleness with which poetry is both egalitarian and power-hungry is contained in the word "leviathan" itself. In Hobbes, it stands for the commonwealth: "the Multitude so united in one Person".[56] But it was also used figuratively since the early seventeenth century for "A man of vast and formidable power or enormous wealth" (*OED*, 1c). As part of a Hobbesian world, the life of poetry internalizes the conflicts and energies that constitute that world, implicating the poet in what Hobbes has called "the NATURALL CONDITION of Mankind":

> For such is the nature of men, that howsoever they may acknowledge many others to be more witty, or more eloquent, or more learned; Yet they will hardly believe there be many so wise as themselves: For they see their own wit at hand, and other men's at a distance. But this proveth rather that men are in that point equall, than unequall. For there is not ordinarily a greater signe of the equall distribution of any thing, than that every man is contented with his share.
>
> From this equality of ability, ariseth equality of hope in the attainment of our Ends. And therefore if any two men desire the same thing, which neverthelesse they cannot both enjoy, they become both enemies; and in the way to their End ... endeavour to destroy, or subdue one another ....
>
> So that in the nature of man, we find three principall causes of quarrell. First, Competition; Secondly, Diffidence; Thirdly, Glory.[57]

Thus, in the lines from Spenser quoted by Keats, "Glory" can evoke Hobbesian associations, just as "Brood" can gesture beyond its primary

54. *Ibid.*, epigraph to Vol III of John of Salisbury's *Policraticus.*

55. *Letters*, I, 193.

56. Thomas Hobbes, *Leviathan*, ed. Richard Tuck, Cambridge, 1991, 120.

57. *Ibid.*, 87-88.

implications of nurturing and creativity towards a more sombre and melancholic meaning.[58] As a phrase suddenly come upon in a familiar poem, "Th' eternal Brood of Glory" could have offered Keats, at a moment of restless diffidence, a scope for identification and self-consciousness far surpassing its authorially intended meaning. It is, once again, the Hobbesian background to this passage and to the image of Milton gormandizing that helps us to link the imagery with the vision of "eternal fierce destruction" in the verse-epistle.[59]

Poetry ceases to be exalted or ethereal when taken up as a form of "employment", or when experienced as a "trade" — both words frequently used by Keats to describe his vocation from 1817 onwards.[60] Keats uses this professional and mercenary register to talk about poetry almost exclusively in his letters to intimate friends (especially Reynolds), reserving for his poetry a more sublime language in which to represent his sense of vocation. But, in a letter to Haydon, written on 10 and 11 May 1817, these two registers come together in a memorable appropriation of Shakespeare that is particularly relevant to Keats's self-image as a young poet:

> I am "one that gathers Samphire dreadful trade" the Cliff of Poesy Towers above me — yet when, Tom who meets with some of Pope's Homer in Plutarch's Lives reads some of those to me they seem like Mice to mine. I read and write about eight hours a day .... Thank God! I do begin arduously where I leave off, notwithstanding occasional depressions: and I hope for the support of a High Power while I clime this little eminence and especially in my years of more momentous Labor.[61]

Keats's stature as a poet fluctuates, in this passage, as his imaginative identifications with the different human elements in Shakespeare's

58. Keats could also have been influenced by Wordsworth's use of "brood" — most memorably in the "Immortality Ode", l. 119. See also Wordsworth's analysis of his own use of this word in the Preface to *Poems* (1815): see *Wordsworth's Literary Criticism*, ed. Nowell C. Smith, London, 1905, 158.

59. In this connection, see *Leviathan*, 88-89: "Out of Civil States, there is alwaye *Warre* of every one against every one." See also *Letters*, II, 79, for another Hobbesian account of human social behaviour.

60. See, for instance, *Letters*, I, 168 and 188.

61. *Ibid.*, I, 141.

theatrical fiction change.[62] When he gathers samphire, he seems, from the point of view of Edgar at the top of the cliff, "no bigger than his head". "Half way down" between the sea and the top, his sense of his own achievement is overwhelmed by a vision of what is yet to be scaled. The fact that the samphire-gatherer "hangs" in this position (a detail made much of by Wordsworth in his important discussion of these lines in the 1815 Preface: *ibid.*, 157) suspends him precariously between activity and powerlessness. But this location within a sublime topography does not exalt the status of his activity, which remains a humble "trade" even though its "dreadful"-ness makes it potentially heroic. In this the samphire-gatherer becomes identified in Keats's mind with Wordsworth's leech-gatherer — a connection made by Wordsworth himself in the 1815 Preface — who also elicits questions from the poet that are brought to bear on the poet's occupation: "How is it that you live, and what is it you do?"[63] After dwelling on the figure of the samphire-gatherer, Keats's identification shifts to the figure of the blinded Gloucester who thinks himself on the cliff-top trying to visualize the diminutive fishermen on the beach below as mice. But Keats's "Mice" are lines from Pope's Homer in one of John and William Langhorne's translations of Plutarch read out to him by his brother Tom. What reaches Keats's ears are at several diminishing removes from the sublime "mistiness"[64] of Greek, Pope's "rocking horse" to Homer's "Pegasus",[65] compared to which the floundering start to his *Endymion* seems more of an original achievement. But, like the cheated Gloucester, his elevation on the "Cliff of Poesy" is unstable and illusory, and a few lines later the cliff shrinks to "this little eminence" (recalling "the bald top of an eminence" in "Resolution and Independence", l. 58), as he projects his "Years of more momentous Labor" into the future. Thus, the transformations in Keats's self-image re-enact Shakespeare's movement from vertiginous sublimity to anti-climax in the Dover Cliff scene. Keats leaves unspecified as to what the "Cliff of Poesy" actually represents: whether it stands for the literary achievements of the past — "the overpowering idea of our dead

62. For the original samphire passage in Shakespeare, see *King Lear*, ed. Kenneth Muir, London, 1972, IV.vi (especially, ll. 11-24).

63. See Wordsworth's "Resolution and Independence", l. 119.

64. *Letters*, I, 274.

65. *Sleep and Poetry*, ll. 186-87.

poets",[66] or whether it is another image for the "vast idea" in *Sleep and Poetry*, for what is yet to be achieved in the projected career of the individual poet.[67]

The letter to Haydon illustrates another aspect of Keats's ambivalent relation to the sublime when representing poetic endeavour and achievement. The element of physical exertion in the samphire-gatherer's trade leads to the idea of "momentous Labor" in climbing the "Cliff of Poesy". Writing poetry is a matter of willed exertion, a form of activity that is the intellectual counterpart of physical labour. This, far from demeaning poetry, actually enhances its claim to dignity and recognition as productive work: "I read and write about eight hours a day ... I do begin arduously where I leave off ...." Recent studies of the sublime by Terry Eagleton, Frances Ferguson and Tom Furniss have concentrated on the role of the idea of labour in the discourse of the sublime.[68] In Part IV of the *Enquiry*, Burke provides the clearest account of the role of pain and terror as requisite forms of labour in the production of the sublime, using the idea of physical exercise or exertion most often metaphorically, but sometimes quite literally:

> Providence has so ordered it, that a state of rest and inaction, however it may flatter our indolence, should be productive of many inconveniences; that it should generate such disorders, as may force us to have recourse to some labour, as a thing absolutely requisite to make us pass our lives with tolerable satisfaction .... Melancholy, dejection, despair, and often self-murder, is the consequence of the gloomy view we take of things in this relaxed state of body. The best remedy of all these evils is exercise or *labour*; and labour is a surmounting of *difficulties*, an exertion of the contracting power of muscles; and as such resembles pain, which consists in tension or contraction, in every thing but degree. Labour is not only requisite to preserve the coarser organs in a state fit for their functions, but it is equally necessary to these finer and more delicate organs, on which, and by which, the imagination, and perhaps the other mental powers act.

---

66. *Letters*, II, 116.

67. Keats returns to this Shakespearean scene in a letter to his publisher Hessey on 8 October 1818, which describes the writing of *Endymion* as a "leap[ing] headlong into the Sea" (*Letters*, I, 374), echoing IV.vi.24 of *Lear*.

68. Terry Eagleton, *The Ideology of the Aesthetic*, Oxford, 1990, ch. 2, "The Law of the Heart: Shaftesbury, Hume, Burke"; see n.4 above for the Ferguson and Furniss references.

He then goes on to theorize, within an empiricist framework of the actual operations of the body or organs of sense, how "modes of terror" or the apprehension of "visual objects of great dimensions" act on the "sensibility" of the subject, producing through the labour of his or her physical and psychological response "an idea of the sublime".[69]

Burke's notion of the sublime, thus, can be seen as representing "a labour theory of aesthetic value", fostering a work ethic of "enterprise, rivalry and individuation".[70] Reading Burke's treatise as "a contribution to the hegemonic struggle of the rising middle class in the first half of the eighteenth century", Furniss extends and historicizes Eagleton and Ferguson's notion of the work ethic to show Burke's aesthetic theory as seeking to create an essentially middle-class and meritocratic ethos embodied in the image of the self-made man of ability without property. This heroic and virtuously labouring subject is a strategic fiction whose sublime aspirations are defined in terms of the distinctions between sublime and beautiful, labour and repose, masculinity and effeminacy, virtue and luxury. Rather than perceiving these oppositions as analogues to the relations between the middle class and the aristocracy, Furniss's deconstructive method sees them as "dramatizing different impulses or potentialities within the bourgeois ethos itself".[71] Thus the Burkean subject is not positioned in a simple alignment to a set of corresponding terms within these binaries, but is constituted by the "uneasy relation" between the terms that make each pair.

Keats's representations of the poet's self-making in the letters and poems use the discourse of the sublime with an awareness of the constituting dialectics that Furniss analyses in his book. His relationship with the sublime in developing a sense of vocation is dialectical in several ways. Firstly, the process of self-definition is necessarily relational for him, constituted by critical engagements with the sublimity of other literary achievements, notably of Shakespeare, Milton and Wordsworth. Secondly, these engagements are often realized in dialogue, as it were, played out within specific human relationships, often through epistolary exchange. The pressure of others' perceptions of one's own achievements and potentials determines self-making as integrally as aspirations engendered within oneself. I will demonstrate the extent to which this is important for Keats by an analysis of the

---

69. *Philosophical Enquiry*, 122 ff.

70. Ferguson, 134, and Eagleton, 54.

71. Furniss, 44.

language of Haydon's epistolary encouragement and of Reynolds's published reviews of Keats, both using the language of the sublime in holding up images of endeavour and achievement for him. Thirdly, Keats's own appropriation of the sublime language of labour and industry exists in an uneasy relation with another set of experiences and aesthetic criteria that derive from the demonized terms in Burke's system of oppositions. Luxury, indolence, idleness and effeminacy are all modes of aesthetic experience for Keats; and although these indulgences bring moments of anxiety or restlessness, they are invariably transformed into affirmations of creative power, reinforcing rather than undermining the seriousness and dignity of his labour.

Keats began his relationship with Haydon by writing two sonnets, "Highmindedness, a jealousy for good ....", and "Great spirits now on earth ...". that assimilate Haydon's image into an iconography of the sublime. In the first sonnet of 1816, although his achievements are presented in national and socially revolutionary terms, Haydon is a powerfully individuated figure whose sublime solitariness is defined in opposition to a vulgar commercialism: "A money mong'ring, pitiable brood" (l. 8). Moreover, the steadfastness of his genius is expressed in Wordsworthian terms as a "singleness of aim", through a quotation from Wordsworth's "Character of the Happy Warrior" (l. 40). Like the "high endeavours" (l. 6) of Wordsworth's exemplary warrior "Among the tasks of real life" (l. 4), Haydon is also what Furniss calls a "heroic and virtuous labourer" who in Keats's sonnet is "toiling gallantly" (l. 10). In the second sonnet, Haydon is brought explicitly in line with the other national heroes, such as Wordsworth and Hunt, and here too the sublimity of his stature combines individuation ("standing apart", l. 9) and heroic exertion ("mighty workings", l. 13). The latter is what Keats especially wishes to imbibe from him: "Your Letter has filled me with a proud pleasure and shall be kept by me as a stimulus to exertion ...."[72] It is significant that Keats sends his Elgin Marbles sonnets, written a few months later in March 1817, to Haydon immediately after composition, because these sonnets describe the difficulty and failure of precisely this kind of exertion in confronting the sublime. In doing so, and especially in addressing the difficulty of producing sublimity from the experience of being humbled by it, Keats comes up against a curious doubleness in Burke's theory.

In Burke, sublimity can be produced at both ends of the aesthetic confrontation. The object confronted and the human subject confronting

72. *Letters*, I, 118.

it could both embody and produce the sublime respectively. But the nature of the sublime objectively embodied and subjectively produced can be radically different although mutually generative. Defining the qualities of the sublime object is the ostensible project of Part II of Burke's treatise, and the result of this theoretical enterprise is a sublimity of superhuman power that could also take the forms of terror, obscurity, vastness or infinity. But what this produces in the human subject is an equally sublime powerlessness, most often manifesting itself in the failure of language and action. Inasmuch as the terrible and the terrified, the eloquent and the speechless, the "Cliff of Poesy" and the samphire-gatherer are both sublime, the sublime can be experienced as at once empowering and incapacitating, stimulating as well as paralysing exertion. Burke's treatise is particularly eloquent about the inadequacy of words in representing the sublime,[73] and Keats's sonnets address the particular difficulty for the poet in using the sublime for description and inspiration.

An acute analysis of this doubleness implicit in Burke's notion of the sublime can be found in Jeffrey's 1811 review of Alison's *Essays on the Nature and Principles of Taste*. Jeffrey's associationist critique of Burke and Payne Knight's aesthetics of the sublime is founded on the pointing out of a "radical error" in their monolithic definition of the sublime as "that sympathetic elevation of spirit which is produced by the contemplation of great might and energy":

> The radical error lies ... in supposing that sublimity can only be of one description; and that all sublime objects must produce one and the same sort of emotion. Now, the fact is, we think, very clearly, that there are at least two sorts of sublimity, in the same way as there are many sorts of beauty; — and that some produce a kind of awe, humiliation and terror, and some a sort of of inward glorying and elevation of the spirit, according to the nature of the suggestions which they supply to the imagination.

Shifting the focus of analysis from the intrinsic qualities of the sublime object to the spectator's state of mind, Jeffrey gives sublimity "a mixed character". It can either "kindle a kind of generous emulation in the minds of the spectators, and to elevate them, by an ambitious sympathy, to the height of the noble daring of which they see that their nature is

73. See *Philosophical Enquiry*, 57, and Part V, especially Section VII.

capable", or "quell and subdue the spirit with a sense of its own weakness and insignificance".[74]

Keats's 1817 sonnets on the Elgin Marbles capture this mixed character of the sublime by using the image of the "sick eagle looking at the Sky"[75] to represent the spirit "oppressed under the load of too overwhelming a sublimity".[76] In Akenside's *The Pleasures of Imagination*, "Nature's kindling breath" fires the "eagle-wings" of "the chosen genius"

> Impatient of the painful steep, to soar
> High as the summit; there to breathe at large
> Aetherial air: with bards and sages old,
> Immortal sons of praise.
>
> (I, 37-43)[77]

In Gray's "The Progress of Poesy. A Pindaric Ode", the eagle reappears as a symbol of proud transcendence "Sailing with supreme dominion/Through the azure deep of air" (ll. 114-17). The lyric poet tries to imitate this flight to rise "Beyond the limits of a vulgar fate" (l. 122).[78] Keats's "sick eagle" invokes this eighteenth-century trope of sublime aspiration in order to point up the limiting impulse within the sublime itself. But the most significant appropriation of Keats's image occurs in Reynolds's review of Keats's 1817 *Poems* published in *The Champion* of 9 March 1817:

> His imagination is very powerful, — and one thing we have observed with pleasure, that it never attempts to soar on undue occasions. The imagination, like the eagle on the rock, should keep its eye constantly on the sun, — and should never be

74. Jeffrey, 41-43.

75. "On Seeing the Elgin Marbles", l. 5; see also "To Haydon with a Sonnet Written on Seeing the Elgin Marbles" l. 3: "Forgive me that I have not eagle's wings".

76. Jeffrey, 43.

77. *The Poetical Works of Mark Akenside*, ed. Alexander Dyce, London, 1845, 87.

78. *The Poems of Thomas Gray, William Collins and Oliver Goldsmith*, ed. Roger Lonsdale, London, 1969, 176-77.

> started heavenward, unless something magnificent marred its solitude.[79]

What, for Keats, is a kind of sickness becomes, for Reynolds, a reassuring virtue. His Addisonian comfortableness with limits contrasts with Keats's Humean restiveness within them. In his verse-epistle to Reynolds, Keats redresses this sanitizing misrepresentation of himself by reinscribing the imagination as essentially transgressive in its engagement with sublimities outside its "proper bound".

Haydon also singles out the eagle image and elaborates on it, but it is in response to *Sleep and Poetry* that he imposes an extraordinary prevision of sublime greatness on Keats: "it is a flash of lightening [*sic*] that will sound men from their occupations, and keep them trembling for the crash of thunder that *will* follow." If the Elgin Marbles sonnets sought to represent powerlessness as a condition of the sublime, Keats is now confronted, in Haydon's "awful encouragement", with an image of himself that combines all the Burkean forms of power.[80] Haydon's attempt to encourage and enthuse Keats sustained this hyperbolic language of Napoleonic self-aggrandizement:

> I always arose, with a refreshed fury — an iron clenched firmness ... that sent me streaming on with a repulsive power against the troubles of life that attempted to stop me, as if I was a cannon shot, darting through feathers ... for I am able and work like a hero ....

His advice to Keats is relentless labour and industry, the only path to sublime achievement:

> God bless you My dear Keats go on, dont despair, collect incidents, study characters, read Shakespeare and trust in Providence — and you will do — you must, you shall ....[81]

This will to self-aggrandizement finds its appropriate trope, within the discourse of the sublime, in the idea of political imperialism or military conquest; and this species of the sublime is most explicitly outlined in Baillie's *An Essay on the Sublime* (1747). For Baillie,

79. *Selected Prose*, 100.

80. *Letters*, I, 122, 125 and 124.

81. *Ibid.*, I, 135,

military conquest is not just a metaphor for "an effort of the *Soul* to extend its *Being*, and hence an *Exultation*, from a *Consciousness* of its own *Vastness*";[82] but it is also used literally, with several examples from history, to illustrate sublime heroism, defined as "Desire" or "Pursuit of Conquest" arising "either from a Desire of Power, or Passion for Fame; or from both". His examples are Alexander and Caesar, the sublimity of the former contrasted with the "Power mean and contemptible, altho' ever so absolute" of Caligula.[83]

The figures of Homer and Cortez in the sonnet "On First Looking into Chapman's Homer" owe their sublimity to this imaginative engagement with imperialistic power in the discourse of the sublime, transposed — as in Longinus and Burke — to the realm of aesthetic response, "a sort of swelling and triumph" that sublime rhetoric induces in the reader or auditor: "that Glorying and sense of inward greatness, that always fills the reader of such passages in poets and orators as are sublime ...."[84] In the verse-epistle to Reynolds, Keats's sense of unreadiness for a certain kind of philosophical poetry is represented through an image that invokes the idea of martial audaciousness and conquest, even as Keats hesitates to measure his achievement in such terms:

> ... For in the world we
> Jostle — but my flag is not unfurl'd
> On the admiral staff — and to philosophize
> I dare not yet!
>
> (ll. 71-74)

Keats's image recalls Milton's Azazel, one of the four standard-bearers in Satan's army, rousing himself for battle:

> Azazel ... a cherub tall:
> Who forthwith from the glittering staff unfurled
> The imperial ensign, which full high advanced
> Shone like a meteor streaming to the wind ....[85]

82. John Baillie, *An Essay on the Sublime*, London, 1747, 8.

83. *Ibid.*, 19-26. See Keats's comparison of the Elizabethans with the moderns in *Letters*, I, 224.

84. *Philosophical Enquiry*, 46-47, in a section called "Ambition".

85. *Paradise Lost*, I, 534-37.

This whole passage (535-65) is underlined in Keats's copy of *Paradise Lost*, and his marginal note expresses a profound sympathy with "the thousand Melancholies and Magnificences of this Page". The fallen angels' "ethiop Immortality" in a "sort of black brightness" comes to Keats's mind just before going on to write about his own experience of being "Lost in a sort of Purgatory blind".[86] In an essay "On Milton", published in *The Champion* of 7 July 1816, Reynolds quotes this passage as an example of Milton's "strong" writing, characterizing his sublimity in terms of "a noble labour" and "heroic atchievements".[87] The Miltonic allusion, then, works in several directions within the verse-epistle. It evokes, primarily, an idea of conquest and advancement that Keats feels unready to take upon himself. But because of his familiarity with Milton's epic, the image brings with it secondary associations, not of power and aggrandizement, but of powerlessness and defeat, and the very different order of sublimity they evoke. Thirdly, because of the use that Reynolds had made of this passage, it is linked in Keats's mind, especially when writing to Reynolds, with yet another kind of sublimity — that of Milton's epic achievement.

Looking into the Plutarchian source also yields interesting results for the discussion of Keats's relation with the sublime. In Plutarch, Alcibiades is principally the embodiment of ambitious military imperialism; and this is the immediate context to Keats's allusion — the battle by sea between the Athenians and Lacedaemonians, in which

> *Alcibiades* [set] up a Flag in the top of his Admiral Galley, to shew what he was ... the ATHENIANS in the end won 30 Gallies of their Enemies, and saved all their own, and so did set up certain Flags of triumph and victory.[88]

Although primarily a sublime figure of individualism and achievement, like Baillie's Alexander and Caesar, Alcibiades had other associations for Keats, also derived from Plutarch. There is an entire section in Plutarch entitled "*Alcibiades* riot" that gives a vivid description of the vain and dissolute side of his character, his "rashness and indolency":

---

86. Reprinted in John Keats, *The Complete Poems*, ed. John Barnard, Penguin, 1973, 519-20.

87. *Selected Prose*, 66-67.

88. Plutarch, *The Lives of the Noble Grecians and Romans*, Cambridge, 1676, 178.

> And following these vain pleasures and delights, when he was in his galley, he caused the planks of the poop thereof to be cut and broken up, that he might lie the softer ... and he carried to the wars with him a guilded Scuchion wherein he had no cognizance nor ordinary device of the ATHENIANS, but only had the image of Cupid in it, holding lightning in his hands.[89]

This dichotomy between heroic prowess and indolent self-indulgence in Alcibiades' public image appealed to Keats's imagination, providing him with "the abstract Idea ... of an heroic painting ... of Alcibiades, leaning on his Crimson Couch in his Galley, his broad shoulders imperceptibly heaving with the Sea".[90] The admiral flag and the "guilded Scuchion" with the image of Cupid on it become objective correlatives of conflicting impulses — like Burke's sublime and beautiful — figuring the ambivalence of Keats's own relationship with the ethic of the sublime.

The relationships between labour and luxury, indolence and industry, work and leisure in the discourse of the sublime provide Keats with a vocabulary for representing some of the tensions and struggles in his "fevrous life alone with Poetry".[91] The story of his most productive year, as it emerges from the letters and poems, can be told in terms of his "1819 temper" — a sustained struggle between what he calls his "industrious humour"[92] and the imperatives of Indolence, the forms of which can range from "supremely careless" fantasies of readerly luxury[93] to a "numbing" of the body and of the creative faculties.[94] But in some of his earlier letters to Reynolds, Keats achieves a kind of serenity, not by resolving or transcending these dichotomies, but by recognizing their imaginative possibilities with a self-awareness that can become an enabling conviction.

The letter written to Reynolds on 19 February 1818 provides a beautiful example of this process. It addresses the problem of the poet's apparent idleness or indolence, compared to other forms of social production. Keats's vision of the paradoxical nature of the poet's labour

---

89. *Ibid.*, 171.

90. *Letters*, I, 265.

91. *Ibid.*, II, 113.

92. *Ibid.*, II, 225.

93. *Ibid.*, II, 78-79.

94. *Ibid.*, I, 287.

is encapsulated in a single phrase — "delicious diligent Indolence"; and he begins by exploring this contradiction in the experience of reading, apparently the most passive of aesthetic activities. Keats, however, transfers this alleged passiveness from the reader to the text, which is represented as a finished and perfected product ("full Poesy", "distilled Prose") having a "mere passive existence". The reader, on the other hand, although seeming to inhabit a world of eternal leisure, brings to this text "a certain ripeness in intellect" — a ripeness distinct from the fullness of the text in that it initiates an active process that is both creative and cognitive, a "voyage of conception". Thus, by establishing the reader's creativity, Keats is already paving the way for a transition from reading to writing, merging the figure of the reader into the figure of the poet. At the same time, the very passiveness of the text becomes a form of agency as Keats affirms the social purpose of "great Works". With the reader and the text both invested with agency, an interaction is set up between them whereby the reader assimilates what the text offers him and produces from this his own "tapestry empyrean". Keats's images for this reciprocity are the forms of intercourse between the flower and the bee, and between man and woman. Both images represent a creative process within a structure that tends to be polarized in terms of the active and the passive: "... let us open our leaves like a flower and be passive and receptive — budding patiently under the eye of Apollo and taking hints from every noble insect that favors us with a visit ...." Passiveness, here, is redefined as the capacity to receive the seeds for subsequent creation, of "taking hints", opening and budding. With this the transition from reception to creation is completed when a letter that has begun with the experience of reading ends with a new poem.

This "beautiful circuiting" between the reader and the text is also embodied in the spider who creates out of his own resources a shelter for himself that has minimal contact with the world outside this sphere of self-sufficiency. Keats's spider represents a fantasy of unalienated labour that can only exist in the natural world, outside the forms of social production in which the poet will always be implicated. This element of fantasy is central to the spirit and tone of the letter, its persistent tendency to situate itself outside the materiality of the actual world (in which reading and writing take place), even while forging a symbolic language from this world's natural processes. Keats's imagery creates a gossamer world of busy, diminutive creatures and talking birds, and quotatations from *The Tempest* and *A Midsummer Night's Dream* deftly sketch the figures of Ariel and Puck into this fantasy scenario. Words like "ethereal", "airy", "empyrean" and "spiritual" give the letter an illusory weightlessness, making it resemble the "tapestry empyrean", tipping with "as few points" the world in which it is written and which it addresses. But this is a willed and knowing rarefaction, deliberately reproducing, "in a finer tone", the most problematic activities and preoccupations of social existence, in which the poet, as "scullion-Mercury", is both a god and a menial. It is this knowledge, an ever-present "sense of real things", that is sustained as an undersong to the letter's consummate "sophistication". The consolation that the thrush offers is built upon a final, redeeming sadness that alone can make idleness other than what it seems to be:

> O fret not after knowledge — I have none
> And yet the Evening listens — He who saddens
> At thought of Idleness cannot be idle,
> And he's awake who thinks himself asleep.[95]

Sadness, and a vigilant responsiveness to its inward springs ("the wakeful anguish of the soul" as Keats puts it in the "Ode on Melancholy", l. 10) become a grave and strenuous labour that transforms the accompanying enervation into something richly humane and creative.

95. *Ibid.*, I, 231-33.

NEWTONIAN AND GOETHEAN COLOURS IN THE POETRY OF KEATS

ALLAN C. CHRISTENSEN

The attitude of the English Romantics to the optics of Sir Isaac Newton emerges amusingly in Benjamin Haydon's famous account of a dinner in his studio on 28 December 1817. They were celebrating the completion of his painting, *Christ's Entry into Jerusalem*, into which he had introduced the likenesses of Keats, Wordsworth and other Englishmen:

> [Lamb], in a strain of humour beyond description, abused me for putting Newton's head into my picture — "a fellow," said he, "who believed nothing unless it was as clear as the three sides of a triangle." And then he and Keats agreed he had destroyed all the poetry of the rainbow, by reducing it to the prismatic colours. It was impossible to resist him, and we all drank "Newton's health, and confusion to mathematics." It was delightful to see the good-humour of Wordsworth in giving in to all our frolics without affectation, and laughing as heartily as the best of us.[1]

Had they been aware of Goethe's recent treatise on optics, the *Farbenlehre*, published in 1810, the company would have found systematic evidence to justify their drinking of confusion to mathematics. Proud of his scientific thoroughness, Goethe had prosecuted his research precisely with the intent of refuting Newton. And if scientists remained unconvinced, the Goethean theory of colours did impress contemporary painters and become a decisive influence, a century later, upon the German Expressionists.[2] His findings may

---

1. *The Autobiography and Memoirs of Benjamin Haydon*, ed. Aldous Huxley, London, 1926, I, 269.

2. For a full and penetrating discussion of Goethe's influence upon painters from Turner to the Expressionists, see John Gage, *Colour and Culture: Practice and Meaning from Antiquity to Abstraction*, London, 1995, 201-12.

interest us, though, especially as a point of reference for the optical theories that figure pervasively in the poetry of Keats. In the European context of speculation about how the imagination brings our world into being, Keats's intuitions regarding colours led him to an almost Goethean position.

But to place Keats first in a more English context, we may define a disagreement that did not emerge at that convivial dinner but that may still have opposed him to another of Haydon's guests. Wordsworth, that is, had expressed in a well-known statement his intention to treat "incidents and situations from common life" in his poetry and "to throw over them a certain colouring of imagination, whereby ordinary things should be presented to the mind in an unusual way". In contrast, Keats would soon affirm in his verse epistle to J.H. Reynolds a wish *not* to project imaginary colours outwards but to absorb the colours of natural phenomena inwards into his dreams: "Oh, that our dreamings all of sleep or wake/Would all their colours from the sunset take" (ll. 67-68). The statement suggests the Keatsian "chameleon poet" that lacks its own colouration and simply soaks up the hues of its external surroundings.

Yet in the epistle to Reynolds, Keats does not desire passively to soak up any old colours whatsoever. He wants specifically to take colours "from something of material sublime" (l. 69), and the emphasis, as in Wordsworth, is upon the value of heightened or more than prosaic and ordinary colouration. Indeed I would argue that his image of the passive chameleon is deceptive. He admires a word in *Paradise Lost*, for example, in its resemblance to "a beautiful thing made more beautiful by being reflected and put in a mist".[3] And his own poetry shows a preference for phenomena in which colours are not only perceived but significantly altered or brought into existence through reflecting and filtering agencies. *Endymion*, in fact, contains innumerable moments in which the light of the moon or of the setting or rising sun is coloured by clouds and mists and even, in Book III, filtered through the depths of the sea. Beneath the waves, Endymion enjoys the rippling effects of the moonlight until with the "rosy veils" of Aurora the "sobered morning came meekly through billows" (ll. 112-16). The watery filter also figures memorably in "To Autumn", as the "Season of mists" conspires with the sun and in the last stanza colours an otherwise desolate setting with tints of beauty: the "barrèd clouds bloom the soft-dying day,/And touch the stubble-plains with rosy hue" (ll. 25-26).

---

3. "Keats, marginal note on *Paradise Lost*, I, 321" (see *Romanticism*, ed. Cynthia Chase, London and New York, 1993, 185).

In a similar way too, the foliage of trees may exercise the effect of filtration — creating the half-lights and shadows that make Keats's many groves and bowers so apparently inviting. Unlike Shelley at the end of *Adonais*, Keats generally turns away from the scorching white light of eternity to create his versions of the many-coloured dome. "'Gainst the hot season", as it is called at the beginning of *Endymion* (l. 18), he seeks a cover that will protect him as well from the opposite danger of chilling exposure "on the cold hill's side" ("La Belle Dame Sans Merci", l. 36).

Rather than simple or womb-like refuges, Keats's veiling and protective settings are rather complicated locations that may figure, as most explicitly in the "Ode to Psyche", the working interior of the mind. In this context, the colouring and filtering elements must represent an aspect of the active imagination or agency of perception. At this point the more systematic formulations of Goethe also become relevant and may helpfully illuminate, as it were, the Keatsian imagination.

Goethe develops his theories, I have said, with particular antagonistic reference to the optics of Newton. In the Newtonian conception white light is composed of the seven prismatic colours that are simply rays with seven different mathematically defined degrees of refrangibility. Disliking for temperamental and philosophical reasons such a consideration of colours as purely objective and mathematical phenomena, Goethe wishes instead to treat them as psychological impressions. The human eye and mind bestow upon our world its colours, which exist in relationships of complementarity and opposition in accord with our desire for a morally significant and philosophically coherent environment.

The complementarity and opposition between green, the simple colour of nature, and red, the most complex and spiritual of colours, is particularly interesting. But the principal opposition from which all colours derive is that between light and darkness, both of which are positive presences and the only two *objective* components of colouration. Our impressions of colours thus depend upon the various combinations of light and darkness as these are further filtered through water vapour and other media of varying degrees of density. So the stance of the perceiving subject with respect to the medium — the subjective point of view — acquires additional significance in the elaboration of the mental result. As for the spectrum of colours, Goethe places yellow at one end, closest to pure light, and blue at the other end, closest to pure darkness. Between the two a porous medium allows neutralization of the opposing elements into green, and a dense medium their convergence into brilliant red, the life-principle of our environment and the colour *par excellence*.

Goethe's *Farbenlehre* also has implications for a theory of acoustics.[4] Just as colours result from combinations of light and darkness, so it would appear that tones derive from combinations of sound and silence. Levels of pitch are accordingly not to be understood in purely mathematical terms of vibrating frequencies. Such acoustical theories may also have repercussions in Keats, as it may be interesting to notice in passing before returning to the topic of colours. Like Goethe, Keats seems at least to prize silence as a positive quality rather than as mere absence of sound and to emphasize subjective activity in the perception of musical tones. When in Book II of *Endymion* an eagle deposits the protagonist in a particularly luxurious bower, he thus transforms the silence into tones: "to his capable ears/Silence was music from the holy spheres" (ll. 674-75). Thanks to the same capable ears, presumably, the Cave of Quietude in Book IV is a place "where silence dreariest/Is most articulate" (ll. 539-40); and we may probably relate the articulations of quietude to the paradoxical "ditties of no tone" discerned amidst the silences of the Grecian Urn (l. 14). It is significant as well, I think, that in the bowers that encourage such auditory capacities the air is often a medium, in the Goethean sense, that odours and dews render utterly dense.

To come back then to Keatsian colours, we naturally find here too that a dense medium secures the best effects. Ideally the seas, clouds and vapours should possess a sufficient force and identity of their own to attract the love of the light. The moonlight seeks in Book III of *Endymion* "to please/The curly foam with amorous influence" (ll. 84-85) and to produce "a stress/Of love-spangles" (ll. 82-83).[5] The phenomenon suggests a process of penetration whereby the medium does not so much diffuse the light and the darkness as fuse with them. Fusion with the media of the particular densities that bring out deep red shades may also seem for Keats as for Goethe to provide some of the loveliest optical results. To prepare for the arrival of Apollo in Book III

4. Gage, 208-209, 235-36, gives some examples of Goethe's relevance to speculations among painters concerning correspondences between colours and sounds (the phenomenon of *audition colorée*).

5. In a letter of 1910, cited by Gage, 207-208, Franz Marc also describes the sexual dimension of encounters between colours close to blue, the male principle at the dark end of the spectrum, and colours close to yellow, the female principle at the light end.

of *Hyperion*, the poet therefore fills the air with music and cries:

> Flush every thing that hath a vermeil hue,
> Let the rose glow intense and warm the air,
> And let the clouds of even and of morn
> Float in voluptuous fleeces o'er the hills;
> Let the red wine within the goblet boil
> Cold as a bubbling well; let faint-lipped shells,
> On sands, or in great deeps, vermilion turn
> Through all their labyrinths; and let the maid
> Blush keenly, as with some warm kiss surprised.
>
> (ll. 14-22)

While incidentally reminding us of Keats's frequent treatment of embarrassment, the maiden's blushing response to the kiss also evinces the poet's concern with the physiology of the phenomenon of colour. In the passage from the first book of *Endymion* regarding the so-called pleasure thermometre too, the medium that seems to glow is not a cloud or an ocean but the human body. The experience of "fellowship with essence" causes the human subject to "shine/Full alchemized" (ll. 779-80); as the light materializes into "an orbèd drop" (l. 806), it dematerializes in its turn the actual body of the observer:

> ... Its influence,
> Thrown in our eyes, genders a novel sense,
> At which we start and fret, till in the end,
> Melting into its radiance, we blend,
> Mingle, and so become a part of it — ....
>
> (ll. 807-811)

The light "thrown in our eyes" irradiates us and dissolves us into a condition of incandescence. For Keats even more than for Goethe, I believe, the incandescence exists not just in the dense media of the external atmosphere but in something kindled physically within us. The variously glowing seas and clouds and the versions of leafy foliage are figures, as I have intimated, for the filtering elements of our own eyes and our bodily responses. It may also be that as "we start and fret" at the assault of the light upon our eyes, our resistance to the incursion is at least as important as any eventual submission to it. Whether they resist or submit, however, our eyes become the site of an encounter that can resemble either a military confrontation or, as in the passage from *Endymion*, an "amorous" meeting. Whereas Goethe locates the encounter between opposing light and darkness in the external environment, Keats opposes a light from without against an equally necessary darkness that is within. Or in some situations, as we shall observe, he reverses the paradigm so that a light that is within radiates outward to counteract an external darkness. In this latter visualization of the phenomenon, incidentally, Keats may approach the Wordsworthian scheme, as Coleridge also summarizes it his "Dejection" ode:

> Ah! from the soul itself must issue forth
> A light, a glory, a fair luminous cloud
> Enveloping the Earth —
> And from the soul itself must there be sent
> A sweet and potent voice, of its own birth,
> Of all sweet sounds the life and element!
>
> (ll. 53-58)

There is a parallel once more between visual and acoustical phenomena, and with respect to the latter, Keats may indicate the "capable ears" as the site wherein silence and sound meet. In this encounter too the locations of the opposing elements may be interchangeable. Either the literal silence without is transformed into unheard melody within, or the noisiness without is hushed by the imagination into something more beautiful. The latter possibility seems to obtain in *The Eve of St Agnes* when the "hall door", as a figure for the ears, briefly admits an agressive din and then "shuts again, and all the noise is gone" (l. 261).

The hushed and darkened chamber of Madeline on St Agnes Eve may provide, indeed, an especially good representation of the mind in the act of perception. While the door suggests the ears, the high casement window naturally implies the eyes of Porphyro. The window admits but perhaps also resists the moonlight as the many-coloured panes stain the "wintry" beams. Porphyro's mind is thereby able creatively to colour and warm into life his image of Madeline, whose beauty eventually kindles in turn his own glowing incandescence — so that he rises "Ethereal, flushed, and like a throbbing star" (l. 318). But to protect the beautiful impression, as I have been suggesting, it is important that Porphyro's organs of perception maintain their capacity not only as taming filters but as barriers too against threats from without. The window is thus in part a defensive weapon, which features a shield as its most central and prominent element — "A shielded scutcheon blushed with blood of queens and kings" (l. 216). Later the device of the bloody shield is even associated explicitly with Porphyro: he promises Madeline to keep up a protective vigilance as "Thy beauty's shield, heart-shaped and vermeil dyed" (l. 336). That blood-red, for Goethe the most vital of colours that derives from the encounter of equally matched light and darkness, may imply the eye's strenuous and combative vigilance. The protecting eye must confront the light, refusing to see unwanted things and so refusing to admit them into the mind.

In many passages of *Hyperion* the eyes figure even more obviously as protagonists that can determine, by their action of seeing or not seeing, what effectively exists. The closed and "realmless eyes" of Saturn (I, l. 19) are later described as "faded" when he opens them to "[see] his kingdom gone" (l. 90). In this case he has not refused to see his kingdom but has simply been unable to see it. The failure may nevertheless have originated in his eyes, so that their realmlessness is the cause and not the effect of the subsequent loss of his kingdom. In Book II, Enceladus therefore emphasizes the need to regain a capacity of vision and rejoices to see new signs of strength in the eyes of the Titans:

> "O joy! for now I see ye are not lost:
> O joy! for now I see a thousand eyes
> Wide-glaring for revenge!" As this he said,
> He lifted up his stature vast and stood,
> Still without intermission speaking thus:
> "Now ye are flames, I'll tell you how to burn,
> And purge the ether of our enemies;
> How to feed fierce the crooked stings of fire,
> And singe away the swollen clouds of Jove,
> Stifling that puny essence in its tent."
>
> (ll. 322-32)

In the battle with Jove, the principal weapon will be the eyes that are now associated not with blood but with fire. The strong eyes of the Titans will burn away the protective clouds that the weaker eyes of the enemy have thrown up and irradiated. At the prospect "a gleam of light" (l. 352) begins indeed to burn in the countenances of the Titans until the arrival of the scornful Hyperion with his even greater brilliance unnerves them once more. On his "granite peak" (l. 367) Hyperion

> stayed to view
> The misery his brilliance had betrayed
> To the most hateful seeing of itself.
>
> (ll. 368-70)

Forced to see themselves as hateful, the Titans effectively become hateful, and they will offer no opposition to what promises in Book III to become the supreme visionary power of Apollo. As he sees truths in the eyes of Mnemosyne, his brain reflects them back in a process that imparts strength and brilliance to *his* eyes as well:

> While his enkindled eyes, with level glance
> Beneath his white soft temples, steadfast kept
> Trembling with light upon Mnemosyne.
>
> (ll. 121-23)

The strong eye that projects the light deriving chiefly from an inward source may receive its most important figuration in Moneta, who replaces Mnemosyne in *The Fall of Hyperion*. Apparently quite oblivious to the external environment, a light from within illuminates her eyes and dominates the observing poet too:

> But for her eyes I should have fled away.
> They held me back, with a benignant light,
> Soft-mitigated by divinest lids
> Half-closed, and visionless entire they seemed
> Of all external things — they saw me not,
> But in blank splendour beamed like the mild moon,
> Who comforts those she sees not ....
>
> (I, 264-70)

Mastered by those half-closed or shielded eyes, the poet is able to intuit enough of what lies behind them to understand a certain paradox. The energy that "fill[s] with such a light/ Her planetary eyes" actually emanates from a dark source — the "high tragedy" that is being enacted "in the dark secret chambers of her skull" (ll. 277-81). There is another paradox too: whereas we have admired in the dark chamber of Madeline a beautifully coloured vision, the light associated with Moneta has lost all colour:

> ... Then saw I a wan face,
> Not pined by human sorrows, but bright-blanched
> By an immortal sickness which kills not.
> It works a constant change, which happy death
> Can put no end to; deathwards progressing
> To no death was that visage; it had passed
> The lily and the snow; and beyond these
> I must not think now, though I saw that face ....
>
> (ll. 256-263)

When he gets behind that face and into the mind of Moneta, the poet will be able in his turn to gain "a power ... of enormous ken/To see as a god sees" (ll. 303-304). The divine vision, as we gather once more, takes in very little from the world without and creates within the mind itself the realms and the colours that the god loftily chooses to perceive. Perhaps this strong imagination also recognizes that there is a tragic beauty that goes beyond the intensely vital colour of blushing blood to decay into the nearly corpse-like whiteness of Moneta's "immortal sickness".

Moneta's decadent whiteness disturbs us too as a reminiscence of what has happened to poor Lamia in the slightly earlier poem. The strongly imaginative Lamia has begun as a creature that is even positively ridiculous in her fantastic colouration:

> ... a gordian shape of dazzling hue,
> Vermillion spotted, golden, green and blue;
> Striped like a zebra, freckled like a pard,
> Eyed like a peacock, and all crimson barred.
>
> (I, 47-50)

After her metamorphosis and her successes in perceiving and creating attractive environments, however, she is finally dissolved by the superior vision of Apollonius into a sick whiteness:

> ... No soft bloom
> Misted the cheek; no passion to illume
> The deep-recessèd vision. All was blight;
> Lamia, no longer fair, there sat a deadly white.
>
> (II, 273-76)

Whereas the vision of Moneta may involve a tragic awe, the power of Apollonius to see through Lamia and drain her body of blood demonstrates the perversity of the strong imagination. Even in their perversity, that is, the implacable glaring eyes which are virtually the entire identity of Apollonius continue to demonstrate a battling imagination. He sees not necessarily what is there but what he determines or pre-determines to see. Of the realm of Lamia, we read, "'twas just as he foresaw" (l. 162), and, in a sense more grim than Saturn's, his eyes have foreseen her final realmlessness. So he can impassively "unweave a rainbow" and resolve all colours and mysteries into "rule and line" (ll. 235-37). Indeed, as Marjorie Levinson has recently argued, he is a Pythagorean that reduces all phenomena to numerical values, thereby returning us as well to an entirely Newtonian optics.[6] Far from the psychological splendours that may exist within our minds, the matter of colours becomes again a merely mathematical reference to degrees of refrangibility. Still to the Newtonian mind that has created it, the mathematical vision must have its own abstract charms.

In his optics, Keats has placed himself amongst the most daring of the Romantics. Wishing to see as a god sees, his protagonists dare to believe that what they observe depends upon their own eyes and wills rather than upon anything that is really out there in space. So they transcend a materialistic and mathematical vision and live in environments dense with vapours and irradiated by mental colours — as in the canvasses of William Turner and the painters that subscribe to Goethean theories. But while they may thus dare to doubt the objective validity of the Kantian *Ding an sich*, they are not precisely solipsists and so must brave encounters with the possibly stronger visions of other observers. Inevitably, it may also seem, they call into being their versions of Nemesis.

At best the Nemesis will be a new order of gods that will triumph through its superior beauty as well as its stronger eyes. At worst it will be the abstractly quantifying and sterilizing vision of a Newtonian Apollonius. Among the competing visions that can never finally be ratified by appeals to something external, the poems propose the tension of oppositions. Never absolute and uncontested, the truth continues to shimmer colourfully or to dissolve towards blankness as itself a phenomenon of ongoing reflection.

6. Marjorie Levinson, *Keats's Life of Allegory: The Origins of a Style*, Oxford, 1988, 272, 278.

KEATS'S LAST WORKS AND HIS POSTHUMOUS EXISTENCE

RALPH PITE

There are three areas I wish to explore in this essay: firstly, I will be pondering how Keats's writing, moods and behaviour in his last year do not fit very well with the picture that biographical and critical studies have presented. These differences particularly inform our understanding of Keats's poem, *The Cap and Bells; or, The Jealousies* and can be illustrated by it. That poem, however, is itself a development from earlier works, especially "The Eve of St Mark" and the revised version of *The Eve of St Agnes* — and this too I want to consider. Thirdly, *The Cap and Bells* is a response to Byron's *Don Juan*; Keats is not recommending us to "open [our] Goethe" necessarily, but like Carlyle he wants us to "close our Byron". Moreover, Keats's poem and Carlyle's *Sartor Resartus* are both preoccupied by the sources of selfhood and both voice themselves indirectly via supposed authors and rapid changes of speaker.

Few critics have had anything good to say about *The Cap and Bells*. To the high Victorian view of Keats, the attempt at satire was innately misguided. Sidney Colvin remarked of the revisions Keats made to *The Eve of St Agnes* that they are "the first sign we find of that inclination to mix a worldly-wise, would-be Don Juanish vein with romance which was soon to appear so disastrously in *The Cap and Bells*".[1] Mixing tones is a suspect "inclination" that Keats would have better restrained; the result is disastrous. This attitude to the poem has lasted because while Colvin thinks of it as a moment of weakness, John Barnard considers the poem as the road Keats did not take:

> [Keats] had the capacity to write the fanciful prose pieces on contemporary life written by Hunt himself, Charles Lamb, and

1. Sidney Colvin, *John Keats: His Life and Poetry His Friends Critics and After-Fame*, London, 1917, 367. J. Middleton Murry explains the hostility to the poem in *Keats and Shakespeare: A Study of Keats's Poetic Life from 1816 to 1820*, London, 1925, 207-209.

> other periodical writers.
>
> But Keats's dedication to a high-minded view of Poetry and Fame meant that any talent for whimsical or light verse, or for satire, went undeveloped.[2]

He could have done better in light verse, only he chose not to; what Barnard calls high-mindedness was for Colvin the poet's "natural" avoidance of attempts at mixed forms. Both critics, therefore, whether or not they endorse the "romantic narrative" of Keats's career, use that structure to judge the poem and to account for its failure. Keats's dedication to Poetry and Fame precludes success either as a hack journalist or as a "flash" Byronic satirist. Poetry and worldly-wisdom are either intrinsically alien to each other or Keats has chosen to make them so.

Keats, however, was no mean journalist: *The Champion* theatre reviews are, of course, exceptionally insightful and revealing now about the poet writing then. Nonetheless, they are convincingly undistinguished: Keats adapts himself and his manner of writing very well to the demands of journalism; more easily than Shelley, for example, or Henry James. Adaptability also made him a helpful collaborator. Stanza 63 of *The Cap and Bells* seems to include, as Jack Stillinger points out, a private joke between Hunt and Keats. The magician Hum produces a fine poetical passage and his master, the Emperor Elfinan pats him kindly on the head:

> "Why, Hum, you're getting quite poetical.
> These *nows* you managed in a special style."
>
> (ll. 559-60)

Hunt's essay in the *Indicator* of 28 June 1820 is entitled "A Now, Descriptive of a Hot Day" and Hunt reports in his *Autobiography* it was "the paper … most liked by Keats …. He was with me while I was writing and reading it to him, and contributed one or two of the passages."[3] Hunt cannot have been writing the paper long before it was

---

2. John Barnard, *John Keats*, Cambridge, 1987, 147-48.

3. John Keats, *Complete Poems*, ed. Jack Stillinger, Cambridge: Mass., 1982, 484. All texts of Keats's poem are quoted from this edition; references are to the book or canto and line-numbers of the poems. All quotations from Keats's letters are from *The Letters of John Keats 1814-1821*, ed. Hyder Edward Rollins, 2 vols, Cambridge: Mass., 1958. Stillinger adopts Keats's preferred title of *The Jealousies* for *The Cap and Bells; or, The Jealousies*: see Stillinger, 481-82. Keats's sonnet

published and this has implications for the dates when we imagine Keats working on the poem.[4] In any case, Keats's participation suggests a more robust and practically resolute final summer than biographers usually present.

As Barnard says, Keats did have quite a talent for jokes and appears to have wanted to develop it. Moreover, the poem, although as Brown says "it was begun without a plan" and "written subject to future amendments and omissions", could be excerpted more readily than any other of his works precisely because of its incidental, spontaneous quality.[5] Stanzas 25-29, about the discomforts of travelling by carriage in London, were published by Hunt in the *Indicator* on 23 August.[6] The beginnings of Keats's success as a poet were obvious during this summer: the 1820 volume was published in the last week of June. As you would expect, Hunt's *Indicator* ran a supportive defence and appreciation of the volume on 2 and 9 August, but favourable reviews were already appearing elsewhere — in *The Monthly Review* in July and Jeffrey's more grudging assessment in the *Edinburgh Review* in August. P.G. Patmore had already written an enormous effusion of praise for *Endymion* for the *London Magazine* in April and in September the *London Magazine* also printed a judicious but highly respectful piece on the 1820 volume by John Scott. In consequence, the *Eclectic Review* was already beginning to sound passé when in September its review of the volume attacked Hunt via Keats and lambasted once again the Cockney school. The extract from *The Cap and Bells* in the *Indicator* responds to this atmosphere. It was as near to a publicity stunt as Keats ever came. Keats's entry into literary London, however, was not simply a compromise with necessity, I think, nor a frantic effort to publish

---

"As Hermes Once Took to His Feathers Light" was published in the same number of the *Indicator*.

4. The date is usually given as November-December 1819. Keats had the poem in mind repeatedly in 1820 (see *Letters*, II, 268, 289-90, 299) and probably added to and adapted it. C.L. Finney, *The Evolution of Keats's Poetry*, 2 vols, Cambridge: Mass., 1936, 732-37, gives a very helpful account of the poem's possible date.

5. Brown is quoted in a note to the poem in *Life, Letters, and Literary Remains, of John Keats*, ed. R.M. Milnes, 2 vols, London, 1848, where the poem first appeared. See also *The Keats Circle: Letters and Papers, 1816-1878*, ed. Hyder Edward Rollins, 2nd edn, 2 vols, Cambridge: Mass., 1965, 71-72, 99.

6. See *The Poems of John Keats*, ed. Miriam Allott, 3rd impression with corrections, London and New York, 1975, 713n.

what he could before he died.

Had Keats known for sure he was going to die, I would expect him to have prepared a last will and testament more carefully. Charles Brown's story is the most famous version of Keats as Stoic, foreseeing and resigning himself to death. Brown says in his life of Keats that, on seeing the blood from the haemorrhage in February 1820, Keats remarked, "I know the colour of that blood; — it is arterial blood; — I cannot be deceived in that colour; — that drop of blood is my death-warrant; — I must die."[7] I doubt whether Keats was actually so melodramatic at the time. One wonders whether Brown is simply misremembering or recording what, in his view, Keats "must have been" feeling.

Keats refers to this supposed conversation on one occasion only. He writes to Fanny: "When I said to Brown 'this is unfortunate' I thought of you."[8] It would be easy and natural for Brown to expand on this blunt, inscrutable comment — to develop what he took to be the unstated meaning of Keats's words. One indication of this likelihood is Keats's own anxiety that "this is unfortunate" might be misunderstood and even misused. In the letter in question, Keats is trying to reassure Fanny that his first thoughts were for her; that he saw immediately how unfortunate his illness was for her as well as for him. She may or may not have been complaining of neglect; in any case, she would have been likely to feel Keats's coolness as a rejection — of her and of their love — particularly if it was reported to her by his jealous friends. She would have seen that Keats's illness threatened to exclude her by throwing him back on his own resources, restricting him to his own part of the house and confining him to the circle of his male friends.

In all these accounts of Keats's illness, then, we are on dubious ground. Keats's comments are influenced by his consideration for the feelings of his lover and his friends; at the same time, their reactions and subsequent recollection are inevitably forms of grief-work, coloured by bereavement. Keats, moreover, recognized his vulnerability to their feelings of loss. His sense of himself as leading a "posthumous existence"[9] can be read as, in part, a wry comment on his powerlessness against other people's elegies. The "changes of sentiment" that come to characterize his last poems and the drive in them towards self-parody are, I suggest, responses to the usurpation of

7. *Keats Circle*, II, 73.

8. *Letters*, II, 254.

9. *Ibid.*, II, 359.

his identity which occurred when Keats became dangerously ill. His writing in the poems as well as in the letters throughout the period of his illness is a way for him to resist people's pity and to contend with the stereotype of the consumptive poet that was imposed on him and on the pattern of his life.

Similarly, his efforts at publication are forward-looking and ambitious. Keats was still trying to make a career for himself: illness was to him a period of enforced idleness in which, to stop himself fretting, he decided to publish much of the best of what he had already written. The hope would be that success now would set him up for the postponed future or help him financially if the illness went on. Similarly, even in Italy in late 1820, Keats continued to fight against the conviction that he was going to die — partly as before in the belief that fighting against it was the best way of staying alive. Keats's conduct in his last year, therefore, was a form of resistance to the plangency of biography. It brings to notice and reflects on the distance between the sorrow of bereavement and the prospect of dying oneself. That consideration, in turn, throws a different light on *The Cap and Bells*, while Keats's persistence in writing comic verse disturbs the image of him as high-minded and unpopular. *The Cap and Bells* is not a disastrous failure and Keats had not unequivocally decided to renounce popularity for art — not in his last year, certainly, and before that only in an uncertain, troubled way if at all. Keats similarly was not at a complete loss what to do after September 1819, when he had completed "To Autumn" and closed the so-called "Living Year". Robert Gittings, in his biography of Keats, entitles the chapter that covers autumn 1819, "Unmeridianed"; Walter Jackson Bate's chapter headings for September 1819 to February 1820 are "The Close of the Fertile Year", "Illness" and, lastly, "Adrift".[10] This view does not square with his practical energy in the autumn and later nor with the confidence of his remark to Fanny Keats (20 December 1819): "My hopes of success in the literary world are now better than ever."[11]

---

10. Robert Gittings, *John Keats*, London, 1968, 515; Walter Jackson Bate, *John Keats*, Cambridge: Mass. and London, 1963, 562, 606, 628. "Unmeridian'd" is quoted from a letter to Severn — 10 November 1819; on 26 October 1819 Keats writes to Fanny Keats, "I am in an i[n]dustrious humour"; on 12 November 1819, in a more worried letter to George and Georgiana, Keats nonetheless observes that "as we get older, each follows with more precision the bent of his own Mind" (*Letters*, II, 227, 225, 230).

11. *Letters*, II, 237.

In 1820, then, Keats continued to work intelligently and prospectively; *The Cap and Bells* is a part of his continuing endeavour and he probably went on writing it until he left for Rome in September. Moreover, the tone of *The Cap and Bells* is not an entirely new departure, for not only was Keats a talented writer of occasional comic pieces, many of his poems in 1819 have satirical elements. In "The Eve of St Mark", for example, which he himself described as evoking the atmosphere of a country town, its quietness, sanctity and peace, Keats introduces a hint of worldly-wise disdain.

> The silent streets were crowded well
> With staid and pious companies,
> Warm from their fireside orat'ries,
> And moving with demurest air
> To even song and vesper prayer.
>
> (ll. 14-18)

Or a moment later, when Bertha looks into the "curious volume" whose "broideries" "Perplex'd her", Keats includes lines that foreshadow T.S. Eliot's quatrain poems of 1920:

> Martyrs in a fiery blaze,
> Azure saints mid silver rays,
> Aaron's breatplate, and the seven
> Candlesticks John saw in heaven,
> The winged Lion of St Mark,
> And the Covenantal Ark,
> With its many mysteries,
> Cherubim and golden mice.
>
> (ll. 31-38)

The aplomb of the cadence and the full-rhyme in "the seven/Candlesticks John saw in heaven" has an arch over-completeness. Keats's "golden mice" evoke and ridicule the baubles and the vulgar superstition that disfigure medieval Christianity. Bertha has, therefore, every right to be perplexed; yet it may not be an instructive confusion, not the wonder and astonishment that lead to insight. There is social commentary in the poem as well as religious scepticism: these churchgoers "Warm from fireside orat'ries" contrast with the "chilly sunset" that "told/Of unmatur'd green vallies cold" (ll. 7-8), whose immaturity is "outstript" by the sycamores and elm trees in the bishop's garden: "By no sharp north wind ever nipt,/So shelter'd by the mighty pile" (ll. 46-47).

The Pre-Raphaelites adopted "The Eve of St Mark" in the same way that they adopted "The Lady of Shalott". As Isobel Armstrong has shown, Tennyson's poem is systematically ambiguous in its rendition of the medieval past.[12] It seems to me that Keats is doing something similar here: he commends the poem to his brother and sister as careless but enjoyable, saying that it is "quite in the spirit of Town quietude. I th[i]nk", he adds, "it will give you the sensation of walking about an old county Town in a coolish evening. I know not yet whether I shall ever finish it."[13] The remark sounds like another invitation to reverie and idleness, similar to the earlier sonnets in praise of wise passiveness and hostile to the bustle of self-determination. Keats introduces the poem as a life of sensations not thoughts and that (we might suppose) is equivalent to Bertha's dazed reading of the book. However, there is a knowingness about his "quite in the spirit of Town quietude" (a knowingness furthered by the internal near-rhyme) as if Keats thought of himself as providing a clichéd idyll; his confidence too is decisive "I *think* it will give you" (my emphasis), not "I hope it will" or "I doubt whether it will".

Indeed the poem does give us something of that sensation: the Pre-Raphaelites were not entirely mistaken about it. Keats makes two words of "evensong" in the line "To even song and vesper prayer". The separation makes the description incantatory, into an invocation of calm. The enchantment seems also to be working as it is spoken because the line manifests the stateliness it describes. Yet the congregation is moving with "demurest air". "Demurest of the tabby kind" is Thomas Gray's description of the favourite and unfortunately drowned cat.[14] Quiet self-satisfaction and composed dignity characterize both the animal and Keats's pious folk. "Demurest" makes his provincials self-regarding, conscious of being watched and satisfied to play their part to the full. They seem fully to enjoy the protection which the bishop's palace offers both to them and to the trees, to the sycamores and elms whose growth is as quick as hothouse flowers. The social edge to the poem alerts its reader to the idea that this quiet, well-protected space is unnatural, artifically well-defended and contrived by power: the

12. Isobel Armstrong, *Victorian Poetry: Poetry, Poetics and Politics*, London, 1993, 12-18, 67, 83-86, 246.

13. *Letters*, II, 201.

14. Thomas Gray, "Ode on the Death of a Favourite Cat, Drowned in a Tub of Gold Fishes", l. 4; note *OED* definition 3: "Affectedly or constrainedly grave or decorous."

Minster, Keats says, is "a *mighty* pile" (my emphasis). Similarly, Bertha looks out on this scene in the intervals of reading her curious volume. The bewildering paraphernalia in the book are repeatedly juxtaposed to this idyllic scene whose artificiality is no more than disguised. Its many mysteries boil down, in fact, to "Cherubim and golden mice". Medievalism, the spirit of Town quietude, is nearly reduced by the poem to another golden mouse: a harmless, whimsical oddity or a quaint entertainment.

Nearly but not quite reduced to this because the poem avoids lampooning the idea or hankering after it or bemoaning the way in which medieval simplicity has become a hackneyed device or been reduced to what Keats would call "mawkishness". There is a curious poise to its ironies that corresponds, I think, to the tone of measured but non-commital confidence with which Keats recommends it to his brother. He is not, he declares, indifferent to it, but he is undeluded by the charms he can work. Hidden within his composure, then, is a vein of self-assertion — his readers may be deluded but he is not — and of aloofness. He stands above and away from both his achievements and his audience.

Marjorie Levinson, in *Keats's Life of Allegory*, says of the Hyperion poems and *Lamia* that "it is not poise we feel but something more like deadlock", a deadlock however that betokens "a qualitatively different kind of knowledge than the sort we've explored in 'La Belle Dame' and 'St Agnes'". She then continues:

> A Romantic restatement of the claim would go something like this: through *Lamia* a crisis poem, Keats acquires his own voice. "The Cap and Bells", an utterance *in propria persona*, is the satiric-comic expression of that critical subjectivity. We see that there is nothing "bad" about the poem, and, sad to say, nothing very good either.[15]

The deadlock is presented as an advance on the earlier poise; according to Levinson, Keats's qualitatively different knowledge (romantically construed as his acquiring his own voice) is gained by facing his conflicts. This engagment is made possible by the narrative form (rather than discursive form) of the Hyperion poems and *Lamia*. Levinson's rejection of *The Cap and Bells*, however, betrays her commitment to the romantic positions she parodies. The poem is not earnest enough for

15. Marjorie Levinson, *Keats's Life of Allegory: The Origins of a Style*, Oxford, 1988, 200, 253.

her; it does not engage in the deadlock which brings knowledge; rather it merely recapitulates a previously attained insight in a "satiric-comic" mode.

It is possible to read *The Cap and Bells* more affirmatively than this: the poem is intelligently suspicious about how far earnest engagement will take you; about how far it will advance not only a career but a process of soul-making. However, in doing so, the poem does extend the trajectory which Levinson suggests; it moves on from deadlock as deadlock had been a move on from poise. Consequently, its "satiric-comic expression" lacks the security that irony can give. The development revealed by the poem consists in its disavowal of the settled position achieved by "The Eve of St Mark". Its peculiar mixing of tones and its suspicions about *depth* both arise from its interest in unsettling poise.

Colvin disparages the revisions Keats made to *The Eve of St Agnes* in September 1819, at the close of the fertile year. His distaste echoes the protests made by Woodhouse, who found in the new ending "a sense of pettish disgust".[16] Keats changed the last lines of the poem from:

> Angela the old
> Died palsy-twitched, with meagre face deform;
> The Beadsman, after thousand aves told,
> For ay unsought for slept among his ashes cold.
>
> (ll. 375-78)

to:

> Angela went off
> Twitch'd with the Palsy; and with face deform
> The beadsman stiffen'd, 'twixt a sigh and laugh
> Ta'en sudden from his beads by one weak little cough.[17]

When Woodhouse objected, Keats replied (Woodhouse tells us) by saying he liked "that the poem should leave off with this Change of Sentiment — it was what he aimed at, & was glad to find from my objections to it that he had succeeded".[18] Woodhouse does not take

---

16. *Letters*, II, 162-63.

17. Quoted from Allott, 479n.

18. *Letters*, II, 163.

this explanation quite seriously — it is to him a typical "Keats-like rhodomontade" whose perversity shows up the eccentricity of what he was trying to do. A "Change of Sentiment" though, whether you like it or not, is undoubtedly brought about by the new ending: "'twixt a sigh and laugh/Ta'en sudden from his beads by one weak little cough." It's a deliberately provocative, near-adversarial way of writing — an attempt to escape the unthinking condescension with which Keats felt himself viewed by his confessedly less "sensitive" friends. Asserting himself against that demure patronage, however, ran the risk of exposing him to it still more, as Woodhouse's deftly supercilious reaction shows. Keats's calculated offensiveness may all too easily be dismissed as pettish, sulky, obstinate or as just a phase brought on by neglect and frustration.

Why, if it was so easily criticized and so unpopular with his friends, did Keats persist in this vein later in the autumn? The reason, I believe, was that changes of sentiment, a moody unpredictability and capriciousness, began to seem to him the customary way people had of sustaining themselves under pressure and social confinement. His letters in the second half of 1819 and the following year dislike London life: its slack extensiveness and the illusory freedom which sheer size can give.[19] He seems to have been shifted from the ironies of quietude to the miseries of society; indeed, of "Saciety" as he called it, imitating in that spelling an upper-class accent, and, by punning "society" with "satiety", sounding as if he had had his fill.[20] Becoming more of a "flexible speaker" is characteristic at this time of Keats and of his poetry: "The Eve of St Mark" includes an Angora cat, a parrot, a macaw, and a feeling of orient silks in the cloistered walks. Such pampered eclecticism is imitated by the poem's impersonation of Chatterton. Similarly, only more so, *The Cap and Bells* is eclectic and flexible, shifting from voice to voice: from Hum's poetic moments to Crafticanto's narrative, from Eban's vulgar refinement to Elfinan's refined vulgarity.[21]

---

19. Cf. his praise of sleep in *Endymion*, Book I, ll. 455-57, "O unconfin'd/Restraint! imprison'd liberty! great key/To golden palaces, strange minstrelsy."

20. See "the State of Saciety", "When once a person has smok'd the vapidness of the routine of Saciety" and "standing at Charing cross and looking east west north and south I can see nothing but dullness" (*Letters*, II, 242, 244 — 15 January 1820. See also *ibid.*, 144, 149, 187).

21. Crafticanto resembles Tom Moore's "Phil. Fudge" in *The Fudge Family in Paris* (1818), especially "Letter IX". Keats may have taken the name "Hum" from Moore's "Fum and Hum, the Two Birds of Royalty", a squib on the Brighton

The fragment purports to withdraw from such a jarring chorus of voices by ending on a promise to resume the story, "Plain in our original mood and tense". Plainness is, however, a naïve hope typical of Keats's narrator, "Lucy Vaughan Lloyd" of "China Walk". She sounds oblivious to the difficulty of what she is proposing and, consequently, idleness and privilege seem to luxuriate in an ideal of impartial utterance. Lucy's blithe energies, though, are roused by this prospect. She is blind to her own freedom from labour when she adds, we will "proceed to tell/Plain .../... *though labour 'tis immense!*" (my emphasis). Her exclamation mark rejoices in the heroism of the attempt. One of the glories of her poetic calling is this arduous work and there is, for her, no question but it will be admired. Her self-congratulation imagines social acceptance and, curiously, seems to produce it. For the Lucy Vaughan Lloyds of this world, there is an audience delighted to endorse the view she has of herself and keen to think of her rambling fancy as an admirable attempt if not a deed accomplished; an audience eager to create poets and poetesses out of whoever has enough unthinking self-confidence to go into print.

The undertones of the poem, then, are as hostile to "saciety", as resentful and vindictive as Keats sounded when he revised *The Eve of St Agnes*. But while the poem pokes fun at women poetasters, it also attacks those who make such confident fun of them — Keats, himself, for instance, and, more eminently, Byron, whose *Don Juan*, Cantos I and II, was published anonymously in July 1819.[22] *The Cap and Bells* responds to the challenge it sets as well as satirizing the posture it strikes. Keats had frequently disliked the mannered theatricality of Byron's poems, though he recognized a force in the work that commanded respect. Earlier, Keats had attacked Byron's poetry as shallow and inauthentic;[23] in *The Cap and Bells*, he seems to think Byron was not being inauthentic enough. Or, at least, he is trying to

---

Pavilion, "that Palace or China-shop (Brighton, which is it?)" (l. 3). Bob Fudge mentions "the Brighton Chinese" in "Letter VIII" of *The Fudge Family in Paris* (*The Poetical Works of Thomas Moore*, ed. A.D. Godley, Oxford, 1910, 452, 476). Elfinan's Chinese toys suggest the Regent directly, and Keats, like Moore, is partly just representing contemporary England when he conflates Orient and Occident. Keats was learning to admire Moore's satire in 1819 (contrast his views in *Letters*, II, 73, 245).

22. Keats knew of the poem's imminent appearance: see *Letters* II, 59 — 14 February 1819.

23. See *Letters*, I, 368, 390; II, 16. Keats comes nearest to admiration for Byron in *Letters*, I, 395 — 14 October 1818.

find out if that criticism of Byron can be made to stick.

Keats referred to *Don Juan* in September 1819 as "Lord Byron's last flash poem".[24] "Flash" meant, at the time, not simply "showy" or "smart" but canting as well: "applied .. to a person .. who has a smattering of the cant, and .. pretends to a knowledge of life which he really does not possess" (1812).[25] Keats resented, perhaps enviously, the social superiority that Byron could turn to his advantage. His use of "flash", however, starts to accuse Byron of facile self-confidence disguising actual ignorance. This was the reason why *Don Juan* had no depth and could offer instead only illusions of depth. Keats's remark is off-hand and studiedly casual, by contrast with the moral panic of his guardian, Richard Abbey. In a conversation between Abbey and Keats, Abbey "began blowing up Lord Byron" and yet, the next minute, conceded that *Don Juan* had some worth: "however Says [*sic*] he the fellow says true things now & then."[26] Keats reporting this sounds tired of the whole business of literary debate, of reputation-mongering and opinion-forming. Abbey is annoyingly typical because he has been drawn into the earnest discussion that the poem set out to provoke and so remained quite blind to its trickery and adroit attitudinizing.[27]

The contempt in Keats's reaction to Abbey extends to Byron as well: the "flash poem" is doubly deceptive, firstly, because its worldly-wisdom is more apparent than real and, secondly, because its outrageousness is contrived. Moreover, *The Cap and Bells* reveals what lies behind both aspects of this dislike. Byron's poem fails according to Keats because "flash" writing depended on and sustained a central consciousness that pulls the strings of the world it creates. Even as *Don Juan* derided the solitary grandeur of the Lake poets, it provided an image of power and independence in the worldly narrator. Byron's posture is fundamentally similar to Wordsworth's, only in some ways more naïve because believing itself more mature.

The Cap and Bells, in consequence, is withering about integrity. This quality in it reappears in the later cantos of *Don Juan* which Keats

---

24. *Ibid.*, II, 192.

25. Quoted in *OED*, definition 3 of "Flash *a*3". Rollins refers to the Preface to Tom Moore's 1819, *Tom Crib's Memorial to Congress*: see *Letters*, II, 192n.

26. *Letters*, II, 192.

27. Charles Lamb's essay, "On the Artificial Comedy of the Last Century", makes the same complaint about the period's blinkered earnestness. Keats and Lamb seem to have got on, sharing similar taste in people and in jokes: see *Letters*, I, 198 and II, 215.

did not live to read. For the same reason, the poem is continually self-parodic. Hum resembles Keats and both he and the emperor, Elfinan, resemble Hyperion (the protagonist of the poem Keats was revising as he wrote *The Cap and Bells*).[28] Crafticanto's narrative towards the end of the poem, for example, includes a tricky encounter with a bat:

> A large bat
> Came sudden 'fore my face, and brush'd against my hat.
> (ll. 674-75)

In *Endymion* Book II, "the sounds again/Went noiseless as a passing noontide rain/Over a bower" (379-80); similarly, in Book I, Keats writes, "when lo! refreshfully,/There came upon my face, in plenteous showers,/Dew-drops" (ll. 898-900). Celebrated Keatsian immediacy is more frightening in the later poem and less illuminating. It seems to be another effect, good for poetry but not necessarily for any higher purpose and by no means a proof of sincerity.

Keats quotes and rehandles many other elements from his own poetry.[29] In a more extreme form than in *The Fall of Hyperion*, he is (as Marjorie Levinson puts it), "translating himself".[30] In the process he turns a key-term that guarantees integrity into the stock in trade of poetry: Bertha in her sleep "Talk'd of one Master Hubert, deep in her esteem" (l. 711); and Hum, that accomplished con-artist, fends off Elfinan's anger with a strange reply:

> " ... I'll knock you — " "Does your Majesty mean — *down*?
> No, no, you never could my feelings probe
> To such a depth!" The Emperor took his robe,
> And wept upon its purple palatine ....
> (ll. 408-11)

Hum's pun is very strained. Elfinan, he says, could not knock him down because he could not plumb his depths. This does not really make sense (interpersonal subtlety is not, perhaps, the first requirement of a

---

28. Cf. *Hyperion*, I 213-24 with *The Cap and Bells*, ll. 176-80 and 624-30.

29. Cf., for example, *The Cap and Bells*, ll. 415-23 with *The Eve of St Agnes*, ll. 264-70, with "Ode to a Nightingale", ll. 17-18 and "Ode on Melancholy", l. 28. Compare too *The Cap and Bells*, ll. 167-71 with "La Belle Dame Sans Merci", ll. 29-36, with *The Eve of St Agnes*, ll. 226-30, and, more remotely, with "To Autumn", ll. 21-22.

30. Levinson, 202.

boxer) but it keeps Elfinan at bay. The trick of the tongue serves its present purpose and that is enough to be going on with.

Hum can talk his way out of any embarrassment and keeps himself afloat (as a magician and respected sage) by a succession of ruses of which this is only the most extreme. The feeling that Hum is supporting himself on thin air corresponds to the poem's interest in flying on magic carpets, in floating and looking down into apparent depths. Eban, the blackamoor servant, crosses town to bring Hum to his master, Elfinan. The streets are paved with pearl:

> and, as he on did pass
> With head inclined, each dusky lineament
> Show'd in the pearl-paved street, as in a glass;
>
> (ll. 263-65)[31]

Eban loves looking at reflections of himself ("he knock'd at the magician's door;/Where, till the porter answer'd, might be seen,/In the clear panel, more he could adore —" [ll. 275-77]). His vanity is effortless, unstoppable and even invigorating. But this narcissism reappears in Crafticanto's description of arriving by magic carpet in Panthea:

> "Onward we floated o'er the panting streets,
> That seem'd throughout with upheld faces paved;
> Look where we will, our bird's-eye vision meets
> Legions of holiday; bright standards waved,
> And fluttering ensigns emulously craved
> Our minute's glance ...."
>
> (ll. 730-35)

The crowds run after the flying cavalcade "With mad-cap pleasure, or hand-clasp'd amaze" while still gazing upward "with hungry eyes" (ll. 724, 722). "Hungry" and "panting" start to bear down on the more innocent desires Crafticanto sees in the crowds below. Their love of emulation turns into a craving; it demands that the nobles behave like royalty in return for the commoners' behaving like subjects. What looks like devotion is, in truth, part of a bargain. The force of their demand emerges more clearly when Crafticanto and Bellanaine land:

31. Cf. *Lamia*, I 378-86.

"A poet, mounted on the court-clown's back,
Rode to the Princess swift with spurring heels,
And close into her face, with rhyming clack,
Began a prothalamion ...."

(ll. 775-78)

Hum's string of "Now"s had described Bellanaine's skiey journey; his poetry, like Crafticanto's patronizing indulgence of the crowd's excitement, is rudely challenged by the "rhyming clack" of the court poet.

It is as if poetry is the magic carpet on which Bellanaine rides. Poetry creates illusions of loftiness or superiority; its lofty perspective enables the readership to view the outside world as if it lay below and in subjection. Poetry, therefore, makes self-involvement look like an elevated sensibility and, by doing so, it obscures and enhances the dream of self-sufficiency with which its readers deceive themselves. Disgust outweighs pettishness at this moment in the poem: Bellanaine's and Crafticanto's reception by the courtiers is like the sad awakening of "La Belle Dame Sans Merci", only worse because the disconsolate cry of the pale knights has been made over into the antics of a performing monkey. There are comparable effects in Gissing's *New Grub Street* and Keats shares with Gissing a bleak reluctance to entertain the dream of personal and artistic freedom; the dream which, both writers perceived, determined the lives of those who believed themselves made free by pursuing such a dream.

Keats's poem, all the same, is less bleak than Gissing's novel. Its disgust is not so much the source of indignation as an emotion he transforms into something more genial by writing the poem. *The Cap and Bells* is less sulky or moody overall than this final incident would suggest because Keats's dislike of pretensions to integrity could readily modulate into a perception that integrity was unattainable. Friends who have been apart "are both altered" when they meet again. Their nature simply changes over time. It is, he admits to George and Georgiana in September 1819, "an uneasy thought that in seven years the same hands cannot greet each other again". But, he adds at once, "All this may be obviated by a willful and dramatic exercise of our Minds towards each other".[32] Keats began *The Cap and Bells* soon after he had given up *King Stephen*. He abandoned the play because, I think, he found the writing of it short-circuited by his dissatisfaction with the staginess of his own and his period's dramatic conventions. Keats could not

32. *Letters*, II, 208-209.

overcome directly the power dramatic conventions had to replicate again and again a fierce apartness and self-sufficiency which he found false and degrading. The fragment of the play that survives is caught between equally unattractive opposites: Stephen's hectic soliloquies and Maud's down-beat *Realpolitik*. The more up-to-date and hardheaded judgements of the Queen are as flat as Stephen's tirades are theatrical. In both, declamation seems to entail an insistence on self which, if once impressive and sublime, now appears to Keats to be simply tiresome. It comes as a relief to find *The Cap and Bells*, by contrast, so full of business and event; the multiple voices of the poem begin to sound like a drama at points but they also manifest a new understanding of the dramatic, one less earnest about negative capability and less convinced than Lucy Lloyd of poetry's ability ever to convey plainly how people behave. This change in *The Cap and Bells* corresponds, moreover, to changes perceptible in Keats's letter to Georgiana from January 1820 where, as he works out the varieties of comic writing, "disinterestedness" is replaced in his vocabulary by liberality.[33] In that move, Keats is replacing an ideal of independence with the virtue of generosity, with a form of kindness to others that manages to avoid both condescension and subservience.

---

33. "The more I know of Men the more I know how to value entire liberality in any of them" (*Letters*, II, 243 — 15 January 1820). On types of comedy, see *ibid.*, 245-47.

FEMALE EMPATHY TO MANLINESS: KEATS IN 1819

JACQUELINE SCHOEMAKER

Victorian artists and thinkers either admired Keats (like the Pre-Raphaelites, for instance, who were deeply influenced by him) or accepted his aestheticism but rated him as an inferior artist (a common response among those who aspired to "high seriousness").[1] Paradoxically, Keats was either appreciated for his "character" and "manliness" or attacked and rejected for his lack of these very qualities. All this tells us more about Victorian values than about Keats. The idea that his famous "Negative Capability" appears to be connected with feminine empathy[2] did not appeal to his Victorian readers and prompted severe critics to ridicule him.

William Michael Rossetti, whose acquaintance with Keats "was born in the glow of the Pre-Raphaelites' admiration for one of their heroes", describes a "virile, courageous Keats, full of 'earnestness and pleasantry', whose flaws were only those of youth and energy".[3] A favourable view of Keats implied a defence of his manliness. The opposite point of view is best represented in Thomas Carlyle's remark that "Keats is a miserable creature, hungering after sweets which he can't get".[4] The publication of Keats's letters to Fanny Brawne in 1878 caused an uproar, not only because they revealed the most private Keats, but also because they showed his most unmanly side. Algernon Charles Swinburne, who had approved of Keats before the publication

1. See Earl R. Wasserman, *The Finer Tone*, Baltimore: Md, 1953, 98.

2. See Alan Richardson, "Romanticism and the Colonization of the Feminine", in *Romanticism and Feminism*, ed. Anne K. Mellor, Bloomington: Ind., 1988, 14-15.

3. William Henry Marquess, *Lives of the Poet: The First Century of Keats Biography*, University Park: Pa, 1985, 79.

4. Quoted in Christopher Ricks, *Keats and Embarrassment*, Oxford, 1974, 120.

of the letters (he had even called him "perfect"), believed that the letters "ought never to have been written", and ended up calling Keats an "effeminate rhymester in the sickly stage of welphood".[5]

Matthew Arnold had a healthier opinion of Keats: he did not share the Pre-Raphaelites' enthusiasm, but though he criticized him, he admired him enough not to wish to go as far as Swinburne in his comments on him. He did not think that Keats's letters to Fanny Brawne should never have been written, only that they should never have been published. He viewed the letters as those "of a youth ill brought up, without the training which teaches us that we must put some constraint upon our feelings and upon the expression of them".[6] Perhaps embarrassed by Keats's display of sensuousness and feeling, he states that "we cannot but look for signs in him of something more than sensuousness, for signs of character and virtue". Arnold wanted to find strength and manliness in Keats and he preferred never to have seen the texts in which he was confronted with his lack of these qualities. To his relief, he discovered that Keats's attitude towards the public was "that of a strong man, not of a weakling avid of praise", and he concluded, almost with pride, that after all Keats did have "flint and iron" in him.

It is no surprise that Keats's lack of manliness was so much discussed. If the Victorians had a problem with Keats's feelings (or his expression of them), so did Keats himself. The period from January until September 1819 was particularly turbulent for Keats in this respect, for during this period he grew more and more convinced that he had to break away from the love of woman in order to write great poetry and this culminated in an unreasonable display of "flint and iron" to Fanny Brawne in August and September 1819. *The Eve of St Agnes* (January 1819) coincides with the beginning of Keats's love for Fanny Brawne and shows his admirable capacity for feminine empathy, "Negative Capability" and confidence in the female Gothic tradition. "La Belle Dame Sans Merci" (April 1819) does not offer a female but a male point of view, in which the knight's fear is foregrounded, and anticipates Keats's agony in his relationship from which he suffered in the summer. The letters he wrote to Fanny Brawne (and to others) during that summer, together with the composition of *Lamia* and the revision of *The Eve of St Agnes* reveal that he was seized by an outburst of manliness.

---

5. Quoted in Marquess, 68.

6. Matthew Arnold, "John Keats", in *Essays in Criticism*, London, 1915, 100-21.

Whereas Victorian literature often tried to deny female sexuality, Gothic literature was in essence an assertion of women's sexual experience. Many Gothic novels deal with the relation between a female character and her surroundings from her point of view. She discovers her nature through her relationship with her often threatening father and lover, but most importantly, she reaches her true self through her connection with her usually absent mother. Identification with the mother plays an important role, not only for the female character within the Gothic novel, but also for male writers in the Romantic period. As Alan Richardson says, "in moving from an 'Age of Reason' to an 'Age of Feeling', male writers drew on memories and fantasies of identification with the mother in order to colonize the conventionally feminine domain of sensibility".[7] We do not know in how far Keats drew on these memories and fantasies in handling his own sensibility: his mother had died when he was fourteen, but he does not mention her often, and there is no clear evidence that he tried to establish his identification with her in the manner suggested by Richardson. What is interesting, though, is that he jokingly refers to Ann Radcliffe as "mother Radcliff[e]".[8] (It is no coincidence that on the whole, the Victorians did not share the Romantics' curiosity about or appreciation of Radcliffe's novels.)

In *The Eve of St Agnes*, Keats makes use of Gothic elements for his theme. We are confronted with the tradition of superstitious belief in the legend of St Agnes, which is passed on from one female generation to another. Madeline

> had brooded, all that wintry day,
> On love, and winged St Agnes' saintly care,
> As she had heard old dames full many times declare.
> They told her how, upon St Agnes' Eve,
> Young virgins might have visions of delight ....
>
> (ll. 43-47)[9]

It is Madeline's inmost wish to see her future husband in her dream, and though she is often called naïve, she succeeds, through the power of

---

7. Mellor, 13.

8. Letter to George and Georgiana Keats, 14 February-3 May 1819, in *The Letters of John Keats*, ed. Hyder Edward Rollins, 2 Vols, Cambridge: Mass., 1958, II, 62.

9. John Keats, *The Eve of St Agnes*, in *The Complete Poems*, ed. John Barnard, Penguin edition, 1987, 312-24.

vision, not only in seeing her lover in her dream but also in accepting his physical reality. Initially, Porphyro is a spellbound spectator of this mysterious tradition, looking at old Angela "Like puzzled urchin on an aged crone/Who keepeth closed a wondrous riddle-book" (ll. 129-30). He wants to be let in on the secret:

> "Now tell me where is Madeline," said he,
> "O tell me, Angela, by the holy loom
> Which none but secret sisterhood may see,
> When they St Agnes' wool are weaving piously."
>
> (ll. 114-17)

He enters her world, and though he takes her out of it and so destroys it, at the same time he helps to fulfil her wish. Whereas the Gothic heroine usually develops from a maiden in distress to mistress of the castle (and so stays within the Gothic atmosphere), Madeline, after a moment of despair ("Porphyro will leave me here to fade and pine": l. 329), leaves the gloomy castle with Porphyro to live with him "o'er the southern moors" (l. 351).

It has often been pointed out that Keats uses imagery in *The Eve of St Agnes* which is reminiscent of the atmosphere in Ann Radcliffe's novels; and indeed when we look closer at the poem, we discover that Keats owed more to Ann Radcliffe and the female Gothic tradition than his use of imagery for decorative purposes. In the introduction to *The Female Gothic*, Juliann Fleenor points out that the Gothic heroine lives in an environment strongly dominated by men, that her aim is not to become independent but to find a husband to whom she can respond, and that spatial imagery is often used to convey her sense of imprisonment.[10] In Keats's poem, Madeline's wish is to discover who her future husband will be. She expresses no wish to leave the castle for reasons of independence. She only leaves when Porphyro has assured her that he has a home for her (stanza 39).

The castle is dominated by violent men:

> barbarian hordes,
> Hyena foemen, and hot-blooded lords,
> Whose very dogs would execrations howl
> Against his lineage ....
>
> (ll. 85-88)

10. *The Female Gothic*, ed. Juliann E. Fleenor, Montreal, 1983, 3-28.

Angela refers to them as "the whole blood-thirsty race" (l. 99) and is convinced that "men will murder upon holy days" (l. 119). Although the violence of these lords is not aimed directly at Madeline but at Porphyro, it serves as an attempt to repress Madeline's sexual development, since it is through Porphyro that this development takes place. If we interpret the spatial imagery in the poem as connoting a sense of inprisonment, it turns out that Madeline is more occupied with liberating herself from her environment than with being miserable and frightened. After the solemn opening of the poem, the scene shifts to a dance which is being held at the castle: "many a door was wide" (l. 29) and the rooms "Were glowing to receive a thousand guests" (l. 33). Madeline cannot at this moment partake in this joyful openness: "She danced along with vague, regardless eyes,/Anxious her lips, her breathing quick and short" (ll. 64-65). She is entranced, locked up as it were in her wish to dream of her lover, "Hoodwinked with faery fancy" (l. 70), not yet ready to deal with the "amorous cavalier[s]" (l. 60). Confused and anxious for success with St Agnes, she retires to her room:

> Out went the taper as she hurried in;
> Its little smoke, in pallid moonshine, died:
> She closed the door, she panted, all akin
> To spirits of the air, and visions wide —
>
> (ll. 199-202)

It is in her closed room (and in the dark) that she prepares to receive the vision. Although Madeline seems confined in the castle, guarded by "hot-blooded lords" (l. 86), her closing the door of her room does not point to inprisonment but to a way out. Madeline has closed herself off from the other inhabitants and we find in her room two elements which together form her liberation. There is a "casement high and triple-arched" (l. 208), through which the moon shines on her and shows her purity. The window offers an opportunity for her to reach a higher state of consciousness (her dream) and refers to her later escape. The presence of Porphyro in her room gives material shape to her dream ("Into her dream he melted": l. 320). After Porphyro has convinced Madeline of his honest love for her, the lovers set about their escape from the castle. The spatial imagery in this passage points to wide or open spaces ("the southern moors": l. 351; "the wide stairs": l. 355; "the wide hall": l. 361) and, finally, to liberation itself:

> By one, and one, the bolts full easy slide —
> The chains lie silent on the footworn stones —
> The key turns, and the door upon its hinges groans.
> (ll. 367-69)

The reality of the love between Madeline and Porphyro is emphasized by their courage and sense of togetherness. The lovers are both in a hypnotic state but at the same time, or perhaps because of this, they know exactly how to find each other and end in a happy union. Porphyro's courage is shown in the fact that he risks his life in coming to search Madeline among the "blood-thirsty race" (l. 99). He does not just enter the castle, he "ventures in" (l. 82). Equally courageous is the fact that he wakes Madeline and shows himself to her, because breaking her "midnight charm" (l. 282) may mean that the sensitive Madeline may refuse him forever. But in order to make her his bride (and this is, after all, what she wants), he has to shake her out of her dream and make her face reality. He nearly fails:

> Her eyes were open, but she still beheld,
> Now wide awake, the vision of her sleep —
> There was a painful change, that nigh expelled
> The blisses of her dream so pure and deep.
> (ll. 298-301)

Madeline is disappointed and wants to return to the safety of her vision. She says to Porphyro:

> How changed thou art! How pallid, chill, and drear!
> Give me that voice again, my Porphyro,
> Those looks immortal, those complainings dear!
> (ll. 311-13)

Her courage lies in her final acceptance of Porphyro as a real lover and husband, in making concrete what she had only dreamt of before. Unlike the male lovers in the Gothic novel, who are either chaste or dangerous, Porphyro represents both daemonic and chaste love, and this makes Madeline's experience of love complete. First, she meets with his physical reality and, like the typical Gothic heroine, she becomes confused and afraid. Later, she realizes that it is safe to love the real Porphyro: he calls her his "bride" (ll. 326 and 334) and promises her a home. The unity of the lovers is emphasized by their leaving the Gothic world of the castle. The storm into which they flee is "an elfin-storm from faery land,/Of haggard seeming, but a boon indeed" (ll. 343-44).

The "elfin-storm" offers new opportunities for the lovers: inspiration, freshness, and a new realm of existence. Porphyro and Madeline succeed because they both have an ardent wish to do so, and in his poem Keats explores exactly those sentiments which are typical of young love (hope, wish, fear of and curiosity about sex, happy union).

Keats wrote *The Eve of St Agnes* shortly after he had fallen in love with Fanny Brawne, when his hope of a happy union with her must have appeared as a relatively carefree reality to him. The poem lacks the agony, disappointment and separation which he expressed three months later in "La Belle Dame Sans Merci". The human Porphyro and Madeline find each other and vanish together, leaving behind the "be-nightmared" (l. 375) barbarians of the castle. In "La Belle Dame", the elfin lady departs alone and the human knight experiences nothing but nightmare and bleak reality. The strong conflict between the sexes which we find in "La Belle Dame" is lacking in *The Eve of St Agnes*: the lovers are not pitched against each other but their warmth together is set against the cold and gloom of their surroundings. The tune Porphyro plays on Madeline's lute, "In Provence called, 'La belle dame sans mercy'" (l. 292), may bring an atmosphere of trance, but has nothing in common with the enthralment of the knight in "La Belle Dame Sans Merci".

In the letters Keats wrote around the time he composed "La Belle Dame Sans Merci", there are no signs of anxiety about his relationship with Fanny Brawne. The Brawnes had moved to Wentworth Place, so it is unlikely that he wrote to her during this period. Later that year, he wrote numerous letters to her from the Isle of Wight and Winchester, expressing his fears and his obsessive love for her. During this period, he also bitterly commented on love and women to others, but in the preceding spring, he either preferred not to venture his thoughts or fears about his love, or simply did not have any. However, "La Belle Dame Sans Merci" shows that his perspective (both the male and female point of view are present in *The Eve of St Agnes*) had changed (we hear only the male point of view in "La Belle Dame"). Indeed, the female empathy with which Keats had explored Madeline's wishes, her vision and experience (set in the female Gothic tradition) gives way to a poem in which a male vision takes the form of an interpretation of a female figure.

Despite the expectation which arises from the title, the lady in the poem is not at all dominant and what is foregrounded is the knight's experience and agony, as the stylistic features of the poem indicate. The lady is "de-centered":[11] what we know about her we learn through his story — what he has to say in response to the questioner. La Belle Dame herself is entirely excluded from the dialogue and is only present in six of the twelve stanzas. In the first three stanzas, the questioner speaks and in the last three, the knight talks about his dream and his present situation. Her actions, therefore, are part of his story and he is the survivor left with little to do but tell the tale. In the middle stanzas (4-9), contrary to the expectation which arises from the warning dream ("'La Belle Dame sans Merci/Thee hath in thrall'"), the interaction between the knight and the lady does not show any dominance of the lady over the knight.[12] She takes him to her "elfin grot", but he takes the initiative in travelling there ("I set her on my pacing steed"). While they are riding, the knight "nothing else saw all day long,/For sidelong would she bend". The idea that the lady deliberately blinds the knight is unreasonable, since later on, "she lulled [him] asleep" and provides him with the opportunity to receive the warning dream. If she really had decided to enthral him, she would not have put him to sleep in order to give him the opportunity to experience his own vision. The dream is entirely his own: she does not occur in it, and it even warns him against her. When she "wept and sighed full sore", the knight's reaction is to "shut her wild wild eyes", and this is the last thing we see of the lady, apart from her "lull[ing him] asleep", whereby the knight returns to his natural, human environment. Since she disappears at this point while his vision continues in his dream, we could say that, by shutting her eyes, he blinds her rather than the other way round.

Karen Swann suggests that the knight may even be harassing the lady in order to become one of the pale warriors and princes, "in whose world 'woman' exists only as a delusive fantasy, a memory of a dream".[13] This seems rather exaggerated, but it is certainly true that in the world of the knight's dream, the lady is absent. The lady's "language strange", her "faery's song", makes it obvious why she does not speak in the poem. She is quoted by the knight only once: "And sure in language strange she said —/'I love thee true.'" How can he be so "sure"? The word "sure" seems to refer to his need to reassure himself rather than to absolute certainty. He also says, "She looked at me as she did love": it looks as if she does, but that is all he knows for certain. There is a gap between the "faery's child" and the human

11. See Karen Swann, "Harassing the Muse", in Mellor, 84.

12. "La Belle Dame Sans Merci: A Ballad" (*The Complete Poems*, 334-36).

13. Mellor, 90.

knight because they are not of the same kind, and do not speak each other's language. That she is "without kindness" does not mean she is cruel but she is without human feelings, not belonging to the same "kind", naturally neutral to good and evil. The knight possesses human fervour and lacks the elf's cool neutrality. The gap between the reader and the fairy is even bigger because all we know about her is his interpretation of her strange words and deeds. We follow the knight, and the lady remains remote.

Keats may have used various sources for "La Belle Dame Sans Merci". What is significant is that the lady in his poem differs on all levels from her predecessors in earlier texts. Keats took from his sources only the outward features, the material for a story, his own story, in which a man's inner experience of love is foregrounded and the woman is moved to the background. In "Thomas Rymer",[14] for example, one of the sources for "La Belle Dame Sans Merci", the lady is of a much firmer and more active nature than Keats's "faery child". In both versions of "Thomas Rymer", the story is told directly, not retold by the male lover. The lady corrects Thomas, who sees her as the "Queen of Heaven", and she herself makes known who she is. She orders him: "True Thomas, ye maun go wi me,/For ye maun serve me seven years" (version A). The lady is in possession of the horse: "She turned about her milk-white steed,/And took True Thomas up behind" (version A). In version C, Thomas is not even allowed a place on the horse: "The lady rade, True Thomas ran." This forms a sharp contrast with Keats's poem, in which the horse belongs to the knight, who consequently has the power to put her on it. Whereas Keats's lady does not provide the knight with any information about herself or his human condition (he is left to discover it all by himself), the lady in "Thomas Rymer" seems to have visionary power. She forbids Thomas to eat the fruit he finds in a "garden green" because she knows the fruit will do harm to humans, and she points out the roads to righteousness and wickedness and also the road that leads to "fair elfland" (version A) or to "our land" (version C). Most importantly, the lady forbids Thomas to speak to others about her. This is an aspect Keats ignored. In his poem, the knight relates the whole story to an outsider. Whereas we take the knight's words to be true (we have no reason to mistrust him),

14. "Thomas Rymer", *English and Scottish Popular Ballads*, eds Helen Child Sargent and George Lyman Kittredge, London, 1904. Two versions of the poem appear in this volume: "Thomas Rymer and Queen of Elfland", from Jamieson's *Popular Ballads* (version A) and "Thomas the Rhymer", from *Scotch Ballads* (version C).

the direct speech of Thomas is associated with error. In version A, he only speaks twice to the lady, once when he mistakes her for the Queen of Heaven and once when he is tempted to eat the forbidden fruit.

Other possible sources for Keats's poem show female figures who also differ widely from Keats's neutral lady. They have obvious intentions, whereas La Belle Dame seems to lack any scheme. Her relationship with the knight is little more than his vision of her and this vision is shattered because of his fear of being enthralled, brought about by his dream. One of the figures seen as a source for La Belle Dame is Spenser's Duessa in *The Faerie Queene*, which is strange because Duessa is not even remotely like Keats's lady, being an obvious symbol of evil, who deliberately misleads the "good" characters by calling herself Fidessa. She leads Redcrosse Knight away from his true love and associates with characters in the House of Pride and in Hell. As she says of herself, she is "the daughter of Deceipt and Shame".[15] Keats's lady possesses none of this evil, let alone the pleasure in it which Duessa reveals. Other evil female figures which have been regarded as sources for La Belle Dame are the malevolent Morgan le Fay, and the lady in version C of "Thomas Rymer", who expresses her evil intentions when she says to Thomas:

> "Ilka seven years, Thomas,
> We pay our teindings unto hell,
> And ye're sae leesome and sae strang
> That I fear, Thomas, it will be yere sell."

The fairies who serve as sources for La Belle Dame are not only of a wicked kind. In Thomas Chestre's *Sir Launfal*, the benevolent Dame Tryamour truly loves her knight and accepts him even though he breaks his promise not to tell anyone about her.[16] This story obviously differs from Keats's poem, since it has a "happy ending", whereas at the end of "La Belle Dame Sans Merci", we know nothing of the misery or happiness of the lady and it is not at all clear whether the knight will perish, resume his ordinary human life or go on to search the lady of his vision.

It needs to be said that there is one figure which does resemble Keats's lady, at least as far as her function in the poem is concerned.

---

15. Edmund Spenser, *The Faerie Queene*, ed. Thomas P. Roche, Jr., Penguin edition, 1987, I.v.26.

16. See Charles I. Patterson, Jr., *The Daemonic in the Poetry of John Keats*, Urbana: Ill., 1970, 137-38.

Coleridge's Life-in-Death in *The Rime of the Ancient Mariner*, like La Belle Dame, is neither evil nor good (she wins the Mariner's soul arbitrarily, in a game of dice). She differs from Keats's lady in that she embodies the Mariner's nightmare, whereas Keats's fairy is already out of sight when the knight has his warning dream. Both these figures (and their corresponding male protagonists) occur in Romantic ballads, which use the form of the folk ballad but are essentially different from it because they add a consciousness of suffering to the story. Both ladies serve as a source of inner discovery and suffering for the Mariner and the knight. The Mariner suffers during his nightmare because he is forced to contemplate his crime; the knight suffers for what he sees in his dream as a dangerous love.

It has often been argued that the main source for "La Belle Dame Sans Merci" was Keats's relationship with Fanny Brawne. John Barnard states with certainty that the poem "is an oblique expression of some aspects of Keats's feelings for Fanny Brawne"[17] and that it should be compared to Keats's previous poem, "A Dream, After Reading Dante's Episode of Paolo and Francesca". In this poem, Keats expresses that in the "sad hell" of his dream,

> Where in the gust, the whirlwind, and the flaw
> Of rain and hail-stones, lovers need not tell
> Their sorrows. Pale were the sweet lips I saw,
> Pale were the lips I kissed, and fair the form
> I floated with, about that melancholy storm.[18]

This passage is reminiscent in atmosphere of "La Belle Dame", but the knight in the ballad does tell his sorrows, which is an essential aspect of the poem. It would be unfair to Keats and his poetry to say that "La Belle Dame Sans Merci" is simply the expression of the poet's feelings for Fanny Brawne, although in his experience of love Keats shares certain characteristics with the knight. But unlike the knight, Keats expresses his feelings directly to her. When we read the letters he wrote to Fanny Brawne from the Isle of Wight in July, we get the impression that he saw her as a source of pleasure and pain rather than as a friend: "Ask yourself my love whether you are not very cruel to have so entrammelled me, so destroyed my freedom."[19] A week later, he

---

17. *The Complete Poems*, Notes, 637.

18. *Ibid.*, 334.

19. *Letters*, II, 123.

writes, "I am miserable that you are not with me: or rather breathe in that dull sort of patience that cannot be called Life".[20] This is very much the bleak realm in which the knight is "Alone and palely loitering". In another letter, written during the same period, he tells her he has been reading a story of an enchanting lady and a city of melancholy men (the theme is very similar to that of his poem):

> How I applied this to you, my dear; how I palpitated at it; how the certainty that you were in the same world with myself, and though as beautiful, not so talismanic as that Lady; how I could not bear you should be so you must believe because I swear it by yourself.[21]

These passages show Keats's fear of becoming enthralled and being cast out of his lady's world. Like the knight in his poem, he suffers in a "dull sort of patience" when the lady's physical presence is out of reach and his happy vision turns into anxiety.

In December 1818, Keats had written to his brother and sister-in-law that women at first seem delightful but always turn out to be a disappointment.[22] In the following summer, he came to feel what he had written. As Edward E. Bostetter comments:

> Fanny's beauty gradually takes on sinister connotations; it enslaves him and threatens to destroy him. He resents what he considers the irresponsible possessor of the beauty, who makes it impossible for him to think of anything else and yet gives him no happiness. It was inevitable that with his intense idealism Keats would violently fall in love and demand what no one could return. It was inevitable that he would discover thereby the darker side of love, no matter who the woman was.[23]

It was not Fanny's beauty as such which enslaved Keats, but his own imagination about that beauty. There is no sign of actual cruelty in Miss Brawne, and if she really had done anything to make Keats miserable or

---

20. *Ibid.*, II, 126.

21. *Ibid.*, II, 130 (the story referred to appears in Henry Weber's *Tales of the East* [1812]).

22. *Ibid.*, II, 18-19.

23. Edward E. Bostetter, *The Romantic Ventriloquists*, Seattle: Wash., 1963, 160.

jealous, he certainly would have mentioned it. Instead, the letters show Keats's over-sensitive reaction to his own fear of being hurt (it is exactly this mood to which Matthew Arnold and others objected). He is obsessed with her: the idea of not seeing her for a while "takes on the appearance of impossibility and eternity".[24] Later, he writes, "You cannot conceive how I ache to be with you", and, as the result of his love for her, he expresses his hatred of the world:

> I have two luxuries to brood over in my walks, your Loveliness and the hour of my death. O that I could have possession of them both in the same minute. I hate the world: it batters too much the wings of my self-will, and would I could take a sweet poison from your lips to send me out of it.[25]

He is also jealous: "I must live upon hope and Chance. In case of the worst that can happen, I shall still love you — but what hatred shall I have for another!"[26] Afraid that she will use her beauty to attract others, he says to her, "let me speak of your Beauty, though to my own endangering; if you could be so cruel to me as to try elsewhere its Power".[27] In another letter, he writes, "If you should ever feel for Man at the first sight what I did for you, I am lost".[28] Keats also revealed a deep-seated insecurity about his character and appearance (the inevitable mate of jealousy): "I cannot believe there ever was or ever could be any thing to admire in me especially as far as sight goes",[29] and later (the beginning of August), "Upon my soul I cannot say what you could like me for".[30]

It was during this period of insecurity and obsession that Keats composed Part I of *Lamia*. Of all the female figures in Keats's poetry, Lamia is perhaps the most real and active "belle dame sans merci". Conflict between the sexes, which was absent in *The Eve of St Agnes* and present in "La Belle Dame Sans Merci", now reaches its height.

---

24. *Letters*, II, 13 (this and all subsequent quotes in this paragraph are from letters Keats wrote from the Isle of Wight in July and August 1819).

25. *Ibid.*, II, 132-33.

26. *Ibid.*, II, 123.

27. *Ibid.*, II, 127.

28. *Ibid.*, II, 132.

29. *Ibid.*, II, 133.

30. *Ibid.*, II, 137.

The imagery with which Lamia is described reveals that Keats had a much more cruel and artful female figure in mind than he had for "La Belle Dame". An overdose of colour shows that Lamia is truly hypnotic:

> She was a gordian shape of dazzling hue,
> Vermilion-spotted, golden, green, and blue;
> Striped like a zebra, freckled like a pard,
> Eyed like a peacock, and all crimson barred;
> ....
> So rainbow-sided, touched with miseries,
> She seemed, at once, some penanced lady elf,
> Some demon's mistress, or the demon's self.[31]

Whereas the lady in "La Belle Dame" is simply a "lady elf", Lamia could represent much more. Her change from serpent to "lady bright" (I 171) is accompanied by a pain and madness which are far beyond La Belle Dame's wildness:

> er elfin blood in madness ran,
> Her mouth foamed, and the grass, therewith besprent,
> Withered at dew so sweet and virulent;
> Her eyes in torture fixed, and anguish drear,
> Hot, glazed, and wide, with lid-lashes all sear,
> Flashed phosphor and sharp sparks, without one cooling tear.
> (I 147-52)

The lady in "La Belle Dame" seems to have no real design on her knight; but Lamia's "brilliance feminine" (I 92) in human shape lures Lycius (not necessarily with evil intentions) with whispers of "woman's lore" (I 325), while "Her soft look growing coy, she saw his chain so sure" (I 256). She has "her tender favourite" (I 291) "tangled in her mesh" (I 295).

The composition of Part II of *Lamia* in August coincided with a change in Keats's attitude to Fanny Brawne. At the end of Part I of the poem, the sage Appolonius is introduced. At the end of Part II, the philosopher saves Lycius from marriage with Lamia by making her vanish. Lycius dies of grief. In order for philosophy to rule, the love between man and woman must die. This seems to have been Keats's conviction at the time, for he felt that a commitment to poetry could not co-exist with his other love and he decided to banish the thought of

---

31. *Lamia*, I 47-50, 54-56 (*The Complete Poems*, 414-33).

Fanny from his mind in order to write. Keats had moved to Winchester and was now absorbed in writing, working on *Lamia*, *The Fall of Hyperion* and *Otho the Great* (together with Charles Brown). He writes to Fanny:

> I have had no idle leisure to brood over you — 'tis well perhaps I have not — I could not have endured the throng of Jealousies that used to haunt me before I had plunged so deeply into imaginary interests. I would feign, as my sails are set, sail on without interruption for a Brace of Months longer ....[32]

Only three weeks before, he had "ached" to be with her, and now he writes that he cannot help being "unloverlike".[33] This does not seem to be unnatural: he had had enough of "aching" and had decided, while he could not be with her, to direct his energy towards writing poetry. But his comment to John Taylor a week later is totally unfair to Fanny: "I equally dislike the favour of the public with the love of a woman — they are both a cloying treacle to the wings of independence".[34] Why this attack on a woman's love? He had thought Fanny cruel because he found her beautiful, now he disliked the love of a woman because his own love had changed direction. He had pined and ached and was tired of it, but he did not seem to realize that he was coping, not with the love of a woman, but with a man's love.

Matthew Arnold would have advised him to control his feelings, but the Romantic spirit in Keats did not find much pleasure or comfort in control and his former adoration changed to dislike. In September, he made a short trip from Winchester to London and though he had promised Fanny to visit her, he wrote her a short letter instead, telling her that he could not see her because he loved her too much. He concludes, "I am a Coward, I cannot bear the pain of being happy".[35]

During this period, Keats revised *The Eve of St Agnes*, which caused an uproar among his publishers and his friends. He was afraid his poem would be mocked for naïvety and so made the lovemaking of Madeline and Porphyro explicit.[36] Taylor did not agree and

---

32. *Letters*, II, 140-41. This and all subsequent quotations are from letters Keats wrote in August and September 1819.

33. *Ibid.*, 141.

34. *Ibid.*, 144.

35. *Ibid.*, 160.

36. See *The Complete Poems*, Notes, 619-20.

Woodhouse wrote to Taylor that he thought the more explicit version of the poem "unfit for ladies", to which Keats replied that he did not want ladies to read his poetry, that he wrote for men.[37] This is a strange statement (Keats had always written about, for and to women as well as men) and it should probably be ascribed to his temporary aversion to love and women. It was also during this period that he wrote "Pensive they sit, and roll their languid eyes", a parody on lovers, in which he ridicules the mood and behaviour of those with whom he could identify only two months before. It seems as if he is trying to get over his own pain and disappointment by looking down on others who find themselves in the same situation. He sent the poem in a letter to George and Georgiana and the comment he added is particularly revealing:

> Nothing strikes me so forcibly with a sense of the r[i]diculous as love — A Man in love I do think cuts the sorryest figure in the world — Even when I know a poor fool to be really in pain about it, I could burst out laughing in his face — His pathetic visage becomes irr[e]sistable.[38]

Later that year, Keats moved back to Wentworth Place with Charles Brown and continued to live next door to Fanny. He continued to love her and, having given in to the demands of his publisher concerning *The Eve of St Agnes*, went on writing for both ladies and men. It is a soothing thought that he did not live to be as old as Thomas Carlyle, since it saved him at least the experience of facing directly the criticism and ridicule of self-controlled Victorians. But then again, had he lived, his letters would probably not have been published at the time. And who knows what passionate and "unmanly" letters Carlyle might have written in 1819?

37. *Ibid.*, Notes, 619.

38. *Letters*, II, 187-88.

"SURE IN LANGUAGE STRANGE": JOHN AND TOM AND FANNY AND EMILY

JANE MALLINSON

The fusions and confusions of literary periods are sometimes illuminated by coincidences of chronology; this essay offers some thoughts on such a coincidence. It focuses on the relationship of two poets, John Keats and Thomas Stearns Eliot, with women who loved them, Fanny Brawne and Emily Hale, in the light of a recent reading of Keats's lines from the first version of "La Belle Dame Sans Merci" which emphasizes the lady's confidence in the expression of her love, rather than the knight's interpretation of her words:

> And sure in language strange she said
> "I love thee true."[1]

Keats wrote the first version of "La Belle Dame Sans Merci" on 21 April 1819, within days of completing the sonnet "A Dream, After reading Dante's Episode of Paolo and Francesca". Before he copied out the poem in a letter to his brother George and sister-in-law Georgiana who had recently emigrated to America, Keats related the effect that this episode of the *Inferno* had had upon him:

> The fifth canto of Dante pleases me more and more — it is that one in which he meets with Paolo and Francesca — I had passed many days in rather a low state of mind and in the midst of them I dreamt of being in that region of Hell. The dream was one of the most delightful enjoyments I have ever had in my life — I floated about the whirling atmosphere as it is described with a beautiful figure to whose lips mine were joined as it seem'd for an age — and in the midst of all this cold and darkness I was

1. The text used is that of *John Keats*, ed. Elizabeth Cook, Oxford, 1990, 273-74. See Andrew Bennet, *Keats, Narrative and Audience: The Posthumous Life of Writing*, Cambridge, 1994, 115.

> warm — even flowery tree tops sprung up and we rested on them sometimes with the lightness of a cloud till the wind blew us away again — I tried a Sonnet upon it — there are fourteen lines but nothing of what I felt in it — o that I could dream it every night —.[2]

Keats was twenty-three and had met Fanny Brawne in November 1818. The Christmas of that year Keats had accepted Fanny's mother's invitation to spend the day with her family and other friends. In recalling that Christmas in a letter to Keats's sister in the year of his death, Fanny remembered it as "the happiest day I had ever then spent", although they were not to be engaged until the autumn of 1819.[3] It was after that Christmas party that Keats composed *The Eve of St Agnes*, the sensuous celebration of imagination and young love fulfilled in a cold and hostile world.

According to Valerie Eliot, her husband first met Emily Hale in 1912.[4] John Mayer's careful discussion of T.S. Eliot's early poems dates "La Figlia Che Piange" to that year.[5]

La Figlia Che Piange

O quam te memorem virgo …

Stand on the highest pavement of the stair —
Lean on a garden urn —
Weave, weave the sunlight in your hair —
Clasp your flowers to you with a pained surprise —
Fling them to the ground and turn
With a fugitive resentment in your eyes:
But weave, weave the sunlight in your hair.

So I would have had him leave,
So I would have had her stand and grieve,
So he would have left
As the soul leaves the body torn and bruised,
As the mind deserts the body it has used.
I should find
Some way incomparably light and deft,

---

2. *John Keats*, 469.

3. Walter Jackson Bate, *John Keats*, Oxford, 1967, 430.

4. *The Letters of T.S. Eliot*, ed. Valerie Eliot, New York, 1988, I (1898-1922), xvii.

5. John T. Mayer, *T.S. Eliot's Silent Voices*, Oxford, 1989, 130.

Some way we both should understand,
Simple and faithless as a smile and shake of the hand.

She turned away, but with the autumn weather
Compelled my imagination many days,
Many days and many hours:
Her hair over her arms and her arms full of flowers.
And I wonder how they should have been together!
I should have lost a gesture and a pose.
Sometimes these cogitations still amaze
The troubled midnight and the noon's repose.[6]

In 1912 Eliot was also twenty-three. He was later to record that Dante had been the most persistent and deepest influence on him since 1910.[7] Writing of Dante's *Inferno* he was to say, "We can understand the first episode that strikes most readers, that of Paolo and Francesca, enough to be moved by it as much as by any poetry, on the first reading". He proceeds to quote lines 127—36 of Canto V.[8] It is, of course, the same episode that so moved Keats.

We have then two poems written by young men of twenty-three whose poetry has yet to win them the fame they desire, who both admire a particular passage of Dante's *Inferno* and who are both in the process of falling in love for the first time. Nearly a hundred years separates these two studies of the power of a female muse to fascinate and to threaten the male poet's imagination. Both are haunted by the presence of Paolo and Francesca, whose failure to constrain physical desire and to transform it into Platonic love condemn them to eternity as a footnote in the history of poetry.

In the earliest version of Keats's poem the woman actually speaks; she utters the fatal words "I love thee true", all be it in language strange, which operate as a curse in the context of "La Belle Dame Sans Merci". It is being loved that damns the knight to death in life, condemned to understand the words of the kings and princes who share his enthralment. This exploration of requited love is the antithesis of that in *The Eve of St Agnes*.

In "La Figlia Che Piange" the woman remains silent, as befits her origin in the stone relief of a girl which Eliot apparently wished to see

6. T.S. Eliot, *The Complete Poems and Plays of T.S. Eliot*, London, 1969, 34.

7. T.S. Eliot, *To Criticize the Critic*, London, 1965, 125.

8. T.S. Eliot, *Selected Essays*, 3rd enl. edn, London, 1951, 245.

during a trip to Italy in 1911, but failed to find. Like “La Belle Dame”, “La Figlia” also describes the separation of lovers, with the male protagonist inextricably identified with the poet who cannot emancipate himself from thoughts of the powerful female figure he has created except by turning it into art. In his discussion of the poem, John Mayer writes, “Eliot casts a cold eye on the conditions of creation, and honestly sets down its cost; like the mind that uses the body and then deserts it, the artist deserts life and love”.[9] In Eliot’s poem the woman’s love is rejected, she is immobilized, translated into a figure of suffering passivity, while the lover-poet can move on to the creative task before him, fulfilling himself in the role of artist.

The female figure of love rejected is present in *The Waste Land*. Here she too speaks:

> You gave me hyacinths first a year ago;
> They called me the hyacinth girl.

Her lover seems overwhelmed by the situation, reducing them both to silence redolent with terror:

> — Yet when we came back, late, from the hyacinth garden,
> Your arms full, and your hair wet, I could not
> Speak, and my eyes failed, I was neither
> Living nor dead, and I knew nothing,
> Looking into the heart of light, the silence.[10]

Lyndall Gordon has carefully mapped the association between the real Emily Hale and the images of women which recur in Eliot’s poetry.[11] Margaret Homans has revived the real Fanny Brawne, only to emphasize Keats fear of her effect on him and his need for impersonal poetic independence. She quotes from the letter Keats wrote to Reynolds in August 1819 when he was living alone in Winchester:

> My own being which I know to be becomes of more consequence to me than the crowds of Shadows in the shape of Man and women that inhabit a kingdom. The soul is a world itself and has enough to do in its own home.

---

9. Mayer, 132.

10. Eliot, *Complete Poems*, 62.

11. See Lyndall Gordon, *Eliot’s Early Years*, Oxford, 1977, paperback edn with corrections, 1988: esp. 55-57.

Homans also quotes from Keats's letter to Shelley the following summer, where he says that an artist "must have 'self—concentration', selfishness perhaps .... My imagination is a Monastery and I am its Monk."[12] In his lecture on Shelley and Keats, Eliot says, "There is hardly a statement of Keats about poetry, which, when considered carefully and with due allowance for the difficulties of communication, will not be found to be true".[13]

Keats and Eliot's preoccupation with the impersonality essential to the poet may account for the posthumous silence imposed upon Fanny and Emily about their own feelings for these men at that time. Fanny's letters to Keats were interred with his body and Eliot had all Emily's letters to him destroyed in 1957; his letters to her will only be available in twenty-five years time.

While Fanny and Emily remain silent, the different fate of the muses they evoked continues to fascinate. The tension between Keats's love and fear is transformed into the Odes of 1819, into the doomed Lamia and into the powerful figure of Moneta in *The Fall of Hyperion*.

In Eliot's poetry the fate of the muse is more disconcerting. Germaine Greer has recently drawn attention to the decay of the classical concept of the muse which she sees reaching its apotheosis in Robert Graves's White Goddess which reduces the male to "a fragile and unstable hypermasculine creature, a one-dimensional man".[14] Greer argues that by confusing gender with self-hood Graves imprisons himself in a condition replete with anxiety. She quotes Graves's lines,

> Woman with her forests, moons, flowers, waters,
> And watchful fingers:
> We claim no magic comparable to hers —
> At best poets; at worst, sorcerers.

Greer goes on to say, "For Graves the female evades his system of classification and mocks him with the partiality of his understanding, fascinating him while she appals". Greer quotes Graves's observation,

12. Margaret Homans, "Keats Reading Women, Women Reading Keats", in *Studies in Romanticism*, XXIX/3 (Fall 1990), 341-70.

13. T.S. Eliot, *The Use of Poetry and the Use of Criticism*, London, 1933, rpt. 1964, 101.

14. Germaine Greer, *Slip-Shod Sibyls: Recognition, Rejection and the Woman Poet*, London, 1995: this and subsequent references come from ch. 1, "The Muse"', 1-35.

"The function of poetry is religious invocation of the Muse, its use is the experience of mixed exaltation and horror that her presence excites". When certain figures of women appear in Eliot's early poetry, Graves observation can give a shock of recognition.

Prufrock and Other Observations was published in 1917. Eliot chose to place "La Figlia Che Piange" at the end of the series, although it had been written years before many of the other poems. In *The Complete Poems and Plays of T.S. Eliot*, "La Figlia" now comes immediately before the poems published in 1920, which includes "Sweeney Erect", where Sweeney's elaborate shaving ritual is instinct with violence towards the women of the brothel. We may recall that in "The Love Song of J. Alfred Prufrock" there will be time, among other things, to murder and create. In *Eeldrop and Appleplex*, a prose sketch published in 1917, the story of the man from Gopsum Street is introduced:

> In Gopsum Street a man murders his mistress. The important fact is that for the man the act is eternal, and that for the brief space he has to live, he is already dead. He is already in a different world from ours. He has crossed the frontier. The important fact is that something is done which cannot be undone — a possibility which none of us realize until we face it ourselves. For the man's neighbours the important fact is what the man killed her with? And at precisely what time? And who found the body? ... But the medieval world, insisting on the eternity of punishment, expressed something nearer the truth.[15]

Later in *Sweeney Agonistes*, Sweeney affirms that:

> Any man has to, needs to, wants to
> Once in a lifetime, do a girl in.[16]

These references are usually ascribed to an emotional turmoil initiated by the unhappiness of Eliot's first marriage to Vivien Haigh-Wood. As A.D. Moody suggests, like the gothic "Elegy" excised from the draft version of *The Waste Land*, "They show the mess he was in, in this

---

15. This quotation is from A. David Moody, *Thomas Stearns Eliot: Poet*, Cambridge, 1979; 2nd rev. edn, 1994, 117. I am greatly indebted to Moody's reading of Eliot's poetry, although the interpretation of Eliot's poetry in this paper is my own.

16. Eliot, *Complete Poems*, 124.

matter of his relationship with a woman".[17]

While there is little doubt of the relevance of these observations, they do not fully account for Eliot's preoccupation with the figure of a woman desired and rejected. I suggest that it is Graves's decadent female muse who is Eliot's victim. "La Figlia Che Piange" can be read as an elegy for her impending loss and "Marina", with it epigraph from Seneca's *Hercules Furens*, recalling the moment Hercules awoke to the enormity of the murder of his own children, may be read as the birth of a muse uncontaminated by erotic love.

The conclusion of this essay, replete with the anachronism of equating Eliot's murdered muse with that of Graves's White Goddess who did not appear in print until 1948, may seem far-fetched. Yet this confusing of literary periods does illustrate how one poet shared the experience of another born nearly a hundred years before him and may also confirm the truth of his own observation that, while "the new (the really new) work of art" modifies the ideal order formed by the existing monuments, yet there is "conformity between the old and the new", even if this involves murder in order to create.[18]

---

17. Moody, 117.

18. T.S. Eliot, "Tradition and the Individual Talent", in *The Sacred Wood*, London, 1920, 50.

SCOTTISH PHILOSOPHICAL SPRINGS OF A ROMANTIC LITERATURE: KEATS'S "OLDER" CONTEMPORARY CARLYLE

RALPH JESSOP

Carlyle was hostile to several contemporary poets, dismissing out of hand much that was best in English Romantic poetry. Obviously Carlyle was mistaken in his judgement and one suspects he did not have an ear for poetry, a suspicion amply supported by his own dismal attempts to write verse and yet which is at odds with his public admiration for Burns and his private enjoyment of the poetry of Byron.[1] Carlyle's hostility to English Romantic poets was not however a lone cry from the wilderness and if he occasionally indulged himself in flyting[2] the Satanic school or Lake school, other Scottish intellectuals similarly issued scathing invectives against leading English Romantics.

In order to reveal something of the Scottish bias against English Romantic poetry it is worth rehearsing some of these vituperative and seemingly impassioned curses issued by Carlyle and by two other Scottish writers, Francis Jeffrey and the Scottish philosopher, James Frederick Ferrier. In an early review of Keats's poetry from 1820, Jeffrey indicated a certain degree of sympathy with and interest in the novelty of Keats's work. However he claimed that Keats's poems were "full of extravagance and irregularity, rash attempts at originality, interminable wanderings, and excessive obscurity".[3] And although Jeffrey inscribed his review with some praise, this mainly served to

---

1. See Charles R. Sanders, "The Byron Closed in '*Sartor Resartus*'", *Studies in Romanticism*, 3 (1964), 77-108.

2. The Scots word "flyte" means to scold, chide, rail; to altercate and can also mean a scolding, a vehement reproof; a scolding match (see *The Compact Scottish National Dictionary*, eds William Grant and David D. Murison, 2 vols, Aberdeen, 1986).

3. Francis Jeffrey, "Keats's *Poems*", *Edinburgh Review*, XXXIV/68 (August 1820), 203.

authorize his condemnation of Keats's promising though still juvenile work:

> it must, we fear, be admitted, that, besides the riot and extravagance of his fancy, the scope and substance of Mr K.'s poetry is rather too dreary and abstracted to excite the strongest interest, or to sustain the attention through a work of any great compass or extent.[4]

Jeffrey could be much harsher with other English Romantic poets. Southey was accused of being too ambitious, his poetry characterized by and blamed for "its infantine simplicity, ... energy, wildness, enthusiasm".[5] Wordsworth received a drubbing as Jeffrey complained that his poetry was "a sort of prosy, solemn, obscure, feeble kind of mouthing", work of slender intellectual value since "The great characteristic of [Wordsworth's works] is a sort of emphatic inanity — a singular barrenness and feebleness of thought".[6] But if Wordsworth received Jeffrey's disdainful censure, he greatly admired the beauty and power of Byron's poetry.[7] Such exceptions aside, Jeffrey had little time for the Romantics in his critical articles for the *Edinburgh Review* if not in his private reading. As we shall see, Romantic feebleness of thought clearly annoyed other Scottish critics including Carlyle. Carlyle wrote very little about Keats though it is clear that he had read some of his poetry.[8] In the "Burns" essay he faintly echoes Jeffrey when he wrote of Keats and his poetry that "the whole consists in a weak-eyed maudlin sensibility, and a certain vague random tunefulness of nature".[9] But

---

4. *Ibid.*, 206.

5. Francis Jeffrey, "Southey's *Madoc: A Poem*", *Edinburgh Review*, VII/13 (October 1805), 17.

6. Francis Jeffrey, "Wordsworth's *Tour*", *Edinburgh Review*, XXXVII/74 (November 1822), 450.

7. See Francis Jeffrey, "Lord Byron's *Giaour*", *Edinburgh Review*, XXI/42 (July 1813), 299-309; "Lord Byron's *Corsair*, and *Bride of Abydos*", *Edinburgh Review*, XXIII/45 (April 1814), 198-99.

8. For example, see *The Collected Letters of Thomas and Jane Welsh Carlyle*, Duke-Edinburgh edn, gen. ed. Charles Richard Sanders, Durham: NC, 1970 -, I, 338.

9. *The Works of Thomas Carlyle*, ed. H.D. Traill, Centenary Edition, 30 vols, London, 1896-99, XXVI: *Critical and Miscellaneous Essays*, I, 277. The original article was not as harsh as this and reads "extreme" instead of "weak-eyed

Carlyle had much more to say against that revered poet, literary theorist, and sage of English Romanticism, Coleridge.

Somewhat famously he described Coleridge in a letter to Thomas Murray in 1824 as "a steam-engine of a hundred horses power — with the boiler burst .... A round fat oily yet impatient little man, his mind seems totally beyond his own controul."[10] Shortly after meeting Coleridge in London in 1824 Carlyle wrote to his brother John of Coleridge that

> He is a kind good soul, full of religion and affection, and poetry and animal magnetism. His chief sin is that he wants *will*; he has no resolution, he shrinks from pain or labour in any of its shapes. His very attitude bespeaks this: he never straightens his knee joints, he stoops with his fat ill shapen shoulders, and in walking he does not tread but shovel and slide — my father would call it *skluiffing* .... There is no method in his talk; he wanders like a man sailing among many currents, withersoever his lazy mind directs him .... I reckon him a man of great and useless genius — a strange not at all a great man.[11]

This notion that Coleridge was out of control and useless would later re-emerge in several other sketches which focused on Coleridge's *acratic* nature and the similar or resultant weakness of Coleridge's philosophic intellect. In 1829 Carlyle compared Coleridge to Novalis:

> Our Coleridge's *Friend* ... and *Biographia Literaria* are but a slight business compared with these *Schriften* [of Novalis]; little more than the Alphabet, and that in gilt letters, of such Philosophy and Art as is here taught in the form of Grammar and Rhetorical Compend; yet Coleridge's works were triumphantly condemned by the whole reviewing world, as clearly unintelligible .... It is admitted too, on all hands, that Mr Coleridge is a man of "genius", that is, a man having more intellectual insight than other men; and strangely enough, it is taken for granted, at the same time, that he has less intellectual insight than any other .... The Cambridge carrier, when asked whether his horse could "draw inferences," readily replied,

---

maudlin" and "pervading" instead of "random" (see "Burns", *Edinburgh Review*, XLVIII/96 [December 1828], 281).

10. *The Collected Letters*, III, 139.

11. *Ibid.*, III, 90. Scots *sklufe* or *skloof* is defined as "trail[ing] the feet along the ground in walking".

> "Yes, anything in reason;" but here, it seems, is a man of genius who has no similar gift.[12]

This last joke against Coleridge's supposed genius and actual failure to manifest it would later receive more elaborate treatment by James Frederick Ferrier, the one-time student of Carlyle's friend Sir William Hamilton.

In his *Life of John Sterling* Carlyle devoted a whole chapter to Coleridge. The chapter begins with noting that for "young inquiring men" Coleridge had "a higher than literary, a kind of prophetic or magician character".[13] Later Carlyle provides descriptions of Coleridge's physiognomy to suggest, once again, his essential weakness of will:

> Brow and head were round, and of massive weight, but the face was flabby and irresolute. The deep eyes, of a light hazel, were as full of sorrow as of inspiration; confused pain looked mildly from them, as in a kind of mild astonishment. The whole figure and air, good and amiable otherwise, might be called flabby and irresolute; expressive of weakness under possibility of strength. He hung loosely on his limbs, with knees bent, and stooping attitude; in walking, he rather shuffled than decisively stept; and a lady once remarked, he never could fix which side of the garden walk would suit him best, but continually shifted in corkscrew fashion, and kept trying both.[14]

Though clearly humorous this could hardly be more damning for weakness is one thing and deserves pity while "weakness under possibility of strength" suggests that Coleridge had squandered his potential strength or had even chosen weakness. Gradually enlarging on the key characteristics of "irresolution" and Coleridge's inability to articulate his learning and properly manifest his genius, Carlyle also mimicked his talk, claiming that it

> was distinguished, like himself, by irresolution: it disliked to be troubled with conditions, abstinences, definite fulfulments; — loved to wander at its own sweet will, and make its auditor and

12. "Novalis", in *The Works of Thomas Carlyle*, XXVII: *Critical and Miscellaneous Essays*, II, 3.

13. *The Works of Thomas Carlyle*, XI: *Life of John Sterling*, 53.

14. *Ibid.*, 54.

> his claims and humble wishes a mere passive bucket for itself! He had knowledge about many things and topics, much curious reading; but generally all topics led him, after a pass or two, into the high seas of theosophic philosophy, the hazy infinitude of Kantean transcendentalism, with its "sum-m-jects" and "om-m-mjects." Sad enough; for with such indolent impatience of the claims and ignorances of others, he had not the least talent for explaining this or anything unknown to them; and you swam and fluttered in the mistiest wide unintelligible deluge of things, for most part in a rather profitless uncomfortable manner.[15]

Further expanding the notion of Coleridge's inability to articulate himself, his possession of a potential strength of intellect not actualized, Carlyle later went on to say:

> To the man himself Nature had given, in high measure, the seeds of a noble endowment; and to unfold it had been forbidden him. A subtle lynx-eyed intellect, tremulous pious sensibility to all good and all beautiful; truly a ray of empyrean light; — but imbedded in such weak laxity of character, in such indolences and esuriences as had made strange work with it. Once more, the tragic story of a high endowment with an insufficient will. An eye to discern the divineness of the Heaven's splendours and lightenings, the insatiable wish to revel in their godlike radiances and brilliances; but no heart to front the scathing terrors of them, which is the first condition of your conquering an abiding place there.[16]

Carlyle harshly diminished Coleridge's intellectual status by characterizing him as a waverer, as self-divided, as linguistically impotent, as a Tantalus figure forever forbidden from obtaining the fruits he could so well discern and for which he constantly yearned. In thus mythologizing Coleridge, Carlyle was stating the principle upon which he claimed Coleridge's whole existence was grounded, the principle of an unresolved contradiction between his inner and outer being — actual "weakness under possibility of strength".

But such mythologizing allows and even relies upon the reader's pity towards this poor father of English Romanticism. And even though I have claimed that Carlyle condemns Coleridge without pity by the suggestion that his "possibility of strength" was squandered or rejected,

---

15. *Ibid.*, 56.

16. *Ibid.*, 60-61.

Carlyle's overweening pity for this poor dud of an intellectual construes Coleridge as yet another victim of "the tragic story of a high endowment with an insufficient will". Sharply in contrast with this display of Carlyle's seductive humanity amidst the crash of a crushing critical demolition, a more pugnaciously sharp attack deploying legalistic precision was mounted some eleven years before the publication of Carlyle's *Life of John Sterling* by the Scottish philosopher, James Frederick Ferrier. In 1840 Ferrier wrote what George Davie has described as a "slashing 'Scotch Reviewer' type of article" which attacked

> the weakest point in the Germano-Coleridgean armour — the anti-professionalism in intellectual matters, the characteristically English refusal to take a serious interest in the question of philosophical foundations, the peculiar idea ... of the critic ... as a kind of inspired purveyor of great ideas picked up ready-made from the Germans.[17]

If Carlyle's remarks worked towards diminishing Coleridge's intellectual status, Ferrier's review was a strong contender for utterly demolishing it by discrediting his claims to originality and the power of his understanding. Ferrier charged Coleridge with intellectual dishonesty and tried him against a barage of textual evidence as testimony to this indictment. In charging Coleridge with plagiarism, Ferrier claimed that he wanted

> to do justice to the claims of foreign philosophy and of individual genius, by showing that one of the most distinguished English authors of the nineteenth century, at the mature age of forty-five, succeeded in founding by far the greater part of his metaphysical reputation — which was very considerable — upon *verbatim* plagiarisms from works written and published by a German youth, when little more than twenty years of age! [Schelling who was born in 1775].[18]

In a rather lengthy display of restrained vitriol, Ferrier accused Coleridge of lacking any philosophical genius since he was unable to

---

17. George Elder Davie, *The Democratic Intellect: Scotland and Her Universities in the Nineteenth Century*, Edinburgh University Publications, History Philosophy and Economics: 12, Edinburgh, 1961; repr. 1982, 263.

18. James Frederick Ferrier, "The Plagiarisms of S.T. Coleridge", *Blackwood's Edinburgh Magazine*, XLVII (March 1840), 288.

elucidate the ideas of the transcendental philosophy. Perhaps echoed by Carlyle's notion that Coleridge was unable to express philosophical ideas with clarity, Ferrier jokingly compared the genius of the philosopher to that of the honey-bee. The genius of the bee was to bring forth honey and gladden the breakfast table, the genius of the philosopher was to explicate fundamental ideas. But Coleridge was unable to produce such honey, except that which he had stolen from the German philosopher Schelling — "*Unlike* the bee, *he* [Coleridge] steals his honey ready made".[19] Ferrier went on to detail several of Coleridge's plagiarisms of Schelling which even included the word "esemplastic", that term which is of such importance to Coleridge's poetics and his theory of the poetic imagination. According to Ferrier this came straight from Schelling's *Darlegung* where the term "*In-eins-bildung* — 'a shaping into one'" was used. In order to disguise his source all that Coleridge had had to do was translate the German into Greek and then claim that he had invented the term "esemplastic".[20] According to Ferrier "the extraordinary number of nineteen full pages [had been] copied almost *verbatim* from the works of the German philosopher, without one distinct word of acknowledgement on the part of the transcriber — an event in the history of literature altogether unprecedented".[21]

In comparison with the savage attacks on several Romantic poets by Jeffrey and on Coleridge by Ferrier, Carlyle's few outbursts against the Romantics are, if not tame, certainly brief or undeveloped. Comparing Carlyle with other Scottish writers reveals that his scurrilities were merely outflashes of fire on a sporadically erupting volcano of Scottish critical ferocity which was at times directed against the leading English Romantic poets. Carlyle himself was aware of such vehemence as something which had been seen as a fault in Scottish writing.[22] So also was Jeffrey who, in an article he wrote with Walter Scott, had condemned for his vituperations on modern sceptical philosophy, one of the more populist proponents of the Scottish philosophy of Common

---

19. *Ibid.*, 292; and see 291.

20. *Ibid.*, 294.

21. *Ibid.*, 296.

22. See, "Burns", in *The Works of Thomas Carlyle*, XXVI: *Critical and Miscellaneous Essays*, I, 288.

Sense, James Beattie.[23] However, criticizing other Scots for impetuosity and the excesses of vehement language, Carlyle and to some extent Jeffrey also gave vent to such impetuous language when attacking some of the more famous leading English romantic poets. Perhaps this was little more than the expression of a certain vigour and outspokenness peculiar to Scottish writers which was inculcated through a vigorous oral tradition, argumentative sermons from the pulpit, debating societies in the universities, and a democratic attitude to liberty of speech which at times was repressed by various brusque actions for silencing disruptive voices. Though outspokenness against the remaining vestiges of Scottish political autonomy (such as the authority of the Kirk) could result in punishment for the subversive, stern condemnation of perceived or constructed evils might be freely enjoyed as healthful signs of vivacity — vituperation and loud wrangling were as much a part of the speech, writing, and cultural vitality of Carlyle's Scotland as the repression of speech and the deep silences which Carlyle himself inlaid with metaphysical significance. The stark opposites of silence and caustic, highly argumentative criticism were therefore part of the critical discourse of Scottish reviewers and this is even detectable in those, such as Jeffrey, who were critical of other Scottish writers for this perceived fault and whose own criticism more generally tended to avoid conspicuous ferocity.

However there seems to have been a certain shared bias against English Romantic poetry and poets. As we have seen, Jeffrey accused Wordsworth of a certain "feebleness of thought". Keats was blamed by Jeffrey for his "extravagance and irregularity" and for his "interminable wanderings". By Carlyle he was accused of "weak-eyed maudlin sensibility". Coleridge was out of control, he was intellectually weak through his irresolution or dispositional indecisiveness, a weakness that disabled his power to articulate his thoughts. For Ferrier, Coleridge was intellectually disreputable in having plagiarized Schelling. Ferrier also shared Carlyle's view that Coleridge was unable to articulate himself adequately. Clearly for these Scottish writers something was rotten in the state of English Romantic poetry and for Carlyle in particular, the failing had to do with ineffectual intellectuality or a pervasive indecisiveness — Coleridge's whole being was weak since grounded on the unstable principle of an unresolved contradiction between his inner and outer self. But this critical characterization of Coleridge was not only the condemnation of a man whom Carlyle clearly found personally

---

23. Francis Jeffrey and Walter Scott, "Sir William Forbes's *Life of Dr Beattie*", *Edinburgh Review*, X/19 (April 1807), 197.

repulsive and pathetic, it was also the condemnation of an aspect of Romanticism concerning the weakening effect of self-division to which Coleridge, Byron, and Burns had all yielded.

This, for Carlyle, was one of the faults of the age, an inherent weakness in Romantic poets. But importantly it was the failure to overcome a condition of irresolution or indecision which, according to several other Scottish writers such as Thomas Reid, James Beattie, Sir James Mackintosh, and Sir William Hamilton, had typified the psychological result or condition of the extreme scepticism which had plagued the eighteenth century at least from the time of David Hume.[24] Hume himself had described as the result of extreme scepticism or Pyrrhonism the theoretical if not practical possibility of a complete stasis of being as the individual became trapped between the horns of a dilemma of contradictory deliverences from the duality of theory and practice which jointly encompassed the entirety of human existence.[25] As Carlyle was using a weaker or less theoretically pure version of such a notion to describe the irresolution of Coleridge, he was nonetheless drawing on a concept of scepticism at the heart of Scottish philosophical discourse which had its roots in Hume and which had been one of the focal points of attack for the Scottish school of Common Sense in attempting to counter Humean scepticism.

Carlyle, Jeffrey, and Ferrier undoubtedly apprise us of a Scottish bias against English Romantic poets that focused on a certain weakness of intellect. As I have suggested this Scottish bias against Romantic poets manifests itself as a set of accusations concerning the weakness of indecision as they were charged with "interminable wanderings, and excessive obscurity", irresolution, and the self-division manifested by an

---

24. For example, compare Thomas Reid, *Inquiry*, VI.v, 139Rd; VI.xx, 183Rb; *Intellectual Powers*, II.xxii, 334Rd; VI.ii, 425Ld-426La (all in *The Works of Thomas Reid*, Preface, Notes, and Supplementary Dissertations by Sir William Hamilton, Edinburgh and London, 1846); James Beattie, "Postscript", in *An Essay on the Nature and Immutability of Truth, in Opposition to Sophistry and Scepticism*, 4th edn, London and Edinburgh, 1773, 492; James Mackintosh, "Stewart's *Introduction to the Encyclopædia*" (Part II), *Edinburgh Review*, XXXVI/71 (October 1821), 260; Sir William Hamilton, "Philosophy of Perception", in *Discussions on Philosophy and Literature, Education and University Reform*, 2nd edn, London and Edinburgh, 1853, 94-95 (first published in *Edinburgh Review*, LII/103 [October 1830], 158-207).

25. See David Hume, *Enquiries Concerning Human Understanding and Concerning the Principles of Morals*, ed. L.A. Selby-Bigge, 3rd edn, Oxford, 1975; repr. 1979, 160.

inability to articulate ideas clearly and with precision, a precision demanded by the Scottish philosophical discipline which in Carlyle's day had influenced every intellectual educated in a Scottish university. But if Carlyle's condemnatory descriptions of Coleridge were somehow informed by the notion that Hume's system of extreme scepticism resulted in the ultimate psychological and social collapse described by Hume as theoretically possible and attacked by his opponents as one of the pernicious results of that scepticism, then Carlyle's Scottish bias against English Romantic poets was implicitly a condemnation of a problem raised and countered in the pre-Romantic Scotland of the middle years of the eighteenth century. Wittingly or unwittingly, Carlyle was therefore reaching back to intellectual sources that predated the Romantic period. But he also reached back to an earlier, Scottish Romantic poet and found in Robert Burns almost the same criticism he had levelled at Coleridge.

Carlyle's article on Burns is highly patriotic, angry, defiant.[26] It celebrates the greatness of Burns, laments the tragedy of his life, the weakness of his poetry and of the man himself. Carlyle lionized Burns as a hero in his potential and capability. At the point when Keats is mentioned, Carlyle states one of the main theories of his argument, namely, the notion of a unity of faculties in which the true poet is one who is "fitted to excel in whatever walk of ambition he has chosen to exert his abilities".[27] Carlyle seems to adapt Coleridge's notion of the esemplastic power of the secondary or poetic imagination without the problematic Lockean language and distinction between "primary" and "secondary" as applied to the imagination in Coleridge's *Biographia Literaria*.[28] Carlyle's notion of the poet is no less problematic however as it is hopelessly general and turns the élitism of the poetic imagination into an élitism of heroic men. For Carlyle the poet is a hero through being more of a man than others, a seer or vates specially endowed with extraordinary powers of perception.[29]

But as Carlyle exemplifies this notion of the poet as hero in

---

26. For example, see "Burns", in *The Works of Thomas Carlyle*, XXVI: *Critical and Miscellaneous Essays*, I, 258-59 and 288-89.

27. *Ibid.*, 277.

28. See *The Collected Works of Samuel Taylor Coleridge*, eds Kathleen Coburn *et al*, 16 vols, Princeton and London, 1971 - , VII: *Biographia Literaria*, eds James Engell and W. Jackson Bate (1983), ch. 13, I, 304-305.

29. See "Burns", in *The Works of Thomas Carlyle*, XXVI: *Critical and Miscellaneous Essays*, I, 272 and 278.

characterizing Burns, certain anti-élitist elements seem to be present, such as the idea that, without education, Burns held certain ideas concerning the mind which were much subtler than that of the mechanistic Associationist psychology which had such a vogue during the late eighteenth-century. Though Burns may have belonged to an élite of heroic men this cut across the boundaries of rank and the privileges of education and birth, a point further ramified by Carlyle's observation that Burns's poetry peculiarly appealed to all classes of society, his popularity extending "from the palace to the hut, and over all regions where the English tongue is spoken".[30] Interestingly the notion of the mind which Carlyle claimed Burns had and which was "subtler ... than the doctrine of association" brings to the fore a notion concerning the mind which Carlyle himself endorsed in his own works and which formed a crucial strand in the thought of Scottish Common-Sense philosophy from the time of Hume's first major critic, Thomas Reid, to that of Carlyle's contemporary and friend, Sir William Hamilton.[31] Carlyle quotes Burns as writing:

> We know nothing ... or next to nothing, of the structure of our souls, so we cannot account for those seeming caprices in them, that one should be particularly pleased with this thing, or struck with that, which, on minds of a different cast, makes no extraordinary impression .... Tell me, my dear friend, to what can this be owing? Are we a piece of machinery, which, like the Æolian harp, passive, takes the impression of the passing accident; or do these workings argue something within us above the trodden clod? I own myself partial to such proofs of those awful and important realities: a God that made all things, man's immaterial and immortal nature, and a world of weal or woe beyond death and the grave.[32]

Thus in attempting to distinguish Burns's theory of the mind from that of the contemporaneous Associationist theory, Carlyle highlighted Burns's declaration that he held to an anti-mechanistic notion of nescience concerning the soul or mind, a notion integrally connected with a form of agnostic belief in a Deity. In this as also in his claim

---

30. *Ibid.*, 267.

31. *Ibid.*, 278. I have recently argued this in "Carlyle's Scotch Scepticism: Writing from the Scottish Tradition", *Carlyle Studies Annual*, Special Issue: "Carlyle at 200", Lectures II (No. 16, 1996), 25-35.

32. *Ibid.*, 279.

that Burns's Romantic poetry was not simply about love but was founded on a "first principle" of love, Carlyle was partaking in the discourse of Scottish Common-Sense philosophy which crucially depended upon and even defined itself in terms of a matrix of first principles of the mind and which, in the works of Reid and in Hamilton, stressed and relied upon an important doctrine of nescience concerning ultimate realities and the precise nature of the relationship between mind and body in the acquisition of knowledge.[33]

But if Carlyle found much to praise in the poetry and in the heroism of Burns as one who very nearly approached the status of a true poet, he also detected a fatal flaw very similar, if much less exaggerated, to that which he found in Coleridge. For one of Carlyle's central arguments concerning Burns involved his claim that "To the last, he wavers between two purposes: glorying in his talent, like a true poet, he yet cannot consent to make this his chief and sole glory".[34] Since manhood was so important to Carlyle's notion of the poet as hero it is worth noting that such wavering between two purposes seems to have been thought of by Carlyle as akin to the war between the Flesh and the Spirit or between other such dualities in which it was a mark of manhood that one had wrestled with and yet somehow harmonized mind and body without being subdued by either term of the duality. According to Carlyle in the "Burns" essay:

> We become men, not after we have been dissipated, and disappointed in the chase of false pleasure; but after we have ascertained, in any way, what impassable barriers hem us in through this life; how mad it is to hope for contentment to our infinite soul from the *gifts* of this extremely finite world; that a man must be sufficient for himself; and that for suffering and enduring there is no remedy but striving and doing. Manhood begins when we have in any way made truce with Necessity; begins even when we have surrendered to Necessity, as the most part only do; but begins joyfully and hopefully only when we have reconciled ourselves to Necessity; and thus, in reality, triumphed over it, and felt that in Necessity we are free.

It would seem that such a truce with and resultant triumph over

33. For example, see Reid, *Intellectual Powers*, VI.v, 442R-452La; VI.vi, 452Lb-461Rd; *Inquiry*, VI.xxi, 187Ld; Hamilton, "Philosophy of the Unconditioned", in *Discussions*, 38.

34. "Burns", in *The Works of Thomas Carlyle*, XXVI: *Critical and Miscellaneous Essays*, I, 291.

Necessity or the realities of physical existence had never been achieved by the Romantics — they had failed to achieve true manhood, had failed to be heroes and had thus failed to become true poets, sinking into or surrendering themselves to Necessity, to their conditions, and thereby negating their freedom as something only possible within constraints upon it. Burns had never learned this lesson fully and had thus not been immunized against "many a bitter hour and year of remorseful sorrow".

Tracing Burns's descent into unspecified wrongdoing, Carlyle remarked that "He loses his feeling of innocence; his mind is at variance with itself; the old divinity no longer presides there; but wild Desires and wild Repentance alternately oppress him".[35] These descriptions of the flaw of wavering between two purposes and failing to harmonize the self with the material, finite conditions of the self's environment in Burns sound very close to what Carlyle said of Coleridge's irresolution, his self-division, and they also sound very close to the fever of doubt which Teufelsdröckh undergoes in *Sartor Resartus*. Teufelsdröckh, during the Everlasting No

> lived in a continual, indefinite, pining Fear; tremulous, pusillanimous, apprehensive of I knew not what; it seemed as if all things in the Heavens above and the Earth beneath would hurt me; as if the Heavens and the Earth were but boundless jaws of a devouring monster, wherein I, palpitating, waited to be devoured.[36]

Thus Coleridge and Burns can be read as Carlyle's factual examples which he fictionalized in *Sartor Resartus* by using Diogenes Teufelsdröckh to symbolize man as riven by doubt, self-divided and wavering between the duality of Flesh and Spirit, Body and Mind.

As Carlyle implicitly reached back to the philosophical discourse of pre-Romantic Scotland in characterizing the fatal flaw of Coleridge and Burns, he was enunciating through his descriptions of them and their fundamental weakness something of the core problem of scepticism which Hume had raised and which his opponents in Reid and the Common-Sense school had striven to counter. Carlyle, in theorizing about Coleridge, Burns, and in fictionalizing and symbolizing their irresolution or self-division through Teufelsdröckh, was therefore grappling with that pivotal problem of scepticism at the centre of the Scottish Enlightenment. Romantic poets are generally well known for

---

35. *Ibid.*, 295-96.

36. *The Works of Thomas Carlyle*, I: *Sartor Resartus*, 134.

their oppositions to the Enlightenment, hostilities to mechanisms in language, materialist philosophy, and their concerns with the collapse of religious faith. Opposing the intellectual and practical crisis which Hume and the sceptical tendencies of Enlightenment thought had generated, Carlyle was as much a Romantic as Coleridge, Keats, Wordsworth, or Shelley. But by sharp contrast with the English Romantics, the sources of Carlyle's Romanticism are much more manifestly at the heart of eighteenth-century Scottish philosophical debate where the contest between Humean scepticism and Common Sense was so eloquently, daringly, rigorously, and at times vehemently promulgated.

According to Carlyle that part of Coleridge's attractiveness "to the young ardent mind" was his "almost religious and prophetic" charm which lamented the signs of the times:

> The constant gist of his discourse was lamentation over the sunk condition of the world; which he recognised to be given-up to Atheism and Materialism, full of mere sordid misbeliefs, mispursuits and misresults. All science had become mechanical; the science not of men, but of a kind of human beavers .... Men's souls were blinded, hebetated; and sunk under the influence of Atheism and Materialism, and Hume and Voltaire.[37]

This was recognized as true by Carlyle but Coleridge and the English Romantic poets had failed to provide any solution to the problems of atheism, Materialism, mechanical philosophy, and scepticism. Coleridge's solution concerning the revival of the Church was, for Carlyle, unworkable and unacceptable.[38] Nevertheless, Carlyle's Coleridge does seem to voice some of the most pressing anxieties raised in Carlyle's early attempt at fiction, "Wotton Reinfred", his major article for the *Edinburgh Review*, "Signs of the Times", and that epic metaphysical poem in prose which in so many ways stands counter to the Enlightenment, *Sartor Resartus*.[39]

---

37. *The Works of Thomas Carlyle*, XI: *Life of John Sterling*, 58.

38. *Ibid.*, 59.

39. For example, see "Wotton Reinfred", in *Last Words of Thomas Carlyle*, with an Introduction by K.J. Fielding, London, 1892; repr. Farnborough, 1971, 102-103; "Signs of the Times", in *The Works of Thomas Carlyle*, XXVII: *Critical and Miscellaneous Essays*, II, 79-80. See Ralph Jessop, "Carlyle's 'Wotton Reinfred': They Talked of Scotch Philosophy", *Carlyle Annual*, 12 (1991), 9-15.

Carlyle, like earlier Romantics before him such as Coleridge and Burns may have been opposed to the Enlightenment but a source of his opposition already existed within the philosophical discourse of eighteenth-century Scotland in the Common-Sense philosophy of Thomas Reid which itself may have influenced Coleridge.[40] The philosophical system of Reid in several ways pre-empted the response to what Romantics found most abhorrent in Enlightenment mechanistic philosophy through its overall position in relation to Hume's metaphysical scepticism and some of the crucial elements which constituted that position. Reid opposed the mechanistic and more generally physicalistic terminologies and theoretical constructs of modern philosophers in their adoption of representationism. He did this by means of a critique of language and of the specious authority of theoretical constructs to account for the workings of the mind as mere arguments by an untenable analogy.[41] Less obviously, he also opposed this language through adopting organicist metaphors of growth and development to illustrate the developmental nature of mental capacities and more importantly the notion of an interfusion of philosophy with common beliefs and the first principles or cognitive capacities of the mind as basic, unrationalizable foundations or starting points of all philosophical discourse and learning.[42]

The Scottish school of Common Sense was also supportive of religious belief and this manifested itself in a variety of ways in Reid, the most important of which for any study of Carlyle's frequent appeals to nescience or the unknowability of immaterial substance and ultimate realities, concerned a strand of agnosticism which received its most definitive statement in the early and contemporaneous writings of Sir William Hamilton.[43] The anti-mechanism and anti-representationism of the Common-Sense tradition in Scottish philosophy crucially relied on a grounding intuitionism at the basis of perception or the act of the mind in cognizing physical entities which were conceived of as distinct yet directly related to the mind.[44] This mind-body dualism held that the

---

40. See Paul Hamilton, *Coleridge's Poetics*, Oxford, 1983, 62-72.

41. For example, see Reid, *Inquiry*, VII, 201-202Ra.

42. For example, see Reid, *Inquiry*, I.iv, 101Rb.

43. For example, see Hamilton, "Philosophy of the Unconditioned", in *Discussions*, 15n.

44. See Hamilton, "Philosophy of Perception", in *Discussions*, 55; and also, for example, Reid, *Inquiry*, V.iii, 122Ld.

radically dissimilar entities of the self and the not-self, the subject and the object were distinct yet correlated. In explaining the relation betwen mind and body in the act of perception, Carlyle's contemporary and friend, Hamilton (who followed, embellished, and developed the philosophy of Reid) argued that mind and body were held in a relation such that their duality was always present to consciousness.[45]

This notion of bi-polarity, a notion at the heart of the Scottish attempts to counter Humean scepticism and the problematization of Cartesián dualism and the Lockean theory of ideas, had a much earlier source than that of Reid and its re-interpretation by Hamilton in the late 1820s and early 30s. According to Hamilton it had been a position maintained by the fifth-century Greek philosopher Heraclitus.[46] It is a position which seems to play an important part in Carlyle's *Sartor Resartus* as several recent commentators have recognized with arguments concerning the use of dualities and bi-polar opposites in the text.[47] Carlyle's various outbursts against the despair of extreme scepticism, the mechanical age and its mechanistic construals of the mind, the totalizing Rationalism and scepticism which threatened to destroy the human soul and intellect and replace all such objects of faith and belief with a clothes-screen existence of superficiality and unmitigated materialism — his objections to all of these, along with the pervasive play on dualism in *Sartor Resartus*, at least partially locates this clearly Romantic reaction to eighteenth-century Scottish thought and what it bequethed to the nineteenth century within the terms of a Scottish philosophical discourse which both generated and opposed such things.

The feebleness of thought in Wordsworth's work complained of by Jeffrey along with several of Carlyle's remarks on the irresolution of Coleridge and his intellectual inability, so strongly endorsed by Ferrier's article on Coleridge's plagiarisms, suggests that if we can speak of a Scottish response to the Romantic poets, one of its primary

45. See Hamilton, "Philosophy of Perception", in *Discussions*, 54-55, and 96.

46. *Ibid.*, 61.

47. For example, see J. Hillis Miller, "'Hieroglyphical Truth' in *Sartor Resartus*: Carlyle and the Language of Parable", in *Victorian Perspectives: Six Essays*, eds John Clubbe and Jerome Meckier, Basingstoke, 1989, 1-20; Vivienne Rundle, "'Devising New Means': *Sartor Resartus* and the Devoted Reader", *Victorian Newsletter*, 82 (1992), 13-22; Joseph Sigman, "'Diabolico-Angelical Indifference': The Imagery of Polarity in '*Sartor Resartus*'", *Southern Review*, 5 (1972), 207-24.

complaints concerned the non-intellectual or intellectually inept nature of poetry's response to what for the Scots in the eighteenth century had been a most stressed philosophical debate between scepticism and Common Sense. That the Scottish complaint concerned Romantic feebleness of thought is also suggested by the very caustic and highly argumentative nature of their literary and philosophical criticism in nineteenth-century journals such as the *Edinburgh Review* and occasionally *Blackwood's Edinburgh Magazine*. For Carlyle in particular, the failing of the Romantics had to do with a pervasive indecisiveness or an unresolved contradiction between the inner and outer self, a contradictory state of being which Hume had outlined as the theoretically possible result of his extreme scepticism and which Carlyle seems to have used in theorizing about Coleridge and Burns and in translating them into the symbolic figure of Diogenes Teufelsdröckh. Carlyle did live to become older than Keats and as Basil Willey argues, as the Victorian period progressed he may have outgrown his earlier connections with Romanticism.[48] But as a younger man writing in Scotland he reached back, as so many contemporary Scottish intellectuals did, to the problems of what is usually thought of as the pre-Romantic era of mid-eighteenth century Scottish Enlightenment. His Romanticism, as thus grounded in and part of a literature produced by Scottish intellectuals from Hume, Reid, Jeffrey, Hamilton, Ferrier and others, distinctively partakes in a Scottish philosophical discourse which is yet similar to the characteristic biases against Enlightenment thought which typify English Romanticism. In this, the Scottish philosophical springs of Carlyle's Romanticism, as even of that against which he was reacting, were older and yet contemporary with, significantly different from and yet similar to, the English Romanticism of Carlyle's tragically maudlin contemporary, Keats.

---

48. See Basil Willey, "Thomas Carlyle", in *Nineteenth-Century Studies: Coleridge to Matthew Arnold*, Cambridge, rpt. 1980, 102.

CARLYLE'S "BURNS"

KEITH WHITE

This is an essay about Carlyle writing about Lockhart writing about Burns. In May 1828 right before the Carlyles moved to the moors of Craigenputtock, Dumfries, Thomas agreed to write an extended review of John Gibson Lockhart's recently published *Life of Robert Burns*. The request came from Francis Jeffrey, co-founder and editor of the *Edinburgh Review*. Carlyle first mentions the assignment in a letter of 10 June to his half brother John A. Carlyle (Jack), who was then in Munich:

> The last two nights we spent in Edinburgh were spent — where think you? In the house of Francis Jeffrey; surely one of the kindest little men, I have ever in my life met with. He and his household (wife and daughter) have positively engaged to come and pay us a visit here this very summer! I am to write him an article on Burns, as well as one on Tasso: but alas! alas! all writing is yet far from my hand .... Lockhart had written a kind of *Life of Burns*, and men in general were making another uproar about Burns: it is this Book (a trivial enough one) which I am to *pretend* reviewing.[1]

Lockhart's extensive piece was part of *Constable's Miscellany* (1828). On 25 August Carlyle again wrote to his brother:

> I am *very* busy, and third part done, with a "fair full and free" Essay on *Burns* for the *Edinburgh Review*; a *Life* of that Poet having appeared by Lockhart. No one can say how bilious I am and am like to be. But I have begun to ride daily on Larry, and so Jeffrey *shall* have his *Article* at the appointed time. That wonderful little man is expected here very soon with *Weib und Kind* [wife and child]! He takes no little interest in us; writes

1. *The Collected Letters of Thomas and Jane Welsh Carlyle*, Duke-Edinburgh edn, gen. ed. Charles Richard Sanders, Durham: NC, 1970 -, IV, 382-83.

> often, and half hates half loves me with the utmost sincerity. Nay he even offers me in the coolest lightest manner the use of his *purse*, and evidently rather wishes I would use it. *Proh Deûm atque hominum fidem* [Ah, faithful to God and man]! This from a Scotsman and a Lawyer![2]

In a letter of 25 September, Carlyle mentions the assignment to Goethe,[3] but by October Carlyle's feeling for Jeffrey had cooled, and the project on Burns was to blame. From Carlyle's letter of 6 October to his mother, Margaret A. Carlyle, we know Jeffrey and his family had made their promised visit.[4] Carlyle elaborates in his letter of 10 October to Jack:

> The Paper on Burns is finished; and I suppose will appear in December; being too late for this present Number. The Proof-sheets of it are even now in the house, and corrected. Jeffrey had clipt the first portion of it all into shreds (partly by my permission), simple [*sic*] because it was too long. My first feeling was of indignation, and to demand the whole back again, that it might lie in my drawer and worm-eat, rather than come before the world in the horrid souterkin shape; the body of a quadruped with the head of a bird; a man *shortened* by cutting out his thighs, and fixing the Knee-pans on the hips!

Carlyle did "*nothing for three days*" and then "by replacing and readjusting many parts of the first sixteen pages ... once more put the thing into a kind of publishable state". He sent it back to Jeffrey with, as he told Jack, "the private persuasion that probably I shall not soon write another for that quarter". Otherwise, Carlyle reported to his brother, "I will keep friends with the man; for he really has extraordinary worth, and likes me, at least heartily wishes me well".[5] Apparently the visit went well, although on 21 November Carlyle told Eliza Stodart that Jeffrey "talked — talked from morning to night, nay till morning again — I never assisted at such a talking since I came into the world; either in respect of quantity or quality".[6] Jeffrey and his

---

2. *Ibid.*, IV, 399.

3. *Ibid.*, IV, 407.

4. *Ibid.*, IV, 409.

5. *Ibid.*, IV, 413-14.

6. *Ibid.*, IV, 417.

wife, their maid, and their dog had arrived in a storm that "forced" them to "dismount from his carriage at some of the *yetts* [gates]", but Carlyle describes the visit as "a fairy time".[7] And despite his initial reservations about Jeffrey's editing, Carlyle, as Fred Kaplan notes, did not "reinsert the deleted material" when he later republished the essay in his collected works.[8]

The Burns piece appeared in the December issue of the *Edinburgh Review* (No. 96). As Carlyle and Jeffrey agreed, "Burns" is a pretence of a review of Lockhart's piece. It reads as part literary criticism, part biography, and part sermon on the role of the poet in society. Written only fifty years after Burns's death, nevertheless it perpetuates many of the myths and misconceptions of Robert Burns's life that were already in place. Although Carlyle wrote it with affection and admiration for "one of the most considerable British men of the eighteenth century", the work may sometimes strike modern readers as sentimental, condescending, and didactic.[9] Because it provides readers with nothing that was not already known about Burns, the piece is often discounted in the biographies of both men. Nevertheless the essay remains one of the earliest defining *post facto* documents of the Romantic movement, and in it Carlyle begins to layout the foundations of what will come to typify Victorian literary taste.

Carlyle's fascination with Burns is attributable, in a large measure, to the circumstances of the poet's life. As Carlyle described the poet to Goethe,

> Perhaps you have never heard of this *Burns*: and yet he was a man of the most decisive genius; but born in the rank of a Peasant, and miserably wasted away by the complexities of his strange situation; so that all he effected was comparatively a trifle, and he died before middle age.[10]

Carlyle had reason to empathize with his fellow Scot. Both were from rural backgrounds and suffered nervous disorders much of their lives.

---

7. *Ibid.*, IV, 414.

8. Fred Kaplan, *Thomas Carlyle: A Biography*, Ithaca: NY, 1983, 145.

9. *The Works of Thomas Carlyle*, ed. H.D. Traill, Centenary Edition, 30 vols, London, 1896-99, XXVI: *Critical and Miscellaneous Essays*, I, 262. All page references given after quotations in the main text are to this edition of the "Burns" essay.

10. *The Collected Letters*, IV, 407.

As early as 1818 Carlyle developed chronic digestive problems that were apparently brought on by nerves.[11] In 1824 he consulted an Edinburgh doctor, who put him on mercury and took him off tobacco.[12] As we can see from the letter of 25 August to Jack, Carlyle was still "bilious", and the move to Craigenputtock had been precipitated by concerns for his health.

Apparent from "The Health Record of Robert Burns" that appears in Robert T. Fitzhugh's *Robert Burns: The Man and the Poet*, Burns also suffered from nervous disorders as young men. His brother Gilbert surmised:

> I doubt not but the hard labour and sorrow of this period of his life, was in a great measure the cause of that depression of spirits, with which Robert was so often afflicted through the whole life afterwards.

Gilbert also recalled Robert's chronic "dull headache, which, at a future period of his life, was exchanged for a palpitation of the heart, and a threatening of fainting and suffocation in his bed, in the night time".[13] In a letter of 27 December 1781 to his father Burns writes, "The weakness of my nerves has so debilitated my mind that I dare not, either review past events, or look forward into futurity".[14] In the submission of March 1784 to his *Commonplace Book*, the poet records:

> There was a certain period in my life that my spirit was broke by repeated losses & disasters, which threatened, & indeed effected the utter ruin of my fortune. My body too was attacked by that most dreadful distemper, a Hypochondria, or confirmed Melancholy.[15]

He also told Dr John Moore (August 1787),

> The finishing evil that brought up the rear of this internal file

11. Kaplan, 59-64.

12. *Ibid.*, 87.

13. Quoted in Alan Bold, *A Burns Companion*, New York, 1991, 424-25.

14. *The Letters of Robert Burns*, ed. J. De Lancey Ferguson, 2 Vols, Oxford, 1931, I, 4.

15. Quoted in Robert T. Fitzhugh, *Robert Burns: The Man and the Poet*, Boston, 1970, 417.

> was my hypochondriac complaint being irritated to such a degree, that for three months I was in [a] diseased state of body and mind, scarcely to be envied by the hopeless wretches who have got their mittimus.[16]

How much of Burns's ailments were caused by his nerves and how much by his alleged rheumatic heart disease, perhaps we never will know.[17] However, we do know that Burns's mental distress continued into the 1790s and that Burns himself attributed it to his circumstances. As he told Gilbert in a letter of 11 January 1790:

> ... I have not in my present frame of mind much appetite for exertion in writing. — My nerves are in a damnable State. — I feel that horrid hypochondria pervading every atom of my body & soul. — The Farm has undone my enjoyment of myself. — It is a ruinous affair on all hands.[18]

He would later (1 June 1796) confide to James Johnson that "Personal & domestic affliction have almost entirely banished that alacrity & life with which I used to woo the rural Muse of Scotia".[19]

In November 1793 he writes to Maria Riddell:

> ... Here I sit, altogether Novemberish, a damn'd melange of Fretfulness & melancholy; not enough of the one to rouse me to passion, nor of the other to repose me in torpor; my soul flouncing & fluttering round her tenement, like a wild Finch caught amid the horrors of winter & newly thrust into a cage. —[20]

And by 25 February 1794, he is ready to tell Alexander Cunningham, "My constitution and frame were, ab origine, blasted with a deep incurable taint of hypochondria which poisons my existence".[21]

"The Health Record of Robert Burns" contains over seventy listings of poor health in the poet. A few of the complaints are typical of those

---

16. *The Letters of Robert Burns*, I, 112.

17. See Fitzhugh, 415-16, for a diagnosis by Stanley Bardwell, M.D.

18. *The Letters of Robert Burns*, II, 1.

19. *Ibid.*, II, 322.

20. *Ibid.*, II, 217.

21. *Ibid.*, II, 234-35.

most humans endure. Whatever the true source of his "Hypochondria" and "Melancholy", Burns was certainly convinced that they were caused by social stress. Importantly, the world's effect on Burns is half of Carlyle's thesis: "In one word, what and how produced was the effect of society on him; what and how produced was his effect on society?" (261).[22] Carlyle makes his investigation "with good will" and proves it by naming Burns a neglected "prodigy" and "one of the most considerable British men of the eighteenth century". Carlyle never seems to be aware that in his attempt to prove that Burns was "no vulgar wonder", he is sometimes guilty of unintentional elitism in such statements as "he found himself in deepest obscurity, without help, without instruction, without model; or with models of only the meanest sort". However, like previous biographers, Carlyle insists on placing Burns within the tradition of Rousseau's "l'enfant sauvage", that seminal character of eighteenth-century Primitivism that appears, for instance, in Behn's *Oroonoko*, Colman's *Inkle and Yarico*, Cumberland's *The West Indian*, Goldsmith's *The Deserted Village*, Inchbald's *The Child of Nature*, and later in Blake's "The Shepherd", Wordsworth's "Michael", Keats's "Old Meg She Was a Gipsey", and of course Burns's own "The Cotter's Saturday Night".

For example, Carlyle contends,

> An educated man stands, as it were, in the midst of a boundless arsenal and magazine, filled with all the weapons and engines which man's skill has been able to devise from the earliest time; and he works, accordingly, with a strength borrowed from all past ages.

He contrasts these advantages with he whose,

> state stands on the outside of that storehouse, and feels that its gates must be stormed, or remain forever shut against him! His means are the commonest and rudest; the mere work done is no measure of his strength .... It is in this last shape that Burns presents himself (262-63).

22. Carlyle's motivation for biography is laid out in an essay of 1832: "How inexpressibly comfortable to know our fellow-creature; to see into him, understand his goings-forth, decipher the whole heart of his mystery: nay, not only to see into him, but even to see out of him, to view the world altogether as he views it; so that we can theoretically construe him; and could almost practically personate him; and do now thoroughly discern both what manner of man he is, and what manner of thing he has got to work on and live on!" ("Biography", in *The Works of Thomas Carlyle*, XXVIII: *Critical and Miscellaneous Essays*, III, 44.)

Carlyle adds that the poet's "heart flows out in sympathy over universal Nature" and fondly refers to him as "The Peasant Poet" (265). Furthermore, he declares, "a certain sterling worth pervades whatever Burns has written; a virtue, as of green fields and mountain breezes, dwells in his poetry; it is redolent of natural life and hardy natural men" (274).

Despite the high praise for Burns's heritage, Carlyle speculates on what Burns might have achieved had his economic circumstances been better:

> Had this William Burns's small seven acres of nursery-ground anywise prospered, the boy Robert had been sent to school; had struggled forward, as so many weaker men do, to some university; come forth not as a rustic wonder, but as a regular well-trained intellectual workman, and changed the whole course of British Literature, — for it lay in him to have done this! But the nursery did not prosper; poverty sank his whole family below the help of even our cheap school-system: Burns remained a hard-worked ploughboy, and British literature took its own course (293-94).

However, even if Carlyle does not fully unmask the rustic persona, he does show that the mask had many and interesting layers. Nevertheless, Carlyle must be careful not to contradict himself with the structure of his argument. He acknowledges that money and education might have propelled Burns to even greater literary accomplishments. But at the same time much of Carlyle's admiration for Burns originates from the poet's success despite the apparently antagonistic circumstances of his environment. Carlyle begins to lay the foundation of his thesis when he writes,

> Is not every genius an impossibility till he appear? ... It is not the material but the workman that is wanting. It is not the dark *place* that hinders, but the dim *eye*. A Scottish peasant's life was the meanest and rudest of all lives, till Burns became a poet in it, and a poet of it; found it a *man's* life, and therefore significant to men (273).

Carlyle believes that the secret of Burns's literary achievement is, in part, "his *Sincerity*, his indisputable air of Truth" (267).[23] By this he

23. In Carlyle's lecture of 19 May 1840, "The Hero as Man of Letters: Johnson, Rousseau, Burns", he repeats the sentiment: "The chief quality of Burns

means Burns avoids "fabulous woes or joys", eschews "wiredrawn refinings, either in thought or feeling". To his credit Burns,

> does not write from hearsay, but from sight and experience; it is the scenes that he has lived and laboured amidst, that he describes: those scenes, rude and humble as they are, have kindled beautiful emotions in his soul, noble thoughts, and definite resolves; he speaks forth what is in him, not from any outward call of vanity or interest, but because his heart is too full to be silent .... This is the grand secret for finding readers and retaining them: let him who would move and convince others, be first moved and convinced himself (267-68).

Thus Burns's art commences from his extraordinary ability to exploit his circumstances. As Carlyle puts it, Burns's gift is "his indifference as to subject", that is, the "power he has of making all subjects interesting" (271). Earlier Carlyle made it clear that for Burns the "rough scenes of Scottish life" are no "Arcadian illusion" (265). (Perhaps this is what he has in mind when he later speaks of Keats's "weak-eyed maudlin sensibility and a certain vague random tunefulness of nature": 277). So Carlyle understands that one is not a poet simply because one has rustic or pastoral sensibilities.

In Carlyle's opinion, Burns's work is free from affectation, that "bane of literature" (268). With this point Carlyle begins his many comparisons of Burns with Byron. Carlyle asks, "Are [Byron's] Harolds and Giaours ... real men; we mean, poetically consistent and conceivable men? ... Perhaps *Don Juan* ... is the only thing approaching to a *sincere* work, he ever wrote." He then reaffirms his opinion that Burns "is an honest man, and an honest writer" (269). However, the critic then asserts that his praise for Burns's art does not extend to his "Letters, and other fractions of prose composition", because he perceives them "as the effort of a man to express something which he has no organ fit for expressing" (270). Carlyle's explanation is that Burns's,

> correspondents are often men whose relation to him he has never accurately ascertained; whom therefore he is either forearming himself against; or else unconsciously flattering by adopting the style he thinks will please them.

---

is the *sincerity* of him" (see *The Works of Thomas Carlyle*, V: *On Heroes, Hero-Worship, and the Heroic in History*, 192).

Significantly, when Burns writes "to trusted Friends and on real interests, his style becomes simple, vigorous, expressive, sometimes even beautiful" (270).

At this point in the essay one realizes that "Burns" is not strictly about the poet of that name but rather is often a dissertation on the prerequisites of good poetry. Sincerity, honesty, lack of affectation, the ability to make all subjects interesting — these are the marks of the true poet. As Carlyle explains,

> The poet, we imagine, can never have far to seek for a subject: the elements of his art are in him, and around him on every hand; for him the Ideal world is not remote from the Actual, but under it and within it; nay, he is a poet precisely because he can discern it there. Wherever there is a sky above him, and a world around him, the poet is in his place; ....

In a word, the poet is a "*vates*".

Carlyle will contend in the latter half of his essay that Burns's social and moral failings arise from his leaving his rustic world, body and soul. It is a rather simplistic premise, but one nevertheless that Carlyle does not treat simply. His argument is that Burns is "a poet of Nature's own making; and Nature, after all, is still the grand agent in making poets". His point is that to be a good poet one must keep one's covenant with the world. He discounts the notions that poets must have "a certain sort of training" (that is, an academic training), that he must be "bred in a certain rank, and must be on a confidential footing with the higher classes" or that he must be born in a certain age (272-73). "Let but the true poet be given us", Carlyle writes, "place him where and how you will, and true poetry will not be wanting". For Carlyle, Burns's covenant with his world is apparent because Burns has "a resonance in his bosom for every note of human feeling" (274). Furthermore "No poet of any age or nation is more graphic than Burns" (275),[24] and his "keenness of insight keeps pace with keenness of feeling". In other words, "his *light* is not more pervading than his *warmth*" (279).

According to Carlyle, the Promethean spark in Burns is

24. Four years later, in his essay "Biography", Carlyle will argue that the "secret for being 'graphic'" is "*To have an open loving heart*" (*The Works of Thomas Carlyle*, XXVIII: *Critical and Miscellaneous Essays*, III, 57).

indignation.[25] By proposing, "The Indignation which makes verses is, properly speaking, an inverted Love", Carlyle transposes Juvenal's "*Si natura negat, facit indignatio versum*" (that is, "If nature refuses, indignation will produce verses"). In other words, the indignation that inspires good verse derives not from hate, but from "the love of some right, some worth, some goodness, belonging to ourselves or others, which has been injured, and which this tempestuous feeling issues forth to defend and avenge". Carlyle's moral is that "No selfish fury of heart, existing there as a primary feeling, and without its opposite, ever produced much Poetry" (281).

For Carlyle, Burns's proper indignation manifests itself in the nationalistic poems such as "Dweller in yon Dungeon Dark", "Bruce's Address", and "Macpherson's Farewell". Of course Carlyle must tread lightly because he is, after all, a Scot living in a country ruled by the British. However, he intimates that Burns is at his best when he is writing like a Scot. This does not mean simply writing about things Scottish. For example, Carlyle has little praise for the celebrated "Tam o' Shanter", a work he declares "a piece of sparkling rhetoric" in which unfortunately "the heart and body of the story still lies hard and dead" (282-83). Instead, Carlyle maintains that "by far the most finished, complete and truly inspired pieces of Burns are, without dispute, to be found among his *Songs*" (285). Again, Carlyle's reasoning is consistent with his faith in Burns's sincerity:

> his Songs are honest in another point of view: in form, as well as spirit. They do not *affect* to be set to music, but they actually and in themselves are music .... (286).

He declares that Burns's "chief influence as an author will ultimately be found to depend" on his songs (287). Here Carlyle is diplomatic (uncharacteristically so), for although he acknowledges that Burns's "Songs are already part of the mother-tongue, not of Scotland only but of Britain, and of the millions that in all ends of the earth speak a British language", he also notes that since Burns the greatest change in British, "particularly Scottish literature" is "its remarkable increase of nationality" (287).

Briefly, Carlyle argues that "For a long period after Scotland

---

25. Teufelsdröch's "Indignation and Defiance" occurs after his assent to the "Everlasting No" and "Baphometric Fire-baptism", and it provides him with "at least a fixed centre to revolve around" (*The Works of Thomas Carlyle*, I: *Sartor Resartus*, 135).

became British, we had no literature" and that Scotland, although "so full of writers", had "no Scottish culture".[26] But it is the French not the British whom Carlyle blames, because Scottish writers modelled themselves after Racine, Voltaire, Batteux, Boileau, Montesquieu, Mably, and Quesnay. Carlyle blames Burns's predecessor's "lack of patriotic affection, nay of any human affection whatever" on their French models:

> The French wits of the period were as unpatriotic: but their general deficiency in moral principle, not to say their avowed sensuality and unbelief in all virtue, strictly so called, render this accountable enough).

However, Carlyle hopes "there is a patriotism founded on something better than prejudice", and thus his metaphor for Motherland is that it is a place that nourishes what is native to its ground (288-89). In his final assessment of Burns the poet Carlyle allows himself a pun: "in no heart did the love of country ever burn with a warmer glow than in that of Burns" (290).

Although the second half of Carlyle's essay still lies before him, nevertheless his discussion of Burns the social animal is fairly elementary. According to Carlyle, Burns's social and moral failings are chiefly the result of his lack of religion and his encounter with the Edinburgh circle. Central to the psychological profile of Burns that emerges is the notion that the poet was a *puer aeternus*, a term never used by Carlyle but one implicit in such statements as "Properly speaking, there is but one era in the life of Burns, and that the earliest" and "We have not youth and manhood, but only youth" (291). Therefore, to the young poet whose psychological development was arrested, "the world still appears to him, as to the young, in borrowed colours: he expects from it what it cannot give to any man". In this and other respects, Carlyle will note, Burns complements Lord Byron, whose life span was one year shorter than even Burns's.

Those who know only Carlyle's famous injunction of 1843 — "Close thy *Byron*; open thy *Goethe*"[27] — and not the context in which he expresses it will be surprised to learn that in "Burns" Carlyle does

26. In "The Hero as Man of Letters" Carlyle astutely observes, "That he should have tempted so many to penetrate through the rough husk of that dialect of his, is proof that there lay something far from common within it" (*The Works of Thomas Carlyle*, V: *On Heroes, Hero-Worship, and the Heroic in History*, 189).

27. *The Works of Thomas Carlyle*, I: *Sartor Resartus*, 153.

not scorn, but pities Byron and compares his fate with Burns. Carlyle argues that Burns's response to life's vicissitudes was to swerve "to and fro, between passionate hope and remorseful disappointment", and hence like Byron, Burns failed to achieve a "moral manhood" (292-93). Like Burns, Byron "has a poet's soul, and strives towards the Infinite and Eternal; and soon feels that all this is but mounting to the house-top to reach the stars!". "Like Burns", Byron "is only a proud man; might, like him, have 'purchased a pocket-copy of Milton to study the character of Satan'; for Satan also is Byron's grand exemplar, the hero of his poetry, and the model apparently of his conduct". In short, Carlyle believes both poets had overreaching spirits:

> As in Burns's case too, the celestial element will not mingle with the clay; both poet and man of the world he must not be; vulgar Ambition will not live kindly with poetic Adoration; he *cannot* serve God and Mammon (315-16)

Although all this anticipates (stereo)typical Victorian moralizing, nevertheless Carlyle is sympathetic: "Byron and Burns were sent forth as missionaries to their generation, to teach a higher Doctrine, a purer Truth." He argues that each "had a message to deliver, which left them no rest till it was accomplished". Thus both poets lived, "in dim throes of pain" with "this divine behest ... smoldering within them; for they knew not what it meant, and felt it only in mysterious anticipation, and they had to die without articulately uttering it". To their detriment, the two men were "in the camp of the Unconverted" and hence not spiritually prepared to be "idol-priests" (316-17).

In Burns's case "the Unconverted" were the "sages and nobles of Edinburgh" (297). Carlyle refers to Burns's exploit in Edinburgh as "the most striking incident in Burns's life." However, (following Gilbert's and Burns's own admissions) Carlyle also stresses the importance of Burns's first trip from home, the one he made in 1781 to Irvine "so early as in his twenty-third year" (293). Burns himself told John Moore, "My twenty third year was to me an important era. — Partly thro' whim, and partly that I wished to set about doing something in my life".[28] This also began another period of the "hypochondriac complaint" that Burns mentions to Moore above. Significantly, Carlyle's digestive disorders and the beginning of a period that lead nearly to a mental breakdown and religious crisis began in November

28. *The Letters of Robert Burns*, I, 112.

1818, a month before Carlyle's twenty-third birthday.[29]

Robert Fitzhugh declares Burns's trip "the arrival of his long-postponed maturity".[30] In effect, the poet went to Irvine a flax farmer and came home a poet. Although this is a bit of a simplification (Burns had already been writing poetry), nevertheless in Irvine he met an adventurous sailor name Richard Brown, who "gave Burns his first thought of publication by suggesting that he send some of his poems to a magazine".[31] But Brown may have encouraged Burns in other ways, for to Moore the poet commented, "He was the only man I ever saw who was a greater fool than myself when WOMAN was the presiding star ... Here his friendship did me a mischief."[32] As Fitzhugh notes, "In Irvine, Burns also went through a religious ferment which must have been at least part cause of the desperate depression ... which accompanied 'alarming symptoms of a Pleurisy or some other dangerous disorder' that afflicted him there".[33] Both Carlyle and Fitzhugh stress that Burns had not been adequately prepared for this new world. Lockhart points out that in Irvine, "a small sea-port", the "adventurous spirits of a smuggling coast, will all their jovial habits, were to be met with abundance".[34] Carlyle maintains that "up to this date Burns was happy", but after quitting "the paternal roof" he ventured,

> forth into looser, louder, more exciting society; and becomes initiated in those dissipations, those vices, which a certain class of philosophers have asserted to be a natural preparative for entering on active life; a kind of mud-bath, in which the youth is, as it were, necessitated to steep, and, we suppose, cleanse himself, before the real toga of Manhood can be laid on him .... [W]e hope they are mistaken (294).

The key ideas in the dissertation that then follows are "manly

29. Kaplan, 59.

30. Fitzhugh, 35.

31. *Ibid.*, 36.

32. *The Letters of Robert Burns*, I, 113.

33. Fitzhugh, 38.

34. John Gibson Lockhart, *Life of Robert Burns*, New York, 1959, 27.

Action", "striving and doing", and most of all "Necessity".[35] It is interesting how closely the clichés and misconceptions (that is, adventure and debauchery) of achieving manhood are still with us today. However, according to Carlyle, one achieves manhood not from "the training one receives in this Devil's-service, but only our determining to desert from it". In what sounds like a page out of Baden-Powell, Carlyle writes,

> We become men, not after we have been dissipated, and disappointed in the chase of false pleasure; but after we have ascertained, in any way, what impassable barriers hem us in through this life; how mad it is to hope for contentment to our infinite soul from the *gifts* of this extremely finite world; that a man must be sufficient for himself; and that for suffering and enduring there is no remedy but striving and doing. Manhood begins when we have in any way made truce with Necessity.

In short, "Necessity" is coming to terms with the world and doing what it requires one to do. Carlyle concludes, "Had Burns continued to learn this, as he was already learning it, in his father's cottage" he would have "been saved many a lasting aberration, many a bitter hour and year of remorseful sorrow" (295).

However, according to Carlyle, Burns was seduced from these truths by those he met in Edinburgh. These "Lion-hunters" (because of their "*Lionism*") as Carlyle despairingly writes in 1840 (in "The Hero as Man of Letters"):

> were the ruin and death of Burns. It was they that rendered it impossible for him to live! They gathered round him in his Farm; hindered his industry; no place was remote enough from them .... They came to get a little amusement: they got their amusement; — and the Hero's life went for it![36]

In "Burns" he succinctly declares, "These men, as we believe, were proximately the means of his ruin" (303).

On one of the very few occasions in "Burns" when Carlyle refers to Lockhart, the two agree that although Burns held his own in this learned

---

35. Carlyle offers more on "Necessity" in *Sartor Resartus*: "happy he for whom a kind heavenly Sun brightens it [i.e., Necessity] into a ring of Duty" (*The Works of Thomas Carlyle*, I: *Sartor Resartus*, 78).

36. *The Works of Thomas Carlyle*, V: *On Heroes, Hero-Worship, and the Heroic in History*, 194-95.

company, nevertheless he came away "maddened still more with the fever of world Ambition" (301). Carlyle's other complaints against the "Lion-hunters" are that "they wasted his precious time", "they disturbed his composure, broke down his returning habits of temperance and assiduous contented exertion", and "Their pampering was baneful to him" (303).

Carlyle also has strong words for the "Dumfries Aristocracy", whom he blames for unjustly ostracizing Burns for alleged sympathies with the Jacobins. Undoubtedly Carlyle is referring to Burns's social reputation after an incident that occurred at a dinner party in December 1793. Fitzhugh recounts it:

> The traditional story of what happened at the dinner ... is that the gentlemen over their wine began to discuss the Rape of the Sabines and decided to enact something similar when they rejoined the ladies. Mrs Carswell, a descendant of Patrick Miller, reports a strong tradition that army officer guests planned the affair as a "rag" to humiliate Burns the Jacobin .... So when Robert had carried out his part with hearty dispatch and all the latitude the occasion called for, he was stupefied to find himself alone.

This is not the place to delve into the complicated issue of Burns's relationship with the Riddell family, at whose house this dinner party took place.[37] Suffice to say that after the event — whatever intelligence Carlyle had of it[38]— Dumfries society "branded him with their veto" (305).

---

37. Fitzhugh, 272-87; for the dinner table incident, see 280.

38. Fitzhugh (277-78) notes a letter from Mrs Basil Montagu (Anna Dorothea Benson), who wrote to Jane Carlyle about some improper remarks Allan Cunningham attributed to her: "This he has put my name to, who have ever represented Burns as incapable of rudeness or vulgarity — on the contrary as gentle, modest in his manner to women, well bred and gentlemanly in all the courtesies of life, with a natural politeness, poorly imitated by the artificial polish of society, since his manner arose out of the chivalric respect and the devotion he bore to the sex — a respect that modulated his voice and veiled the flashing of his eyes, and gave a winning grace to the most trifling of his attentions; this and a thousand other things all in commendation have I, from time to time, endeavoured to infuse into the dense faculty of honest Allan; and, above all that, during the Carnival of the Caledonian Hunt, 'when Universal Scotland all was drunk', I never saw Burns once intoxicated, though the worthy Member for Dumfries, and the good Laird of Arbigland, and twenty more that might be named, were much more tipsy than Tam o' Shanter, for he could see witches and warlocks, but they could neither see or stand, and were brought home in a state of inglorious insensibility. I

Throughout this essay I have held that Carlyle's fondness for Burns is connected to similarities in their lives (for instance that he was a fellow rural Scot, suffered chronic mental health problems, and a spiritual crises in youth). One cannot help but wonder if Carlyle's sympathy for Burns is also connected with the critic's own experience with his wife's family. The courtship of Carlyle and Jane Welsh is well-documented in the biographies:

> Carlyle's unsuitability as a suitor had been apparent from the beginning. With his constant complaints about his health, his rustic manners, and his lack of a practical vocation, he had little to recommend him except his "genius," his aggressive compliments, and his desire to serve. Cautious in most things, he now became reckless in his rhetoric while soberly recognizing that the son of a farmer could not present himself as a suitor to the daughter of a doctor unless he had more auspicious prospects.[39]

It took Carlyle five years (from May 1821 to October 1826) to win Jane's hand. Thus in Burns and Carlyle have we two rural Scots whose talents and pretensions to rise above their stations is impeded by social prejudice. Perhaps then there is more about Carlyle than Burns in the critic's lament:

> Alas! when we think that Burns now sleeps "where bitter indignation can no longer lacerate his heart," [after Swift's Epitaph], and that most of those fair dames and frizzled gentlemen already lie at his side, where the breastwork of gentility is quite thrown down, — who would not sigh over the thin delusions and foolish toys that divide heart from heart, and make man unmerciful to his brother! (305)

Equally likely is that Carlyle's contempt for the Burns's Edinburgh and Dumfries society is linked to his own ambiguous feelings about his debt to Francis Jeffrey. Carlyle first met Jeffrey, who was his elder by

---

have to him twenty times that Burns always left a dinner party, if there were women, for the drawing room long before any other man joined it; and this in his thick skull has produced the following brilliant remark from Mrs Montagu: 'He drank as other men drank.' ... Poor Burns! Misfortune pursues thee even to the grave! — So it is with almost all great men; reverence keeps silent all who loved them, and Traders take up the theme."

39. Kaplan, 72.

more than twenty-years, in February 1827.[40] Carlyle had received a letter of introduction to the man from Bryan Waller Procter,[41] and as Carlyle told his mother later that month, "The little man received me in his kindest style; talked with me for an hour ... and proved himself by much the most agreeable citizen of Edinburgh that I had ever met with".[42] However, Jeffrey was in fact Lord Jeffrey (Carlyle would later turn down a knighthood) and a man of considerable power and influence. In a letter of 17 August 1828 to Anna D.B. Montagu, Carlyle speaks gratefully of Jeffrey's efforts to secure him a professorship at London University.[43] Carlyle continued to rely on Jeffrey's support but in December 1833 was angry with the man for not supporting his application to a position at the astronomical observatory in Edinburgh.[44] Nevertheless they remained acquaintances until Jeffrey's death in January 1850, and Carlyle included him in his *Reminiscences*. "Our poor little Jeffrey is no more! I know not when I got such a stroke out of a Newspaper", Carlyle wrote to Jane on 29 January.[45] However their initial warmth for one another cooled after the "Burns" piece largely because of Jeffrey's opinion of Carlyle's distinctive writing style (his "Carlylese").[46]

"It seems dubious to us whether the richest, wisest, most benevolent individual could have lent Burns an effectual help", Carlyle says of Burns, and the critic is magnanimously ready to "pity and forgive" the poet's transgressors. Carlyle does so with the conviction that ultimately Burns is responsible for the causes of his downfall, that is, his "want of unity, of consistency in his aims" (307). He reminds the reader that "Locke was banished a traitor", Milton was "Not only low, but fallen from height", Cervantes "finished his work in prison", but these men prevailed where Burns failed because "They had a true, religious principle of morals; and a single, not a double aim in their activity" — that is, "They were not self-seekers and self-worshippers; but seekers and worshippers of something far better than Self". What Carlyle has in

---

40. *The Collected Letters*, IV, 190.

41. *Ibid.*, IV, 185.

42. *Ibid.*, IV, 190.

43. *Ibid.*, IV, 388-89.

44. *Ibid.*, VII, 84.

45. Trudy Bliss, *Thomas Carlyle: Letters to His Wife*, Cambridge: Mass., 1953, 281.

46. Kaplan, 368.

mind, of course, is Burns's enjoyment of earthly pleasures. Without mentioning the women, the illegitimate children, and alcohol, nevertheless Carlyle makes his point: "His morality, in most of its practical points, is that of a mere worldly man; enjoyment, in a finer or coarser shape, is the only thing he longs and strives for" (312-13). By "religion" Carlyle has nothing as narrow as organized worship in mind, "For Poetry, as Burns could have followed it, is but another form of Wisdom, of Religion" (314).

In the final analysis Carlyle depicts Burns as a tragic victim of "an age, not of heroism and religion, but of scepticism, selfishness and triviality, when true Nobleness was little understood, and its place supplied by a hollow, dissocial, altogether barren and unfruitful principle of Pride" (311). This is the age that blackens the church walls in Blake's "London", and the age of "selfish men" that Wordsworth complains about in "London, 1802". In "The Hero as Man of Letters" Carlyle writes, "The Eighteenth [century] was a *Sceptical* Century; in which little word there is a whole Pandora's Box of miseries".[47] If Burns was hapless enough to be born at such a time, he was doubly cursed to be born "a true Poet and Singer, worthy of the old religious heroic times". Ultimately, Carlyle decides, Burns "spent his life in endeavouring to reconcile these two; and lost it" (311-12).

Carlyle's moralizing may in fact be a mask. In addition to the obvious points of kinship that Carlyle shared with Burns, it must have galled him to see a poet of Burns's ilk waste his days on farming and his nights on carousing. No biographer has been able to exonerate Burns of his philandering, although apparently the matter of his alcohol consumption is debatable.[48] In "Burns" Carlyle declares that he is "far from regarding him as guilty before the world", but in *Sartor Resartus* Carlyle advises,

> Be no longer a Chaos, but a World, or even Worldkin. Produce! Produce! Were it but the pitifullest infinitesimal fraction of a Product, produce it, in God's name! Work while it is called Today; for the Night cometh, wherein no man can work.[49]

Carlyle can hardly be singled out for his occasional patronizing

47. *The Works of Thomas Carlyle*, V: *On Heroes, Hero-Worship, and the Heroic in History*, 170.

48. See "Burns and Alcohol", in Bold, *A Burns Companion*.

49. *The Works of Thomas Carlyle*, I: *Sartor Resartus*, 157.

attitude toward his subject. The world still wonders that poverty and an apparent lack of formal training can produce a Shakespeare, an Abraham Lincoln, a Mark Twain, etc. Perhaps with the success of Chatterton's and Macpherson's primitive forgeries, Burns himself was encouraged to play the role of "sagacious country farmer of the old Scotch school" as Scott remembered him forty years later (299).[50]

However, Burns was by no means the unlettered "rustic wonder" Carlyle construes, as Gilbert Burns's brief memoir attests. Thus with well intentioned but misplaced presumption Carlyle deprives his hero of self-determination, of the right to make choices however poor they may appear to posterity. (The matter is worsened when one remembers that in 1828 Carlyle was still six years younger than the man he judges.) A significant implication of "Burns" is that apart from drawing similarities in Burns's and Byron's moral development, Carlyle does not associate Burns with Blake, Wordsworth, Coleridge, Keats, or Shelley, as we do today. Perhaps Carlyle stood too near. Perhaps we stand too far. This matter of the biographer's distance from his subject appears in the first of Carlyle's essay's many clever aphorisms: "For it is certain, that to the vulgar eye few things are wonderful that are not distant". As he explains, "It is difficult for men to believe that the man, the mere man whom they see, nay, perhaps painfully feel, toiling at their side through the poor jostlings of existence, can be made of finer clay than themselves" (259). In "Burns" Carlyle concludes, "The world is habitually unjust in its judgment of such men [as Burns] .... It decides, like a court of law, by dead statues" (317-18). However, from the even greater distance of "The Hero as Man of Letters", Carlyle proclaims that Burns failed to receive his due from his own age because he lived in an age of "*spiritual paralysis*".[51]

---

50. See also Lockhart, 81.

51. *The Works of Thomas Carlyle*, V: *On Heroes, Hero-Worship, and the Heroic in History*, 170.

GOETHE TRANSLATED: CARLYLE'S *WILHELM MEISTER*

HELGA HUSHAHN

Goethe's *Wilhelm Meisters Lehrjahre*, begun in February 1777, was eventually published in four volumes, each containing two of the novel's eight Books, consecutively in January, May and November 1795 and in October 1796.[1] For the most part, therefore, it appeared in public in the same year that Thomas Carlyle, who first translated this earliest and possibly most renowned *Bildungsroman* into English, was born. *Wilhelm Meisters Lehrjahre* had been preceded by an earlier version, *Wilhelm Meisters Theatralische Sendung*, which, since the manuscript had been lost, was not published until 1911.[2] *Wilhelm Meisters Wanderjahre oder Die Entsagenden* has also two versions, the first, the "Urfassung", appearing in 1821; and it was this version that Carlyle translated as *Wilhelm Meister's Travels: or The Renunciants*, which he published together with other translations from German in *German Romance* in 1827; Goethe's more extended version of 1829 he did not translate. In this essay I am limiting my concern to Carlyle's translation of *Wilhelm Meisters Lehrjahre*, and will be attempting a preliminary exploration of the meeting of minds that any translation involves — in this case the minds of two men representing distinct but overlapping generations evolving in cultures that were diverse but also self-consciously akin.

The popularity of German literature in Britain throughout the 1790s, mainly inspired by the many translations of Kotzebue's sentimental

1. *Goethes Werke*, ed. Erich Trunz, Hamburger Ausgabe, Munich, 1982, VII, 613 and 617.

2. See Goethe's two letters to Karl Ludwig von Knebel: in the first of 27 July 1782 he writes, "Das zweite Buch von *Wilhelm Meister* erhältst Du bald, ich habe es mitten in dem Taumel geschrieben", and in the second of 21 November 1782, "Du sollst bald die drei ersten Bücher der *Theatralischen Sendung* haben" (*Goethes Werke*, VII, 614). See also *The Oxford Companion to German Literature*, eds Henry and Mary Garland, Oxford and New York, 1986, 988.

dramas and the craze for Gothic fiction in novels and on the stage, and stimulated by translations and adaptations of Schiller, had declined by the end of the first decade of the nineteenth century.[3] British audiences and readers knew little of Goethe's works apart from his early *Die Leiden des jungen Werther* (*The Sufferings of Werther*), originally published in 1774 and translated many times from 1779 onward, and *Götz von Berlichingen* (1773) translated into English twice in 1799; English versions had also appeared of *Iphigenie* (1793), *Clavigo* and *Stella* (both in 1798), and *Hermann und Dorothea* (1801).[4]

As the Preface to the first edition of Carlyle's translation of Goethe's *Wilhelm Meisters Lehrjahre* indicates this rising wave of interest in German literature and its decline, and something of the nature of this popularity where it had existed or continued to exist was not unknown to him:

> ... we disdain to be assisted by the Germans, whom, by a species of second-sight, we have discovered, before knowing anything about them, to be a timid, dreaming, extravagant, insane race of mortals; certain it is, that hitherto our literary intercourse with that nation has been very slight and precarious. After a brief period of not too judicious cordiality, the acquaintance on our part was altogether dropped: nor, in the few years since we partially resumed it, have our feelings of

---

3. Schiller's *Die Räuber*, translated as *The Robbers* by Alexander Frazer Tytler, appeared in 1792, and another translation in 1799; *Der Geisterseher* appeared in English as *The Ghost-Seer* in 1795 and as *The Armenian, or the Ghostseer* in 1800; Matthew Gregory Lewis, the author of *The Monk* and a play, *The Castle Spectre* (1798), partially based on *The Robbers*, translated *Kabale und Liebe* as *The Minister* in 1797; but there is also an earlier anonymous translation of Schiller's play as *Cabal and Love* from 1795. Coleridge translated *Die Piccolomini* and *Wallensteins Tod* in 1798-99. Translations of Kotzebue were numerous, the most popular being *Das Kind der Liebe* (translated three times in 1798, most famously as Mrs Inchbald's *Lovers' Vows*), and Sheridan's two adaptations, *The Stranger* (*Menschenhass und Reue*) and *Pizarro* (*Die Spanier in Peru*), produced at Drury Lane in 1798 and 1799 respectively (see *The Revels History of Drama in English, VI: 1750-1880*, eds Michael Booth *et al*, London, 1975, 188-89). Probably as many as forty of Kotzebue's plays were translated in many different versions in the 1790s and at the beginning of the new century.

4. A glance at Appendix B: Chronological List of Translations in Violet Stockley's *German Literature as Known in England 1750-1830*, New York and London, 1929, rpt. 1969, 324-30, indicates an enormous increase of translations in the 1790s, followed by a decline after about 1805 and another resurgence in the 1820s.

affection or esteem been materially increased. Our translators are unfortunate in their selection or execution, or the public is tasteless and absurd in its demands; for, with scarcely more than one or two exceptions, the best works of Germany have lain neglected, or worse than neglected, and the Germans are yet utterly unknown to us. Kotzebue still lives in our minds as the representative of a nation that despises him; Schiller is chiefly known to us by the monstrous production of his boyhood; and Klopstock by a hacked and mangled image of his *Messias*, in which a beautiful poem is distorted into a theosophic rhapsody, and the brother of Virgil and Racine ranks little higher than the author of *Meditations among the Tombs*.

But of all these people there is none that has been more unjustly dealt with than Johann Wolfgang von Goethe. For half a century the admiration, we might almost say the idol of his countrymen, to us he is still a stranger ....[5]

It was when Thomas Carlyle was seeking spiritual and moral guidance in his early twenties, and came upon Dugald Stewart's *Dissertation on the Progress of Metaphysical, Ethical, and Political Philosophy*, which he read "twice within two years",[6] that he was pointed in the direction of Madame de Staël's *De l'Allemagne*, a work which was not only to inspire Carlyle's curiosity about German literature, but also to revive a more widespread interest in German writing and culture in the first half of the nineteenth century. Carlyle read *De l'Allemagne* in 1817; by February 1819 he was taking German lessons, or as he expresses it in a letter to a friend, acquiring "a slight [tinc]ture of the German language ... from one Rob*t* Jardine of Göttingen (or rather Applegarth), in return for an equally slight tincture of the French which I communicate".[7] On 23 February he reported to his brother Alexander that he studied German until "eleven o'clock" (after which he went for a stroll around the environs of Edinburgh), and on 29 March he tells him that he is "still at the German":

5. *The Works of Thomas Carlyle*, ed. H.D. Traill, Centenary Edition, 30 vols, London, 1896-99, XXIII: *Wilhelm Meister's Apprenticeship and Travels*, I, 3-4.

6. Charles Frederick Harrold, *Carlyle and German Thought: 1819-1834* (1934), London, 1963, 33-34. Carlyle read the "work in the summer of 1816 and in June, 1818" (*ibid.*, 256 n.32). See *The Collected Letters of Thomas and Jane Welsh Carlyle*, Duke-Edinburgh edn, gen. ed. Charles Richard Sanders, Durham: NC, 1970 -, I, 84 and 133.

7. *The Collected Letters*, I, 160.

> My teacher is not a man (any more than he was a boy) of brilliant parts; but we go on in a loving way together — and he gives me the *pronunciation* correctly, I suppose. I am able to read books, now, with a dictionary. At present I am reading a stupid play of Kotzebue's — but to-night I am to have the history of Frederick the Great from Irving.[8]

By May he was reading Klopstock's *Messias*, and by January 1821 he wrote to Alexander that he has "translated a portion of Schiller's History of the thirty years war ... ; and sent it off, with a letter introduced by Tait the Review-bookseller, to Longman and Co London".[9] From this point on, Carlyle refers regularly in his letters to German literature or German writers, especially Schiller. By January 1822 he was already engaged in writing a critical account of Goethe's *Faust* for "the Review people".[10] In July 1822 he asked his brother John to find him and send "Schiller's Tragedy of *Wilhelm Tell*", as "Oliver & Boyd have agreed to go half with [him] in printing a poetical Translation of this work!".[11] And although this translation never appeared, indirectly it led to Carlyle's *Life of Schiller*. On 26 February 1823, he reported to Jane Welsh that he has been approached by Boyd "the pursy Bookseller" to translate Goethe's *Wilhelm Meister*.[12] At this stage Carlyle was positively enthusiastic about Goethe which he expresses in a letter to Jane Welsh on 6 April 1823:

> Goethe lies waiting for your arrival. You make a right distinction about Goethe: he is a great genius and *does not make you cry*. His feelings are various as the hues of Earth and sky, but his intellect is the Sun which illuminates and overrules them all. He does not yield himself to his emotions, but uses them rather as things for his judgment to scrutinize and apply to purpose. I think Goethe the only living model of a great writer. The Germans say there have been *three* geniuses in the world since it began — Homer, Shakespear, and Goethe! This of course is shooting on the wing: but after all abatements, their countryman is a glorious fellow. It is one of my finest day-

---

8. *Ibid.*, I, 167, 172-73.

9. *Ibid.*, I, 178 and 301.

10. The *New Edinburgh Review*, where Carlyle's article appeared in April 1822 (see *The Collected Letters*, I, 421 and n. and II, 9).

11. *Ibid.*, II, 153.

12. *Ibid.*, II, 316.

> dreams to see him ere I die.[13]

A month later he informed John that he has "*almost* engaged to translate" *Wilhelm Meister*.[14] However, translating it seems to have caused him a great deal of trouble, which is hardly surprising since he had embarked on rendering into English an example of Goethe's mature prose writing which still makes intellectual demands on the native German speaker. On 18 September Carlyle complained to Jane Welsh:

> Meanwhile I go on with Goethe's Wilhelm Meister; a book which I love not, which I am sure will never sell, but which I am determined to print and finish. There are touches of the very highest most etherial genius in it; but diluted with floods of insipidity, which even *I* would not have written for the world. I sit down to it every night at six, with the ferocity of hyaena; and in spite of all obstructions my keep-lesson is more than half thro' the first volume, and travelling over poetry and prose, slowly but surely to the end.

He declared that "Some of the poetry is very bad", but granted that "some of it [is] rather good"; he picked out as being particularly "mediocre — the worst kind", "Who never ate his bread in sorrow" (the harper's song in *Wilhelm Meister's Apprenticeship*).[15] But in a letter to James Johnstone written a few days later his criticism is sharper and even despairing:

> In the meantime I am busily engaged every night in translating Goethe's Wilhelm Meister; a task which I have undertaken formally and must proceed with, tho' it suits me little. There is poetry in the book, and prose, prose forever. When I read of players and libidinous actresses and their sorry pasteboard apparatus for beautifying and enlivening the "moral world", I render it into grammatical English — with a feeling mild and charitable as that of a starving hyaena. The Book is to be printed in winter or spring. No mortal will ever buy a copy of it. *N'importe* [No matter]! I have engaged with it to keep the fiend from preying on my v[itals,] and [with th]at sole view I go along with it. Goethe is the grea[test ge]niu[s that has] lived for a century, and the greatest ass that [has l]ived for th[ree. I] could

---

13. *Ibid.*, II, 326.

14. *Ibid.*, II, 349.

15. *Ibid.*, II, 434-35.

> sometimes fall down and worship him; at other times I could kick him out of the room.[16]

Finally, on 13 January 1824 he reported to his brother, Alexander, that the "printing of *Meister* commences immediately on my arrival"; and on 25 June he asked him whether he has received "*Meister*, and how do you *dis*like it?":

> For really it is a most mixed performance, and tho' intellectually good, much of it is morally bad. It is making way here perhaps — but slowly: a second edition seems a dubious matter.

The publication of the translation, anonymously in three volumes, was probably 4 June or thereabouts, since it was on that date that Carlyle asked David Hope to send a promised copy to William Grahame.[17] Carlyle's lack of confidence in his labours was partly due to his own personality and attitude to life, which differed immensely from Goethe's when he wrote *Wilhelm Meisters Lehrjahre*. But without Carlyle's courageous endeavours there probably would not have been such an early translation of the work — Carlyle dispatched a copy of it to Goethe on 24 June.[18]

I wish now to consider how and in what manner Carlyle treats a number of features, sections and elements in his translation: does he always arrive at the adequate expression of Goethe's original text, and if it is adequate, is this only in respect to the work itself or in respect to something else? For is the style of expression to be found in the translation not always bound as much, if not more, to the translator and his period than to the original text emanating from its author bound in his particular time? Goethe had written *Wilhelm Meister* nearly thirty years before Carlyle translated it and Weimar was in most respects a long way from Edinburgh.

In the first chapters of *Wilhelm Meister* Goethe plunges the reader immediately into the vivid ebullience of the story; and indeed any reader of the same portion of Carlyle's translation will soon find him or herself immersed in the narrative in the same way, and forgetting that it is a translation. Carlyle is able to invoke a similarly animate picture as

---

16. *Ibid.*, II, 437.

17. *Ibid.*, III, 12 and 96; and 74 and n.

18. *Ibid.*, III, 86-87.

Goethe, but then, unexpectedly, through minor differences in tone or by the choice of various shades of expression, the translation takes on a jarring quality. For example, take the question of the mode of address, always more complicated in German, with its distinctions of intimacy and formality in its use of personal pronouns, than in English, and even more complex in the eighteenth century. Wilhelm and Barbara, Mariana's old nurse, servant and confidante, except at the very beginning of the story, employ the intimate form when they address the actress, Mariana, Wilhelm's mistress. When Barbara asks her, in Carlyle's version, "What ails thee, my darling?", already differences between the two versions become apparent. First, in nineteenth-century English "thee" as a form of address seems already obsolete and self-consciously "literary", while the verb "to ail" implies sickness. Goethe uses "was hast du", a much more neutral way of asking what the trouble is when a facial expression indicates that something is wrong.[19] As Carlyle is perfectly at ease with the modern form of "you" in his letters to his family and friends, it is puzzling why he chose an awkward old-fashioned term of address. Another little problem reveals itself in the description of Barbara, who in Goethe's version is referred to as "die alte Barbara" or "die Alte". Translated, this becomes "old Barbara", or "the old damsel" or "the old dame", which even to early nineteenth-century ears probably sounded rather quaint, and patronizing, whereas the original German terms did not lack respect. Perhaps, these trifles hardly merit attention, since there are other parts of the text where differences between the original and the translation become more conspicuous.

Goethe uses different narrative techniques in order to seem objective and detached. At times a third-person narrator is used, while on other

---

19. *The Works of Thomas Carlyle*, XXIII: *Wilhelm Meister's Apprenticeship and Travels*, I, 36; *Goethes Werke*, VII, 9-10. Since there will be frequent references to both of these editions throughout this essay, from this point on they will simply be referred to as "Carlyle" and "Goethe". It is appropriate at this point to state that throughout this article I have based my consideration of Carlyle's translation of Goethe's text on the basis of the text in the Centenary Edition, on the assumption that it represents the translator's final and possibly best effort to represent the character of the original. In his Preface, "To the Reader", to the 1842 revised edition of the translation (reprinted in Carlyle, I, 1), Carlyle says that he has "made many little changes". This suggests that yet another article might be contemplated studying Carlyle's revisions of his own text. This would involve not only the first and second editions of 1824 and 1842, but also the edition of 1871, which from internal evidence appears to be the copy text of H.D. Traill's Centenary Edition.

occasions to recount the exploits of his youth the hero, Wilhelm, takes over. Since the distance between protagonist and his account then becomes blurred or even entirely absent, the narrator cannot any longer be thought of as someone taking responsibility for his tale. When Wilhelm tells the young actress Mariana and Barbara about a youthful poem of his "where the Muse of tragic art and another female form, by which I personified Commerce, were made to strive very bravely for my most important self",[20] he is unconsciously reflecting the very predicament that he and the two women are in. For at the very beginning of the novel, Mariana has had an angry altercation with Barbara over the latter's mercenary attitude to the young actress's admirers, in particular over her self-confessed passionate love for Wilhelm (described by Barbara in Goethe's text as "unbefiedert", meaning "penniless", and in Carlyle's as "callow").[21] The effect of Wilhelm's poem mirroring the situation in the novel is comical; but Carlyle does not seem to notice its parodic nature. Goethe allows the protagonist to express himself in a light-hearted as well as in a theatrically exaggerated manner; whereas Carlyle's translation has a far more earnest and ponderous tone, as the passage in which the lovely muse is depicted shows:

> And how differently advanced the other! What an apparition for the overclouded mind! Formed as a queen, in her thoughts and looks she announced herself the child of freedom. The feeling of her own worth gave her dignity without pride: her apparel became her, it veiled each limb without constraining it; and the rich folds repeated, like a thousand-voiced echo, the graceful movements of the goddess. What a contrast! How easy for me to decide! Nor had I forgotten the more peculiar characteristics of my muse. Crowns and daggers, chains and masks, as my predecessors had delivered them, were here produced once more. The contention was keen; the speeches of both were palpably enough contrasted, for at fourteen years of age one usually paints the black lines and the white pretty near each other. The old lady spoke as beseemed a person that would pick up a pin from her path; the other, like one that could give away kingdoms. The warning threats of the housewife were disregarded: I turned my back upon her promised riches; disinherited and naked, I gave myself up to the muse; she threw

20. Carlyle, I, 60.

21. Carlyle, I, 37; Goethe, VII, 10.

her golden veil over me, and called me hers.[22]

The difference between the two versions depends on but a few choices of expression. For instance, Wilhelm's second enthusiastic exclamation, in Carlyle's version "What an apparition for the overclouded mind!", seems to be more solemn than Goethe's "Welche Erscheinung ward sie dem bekümmerten Herzen". "Apparition" gives the impression of a phantom or ghost, while Goethe only means a beautiful image or appearance. "The overclouded mind" for a "bekümmertes Herz" stresses the intellect rather than a sense of heart-ache. In this passage "die Alte" becomes "the old lady", and "die warnenden Drohungen der Alten" is translated into "the warning threats of the housewife", when perhaps "old woman" would have been the acceptable expression in order not to make her appear more meanly avaricious than she is meant to be (in the paragraph before, Goethe had used the term "die alte Hausmutter", which is altogether more affectionate). In the last sentence of this passage Carlyle even shies away from translating "nakedness": "enterbt und nackt übergab ich mich der Muse, die mir ihren goldnen Schleier zuwarf und meine Blöße bedeckte" becomes "disinherited and naked, I gave myself up to the muse; she threw her golden veil over me, and called me hers". Rather than emphasizing "nakedness" ("Blöße" in the original), since the sense is already there (in "nackt"), Carlyle manages to produce a version that will reduce the danger of the reader blushing. But as a consequence, the sense of amusing banter eludes Carlyle, and the levity of Wilhelm's own ludicrous sketch of his adolescent poem is lost.

The range and wealth of Goethe's female characters is quite amazing, but some of them seem to be a stumbling block for Carlyle, especially the "libidinous actresses". Of these, of course, Mariana is one, but she does not get away with being sexually emancipated. However, Goethe goes out of his way to depict the attractiveness of Philine, one of the two "darlings" introduced in the fourth chapter of the second book, who has possibly more than one lover, and lacks Mariana's tenderness of heart, despite her disorderliness and her disorganized style of living. When Wilhelm catches sight of Philine for the first time, she is looking out of the window of an inn; Goethe's and Carlyle's descriptions of her are very similar, except "ein wohlgebildetes Frauenzimmer" becomes "a handsome young lady". Since Philine's origins are not genteel, in this instance "young woman"

22. Carlyle, I, 60: Goethe, VII, 32-33.

or “young female” would have been more appropriate.[23] Wilhelm becomes acquainted with Laertes, one of Philine’s fellow actors, who formally introduces Wilhelm to her. The short account of her attire gives an impression of an appealing yet casual young female. Goethe furnishes her with a pair of “leichte Pantöffelchen”, which in Carlyle’s version become “tight little slippers” (rather than the more accurate “light” or “flimsy”).[24] In the following sentence her lack of cleanliness is pitted against the prettiness of her feet:

> She had thrown a black mantle over her, above a white négligé, not indeed superstitiously clean, but which, for that very reason gave her a more frank and domestic air. Her short dress did not hide a pair of the prettiest feet and ankles in the world.[25]

Carlyle changes the decorative black mantilla of Goethe’s original (“eine schwarze Mantille”) with its suggestion of exotic Spanish lace into a more commonplace “mantle”, as if it were a cloak to hide her soiled négligé. The white négligé like Philine herself is not immaculate, but Goethe’s version, “nicht ganz reinlich”, is comparatively, if somewhat ironically restrained, compared with Carlyle’s rather heavy handed, sarcastic rather than ironic, “not indeed superstitiously clean”. A carefree person like Philine would hardly be expected to be over-observant in her cleanliness; but Goethe grants that her touch of slovenliness has the advantage of giving her “häusliches und bequemes Ansehen” (“a domestic and comfortable appearance”), which Carlyle translates into “a more frank and domestic air”. Whereas Goethe depicts her with the prettiest feet of the world (“die niedlichsten Füße von der Welt”), Carlyle has to add a pair of ankles as well. Goethe creates a pleasing impression of an attractive young woman which he delicately undermines with his irony, while Carlyle presents her as a rather more stereotyped actress. The addition of the ankles to the “pair of prettiest feet” can possibly be explained by differences in national cultures at the time: whereas Germans were expected to be enthralled

---

23. Carlyle, I, 120-21: Goethe, VII, 90-91.

24. One might well suppose that this is a printing error that has never been corrected in Carlyle’s translation. It is highly unlikely that he inadvertently or deliberately mistranslated “leichten”; and it is possible that his “light” has been misread “tight” either by Carlyle himself in preparing a fair copy or by the printer. There is a possibility, however, that Carlyle found the idea of tight high-heeled slippers more erotically suggestive than flimsy slippers.

25. Carlyle, I, 123; Goethe, VII, 93.

by small and dainty feet, an Englishman or a Scotsman were more attracted to slim ankles.

Since Philine likes to have more than one admirer, she sets out to seduce Wilhelm when she takes over the task of dressing his hair from her "little servant", who is resentful at being asked to perform the task. No wonder Wilhelm feels more than once tempted to "imprint a kiss" on her bosom, that so often approaches his lips while she is "frizz[ling] Wilhelm's locks".[26] Two days later Wilhelm is more than ever intrigued by the "mysterious presence of the child" (Mignon) and Philine's "siren charms". For the latter phrase, Goethe uses "frevelhaften Reize", words which are open to a variety of interpretations, since "frevelhaft" may denote something like "iniquitous" or "sacrilegious" or "wicked", but may also have the more affirmative sense of "bold", "daring" or "audacious", at the same time it implies "foolhardiness" and "recklessness".[27] Goethe's characters are multi-facetted, and "bold" or "reckless" would be more true to his ambiguous portrait of Philine's character. Carlyle's phrase "siren charms" only conveys her teasing or tantalizing aspects, and tells us nothing about her except that she was a truly "tempting temptress". When Goethe touches on her sexual nature or attraction, Carlyle, who indeed has no great sympathy for Philine, holds back and either changes the risqué expression or leaves it out completely. At the beginning of Chapter 12 in Book II, Philine is sitting beside Wilhelm attempting to entice him. When he does not react, she refers to him as "the stone man" who will still be sitting "on the stone bench" when she returns. At this point in Goethe's text we are told that, in fact, she was doing him an injustice, for at that moment he was doing his very best not to respond to her enticements, and he admits to himself that had he been alone with her in a summer-house probably he would not have been indifferent to her and would have returned her caresses:

> Diesmal tat sie ihm Unrecht; denn so sehr er sich von ihr zu enthalten strebte, so würde er doch in diesem Augenblicke, hätte er sich mit ihr in einer einsamen Laube befunden, ihre Liebkosungen wahrscheinlich nicht unerwidert gelassen haben.

This important insight Carlyle leaves out, which simplifies Wilhelm's ambivalent feelings, implied in the following paragraph when we are

26. Carlyle, I, 124; Goethe, VII, 94.

27. Carlyle, I, 137; Goethe, VII, 107.

told, in Goethe's text, that "vielmehr hatte ihr Betragen einen neuen Widerwillen in ihm erregt". This too is reduced to a sharper less complex form in Carlyle's version — "her conduct had excited fresh aversion in him" — since Goethe's "Widerwillen", may suggest hostile dislike, but primarily "resistance", which again suggests that Wilhelm may be more torn than he or Carlyle would wish to admit.[28]

In another episode Carlyle translates "Liebhaber" ("lover") as "amateur", and by so doing unfortunately obscures one of Goethe's revealing plays on words, which once more indicates his delicately ironic attitude to Philine. The Count and Countess surprised at the small number of assembled actors, inquire whether it is indeed the whole company. Melina, who has taken over the directorship, replies that some are absent; to which Philine adds, "Es ist noch ein recht hübscher junger Mann oben, der sich gewiß bald zum ersten Liebhaber qualifizieren würde". From the context it is clear that Philine means that although Wilhelm, the "pretty young man" is not a professional actor, he could soon learn to play the part of lover, either on the stage or off it. Carlyle's version — "There is a very pretty young man above, who without doubt would shortly become a first-rate amateur" — flattens the delicious innuendo of the original text, either inadvertently or deliberately.[29]

Some time later when the company is preparing to perform *Hamlet* in the public theatre in a large commercial city, Philine has been given the role of the Duchess in what Goethe, without any explanation, describes as "der kleinen Komödie" (and Carlyle translates as "the small subordinate play"), by which is meant presumably the play within the play, "The Mousetrap", by means of which Hamlet seeks to "catch the conscience of the king".[30] She tells the other actors (in the words

---

28. Carlyle, I, 165; Goethe, VII, 134.

29. Carlyle, I, 181; Goethe, VII, 150. Perhaps this is just one of the unavoidable losses of translation: despite the etymology of "amateur", even in Carlyle's day it is unlikely that the reader of his translation would have seen the implication of Philine's remark, which could have only been made clear (and therefore spoilt) by elaborate paraphrase.

30. Carlyle, I, 338; Goethe, VII, 300. One wonders why Goethe offered no reason for the inclusion of "der kleinen Komödie" in Shakespeare's play: did he assume that all his readers would be so familiar with *Hamlet* that they would understand at once what he is referring to? Since no note is even offered in the modern Hamburg Ausgabe, present-day editors presumably think the same. Nevertheless, one wonders how many readers of *Wilhelm Meisters Lehrjahre* have understood the reference.

of Carlyle's close translation):

> "I will show it so natural ... how you wed a second without loss of time, when you have loved the first immensely. I hope to gain the loudest plaudits, and every man shall wish he were the third."[31]

Aurelie, the sister of the theatre director, Serlo, and a great tragic actress, finds these utterances repugnant, but her brother reacts wittily by saying what a pity it was that they could not have a ballet, with a "pas de deux" for her with both her husbands, "und der Alte sollte nach dem Takt einschlafen, und Ihre Füßchen und Wädchen würden sich dort hinten auf dem Kindertheater ganz allerliebst ausnehmen". In his translation Carlyle makes more explicit what is implied in the first part of the German text, "and the first [husband] might dance himself to sleep by the measure", thereby allowing his rival access to his wife either by taking a nap or by dying (the one preceding the other both in "The Mousetrap" and in *Hamlet* itself). The rest of the sentence Carlyle translates: "and your bits of feet and ankles would look so pretty, tripping to and fro upon the side stage" (thus preferring "feet and ankles" to Goethe's "feet and calves"). This sally provokes Philine to place her exquisite slippers of "of Parisian workmanship", that she had had as a present from the Countess, in front of him. Serlo begins to play with them, drops them on to the table and begins a speech of some twenty-two lines in the modern Hamburg Ausgabe (more than half a page) of wanton badinage:

> "Darf ich sagen" versetzte er mit verstellter Bescheidenheit und schalkhaftem Ernst, "wir andern Junggesellen, die wir nachts meist allein sind und uns doch wie andre Menschen fürchten und im Dunkeln uns nach Gesellschaft sehnen, besonders in Wirtshäusern und fremden Orten, wo es nicht ganz geheuer ist, wir finden es gar tröstlich, wenn ein gutherziges Kind uns Gesellschaft und Beistand leisten will. Es ist Nacht, man liegt im Bette, es raschelt, man schaudert, die Türe tut sich auf, man erkennt ein liebes pisperndes Stimmchen, es schleicht was herbei, die Vorhänge rauschen, klipp! klapp! die Pantoffeln fallen, und husch! man ist nicht mehr allein. Ach der liebe, der einzige Klang, wenn die Absätzchen auf den Boden aufschlagen! Je zierlicher sie sind, je feiner klingt's. Man spreche mir von Philomelen, von rauschenden Bächen, vom Säuseln der Winde

---

31. Carlyle, I, 338.

> und von allem, was je georgelt und gepfiffen worden ist, ich halte mich an das Klipp! Klapp! — Klipp! Klapp! ist das schönste Thema zu einem Rondeau, das man immer wieder von vorne zu hören wünscht."[32]

Philine takes her slippers back, flirts with them and with Serlo, eventually rapping him over the knuckles with the heels. This is a passage of sprightly eroticism which ends with her long hair coming loose and a chair toppling over, while she "artfully contested with a show of serious reluctance" the many kisses the theatre-director "plunder[s]" from her. Needless to say, the sister is not amused. However, the reader is; and one must acknowledge Carlyle's willingness (perhaps he couldn't avoid going along with it since it is the necessary conclusion to the chapter) to give the final moments of erotic farce as full a realization in English as possible. In this respect he is able to rise to the challenge of Goethe with his subtle blend of the sentimental, the sensual and the absurd, all under the shadow of the tragically passionate loves and betrayals of *Hamlet*. However, Serlo's long speech, quoted in full above, brimming with salacious insinuations was clearly too much for Carlyle, since he completely omits it.[33]

---

32. Goethe, VII, 301.

33. Had he not been shy of including it, Carlyle might have translated the paragraph given above in the following manner:

> "May I say," he responded with feigned modesty and a roguish earnestness, "we bachelors, are usually lonely at night, and, just like other people, still are frightened in the dark and long for company, especially in inns and in strange places, where it is a little frightening; we find it really consoling, when a compassionate young woman is willing to keep us company and support us. At night, one is lying in bed, there is rustle of sound, one shudders, a door opens, one recognizes a dear little voice whispering, someone is stealing up, the curtains rustle, clip! clop! the slippers drop, and in a flash! one is not alone any longer. O the precious, single sound, when the little heels rap on the floor! The daintier they are, the more exquisite they sound. Don't speak of Philomele, of the murmuring stream, of the rustling wind and of all that ever has droned and whistled, I maintain that clip! clop! — Clip! Clop! is the most beautiful theme for a rondeau that one might ever wish to hear from the beginning again and again."

Carlyle seems not to have been the only English translator to be diffident of Serlo's imputations. In R.O. Moon's translation of *Wilhelm Meister's Apprenticeship and Travels* (London, 1947), only the last sentence (four or five lines) of the speech

The character of Mignon, epitomizing mystery and brittleness in the romantic imagination, seems to have had a real impact on Carlyle; and in the Preface to his translation he dedicates half a page entirely to her:

> But above all, let him [the reader] turn to the history of Mignon. This mysterious child, at first neglected by the reader, gradually forced on his attention, at length overpowers him with an emotion more deep and thrilling than any poet since the days of Shakespeare has succeeded in producing. The daughter of enthusiasm, rapture, passion and despair, she is of the earth, but not earthly. When she glides before us through the light mazes of her fairy dance, or twangs her cithern to the notes of her homesick verses, or whirls her tambourine and hurries round us like an antique Mænad, we could almost fancy her a spirit; so pure is she, so full of fervour, so disengaged from the clay of the world .... Her little heart, so noble and so helpless, perishes before the smallest of its many beauties is unfolded; and all its loves and thoughts and longings do but add another pang to death, and sink to silence utter and eternal .... The history of Mignon runs like a thread of gold through the tissue of the narrative, connecting with the heart much that were else addressed only to the head. Philosophy and eloquence might have done the rest; but this is poetry in the highest meaning of the word. It must be for the power of producing such creations and emotions, that Goethe is by many of his countrymen ranked at the side of Homer and Shakespeare, as one of the only three men of genius that have ever lived.[34]

In representing Mignon in English, Carlyle exerted himself to come as close as possible to the original. But still his peculiar marks are to be observed in the translation. Wilhelm first sees Mignon almost immediately after he has had an initial glimpse of Philine. Goethe describes the neat fit of Mignon's clothes, which is important because of her youth and the fact that she has to look after herself, and naturally it enhances her contrast with the more casual Philine. Carlyle's transformation of Goethe's description of her "lange Beinkleider mit

---

remains, and sounds particularly innocuous: "People may talk of nightingales, of bubbling brooks, of the murmuring of winds and of all the sounds of organ and pipe — I keep to the click-clack! click-clack! It is the most beautiful subject for a roundelay that one ever wishes to hear in front of one" (I, 259). In the whole last scene, although marginally more accurate in his translation of the German than Carlyle, Moon is nothing like as lively or as graphically appealing.

34. Carlyle, I, 9-10.

Puffen" ("long trousers with puffs") into "tight trousers with puffs" is a trivial change, made for whatever reason. What is more puzzling is his changed version of what happened when Mignon passed Wilhelm on the stairs of the inn. Goethe tells us that Wilhelm "hielt sie auf, da sie bei ihm vorbeikam" (Wilhelm "stopped her, when she passed him"), but Carlyle says his hero "took her up in his arms", which at first sight suggests that he is moving the text into a more rather than a less erotic direction. As a result of Wilhelm's action in Carlyle's version, Mignon has to "[push] herself out of his arms". It may be, however, that Carlyle is after all displaying a protective attitude towards this slight young creature, since as the German text has it, as Wilhelm "ging ... nach seinem Zimmer die Treppe hinauf" (Carlyle: "he was going up-stairs to his chamber"), "ein junges Geschöpf ihm entgegensprang" (Carlyle, again quite literally: "a young creature sprang against him").[35] Perhaps Carlyle considered it more appropriate to have Wilhelm prevent Mignon from falling down the stairs, and since she is such a boyish androgynous figure, he did not feel that any sexual implication was involved.

Carlyle on several occasions reveals a protective attitude towards Mignon. When she has to display her acrobatic skills, Wilhelm, as he witnesses the contortions Mignon has to subject her body to, feels the "deepest pity" for her. Carlyle translates this into "deepest sympathy" since the positions she has to perform are of "considerable difficulty", while the original German has "mit einiger Mühe" ("with some effort"). Carlyle's protectiveness declares itself even in minute alterations to the text in translation, as, for instance, in the episode when, since Wilhelm seems to be very much interested in this strange young girl, Philine invites the "enigma" (as Carlyle translates Goethe's "Rätsel"), Mignon, up to her room after a performance. Wilhelm tries to set her at ease and says, "Fear nothing, my little dear". However the possessive "my" is not to be found in Goethe, who has "Fürchte dich nicht, liebe Kleine" (literally, "don't be afraid, dear little one"). Mignon's southern looks appeal to Wilhelm, but he also notices that "sie manchmal mit den Lippen nach einer Seite zuckte" (literally, "sometimes her lips twitched to one side"). Since this comes in the course of a description which considers whether her mouth is not too much closed for one so young, Carlyle omits the reference to the lips, and associates the sudden movement with the mouth: "her mouth, although it seemed too closely shut for one of her age, and though she

35. Carlyle, I, 121; Goethe, VII, 91.

often threw it to a side, ... ". Goethe's "manchmal" ("sometimes"), in Carlyle becomes "often", which has the effect of increasing the frequency of this particular sign of strain; yet, at the same time, by using the somewhat periphrastic "she often threw it to a side" instead of the more vivid, and more accurate, word "twitch" or "quiver", he seems to be playing down the disturbing nature of this nervous tick.[36] Perhaps by suggesting that it is a constant feature of Mignon's appearance, alongside the eccentricities of her dress, it is to be taken as something quite normal, and not as an indication of Mignon's continuous anguish.

Carlyle's particular compassion for Mignon is indicated by the very small change he makes in the account of the way Mignon is treated, observed by Wilhelm the evening following his introduction to her: since she refuses to perform her "egg dance", "the master of the rope-dancing company [dragged] poor Mignon by the hair out of the house, and unmercifully beating her little body with the handle of a whip". The occurrence is portrayed in all its brutality both in Goethe's text and in Carlyle's; but "poor Mignon" is Carlyle's more touchingly engaged rendering of Goethe's more reserved phrase, and in the context strangely aloof, phrase, "das interessante Kind" ("the interesting child").[37] As a result of the way he sees her being treated, Wilhelm purchases her freedom, although she voluntarily acts as his man servant. A little later, at a time when Wilhelm is preoccupied with Philine, the vulnerable Mignon, fearing that she will be neglected and even abandoned, breaks down and has a fit. Very graphically, Goethe describes Wilhelm's sympathy for Mignon's distress: yet although Carlyle's translation does full justice to this epitome of the literature of sensibility, one sentence seems to be too much for him: "Er schloß sie an sein Herz und benetzte sie mit Tränen."[38] Although by the time that *Wilhelm Meisters Lehrjahre* appeared "Empfindsamkeit" ("sensibility") had had its day, in this scene it reveals its continued presence and power.[39] But nearly thirty years later, however moved Carlyle may have been by Goethe's "interesting child", clearly the future author of "Characteristics" is here pushed to the limits of his sympathy: the

36. Carlyle, I, 128-29; Goethe, VII, 98-99.

37. Carlyle, I, 133; Goethe, VII, 103.

38. Carlyle, I, 174-75; Goethe, VII, 143. Moon, however, translates Goethe's sentence: "He clasped her to his heart and bedewed her with his tears" (123).

39. Goethe himself had written a satirical play, *Der Triumph der Empfindsamkeit*, probably in 1778 (published 1787).

image of the young man, Wilhelm, poetically "bedewing" the forlorn young woman with his tears is something the translator has to pass over in silence.

Mignon is, of course, most famous for her two songs and a poem. The morning after her breakdown which culminates in Wilhelm adopting her as his child, accompanied by the harper, she sings to him "Kennst du das Land, wo die Zitronen blühn".[40] Famously, poetry is what gets lost in translation, despite many attempts, sometimes successful to prove otherwise. Mignon's first song is three stanzas, each in three rhyming iambic pentameter couplets; the first four and a half lines of each stanza consists of one or more questions, beginning "Kennst du ...?", with the final line and a half in the form of an exclamatory response, "Dahin! Dahin! ..", which concludes with the somewhat edgy near rhyme, "ziehn!". Carlyle attempts to reproduce this same structure in his translation, although he abandons the attempt to find even a half rhyme for the final couplet of each stanza, rhyming instead "there" with "go!". Elsewhere in the translation, slight shifts in tone and mood if not in meaning is generated in order to maintain the form. Goethe's "blühn", at the end of the first line, is easily Englished as "bloom"; but Carlyle then needs to find a rhyme and must have found it very difficult to resist "gloom", which corresponds with the adjective in "Im dunkeln Laub" at the beginning of Goethe's (or Mignon's) next line. The problem with this is that by coming at the end of the line as a rhyme word it is given more emphasis in Carlyle's version that in the original, where the "dark foliage" is overridden by the "oranges' golden glow" at the end of the line. In first line of the second stanza, the house, possibly a classical or Palladian house, with its "roof resting on pillars" is reduced somewhat to a less noble edifice celebrated for "its porch with pillars tall" — tall the pillars may be, but this sounds almost like a homely farmstead, with its convenient veranda. The third line, "And marble statues stand, and look me on" is a verbatim translation of "Und Marmorbilder stehn und sehn mich an", but Carlyle is forced into an appalling inversion; and he cannot reproduce the internal rhyme of "stehn und sehn". Carlyle offers a "bridge that hangs on cloud" for Goethe's "Wolkensteg" ("path of clouds" in the first line of the third verse, and "the crag leaps down" for "Es stürzt der Fels" ("the rock falls down") in the fourth line. Perhaps it is too much to say that as a Scotsman, Carlyle preferred the

40. Carlyle, I, 176; Goethe, VII, 145. This is a text that has inspired many settings by such composers as Beethoven, von Reichardt, Schubert, Schumann, Himmel and Hugo Wolf, amongst others.

Celtic word "crag" to the plainer, less resonant "rock", and his choice of "leaps" too was possibly made because it sounds more conventionally poetic than "falls", and altogether a "leaping crag" sounds more threatening than a tumbling of falling rock. One could argue that since Carlyle cannot match the impact of Goethe's "Berg und ... Wolkensteg" in the first line of the stanza, with its immediate and simple evocation of alpine perspective and the dangers of travelling at such an altitude, nor find an equivalent for the vivid alliteration of "Fels" and "Flut" in the later line, within the restraints of the stanza form that he is trying to stick to, he is justified in raising the romantic dramatic impact by other means.[41]

---

41. In later revisions of his translation of *Wilhelm Meister*, Carlyle went on struggling to produce an effective English version of this famous lyric; but this is not the occasion to discuss his various attempts. The present discussion is of the final version of the poem as it appears in the Centenary Edition, which is some way from the original 1824 version, and is basically the 1842 revised text with a few significant changes. Since this same text appears in Chapman and Hall's 1871 edition (p.118), the changes must have originated in that edition, presumably made by Carlyle himself. But this 1871 edition must also have created the misprint in line 16, carried over to the Centenary Edition and possibly later editions. The syntax of "Know'st thou the mountain, bridge that hangs on cloud?" clearly does not make much sense. In his Introduction to the Centenary Edition (Carlyle, I, x), H.D. Traill, says "It is not without significance that Carlyle — to whom, though he abounded in the matter of poetry, its form was always more or less of a stumbling-block — should have been inspired, perhaps for the first and last time, as a verse translator by Mignon's famous song. For with more than one weak and metrically halting line Carlyle's version of that wild and haunting lyric fairly holds its own among innumerable others. Never, at any rate, have the opening lines of the concluding stanza —

> Kennst du den Berg und seinen Wolkensteg
> Das Maultier sucht im Nebel seinen Weg,

been more finely rendered than by —

> Know'st thou the mountain-bridge that hangs on cloud?
> The mules in mist grope o'er the torrent loud,

a couplet which reveals the whole scene as by a single touch of magic to the eye and ear." Despite the fact that the Centenary Edition, unlike previous editions by Chapman and Hall who were clearly cashing in on Carlyle's fame and popularity near the end of his career, was reset, Traill seems to have made no attempt to correct the misprint in the main text of Carlyle's translation, by substituting the hyphen for the comma between "mountain" and "bridge" (as it was reproduced in his own Introduction). Alas, this is characteristic of Traill's irresponsible attitude at

For "Heiß mich nicht reden, heiß mich schweigen" (literally, "Ask me not to speak, ask me to be silent") which Mignon recites to Wilhelm before he leaves the children — his son Felix and Mignon — to find the nobleman, Lothario, Carlyle produces absolutely regular verse form, each line of the three quatrains, rhyming ABAB, has four stresses, with an additional unstressed syllable at the end of the first and third lines in every stanza. Goethe's basic line in this lyric is iambic pentameter, but there are many variations: for instance, stanza 1 has a falling stress in the rhyme words of lines 1 and 3 ("schweigen" and "zeigen"), whereas the other two stanzas shifts this pattern to the even lines ("erhellen" and "Quellen", "ergießen" and "aufzuschließen"). The first quatrain, which probably gave Carlyle a hint for his metrical pattern, does not clearly establish the pentametrical form of the stanza at all, since the first line has nine syllables and a very uncertain pattern of stresses, lines 2 and 4 are tetrameters, and the third line has eleven syllables but a clear iambic rhythm. The fourth line of the second quatrain has thirteen syllables, and six stresses. It would be asking too much to expect Carlyle to imitate Goethe's expressive rhythmic flexibility, since he has a difficult enough task in finding the words and phrases to equal Mignon's alternation between wishing to reveal and to withhold her secret (a secret which is in indeed greater and more calamitous than she ever discovers). She believes that she is obliged by fate not to disclose her origins since she had previously come to harm by disclosing them. Goethe's first line, which already indicates Mignon's double imperative, and therefore, by implication, her doubtful will, Carlyle simplifies to turning it into a single command, "O, ask me not to speak, I pray thee!", weakened further by the rather self-consciously literary entreaty, "I pray thee!"; the more enigmatic paradox of Mignon's second line, "Denn mein Geheimnis ist mir Pflicht" ("for my secret is my duty"), is obscured by Carlyle's more commonplace "It must not be reveal'd but hid", where the auxiliary verb "must" certainly does not have the same ring as "duty".[42] Characteristic of Carlyle's general weakening and simplification of Goethe's powerful lyrical expression of Mignon's struggle is to be found in his version of that emphatic long fourth line in the second quatrain, "Mißgönnt der Erde nicht die tiefverborgnen

---

least to the text of *Wilhelm Meister* in the Centenary Edition, where at the beginning of the volume he simply records that the work was "*Originally published* 1824" and leaves the reader completely in the dark as to what parts of the text may reflect Carlyle's later revisions. One might have expected the editor of such an edition to have been more conscious of the publication history of the text.

42. Carlyle, I, 396; Goethe, VII, 356-57.

Quellen". This line looking forward to a time when the hard rocks ("Der harte Fels" of the previous line) "will not grudge surrendering to the earth its deeply hidden sources", with conspicuous implications for Mignon's plight, is flattened in Carlyle's version of the poem to "Gives up to earth its hidden wells".

The third and fourth lines of the first verse of Mignon's third poem, or *Lied*, in which she contemplates her death,[43] are

> Ich eile von der schönen Erde
> Hinab in jenes feste Haus.

On this occasion the touching simplicity of Goethe's lines (literally, "I hasten from the beautiful earth/Down into that secure house"), Carlyle rather ineptly dresses up:

> Soon from this dusk of earth I flee
> Up to the glittering lands of day.

For some reason, "the beautiful earth" becomes dusky,[44] while "the secure house" in the ground, the grave, he omits, and substitutes a doubtfully dressed up image of Heaven. For Goethe's "Dort ruh' ich eine kleine Stille" (the first line of the second stanza), Carlyle produces the clumsily inverted, "There first a little space I rest". The restraint maintained by Goethe in the last two lines of the third quatrain —

> Und keine Kleider, keine Falten
> Umgeben den verklärten Leib —

is translated by Carlyle into

> No robes, no garments there are worn,
> Our body pure from sin's alloy.

Here "clothes", in different forms, is repeated; "den verklärten Leib" ("the transfigured body") is replaced by the less exalted "body pure"; while the word "sin", fortified by the repugnant notion of "alloy", is introduced. Considering that Mignon as someone more sinned against than sinning, this last image is particularly offensive and far from Goethe's perception of her character: as a whole Carlyle's conception of

43. Carlyle, II, 95-96; Goethe, VII, 515-16.

44. In the 1824 edition Carlyle had "dreary earth".

Mignon's bearing towards her death seems to be rather based on his narrow chapel view of the flaws of humanity than upon a proper appreciation of Goethe's sensitive poetic touch in this song. Yet despite Carlyle's shortcomings, particularly in his translation of the poetry, one's overall impression is that he has gone a fair way to capturing the fragile and vulnerable beauty of Mignon.

Book VI of *Wilhelm Meisters Lehrjahre* consists of the "Bekenntnisse einer schönen Seele" ("The Confessions of a Beautiful Soul"), which seem a large digression and might easily have been omitted by Carlyle, without his readers being either disturbed or even noticing. At the same time, the woman's account of herself is such an incredibly edifying tale of her search for and coming to terms with moral authority, that it is unlikely that Carlyle would have thought of leaving it out. Moral authority is conceived not in demanding Kantian terms, but in the manner that Goethe and Schiller explored the concept as a means of bringing duty and inclination into harmony. The title of this book is not given by the woman herself, but by somebody knowing of her experiences from the outside. In translating the title, "Bekenntnisse einer schönen Seele" into "Confessions of a Fair Saint", Carlyle already misses a key point concerning how we are to interpret this account: from her own volition, the beautiful soul had come to incorporate duty into her life through a physical and spiritual struggle. From the outset, she has virtuous qualities, but in the end fails to achieve sainthood, although she does become a dedicated pietist and turns her worldly nature into an introspective one.

In the translation of this part of the novel many small eccentric deviations occur, as, for instance, when the narrator as a young woman writes about the books she was reading at that time. Among them is the *Römische Oktavia*, which she prized above all other volumes. She admits that "Die Verfolgung der ersten Christen, in einen Roman gekleidet, erregten bei mir das lebhafteste Interesse", which Carlyle conveys to the reader as "The persecutions of the first Christians, decorated with the charms of a romance, awoke the deepest interest in me".[45] "Decorated with the charms of a romance" goes much further in suggesting a degree of reprehensible self-indulgence than the neutral description the woman conveys with her statement that the Octavia's story was "dressed in the form of a novel"; Carlyle's addition that the story was "decorated with charms", and it was a romance suggests a level of frivolity Goethe's text does not warrant. Another small oddity

45. Carlyle, I, 399; Goethe, VII, 360.

occurs when the Fair Soul reports the death of the Marshal of the Court's two sons, adding in Carlyle's text, "I lamented sore; however, in a short time I forgot".[46] Goethe has the woman say "Es tat mir weh, aber bald waren sie vergessen", a much more casual and factual statement about the death of the two boys: she does not lament at all, but admits only that "it hurt" or that "she felt the pain". As is frequently the case, Carlyle's chooses a hyperbolic expression, which cannot but be thought of as highly personal.

In a paragraph in which the woman is talking about her reading, surprisingly she confesses that she gained all her carnal knowledge (described in a periphrastic way as "der natürlichen Geschichte des menschlichen Geschlechts": "the natural history of mankind") from the Bible. Aided by her thirst for knowledge and her gift for putting two and two together, she had discovered the truth of words and things even in doubtful and dangerous parts ("Bedenkliche Stellen", a phrase which is given prominence at the beginning of a difficult sentence) of the holy text; adding that had she known about witches, she would have been equally compelled to find out about witchcraft.[47] Whether through shock, through modesty or disbelief, or a combination of all three, Carlyle leaves out these two and half sentences, and with some relief, moves on to the next part of the confession in which the woman describes her first steps in cooking and her delight in cutting up hens and pigs and taking the entrails to her father.[48]

In the Preface to the first edition of *Wilhelm Meister's Apprenticeship*, Carlyle mentions Shakespeare three times and the character of Hamlet once. To gain the good will of the English reader of the work, he acknowledges "the disfigurement of a translation", but at the same time asks the reader for "long and patient and intense examination", by which he will be rewarded by "descry[ing] the earnest features of that beauty, which has its foundation in the deepest nature of man, and will continue to be pleasing through all ages". He continues:

> If this appear excessive praise as applied in any sense to *Meister*, the curious sceptic is desired to read and weigh the whole performance, with all its references, relations, purposes; and to pronounce his verdict after he has clearly seized and appreciated them all. Or if a more faint conviction will suffice, let him turn

---

46. Carlyle, I, 402; Goethe, VII, 363.

47. Goethe, VII, 360.

48. Carlyle, I, 399.

> to the picture of Wilhelm's states of mind in the end of the first Book, and the beginning of the second; the eulogies of commerce and poesy, which follow; the description of Hamlet; the histrionic life in Serlo and Aurelia; that of sedate and lofty manhood in the Uncle and Lothario.[49]

The passages dedicated to *Hamlet* and its eponymous tragic hero obviously give a great deal of pleasure to Carlyle, and he translates them with ease and grace. When Wilhelm is with the actors at the Count's castle, he stages several nondescript French plays and is entirely ignorant of Shakespeare. Jarno, the favourite if not the natural son of a Prince who is about to visit the Count and Countess, is critical of the shallow repertoire, remarking, "Es ist schade, daß Sie mit hohlen Nüssen um hohle Nüsse spielen" (Carlyle: "It is pity that you should play with hollow nuts, for a stake of hollow nuts").[50] And later we learn, as Carlyle puts it, that "the Prince showed an exclusive inclination for the French theatre; while a part of his people, among whom Jarno was especially distinguished, gave a passionate preference to the monstrous productions of the English stage"[51] — the last judgment reflecting Voltaire's well-known bias. Later when Wilhelm honours the Prince by showing his appreciation of Corneille and Racine, Jarno takes him aside and asks him whether he has ever seen a play by Shakespeare. On Jarno's advice, the hitherto ignorant Wilhelm starts to engross himself with Shakespeare especially with *Hamlet*. While Wilhelm is so engrossed, the narrator renders with stunning simplicity the young man's spellbound state, which Carlyle matches in his version:

> We have heard of some Enchanter summoning, by magic formulas, a vast multitude of spiritual shapes into his cell. The conjurations are so powerful that the whole space of the apartment is quickly full; and the spirits crowding on to the verge of the little circle which they must not pass, around this, and above the master's head, keep increasing in number, and ever whirling in perpetual transformation. Every corner is crammed, every crevice is possessed. Embryos expand themselves, and giant forms contract into the size of nuts.

---

49. Carlyle, I, 8-9.

50. Carlyle, I, 208; Goethe, VII, 175.

51. Carlyle, I, 209; Goethe, VII, 176.

> Unhappily the Black-artist has forgot the counter-word, with which he might command this flood of sprites again to ebb.[52]

Again, however, Carlyle is inclined to go for what appears to him to be a more startling contrast, preferring "Embryos" and "nuts", as a means of expressing small evocative forms, for Goethe's "Eggs" and "mushrooms" — "Eier dehnen sich aus, und Riesengestalten ziehen sich in Pilze zusammen".

Some time later, we find Wilhelm discussing Hamlet's state of mind: "Das zuverlässige Bild, das sich ein wohlgeratenes Kind so gern von seinen Eltern macht, verschwindet; bei dem Toten ist keine Hülfe, und an der Lebendigen kein Halt." Carlyle even manages to work the alliteration of "Halt" and "Hülfe" into his version, with "hold" and "help". But as we find elsewhere, and perhaps it is unavoidable when one considers the differences between the syntax of German and English, Carlyle breaks up Goethe's single sentence (admittedly, already divided by a semicolon) into two:

> The trustful image, which a good child loves to form of its parents, is gone. With the dead there is no help; on the living no hold.

At the same time, rhetorically, this split does help to stress the dramatic point. On other occasions, it is Carlyle who breaks up Goethe's single sentences with a semicolon, as we find a couple of sentences later, when Goethe's "Nun erst fühlt er sich recht gebeugt, nun erst verwaist, and kein Glück der Welt kann ihm wieder ersetzen, was er verloren hat" becomes "Now first does he feel himself completely bent and orphaned; and no happiness of life can repay what he has lost".

In the sentence between these two we find an example where Shakespeare's own words, justifiably, exert their influence on Carlyle's treatment of Goethe's text: "Sie ist auch ein Weib, and unter dem allgemeinen Geschlechtsnamen Gebrechlichkeit ist auch sie begriffen" becomes "She also is a woman, and her name is Frailty, like that of all her sex", inevitably echoing Hamlet's cry in I.ii.146.[53] Similarly, a few paragraphs later Wilhelm's quoting Wieland's prose translation of *Hamlet*, "Die Zeit ist aus dem Gelenke; wehe mir, daß ich geboren

---

52. Carlyle, I, 218-19; Goethe, VII, 185.

53. Carlyle, I, 280-81; Goethe, VII, 245. William Shakespeare, *Hamlet*, ed. Harold Jenkins, The Arden Edition, London and New York, 1982, 188.

ward, sie wieder einzurichten", is naturally rendered in Shakespeare's own version:

> The time is out of joint: O cursed spite,
> That ever I was born to set it right!

Aurelie, who is to play Ophelia, is puzzled why, when she is mad, the poet has put "Zweideutigkeiten und lüsterne Albernheiten in dem Munde dieses edlen Mädchens" (Carlyle: "double meanings and lascivious insipidities ... in the mouth of such a noble-minded person"), and not given her other songs instead, "Fragmente aus melancholischen Balladen" ("fragments out of melancholy ballads"). Almost in the manner of a modern psychiatrist, Wilhelm answers that the sounds of desire that earlier clamoured through her mind, but which she could keep it at bay in her sanity, in her madness are unrestrained, since now "the secrets of her heart are hovering on her tongue" and "that tongue betrays her". Again, as one might expect, Carlyle moves away from Goethe's text, "vom Mädchen, das gewonnen ward; vom Mädchen, das zum Knaben schleicht" (literally, "the girl, who was conquered; the girl, who slinks to the boy") to Shakespeare's "*Tomorrow is Saint Valentine's day*; and *By Gis and by Saint Charity*".[54]

A famous crux in Shakespeare's text (although not recognized by Goethe or his characters, or even Carlyle as such), leads to some amusing reflections on Hamlet's physical as well as mental state, and the relationship between the two. The crux in question is the Queen's remark about her son in the last scene of the play, in the midst of the duel, quoted in Carlyle's text that "He's fat and scant of breath". In an extended note in the Arden edition, Harold Jenkins remarks that "few now see in it an allusion to the actor's corpulence", and proposes, with some qualification, that the word "fat" refers to Hamlet sweating, or, possibly, to his being out of condition.[55] Wilhelm defends his belief that the Dane is "fair-haired and blue-eyed" on the grounds of his Nordic descent, but more curiously because he is plump:

> "Ihm wird das Fechten sauer, der Schweiß läuft ihm vom Gesichte, und die Königin spricht: 'Er ist fett, laßt ihn zu Atem kommen.' Kann man sich ihn da anders als blond und wohlbehäglich vorstellen? denn braune Leute sind in ihrer Jugend selten in diesem Falle."

---

54. Carlyle, I, 291-92; Goethe, VII, 255. *Hamlet*, IV.v.48-66 (350-51).

55. *Hamlet*, V.ii.290 and note (412 and 568-69).

But not only is Wilhelm able to impute that blonds are more likely to be fat than brunettes, and since Hamlet is fat, evidently he must be a blond, this fair-headed corpulence comports more easily with his character:

> "Paßt nicht auch seine schwankende Melancholie, seine weiche Trauer, seine tätige Unentschlossenheit besser zu einer solchen Gestalt, als wenn Sie sich einen schlanken, braunlockigen Jüngling denken, vom dem man mehr Entschlossenheit und Behendigkeit erwartet."

As Carlyle puts it:

> "... Brown-complexioned people in their youth are seldom plump. And does not his wavering melancholy, his soft lamenting, his irresolute activity, accord with such a figure? From a dark-haired young man you would look for more decision and impetuosity."

Aurelie is aghast and cries:

> "You are spoiling my imagination ... away with your fat Hamlets! do not set your well-fed Prince before us! Give us rather any succedaneum that will move us, will delight us ..."

From a man such as Carlyle, with his endless epistolary complaints of aches and pains and his familiarity with tinctures and potions, and a variety of health restoring mixtures, substitutes, "succedaneum" as a medicinal substitute, or drug, is the ideal translation for Goethe's (and Aurelie's) the "Quiproquo, das uns reizt, das uns rührt".[56]

Likewise one has to accept that any translation, Wieland's of Shakespeare, Carlyle's of Goethe, also cannot be anything but a "succedaneum"; but will always work, to a certain extent, as a substitute for the original as long as it pleases us, as long as it moves us. Just as Aurelie says at the end of her exclamation, which draws the chapter to a close, "Die Intention des Autors liegt uns nicht so nahe als unser Vergnügen, und wir verlangen einen Reiz, der uns homogen ist". This may be the pragmatic view of the actor determined to win the attention and approbation of the audience, and may not satisfy the more critically-inclined academic, nevertheless, perhaps it is not such a bad

---

56. Carlyle, I, 343-44; Goethe, VII, 306-307.

rule for translators contemplating their likely readership: “The intention of the author is of less importance to us than our own enjoyment, and we need a charm that is adapted for us.” For someone reluctant to face the challenge of Goethe’s text, perhaps, after all, Carlyle’s charming, and more or less accurate, adaptation, which does not neglect the original author’s intention, even if it occasionally bends or blunts it, remains a work still worth our attention.

POISED ON THE CUSP: THOMAS CARLYLE — ROMANTIC, VICTORIAN, OR BOTH?

MARGARET RUNDLE

In Thomas Carlyle's *Sartor Resartus* (completed in 1831), Teufelsdröckh's exhortation "Close thy *Byron*; open thy *Goethe*"[1] announces the movement, here crystallized, from a Romantic to a Victorian sensibility. This announcement catches the spirit of a transitional moment remarked on by many, like John Stuart Mill in his "Spirit of the Age" (1831), for instance. And Edward Bulwer Lytton in his "View of the English Character" (1833) in *England and the English* proclaims that

> great changes have been over the world .... Those changes which have wrought such convulsions in states have begun by revolutions in the *character* of nations .... The English of the present day are not the English of twenty years ago.[2]

While in their scope these reflect on changes in the constitution of the body social and politic, at the core of each is what lies at the crux of Carlyle's "Satirical Extravaganza on Things in General":[3] modification in the constitution of the self. For through the formal use of a Schlegelian Romantic Irony, *Sartor Resartus* traces the perceptual motion of a self journeying from Romantic to Victorian definition.

Lytton's discrimination between the English of the "present day" and of twenty years before notwithstanding, both he and Mill primarily distinguish between the organization of the *ancien régime* and the

1. *The Works of Thomas Carlyle*, ed. H.D. Traill, Centenary Edition, 30 vols, London, 1896-99, I: *Sartor Resartus*, 153.

2. Edward Bulwer Lytton, *England and the English*, New York, 1833, I, 14.

3. Thomas Carlyle to James Frazer, 27 May 1833, in *The Collected Letters of Thomas and Jane Welsh Carlyle*, Duke-Edinburgh edn, gen. ed. Charles Richard Sanders, Durham: NC, 1970 -, VI, 396.

reconstituted post-Revolutionary arrangement of politics and society. Essentially, they describe the break with an "old", "ancestral" order, feudalistic, medieval in nature. But in the continuum of literary history, Carlyle's *Sartor Resartus* demarcates a finer periodic distinction and thus stands as a text of watershed significance; it punctuates a shift from Romantic to Victorian ideas about both form and substance. Indeed, as Kerry McSweeney and Peter Sabor (the editors of the 1987 edition) remark, *Sartor Resartus*, as sharply as Wordsworth's Preface to the *Lyrical Ballads* had done, designates the closure of an old literary order and the inauguration of a new. Unlike the Preface, which declared a radically different approach, *Sartor Resartus*, despite its patently Romantic features, enacts what McSweeney and Sabor call the "dislocations of the passage"[4] through a collapsing of the previous and the imminent. Interestingly, this "dislocation" signifies a personal as well as a periodic transition. For *Sartor Resartus* carries the original voice Carlyle had increasingly sought in the late 1820s, when translating and interpreting Teutonic thought had grown insufficient to his authorial needs. As Friedrich Althaus remarks in his 1866 biographic sketch for *Unsere Zeit*: "[*Sartor Resartus*] is a memorial to past struggles and a guide to his future life and work".[5] It may well be imagined that the attempt to redefine an authorial self lent a peculiar, compelling intensity to the portrait of the British self in transition that, in *Sartor Resartus*, Carlyle seeks to limn.

That original voice is critical to a reading of the text as ironic, more particularly — as critics like Janice Haney maintain — as Romantic Ironic. Other interpretations of *Sartor Resartus* seem to miss out this larger Ironic context[6] that accounts for its apparent disparities and

---

4. "Introduction" to *Sartor Resartus*, eds Kerry McSweeney and Peter Sabor, Oxford, Oxford, 1987, viii.

5. Thomas Carlyle, *Two Reminiscences of Thomas Carlyle*, ed. John Clubbe, Durham: NC, 1974, 83.

6. Other critics have cast *Sartor Resartus* in various interpretive lights. For instance, Gerry Brookes has placed it in the framework of the persuasive essay (*The Rhetorical Form of Carlyle's "Sartor Resartus"*, Berkeley: CA, 1972); M. H. Abrams has traced there the course of the Romantic circuitous journey (*Natural Supernaturalism: Tradition and Revolution in Romantic Literature*, New York, 1971); and George Levine — while recognizing the oppositional dualism at the heart of Romantic Irony — never identifies the theory by name and reads the use of such a technique as creating a fictional front. He sees the creation of this front as part of a quintessentially Victorian impulse for the author at one and the same time to attract the reader and to protect him- or herself ("*Sartor Resartus* and the

formal extravagances. And none credits the serious self-mockery in Carlyle's own private declaration of intention: "I am going to write — Nonsense. It is on 'Clothes.' Heaven be my comforter!"[7] None gives deserving accord to the importance of the Romantic Irony at work in *Sartor Resartus*, to both the formal device and the "ambiguous status of artistic illusion", signalling, as Haney contends, a "reinterpretation of existence and creation, a reinterpretation that has both philosophical and historical significance".[8]

As this comment suggests, the appearance of Romantic Irony itself, as well as the implications of its use in *Sartor Resartus*, was significant, in fact, revolutionizing. A theory of Romantic Irony was most completely articulated in the late eighteenth and early nineteenth century and was part of a German intellectual revolution as startling in its effect on a philosophical and artistic approach as the French Revolution had been on a political one. Varied as this revolutionary speculation was, change and the dynamism of evolution were seen by all as necessary to progress. Concomitantly, the nature of the self, indeed of the whole human condition, was recognized as contradictory and paradoxical. When coupled, these perceptions contravened earlier notions of stasis and denied both the potential for resolution in a single total metaphysical formula and a Kantian view of existence as defined through mutually exclusive antimonies; rather than a classicist effort to avoid extremes, the impulse was to combine them in what Douglas Muecke terms a "harmony of opposites".[9]

Friedrich Schlegel caught the spirit of this revolution in his theory of an aesthetic account of progressive change and paradox or contradiction. His Romantic Irony is open-ended and dynamic in its representation. He declares, "Irony is the form of paradox".[10] An

---

Balance of Fiction", in *The Boundaries of Fiction: Carlyle, Macaulay, Newman*, Princeton: NJ, 1968).

7. Thomas Carlyle, *Two Notebooks of Thomas Carlyle*, ed. Charles Eliot Norton, New York, 1989, 176.

8. Janice L. Haney, "'Shadow-Hunting': Romantic Irony, *Sartor Resartus*, and Victorian Romanticism", *Studies in Romanticism*, 17 (1978), 308.

9. Douglas C. Muecke, *The Compass of Irony*, 1969; rpt. London, Methuen, 1980, 188. Schlegel's aphorism (no. 74) encapsulates this idea: "Combine the extremes and you will have a true center" ("Selected Ideas" [1799-1800], in *Dialogue on Poetry and Literary Aphorisms*, trans. Ernst Behler and Roman Struc, University Park: PA, 1968, 155).

10. Aphorism no. 48, in *Dialogue on Poetry*, 126.

artistic medium for a metaphysical message, this Irony reveals a self-conscious scrutiny born of awareness about the relationship of the individual — in a finite condition — to the Infinite.

Rejecting Kant's either/or predicament — that either the Infinite *or* the Finite constitutes reality — Schlegel discerns shadings and fluctuations and so proposes *becoming* as an alternative to *being*. The concept of *becoming* shears the closure of a static *being* to open the way for change, for developmental motion. *These* become the ground of substance and reality. Denying neither the Absolute nor coherent order in the universe, Schlegel's proposal identifies human perception of these as necessarily limited, fragmentary, and capable of seeing only chaotic organization. But chaos here sloughs off pejoratives to reassume the original Greek sense of primordial fusion, a diverse richness[11] that defies the superimposition of a system. Romantic Irony's form functions so as to recognize a malleable being.

Process, not product, becomes the aim, then, of spiritual activity and necessitates understanding that everything posited is finite and so must constantly be reformulated to be accurate and appropriate. Further, it requires a dual vision that recognizes the perpetual oscillations between opposites, such as system and chaos, rapture and doubt. Most keenly aware of the dualities of mind and body, mind and world, and of the restricted self, the Romantic Ironist especially is to maintain this dual vision and is to remember that, although the ability to know is limited, this entrapment may be vaulted through acknowledgement of reversals and through self-transcendence. Herein lies part of the Ironist's power, the other part of which derives from the ability the Ironist's work has to mediate between the Infinite and the Finite, since the relationship suggested in the text duplicates that between God, the infinite creator, and *His* finite creation. Through the imagination, the Ironic author creates a new "reality".

When metaphysics is transferred to art, the authentic creative production must reflect the conflicting tensions in the self and the world and must give a sign of the artist's continued striving to represent them. Romantic Irony serves best here, since it opens the text to accommodate these. In addition, it permits the work simultaneously to have and not to have a system, thus allowing the Ironist to escape systematic death through self-transcendence. The Ironic work, reflecting moments of insight and doubt, the author's creating and de-creating, at once mirrors and replicates reality's developmental progress. It is the formal

---

11. For the Greek association of "chaos", see Behler and Struc's introduction to *Dialogue on Poetry*, 10-11.

representation of these positive tensions that Schlegel names an "arabesque".

Thus at least part of the motion in Romantic Irony is the author's. To represent a partial and discontinuous reality and the irreconcilable rift between the absolute and the relative, the writer employs fragments, varied literary constructions, multiple frameworks, and confessional interruptions to disrupt lines of cause and effect. These devices convey at once Schlegel's "impossibility and necessity of total communication" and attest to his "freest of all liberties", the self-parody which allows the author's vaulting of limitations to maintain power over the text. The other part of the motion is the reader's. The fragmentary form of the text jogs the reader into active engagement with it and encourages understanding of it as only a starting point for his or her own striving to develop meaning. In this search, the reader moves toward the truth the author is holding out; consequently, theirs becomes a shared philosophizing, fulfilling German Romantic ideas about art's essential obligation: to encourage self-knowledge and self-cultivation.

This brand of Irony is peculiarly Romantic because of its metaphysical reference and its championing of the creative ego. The German approach, like the English visionary one, recurs to transcendental categories and holds literature and philosophy as clearly legitimate modes of discourse. However, views of the transcendental realm and the operation of consciousness are different. British perspective sees a transcendental pattern, more or less fixed; the Romantic Ironic, a realm moving in the continuous flux of *becoming*. Therefore, with the English, meaning is shaped in an ideal form; with the German, it is denied fixity or any stable centre. The English apotheosize Nature as either the great signifier of the transcendental or as that very realm itself. A Being, a mind, an order are described. If Nature is not recurred to for meaning, the unifying or unified self, portrayed as character or ideal consciousness, is. Coleridge, a typically English Romantic here, speaks of the synthetic power of the poet which fuses internal opposites and external disjunctures in the spirit of unity. Imagination "blends and harmonizes the natural and the artificial, still subordinates art to nature; the manner to the matter; and our admiration of the poet to our sympathy with the poetry".[12] The German views actual or "real" nature, ceaselessly created and destroyed, as moving in the process of *becoming*, a demonstration of its revolutionary capability.

---

12. *The Collected Works of Samuel Taylor Coleridge*, eds Kathleen Coburn *et al.*, 16 vols, Princeton and London, 1971 - , VII: *Biographia Literaria*, eds James Engell and W. Jackson Bate (1983), ch. 14, II, 14-15.

The self is contradiction itself and, when it is the creating self, has tantamount rather than subordinate importance with the work. Schlegel calls for a portrait of the "producer along with the product" in philosophy; similarly, in poetry, he would have a "poetic theory of the creative power with the artistic and beautiful self-mirroring, which is in Pindar ...".[13] Finally, with the English Romantics, time follows the line of a literary temporality, prefigured and ideal, suggesting that the action of existence is predetermined, providential; with the German, time is represented as the interrupted and diverted sequence of an actual story.

Commitment to self-consciousness, to the reversals of Irony reflecting the true nature of existence, to the concept of *becoming* was more congenial to Carlyle than to the English Romantics' favouring of pattern over process, stasis over dynamism. Certainly, the tenets of Romantic Irony operate critically in *Sartor Resartus* to propel consciousness from an older, that is, English Romantic, means of formulating meaning to a new.

In 1829, catching the tenor of Teutonic thinking and anticipating the spirit of *Sartor Resartus* (begun the following year), Carlyle wonders whether the "mind has its cycles and seasons like Nature, varying from the fermentation of *werden* to the clearness of *seyn*; and this again and again; so that the history of man is like the history of the world he lives in?"[14] By 1830, material and psychic fermentation, external and internal chaos, had converted to the fertile abundance from which creation would ensue.[15] Carlyle confesses to Goethe that there is a "wonderful chaos" within him "full of natural Supernaturalism, and all manner of Antideluvian [*sic*] fragments", that increasingly he sees the universe as mysterious and august and external influences as "more heterogeneous and perplexing". While not sure of what, he says that he can "only conjecture from the violence of fermentation that something strange may come".[16]

Demonstrating the detachment and dual vision of the Ironist at work and the consciousness of a "wonderful Chaos", "heterogeneous and perplexing", Carlyle's *Sartor* denies fixity, determinate answers, and an

---

13. Aphorism no. 238, in *Dialogue on Poetry*, 145.

14. *Two Notebooks*, 132.

15. Carlyle had written "On Clothes" by 28 October 1830 and used it as a draft for *Sartor*, completed by the end of July 1831.

16. *The Collected Letters*, V, 153-54.

unshifting meaning. Rather, it embodies Schlegel's harmony of extremes achieved through the continued transformation that comes with transcendence. Indeed, generally, *Sartor Resartus* seems to demonstrate Schlegel's arabesque, that formal representation of positive tensions. It is a work of textual layerings, complex narrative frames, multiple voices, fragments, disrupted lines of cause and effect, and confessional interruptions. The contributory voices there create the semblance of realistic simultaneity, shattering the line of single-voiced narrative. Oliver Yorke and Hofrath Heuschrecke, although heard but rarely, are reminders of the world waiting for the Professor's retailored text. But it is the layerings of fiction that evince Schlegel's "beautiful self-mirroring" and signal the true beginning of Romantic Irony. It is a work replete with continuous reflections and refractions: Teufelsdröckh's *Die Kleider* is material for the editor's book out of which Carlyle fashions *Sartor Resartus*. This stratification of fiction combines with the oppositional imagery of chaotic ocean journeying and stable islands of arrival.[17] Add, then, the fragmented style of "circumlocutions, repetitions", of sentences "not more than nine-tenths [of which] stand straight on their legs", the rest of which are "quite broken-backed and dismembered".[18] These devices construct a Romantic Ironic surface and help create the scene for questioning the relationship between self and system and between the self's conflicting elements. They divert attention away from an orthodox discursive argument for the system of the Clothes Philosophy to centre it instead on the relation of both Teufelsdröckh and the editor to that philosophy. At the very centre of the work's Irony is their dialogic interplay.

Undoubtedly, Carlyle's purpose was to proselytize, but these devices constitute a new means of conversion to fit the temper of the times. Like the period in which Schlegel's theory of Irony appears, that of Carlyle's *Sartor Resartus* was yearning for reform and was seized by the impulse for revolution. In literature, a Wordsworthian promise of a quotidian language to reach and celebrate the individual would no longer suffice. With enfranchisement as one watchword of the early 1830s, the Ironic devices in *Sartor Resartus* — designed to *show* not *tell*, to involve the reader in the exercise of philosophizing — were

---

17. For a treatment of geographic metonymy and metaphor as part of the spatial symbolism in the text, see Elizabeth Waterston, "Past and Present Selves: Patterns in *Sartor Resartus*", in *Thomas Carlyle 1981: Papers Given at the International Thomas Carlyle Symposium*, Frankfurt-am-Main, 1983, 111-24.

18. *The Works of Thomas Carlyle*, I: *Sartor Resartus*, 24.

better calculated to convert. The text's progressive unfolding ideally insures reader engagement and encourages exploration rather than demanding compliance. Arrival, therefore, does not supersede the importance of the journey; means are at least tantamount to ends; and all have a vote in the epistemological election. The dialectical presentation in *Sartor Resartus* creates a scene where self vies with self as a metaphysical and aesthetic Teufelsdröckh faces off against an empirical editor, Carlyle's "Conservative (tho' Antiquack) character". Their conjoined search for meaning propels the work's evolutionary motion.

Critical in this search is the editor. In one crucial sense, he exists as the principal fiction of the text; indeed, Carlyle designates him the "main Actor in the business".[19] Through responses to fragmentary offerings of doctrine or biography, in some measure, he simulates the reader voicing hesitations or objections. Through selecting and ordering the material in those six paper bags, he shapes chaos into some kind of intelligible form. Further, if Teufelsdröckh seeks to evolve ideas about the self and Natural Supernaturalism, the editor attempts "to evolve printed Creation out of a German printed and written Chaos".[20] Teufelsdröckh's prophetic cries of enthusiastic self-creation and the editor's self-restraint alternate in Schlegel's "beautiful self-mirroring" as the two engage in an allied quest for meaning.

But the double vision of the text's Irony is also maintained through Teufelsdröckh, who — oscillating between transcendental and descendental views — on the one hand, degrades "man below most animals" and, on the other, exalts "him beyond the visible Heavens, almost to an equality with the Gods".[21] This motion reflects on a small scale the dialectic of rapture and doubt in the text at large. Further, as these oscillations occur in the Professor's regard for humanity, they also replicate the movements between de-creation and re-creation, the wellsprings of his own prophetic utterances about society — past, present, and future. Thus Diogenes Teufelsdröckh, whose oxymoronic name recalls the contradictory constituents of all being, is prototypic at once of humanity generally and of the Romantic Ironist.

Being aware of this dualism means being aware generally that humans are fitted into an ontological universe run on a divine impulse. Every motion and event in what Carlyle calls the "mighty, billowy,

---

19. *The Collected Letters*, VI, 396.

20. *The Works of Thomas Carlyle*, I: *Sartor Resartus*, 63.

21. *Ibid.*, 51.

stormtost Chaos of Life" is vitalized by the greater power that joins all in continuous, interconnected metamorphosis: "all ... works together with all; is borne forward on the bottomless, shoreless flood of Action, and lives through perpetual metamorphosis."[22] Certainly this retains something of the British Romantic sense of being "Rolled round in earth's diurnal course,/With rocks, and stones, and trees".[23] But consciousness of duality as the prime mover of change, progress, metamorphosis distinguishes this approach. Only through the proportionate balancing of opposed forces — destruction as critical as creation — and the movement between them, can the transcendence out of a trapped condition be achieved. Throughout the universe, Teufelsdröckh proclaims, "all things wax, and roll onwards; Arts, Establishments, Opinions, nothing is completed, but ever completing";[24] the tailor and the clothes are repeatedly retailored.

A further distinction between British Romanticism and Irony is to be discerned in *Sartor Resartus*. Carlyle uses this Irony to support what Anne Mellor calls the "ever-increasing and infinitely increasable freedom of the human spirit".[25] Carlyle's finding the mere ruminations of a British Romantic self insufficient, this freedom denotes life itself and is reified in Teufelsdröckh's "*Welldoing*", or "conduct, a visible, acted Gospel of Freedom", in work.[26] Work and the movement toward freedom it entails, like all else, involve those reversals of the self-immolating phoenix — Carlyle's central emblem of regenerative process — consumed in conflagration in order to rise from the ashes. The universe, society, the self swirl "In that Fire-whirlwind, Creation and Destruction proceed together; ever as ashes of the Old are blown about, do organic filaments of the New mysteriously spin themselves ...."[27] In the tenor of Schlegel's positive philosophical alternative, Teufelsdröckh asserts that "all that Mankind does or beholds, is in continual growth, regenesis and self-perfecting vitality".[28]

But Teufelsdröckh also recognizes that nature's infinite abundance

---

22. *Ibid.*, 56.

23. See "A slumber did my spirit seal", in *The Poetical Works of William Wordsworth*, ed. E. de Selincourt, 2nd edn, Oxford, 1952, II, 216.

24. *The Works of Thomas Carlyle*, I: *Sartor Resartus*, 197.

25. Anne K. Mellor, *English Romantic Irony*, Cambridge: MA, 1980, 115.

26. *The Works of Thomas Carlyle*, I: *Sartor Resartus*, 146.

27. *Ibid.*, 195.

28. *Ibid.*, 31.

and its divine intimations are to be caught only in fragments, in glimpsing moments and, therefore, that it is impossible to impose a system: "The course of Nature's phases, on this our little fraction of a Planet, is partially known to us: but who knows … what infinitely larger Cycle (of causes) our little Epicycle revolves on?"[29] Thus, like the Ironic artist, humans generally have only "rare half-waking moments", when "Dream and Dreamer" are seen, moments that shudder humans from sleep "in a boundless Phantasmagoria and Dream-grotto".[30] But in those moments emerges the creative power of that god-like ME — Fichte's *Ich* actively striving toward the Divine Idea and, in *Biographia Literaria*, Coleridge's finite parallel to the "infinite I AM".[31] The rapture of these moments counterbalances the despair in limited knowledge and the inevitable stoical conclusion that mortality does not signify in the context of life's infinite abundance. It inspires the self with enthusiasm to participate in the continuing divine process that vitalizes the world. Further, though, as Anne Mellor notes, this consciousness of the self's divine portion is essential to Teufelsdröckh's theory of natural supernaturalism. The *Me* clothed in that Goethean "Garment of the Flesh" is a "force, a power",[32] and understanding of the divine element there enables the self to penetrate the material trappings of the world and so to gain proper perspective. Teufelsdröckh, the editor relates, "has looked fixedly on Existence, till, one after the other, its earthly hulls and garnitures have all melted away; and now, to his rapt vision, the interior celestial Holy of Holies lies disclosed".[33]

But the body, however illusory, must not be ignored. No mere counterpart of the spiritual self, the body is the concretion of spiritual essence, a "revelation to Sense of the mystic god-given force that is in … [man]; a 'Gospel of Freedom' … ". It is, indeed, a symbol, which, like all other symbols is at once revealing and concealing. The doctrine of symbols is the axis on which the Clothes Philosophy's metaphysics turns. For symbols mediate the gap between the Infinite and the Finite, embodying both and so giving constant reminder of their interplay: "the Infinite is made to blend itself with the Finite, to stand visible, … as it

---

29. *Ibid.*, 205.

30. *Ibid.*, 42 and 41.

31. *Biographia Literaria*, ch. 13, I, 304.

32. Mellor, 116.

33. *The Works of Thomas Carlyle*, I: *Sartor Resartus*, 203.

were, attainable there."[34]

Incomplete ability to know the dimensions of boundless creation is complicated by the resistance to interpretation of symbols themselves. This inability is the impetus for their perpetual metamorphosis, the retailoring *Sartor Resartus* calls for. Hedging definition with qualifiers, Teufelsdröckh declares that symbols are "more or less ... some embodiment and revelation of the Infinite". So humans — in the search for greater figurative accuracy — must extend the boundaries of knowledge. And symbols — to keep pace with universal and individual ontology — must periodically undergo the transformation of Palingenesia. Like all terrestrial garments, if truly modified, they must be alternately destroyed and created. From the ashes of the disused signifier are thrown out the organic filaments of reborn expression. Thus perception of the Infinite transcends limits, just as the self hurdles restrictions of its own imaging. Old form is immolated to create new "in this so solid-seeming World, which nevertheless is in continual restless flux ... ".

Language is the principal symbol, since humans have access to the Infinite primarily through it. To some degree, it allows the Infinite to be materially conceptualized, the starting point of apprehension. For Teufelsdröckh, the word has omnipotence "in this world". Through use of the word "man, thereby divine, can create as by a *Fiat*".[35] Anne Mellor rightly observes that even to intimate the depth and breadth of the impalpable, symbols must be complex and imaginative. In language, metaphors seem best to answer to this need because of their inherent richness in allusive possibility. The mechanisms of discursive and logical argument are mere "faded raiment"; metaphors, though, are the effectors of vital movement in language, the "Flesh-Garment" or body of thought, working in that verbal clothes-body as "its muscles and tissues and living integuments".[36]

To retain their vital potential, however, words, like other symbols, must be regarded with dual vision. On the one hand, they imply an Infinite *becoming* and so elicit wonder; on the other, both indirect and incomplete and so, in some measure, distorting the view, they arouse suspicion. It is incumbent on the Ironic author principally to maintain such ambivalence toward the word and the fictional systems in which it operates. Mellor points out that the creative artist is both Prometheus

---

34. *Ibid.*, 175.

35. *Ibid.*, 158.

36. *Ibid.*, 57-58.

and Orpheus, both the "savior of mankind and the unacknowledged legislator of human society",[37] a view in keeping with that of Shelley and Byron.[38] In such a position of power, the author must maintain double vision toward a work that is becoming, if it is to be the "Godlike rendered visible".

The inevitable failure to communicate fully causes distrust in linguistic revelation and accounts for the Ironic fragmentation of form. In *Sartor Resartus*, the editor's presence crucially enunciates this dilemma. His retailoring gives scope at once to the euphoria of Teufelsdröckh's metaphorically charged pronouncements of a transcendental vision and to the editorial reservations. Enthusiasm is reined in by scepticism. Indeed, the editor's complaints about the biographical material in those six paper bags are like those about the Professor's literary refractoriness generally: "Nothing but innuendoes, figurative crotchets: a typical Shadow, fitfully wavering, prophetico-satiric; no clear logical Picture."[39] For the editor, Teufelsdröckh is guilty, "by omission and by commission", of needless obscurity, an "eye-bewildering *chiaroscuro*"; his *Die Kleider* is chaotic, having an "almost total want of arrangement", a "mad banquet, wherein all courses had been confounded".[40] These objections periodically disrupt presentation of Teufelsdröckh's comments. They discourage belief in a wholly successful statement and encourage the reader to persist. In some measure, they reduce the reader's difficulty with and resistance to those initially disturbing extravagances in the Professor's expression: Teutonic diction, neologisms, and hyperbolic extremes of sentiment and phrasing.[41] The editor's criticisms help dissipate resentment and assist the reader to adopt what Mellor terms a "suspension of disbelief",[42]

---

37. Mellor, 118.

38. See Shelley's *Prometheus Unbound* (IV, 415-17) and Byron's "Prometheus" (ll. 45-47). For Teufelsdröckh's references to Prometheus and Orpheus respectively, see *Sartor*, 179, where the poet "Prometheus-like, can shape new Symbols, and bring new Fire from Heaven to fix it there", and 210, where the "still higher Orpheus, or Orpheuses ... in past centuries, by the divine Music of Wisdom, succeeded in civilizing Man".

39. *The Works of Thomas Carlyle*, I: *Sartor Resartus*, 148.

40. *Ibid.*, 26 and 27.

41. See Jerry Allen Dibble, "Carlyle's 'British Reader' and the Structure of *Sartor Resartus*", *Texas Studies in Literature and Language*, XVI/2 (Summer 1974), 300; Levine, 55-56; and Mellor, 121. All concur on this point.

42. Mellor, 120.

without which the reader might be lost to the text and the text to the reader. The editor's oblique and unorthodox enticement encourages examination of Teufelsdröckh's philosophy through that Schlegelian exercise of "symphilosophy or sympoetry", that "solemn relationship between the author and the reader where the writer is to elicit interest and the reader, to strive toward the artistic creator's revelations".[43]

This "solemn relationship" is further encouraged by Teufeldsdröckh's championing of the imagination, the workings of which produce his "piebald, entangled, hyper-metaphorical style". Such a style is conducive not only to a valid rendering of his complex metaphysics but also to a means of encouraging the reader to try the harder, indirect route to truth, to join in the epistemological exercise, and to realize, as Mellor says, that "there are more things in heaven and earth than are dreamt of in a rationally systematic philosophy".[44] Guiding rather than badgering the reader into insight and belief allows him or her to discover the text's truths with individual clarity, a method that leads Lee Baker to identify Carlyle's role and *Sartor*'s technique as maieutic, as midwife in the birth of understanding. Baker maintains that the continual Ironic play with symbols leads the reader "to a stage of enlightenment whereby he begins to see the Open Secret of the Clothes Philosophy".[45]

If generally through *Sartor Resartus* Carlyle acts as midwife on the authorial level, inside the text the editor performs this task. Attempting to create order from chaos by building bridges, he urges the reader to progress through Teufelsdröckh's confused material, "fished-up from the weltering deep, and down from the simmering air ... and cunningly cemented, while the elements boil beneath".[46] There is double significance in the editor's confession toward the end of *Sartor Resartus* that his attempt to "build a firm Bridge for British travellers" has resulted merely in the construction of "some zigzag series of rafts floating tumultuously".[47] It reaffirms that, in the face of an expansive universe, abundant and dynamic, linear logic is insufficient for both an accurate portrayal and for the symbolic profusions of language. In

---

43. Aphorism no. 112, in *Dialogue on Poetry*, 131-42.

44. Mellor, 120.

45. Lee C.R. Baker, "The Open Secret of *Sartor Resartus*: Carlyle's Method of Converting His Reader", *Studies in Philology*, LXXXIII/2 (Spring 1986), 222.

46. *The Works of Thomas Carlyle*, I: *Sartor Resartus*, 63.

47. *Ibid.*, 62 and 214.

short, logical rhetoric artificially delimits the Infinite and so perverts realistic representation. Further, though, the editor's admission of failure calls on the reader's power to make imaginative leaps, as Baker says, "from the fragmented, raft-like guidance which the Editor has provided him".[48]

The incentive to make imaginative leaps comes, in part, from an awareness of paradox. With paradox comes the inexorable challenge to examine all symbolic creation. In the proverbial blink of an eye, to some extent, all semiotic systems must be consigned to history. They become outmoded and insufficient at shadowing forth the dynamic truth they seek to embody. The maieutic technique triumphs precisely because it encourages the reader to create, de-create, and re-create self-evinced truths. Guided to Ironic understanding, ideally the reader strives for independent and ever-new interpretations. Although, like the author's, these are never *fait accomplis*, in the very act of invention they celebrate the potential for continual rebirth from the ashes of self-immolation. While the editor congratulates those few "labourers", British readers who have "cleared the passage" to the import of the Clothes Philosophy, he quickly reminds them that there is continued and more original deciphering of the hieroglyphs still at hand: "By degrees the eye grows accustomed to its new Whereabout; the hand can stretch itself forth to work there: it is in this grand and indeed highest work of Palingenesia that ye shall labour, each according to ability."[49] Thus the editor would have the reader call on the divinatory power of the self in a ceaseless search for meaning in much the same way Schlegel does at the end of his *Selected Ideas*. He says there that he has saluted the dawn in his own way; now it is up to the reader to do so "in his way, from his point of view".[50]

Critics like Wayne Booth hold that Romantic Irony operates rhetorically. Hence, the editor's role would be that of mere rhetorical tool. But one principal difficulty with this reduction is that it dislocates the apparent aim of *Sartor Resartus*, robbing the text's final statements of their importance. With such reduction, *Teufelsdröckh* becomes the "main Actor"; the Clothes Philosophy, the quintessential Carlylean utterance, a supposition borne out if one views "Natural Supernaturalism" as the culminating chapter. What follows in the searing Swift-like social commentary and in the farewell is seen then as

48. Baker, 227.

49. *The Works of Thomas Carlyle*, I: *Sartor Resartus*, 214.

50. Aphorism no. 155, in *Dialogue on Poetry*, 160.

a lapse from that high philosophical stance, what Janice Haney calls a collapse of the imaginative donnée of the work.[51] Closer to a British Romantic than a German conception of the self, in this chapter, Teufelsdröckh appears a unified character, who, having transcended the comportment of a fluctuating Ironic self, has apparently reached the unshakable position of prophet. In "Natural Supernaturalism", the editor tells us, the "Professor first becomes a Seer".[52] In the outworks of his philosophy here, Teufelsdröckh offers a visionary perception of undifferentiated unity, an absolute eternity, complete and stable. Teufelsdröckh achieves the rapt Transcendental vision of the pure mystic to whom the "interior celestial Holy of Holies [now] lies disclosed".[53] The progress toward this vision has given primacy to ontology. But with this "last leap" into the realm of mysticism, change, flux, and time are seen as belonging exclusively to phenomenological existence, and perception has been stripped clean of its contradictory intrusions. Here, the only half-revealing nature of emblems, the bodily presence of the universe, dissolves as the spiritual presence shines forth. Greater or smaller, all in "this fair Universe ... is in very deed the star-domed City of God; ... through every star, through every grass-blade, and most through every Living Soul, the glory of a present God ... beams". With this "last leap" into mystical vision, perception becomes fixed and the mortal coil evaporates under a present gaze. Teufelsdröckh declares it "mysterious, ... awful to consider that we not only carry each a future Ghost within Him; but are, in very deed, Ghosts!".[54] The Ironist's double vision is left behind; instead, there comes the single vision of complete communication. As Haney remarks, "In seeing all, man also sees nothing".[55] The literary upshot of this mystical vision, Teufelsdröckh's *Palingenesia*, the response to his own call for a new mythus, predicts an imminent epoch of social rebirth. Unity rather than contradiction will rule because of a reincarnated

---

51. Haney, 327. Numbered among those who see these chapters as a collapse are G.B. Tennyson, *Sartor Called Resartus: The Genesis, Structure, and Style of Thomas Carlyle's First Major Work*, Princeton: NJ, 1965, 318 ff. and Albert J. LaValley, *Carlyle and the Idea of the Modern: Studies in Carlyle's Prophetic Literature and Its Relation to Blake, Nietzsche, Marx, and Others*, New Haven: CT, 1968, esp. 103-105.

52. *The Works of Thomas Carlyle*, I: *Sartor Resartus*, 202.

53. *Ibid.*, 203.

54. *Ibid.*, 210-11.

55. Haney, 322.

conviction, a new religion inspiring the communion of all humans, of self and world, of the individual with the Deity. In this conception, clothes are transformed from finite "time figures" into unmediating visible emblems, communicating directly.

But *Sartor Resartus* does not conclude with these reflections; "Natural Supernaturalism" is not the coda of Carlyle's text, as some critics would claim. The work ends with the glories of neither a completed self nor with an indisputable doctrinal conception. For all Teufelsdröckh's assurances of a harmonic future and a hope that pure reason can resolve contradiction, reality remains charged with conflict: the individual "is revealed to his like, and dwells with them in UNION and DIVISION ...".[56] The creation of that prophetic work is deferred; total communication, never realized. Teufelsdröckh's philosophical system is insufficient to banish the circumscribing world of time and space. He must call on the magic of Fortunatus' hat to disperse its illusory presence and can speak only in the subjunctive: "*Were* [emphasis mine] a Hatter to establish himself", transport to "Any*where*" and "Any*when*" would be possible.[57] Absolute insight and complete communication, except in the subjunctive, remain merely a fond wish.

The real challenge to this visionary absolutism is the process of Irony operating in *Sartor Resartus*, a process in which the editor's "yeas" or "nays" are continually heard. The very form of the work, in other words, refutes both the idea that *Sartor Resartus* ends with the mystic's complete message and that the British Romantic epistemology — to appropriate Haney's distinction, *making* rather than *finding* meaning — is tenable. *Sartor*'s form urges interpretation beyond such stability and Carlyle's own distrust of systems and disaffection with mystics like Coleridge, who retreat from the world and into philosophy, are not to be forgotten. The editor's presence underscores these Carlylean attitudes and works as a reminder that mystifications of narrative are to be scrutinized. Up until the last, the editor maintains a critical distance. No dupe like Hofrath Heuschrecke, who mistakes the hieroglyphical for the literal, the editor asks:

> Could it be expected, indeed, that a man so known for impenetrable reticence as Teufelsdröckh, would all at once frankly unlock his private citadel to an English Editor and a German Hofrath; and not rather deceptively *in*lock both Editor

56. *The Works of Thomas Carlyle*, I: *Sartor Resartus*, 51.

57. *Ibid.*, 208.

> and Hofrath in the labyrinthic tortuosities and covered-ways of said citadel ... to see, in his half-devilish way, how the fools would look?[58]

Further, though, the political exigencies present another challenge to the mystic's singular vision, his quietism after long wanderings, and a reading of *Sartor Resartus* as ultimately championing a providential story or a unified self. The political discord of the day, the context of reality, frames the more self-directed scene of aesthetic and metaphysical exploration. *Sartor Resartus* roughly rearticulates Carlyle's "Signs of the Times" imperative that reform begin with the self. But further it suggests that without this initial movement any social expression through action, work, risks being vacant of purpose. These background political insistences tacitly promote this idea while supporting a Romantic Ironic perspective, which casts suspicion over the feasibility of Teufelsdröckh's unconflicting visionary system. The political scene is fraught with "Catholic Emancipations, and Rotten Boroughs, and Revolts of Paris", deafening the French and English ear. The reader is assured that it is a "blessing in these revolutionary times" to have one country

> where abstract Thought can still take shelter ... [where] the German can stand peaceful on his scientific watch-tower; and, to the raging, struggling multitude here and elsewhere ... tell the Universe ... what o'clock it really is.[59]

But Teufelsdröckh's final movements, in keeping with the open-ended nature of Romantic Ironic texts, belie these earlier assertions. He descends from the tower from which he has only surveyed human activity and removes to England to join the political fray. So he begins his "*public* [emphasis mine] History", thus disputing the idea that sheltering thought is a "blessing". In short, the evolutionary impetus and contradictory complexities here argue against the stasis and single-line clarity of Teufelsdröckh's own philosophy.

In the light of Carlyle's demand for the retailoring of symbols to suit each generation, Teufelsdröckh's epistemology appears egregiously outmoded. While perceptions of the Infinite *ideally* recognize unity, immutability, and completion, these are to be held in the mind only as absolutes. Consciously or not, Carlyle seems, however, to have shared

---

58. *Ibid.*, 161.

59. *Ibid.*, 3.

Schlegel's conviction that "absolute perfection exists only in death".[60] Thus the metaphysics of *becoming* has a working validity, since, in the imperfect strainings of the human mind to conceptualize the Infinite, any understanding of its truths must constantly change. Any *vital* apprehension bears the marks of motion and development. Ultimately, the implications of "Natural Supernaturalism" retain the prerogative of only a lifeless ideal.

Further, the real is the province of human existence and so can not be ignored. The promise of absolute identity — what Teufelsdröckh holds out in that apparently resolving chapter — is specious and fatal to a continued search for meaning. The editor brings the counterbalance of a vitalizing force. Interjections prevent the reductivism of linear logic. They challenge the perfection of the Professor's visions, thereby reviving consciousness of the contradictions and multiplicity of life itself. And the editor's own failed effort to order the chaos of Teufelsdröckh's material reveals the limitations of both language and imposed systems. Boon rather than bane, this necessitates striving, the vital voyaging in the activity of renewed perception. Just as the rumblings of revolution challenge order and codification on a political level, so the editor's presence does on an aesthetic and metaphysical one.

Despite mapping disparate paths, the editor and Teufelsdröckh are in final agreement about work. It is rooted in the real and endorses the tenets of *becoming*, since it demonstrates process, what animates all creation. It precludes notions about closure, since genuine involvement in it dictates that humans declare "to Cant, Begone ... and to Truth [*immer wird, nie ist*], Be thou in place of all to me ...". Its physical grounding confirms the importance of the real and so contravenes the dissolving of the material in Teufelsdröckh's visionary insight. However limited the opportunity for absolute reckoning, the potential for help in the real is not: "Infinite is the help man can yield to man." The thoroughgoing social harmonics of the Professor's prophecy may never be realized, but certainly in the real a united effort in work brings a productive communion: "ten men, united in Love ... [are] capable of being and doing what ten thousand singly would fail in."[61] As it affirms the striving in work, in one sense *Sartor Resartus* explicates the injunction to "Close thy *Byron*; open thy *Goethe*". *This* becomes the aim of the human quest, not the complete communication nor the

---

60. "Dialogue on Poetry", in *Dialogue on Poetry*, 54.

61. *The Works of Thomas Carlyle*, I: *Sartor Resartus*, 234-35.

absolute codified meaning of Teufelsdröckh's proposal. Mellor rightly claims that *Sartor Resartus* "is intended not as a monument of truth but as a goad to action".[62]

In the last three chapters of *Sartor Resartus*, both the type and locus of work are modified, a movement which makes eminently clear the text's transitional quality and its importance as a watershed work. For rather than a lapse from the high philosophy of "Natural Supernaturalism", still with the transcending impulse of Romantic Irony, there is a "last leap" into the realm of social actuality and history as epistemological reference. Interestingly, Gerald Bruns defines the difference between the Romantic and the Victorian writer as lying in the way each sees him- or herself constituted. The Romantic writer, like Wordsworth, develops and identifies meaning through consciousness or nature; the Victorian, by reference to history or social circumstances. These final chapters trace the journey beyond an outmoded British Romantic conception, beyond a problematic German self-conscious Irony to a Victorian strategy for constructing meaning.

Certainly there are other elements that adumbrate this "last leap". Teufelsdröckh's transition from the lone British Romantic figure roaming the earth to a self that "clutches ... on the NOT-ME for wholesomer food"[63] and his altered conviction — away from the belief in the British Romantic precept "*Know thyself*" toward the Victorian "*Know what thou canst work at*" — prefigure those final transformations. But the operation of Romantic Irony as the context for *Sartor Resartus* and its function as a formal maieutic move understanding from one sensibility to another. Its challenge to a visionary British Romanticism and its insistence on a metaphysics and an aesthetic that reflect reality assist the birth of an open rather than a closed perception. Its championing of self-activity allows Carlyle, disaffected with a Romantic self-absorption, to suggest an extension beyond the self, a vaulting of self-consciousness into social consciousness, in whose birth Irony also assists. Developmental progression is to be the hallmark of a social as well as individual culture. If the individual is to become a worldkin, those initial, crucial reforms must carry that individual into participation in a social context and an historical continuum. Carlyle's sense of urgency to respond to the need of the times seems clearly evinced here. Limited though the self's reforming potential may be, it is irresponsible not to recognize an

62. Mellor, 133.

63. *The Works of Thomas Carlyle*, I: *Sartor Resartus*, 136.

obligation to others and the exponential benefit in united striving.

Finally, the physical realities of the text belie those apparent evidences of the editor's concession to the Professor's thinking, of the triumph of Teufelsdröckh's visionary philosophy. In "Farewell" the editor speaks of his lesser mind's being sucked into the whirlpool of Teufelsdröckh's greater.[64] But the Professor descends from the reclusive world of the mystic's tower, not unlike those hermetically sealed retreats in British Romantic poetry. His final Swiftian comments have to do with class division, social actuality, as he warns of the possibility of imminent class war. Taking up the challenge of a politically insurgent time, he moves toward London and the editor and thereby concedes symbolically to the editor's sense of the pragmatic and the real. Vaulting attention to the metaphysical and aesthetic, the Professor concentrates on the scene of reality and so embarks on a new journey for meaning. This scene provides substance for the forms of proposition, a grounding that is vital if action, work, is to be significant.

I would not argue that, in these last stages, Carlyle repudiates a Romantic Ironic consciousness. The actualities of *Sartor*'s revolutionary scene carry those conflicts central to the Ironist's appreciation of contradictory reality. Both London's and Teufelsdröckh's unfinished history bespeak the evolutionary recognition vital to Ironic thinking. Teufelsdröckh's final utterance "*Es geht an* (It is beginning)"[65] is remarkably like the inconclusive conclusion of Schlegel's own last living word, "but", that opened the way for new meaning. Rather, I would maintain that Irony not only assists the birth of a new sensibility but is one legacy critical in its formation. Janice Haney observes that Victorian texts "tend to present history and society as a dynamic interplay of opposing forces: ... Hebraism and Hellenism, feudalism and democracy",[66] and that "earlier categories of meaning" figure here. At a moment fraught with the contradictions of conflict, Carlyle could find a means through Irony of achieving a harmony of opposites, a kind of compromise that does not seek to eliminate extremes through the paling gesture of synthesis but rather works to accommodate their most radical possibilities. Such a method alone, I would maintain, could catch the transitional spirit of the age, could allow Carlyle to write a

64. *Ibid.*, 234.

65. *Ibid.*, 236.

66. Haney, 332.

text tracing the passage from a British Romantic to a Victorian period, poised, as that work is, on the cusp.

THE MULTIPLE HISTORIES OF THOMAS CARLYLE

ANN RIGNEY

In 1818, Jules Garinet published a history of beliefs relating to sorcery and diabolic possession, entitled *Histoire de la magie en France, depuis le commencement de la monarchie jusqu'à nos jours*.[1] In keeping with more traditional histories of France, Garinet divided up his material according to the different reigns of successive monarchs and not according to distinctive phases in the history of thinking about magic. The underlying assumption would seem to be that all history marches to the same tune, that ideas of witchcraft follow the rhythm dictated by politics, and that they must therefore enter a new phase whenever a new king comes to power. Garinet's innovative willingness to explore the history of magic is thus firmly anchored in a belief in the underlying unity of History.

By now, almost two centuries later, there is much less certainty among theorists of history about the tenability of such a belief. Historical research and writing remains premised on the objectivity of past events, by which I mean their existence beyond the imagination of those writing about them. And to the extent that historical research and writing supposes the objectivity of events, it also supposes the commensurability of all truthful accounts of those events. This means, on the one hand, that two accounts of the past cannot both be taken as even provisionally true if they contradict each other and, on the other hand, that accounts of different aspects of the past belong together as parts of some over-arching History-with-a-capital-H.[2] But while History can thus be described in theory as singular and unified, there has been a growing awareness of the difficulties in practice of knowing that History

1. Jules Garinet, *Histoire de la magie en France, depuis le commencement de la monarchie jusqu'à nos jours*, Paris, 1818.

2. See further on this point, Joyce Appleby, Lynn Hunt, and Margaret Jacob, *Telling the Truth about History*, New York, 1994, 259.

completely and subsequently representing it in the form of some single narrative.

In the short-term of practice, there is no singular "History", but only histories of different subjects, which may or may not be synthesized into some more all-encompassing point of view at a later date. Thus Paul Veyne, among others, has argued that there are as many histories to be written as there are new subjects which historians can come up with, and the same phenomena may be pertinent to many different histories. As Veyne puts it, the field of events is a limitless network through which we can track out any number of itineraries depending on our focus of interest — a theoretical point which reflects the historiographical practice of the last decades, characterized as it has been by a far-reaching extension of historical inquiry into domains of experience which had traditionally been ignored by historians. In face of the *de facto* multiplication of histories, historians are being forced to come to terms with the fact that they are "Beyond the Great Story", to invoke the title of a recent book.[3] The attempts to come to terms in theory and in practice with the condition of being "Beyond the Great Story" is often referred to as historiographical postmodernism. But the problem itself is not new, as I shall be arguing here.[4]

A concomitant of the notion that there are many histories to be written even within roughly the same chronological parameters is the notion that historical phenomena may not always develop at the same pace. Fernand Braudel's tripartite division of historical time (the quick, the slow, and the almost immobile, corresponding to the level of particular events and the experiences of individuals, economics, and environment) gives expression to this layeredness of History.[5] Indeed, the idea that History is multi-tracked, and that the various tracks follow different rhythms, can also be illustrated by the case of literary history. The organization of literary and cultural phenomena into periods has sometimes supposed a convergence between artistic and political developments ("Victorianism", for example), but has just as often

---

3. Robert Berkhofer, *Beyond the Great Story: History as Text and Discourse*, Cambridge: Mass., 1995.

4. On the fragmentation of the historical discipline, see Peter Novick, *That Noble Dream: The "Objectivity Question" and the American Historical Profession*, Cambridge, 1988; see also the discussion of the way in which the increase in the number of group histories has led to a loss of confidence in the possibility of writing a unified national history in *Telling the Truth*, 158-59.

5. Fernand Braudel, *Écrits sur l'histoire*, Paris, 1969, 11-38.

deviated from them ("Modernism", for example).[6]

Given the huge number of histories which might be written about the past, biography has often seemed to offer some sort of solid ground, a fixed itinerary through the field of events: your subject is clearly identified, you know when it begins (birth) and when it ends (death). Not surprisingly, then, biographies in one form or another have traditionally been the backbone of historical writing, including literary history with its man-and-work paradigm. Even when the historians in question were supposed to be dealing with some generalized, collective phenomenon, they often produced what were in effect "serial biographies". The perennial appeal of the biographical model as a focus for historical writing and research is also reflected in the current revival of interest in biography among historians who previously concentrated on slowly-moving societal structures (Jacques Le Goff's recent work on the life of Saint Louis is a case in point).[7]

The belief in a special relationship between history and biography is often associated with the name of Carlyle. Indeed, judging by Fritz Stern's classic *Varieties of History: From Voltaire to the Present*, which presents extracts from Carlyle's writings under the title "Biography and History", this is Carlyle's principal legacy, along with the associated

---

6. "Periods" are conceptual constructs, colligatory fictions allowing us to see similarities between different phenomena, and not clear-cut divisions inherent in events. For this reason, the beginnings and ends of periods are usually fuzzy, as is the degree of overlap between one sort of period and another. On this point, see Robert C. Stalnaker, "Events, Periods, and Institutions in Historians' Language", *History and Theory*, VI (1967), 159-79; Daniel Milo, *Trahir le temps (histoire)*, Paris, 1991; and, with specific reference to literary history, David Perkins, *Is Literary History Possible?*, Baltimore: MD, 1992, esp. 139-43.

7. Jacques Le Goff, *Saint Louis*, Paris, 1996. On the contemporary interest in biography, see the same author's "After *Annales*: The Life as History", *Times Literary Supplement*, 4489 (14-20 April 1989), 394-405; Giovanni Levi, "Les usages de la biographie", *Annales*, 44 (1989), 1325-36; Jacques Revel, "L'histoire au ras le sol", in Giovanni Levi, *Le pouvoir au village: Histoire d'un exorciste dans le Piémont du XIIe siècle*, Paris, 1989, i-xxxiii. On the metaphorical uses of biography in the writing of collective history, see Ann Rigney, "Muddying the Waters: Metaphor in History", in *Metaphor and Rational Discourse*, eds Bernhard Debatin, Timothy R. Jackson, and Daniel Steuer, Tübingen, 1997, 169-77. The topicality of biography is reflected among other things in the fact that it was one of the themes selected for particular attention at the 17th International Congress of Historical Sciences, Madrid 1992.

idea of the importance of the heroic in historical study.[8] His "history is the essence of innumerable biographies", is a bit of a cliché, the equivalent of a catch phrase "play-it-again, Sam" among historians. However, those who invoke this phrase often do so out of context and as an indication of naïvety or of an ever-incipient Hero-worship. They tend to forget that Carlyle did more than simply point out the centrality of biography to historical understanding. His argument was also that "History" (the unitary History-with-a-capital-H to which I referred earlier) had to be *distilled* from *innumerable* biographies. And not only were the biographies innumerable, but not one of them had a ready-made structure or coherence:

> Social Life is the aggregate of all the individual men's Lives who constitute society; History is the essence of innumerable Biographies. But if one Biography, nay, our own Biography, study and recapitulate it as we may, remains in so many points unintelligible to us; how much more must these million, the very facts of which, to say nothing of the purport of them, we know not, and cannot know![9]

Birth and death may be relatively clear-cut, but the coherence of what lies in between is anything but obvious. In this way, Carlyle himself provides a warning against treating his own life or *œuvre* as a monolithic entity, held together by some single principle by which he can be consigned definitively to one literary period or another.

In what follows, I want to take this Carlylean principle to heart. So instead of dealing with his *œuvre* as a whole, I shall consider just one aspect of it: his work as historian and theorist of history. In focusing on this aspect of his life, I shall consider its place within the history of historical writing, a history where Victorianism, for example, is not an immediately relevant category.[10]

---

8. *The Varieties of History: From Voltaire to the Present*, ed. Fritz Stern, Cleveland: OH, 1956.

9. "On History", in *The Works of Thomas Carlyle*, ed. H.D. Traill, Centenary Edition, 30 vols, London, 1896-99, XXVII: *Critical and Miscellaneous Essays*, II, 86.

10. My account of Carlyle's work below is a reduced version of an argument which I have developed at much greater length in "'The Untenanted Places of the Past': Thomas Carlyle and the Varieties of Historical Ignorance", *History and Theory*, XXXV (1996), 338-57.

In his 1830 essay "On History", Carlyle asked rhetorically:

> Which was the greatest innovator, which was the more important personage in man's history, he who first led armies over the Alps, and gained the victories of Cannae and Thrasymene; or the nameless boor who first hammered out for himself an iron spade? When the oak-tree is felled, the whole forest echoes with it; but a hundred acorns are planted silently by some unnoticed breeze. Battles and war-tumults, which for the time din every ear, and with joy or terror intoxicate every heart, pass away like tavern-brawls; and ... are remembered by accident, not by desert. Laws themselves, political Constitutions, are not our Life, but only the house wherein our Life is led: nay, they are but the bare walls of the house; all whose essential furniture, the inventions and traditions, and daily habits that regulate and support our existence, are the work not of Dracos and Hampdens, but of Phoenician mariners, of Italian masons and Saxon metallurgists, of philosophers, alchymists, prophets, and all the long-forgotten train of artists and artisans ....[11]

This preference for "the long-forgotten train of artists and artisans" above the military heroes of history places the Carlyle of the early essays alongside someone like Garinet as part of an Enlightenment attempt to extend the domain of the historian from "battles and tumults" to the domain of culture — a project which had been initiated by Montesquieu and Voltaire, and pursued in various ways in eighteenth-century antiquarianism.[12] Thus Carlyle concluded his essay by advocating the exploration of all conceivable domains of human experience and praising the work of a number of eighteenth-century scholars who had shown that all types of themes were possible, from the history of law, chivalry, and monastic life, to technological inventions (Beckmann's *Beyträge zur Geschichte der Erfindungen* [1786-1805] and Goguet's *De l'origine des lois* [1758] came in for particular praise as an indication of all the exciting things to come). Historians

11. *The Works of Thomas Carlyle*, XXVII: *Critical and Miscellaneous Essays*, II, 86.

12. On the extension of historiographical activity in the latter half of the eighteenth century, see Thomas Preston Peardon, *The Transition in English Historical Writing 1760-1830*, New York, 1930. For an account of the antiquarian branch of this new history, see Stuart Piggott's *William Stukely: An Eighteenth-Century Antiquary*, revised edition, London, 1985; also Susan Stewart, *On Longing: Narratives of the Miniature, the Gigantic, the Souvenir, the Collection*, Baltimore: MD, 1984.

must pass through the field of events in all different directions, Carlyle argued, his enthusiasm for histories-in-the-plural only tempered by a passing apprehension that with all this diversity, the hope of a unitary Philosophy of History might be lost altogether:

> Praying only that increased division of labour do not here, as elsewhere, aggravate our already strong Mechanical tendencies, so that in the manual dexterity for parts we lose all command over the whole, and the hope of any Philosophy of History be farther off than ever ....[13]

While Carlyle's concern with extending the work of the historian into the cultural domain was a continuation of an Enlightenment project, it also involved a radicalization and modification of that project. This places Carlyle in the company of other Romantic historians who shared a common awareness of the alterity of the past and an historicist interest in examining the past for its own sake. This historicism was absent, for example, from Garinet's history of magic which described the long-awaited disappearance of superstition and, with an Enlightenment confidence in universal reason, made little or no attempt to understand such superstitions from the inside out.

Carlyle's historicism can be illustrated by reference to his article on "Biography" (1832) where he comments, in the course of his discussion of the biographical dimension to history, on a very brief reference made by Clarendon in his *History of the Great Rebellion* to the king's encounter with a "nameless peasant":

> This, then, was a genuine flesh-and-blood Rustic of the year 1651; he did actually swallow bread and buttermilk (not having ale and bacon), and do field-labour: with these hobnailed "shoes" has sprawled through mud-roads in winter, and, jocund or not, driven his team a-field in summer .... How comes it, that he alone of all the British rustics who tilled and lived along with him, on whom the blessed sun on that same "fifth day of September" was shining, should have chanced to rise on us; that this poor pair of clouted Shoes, out of the million million hides that have been tanned, and cut, and worn, should still subsist, and hang visibly together? We see him but for a moment; for one moment, the blanket of the Night is rent asunder, so that we

13. *The Works of Thomas Carlyle*, XXVII: *Critical and Miscellaneous Essays*, II, 95.

> behold and see, and then closes over him —— forever.[14]

To begin with, this passage illustrates the importance Carlyle attached to visualization as a means to historical understanding: "We see him but for a moment; for one moment the blanket of the Night is rent asunder, so that we behold and see ...." Elsewhere in the same essay, Carlyle made this link between seeing and knowing explicit, arguing that the past to which a historical writer refers must be both *real* and *really seen*. In support of this case, he follows up his discussion of Clarendon with a comparable incident from James Boswell's famous biography of Dr Johnson in which the learned man is briefly accosted by a prostitute in the street; then the "wretched one, seen but for the twinkling of an eye, passes on into the utter Darkness".[15] This brief *seeing* is enough to grant her a place in history. Through the invocation of such scenes focused on concrete details, Carlyle invites the reader to picture the past in such a way as to be momentarily transported back into it — his focus on the peasant's hobnail boot is typical of this strategy. In the use of such a highly visual style, Carlyle was following a contemporary trend initiated by Walter Scott. The French historian Prosper de Barante, for example, had declared his intention in 1824 to reconstruct the past in such a way that the reader could get "that intimate knowledge which comes from *see*ing and *hear*ing living beings".[16] This tradition of representing the past so vividly that it might become accessible to the senses extends down to the "touchy-feely" museums of recent decades with their offers of a direct experience of life in times gone by. Underlying all such attempts to "sensualize" the past is a populistic belief that history should be made interesting for the public at large (this was of particular importance for historians writing in the wake of the French Revolution), and that historical knowledge involves a sort of personal encounter with the past in its otherness. The interest shown by Carlyle and his contemporaries in techniques of representation which would allow the distance between past and present to be bridged can be seen both as a reflection of the importance they attached to such

---

14. "Biography", in *The Works of Thomas Carlyle*, XXVIII: *Critical and Miscellaneous Essays*, III, 55.

15. *Ibid.*, 56.

16. Prosper de Barante, *Histoire des Ducs de Bourgogne de la maison de Valois 1364-1477* [1824], 2 vols, Brussels, 1838, I, 10: "cette connaissance intime de ce qu'on a vu vivre, de ce qu'on a entendu parler." Emphasis and translation mine.

encounters and of their awareness of the difficulties involved in orchestrating them.

Carlyle's evocation of Clarendon's "nameless peasant" not only illustrates the importance he attached to sensory details as a way of bridging the gap between past and present, it also exemplifies his thematic priorities. In focusing on the background to the battle, rather than the battle itself, Carlyle gave expression to the belief that hitherto marginalized phenomena relating to everyday experience were the most important part of history and not merely a supplement to traditional histories, focused on political and military events and involving members of the élite (as we've seen above, Carlyle dismissed these as mere "tavern brawls"). The value Carlyle attached to recuperating whatever had been marginalized in existing representations of the past and the negative definition he thus gave to his task is also something he shared with other historians of the Romantic period. Thus Macaulay, in his 1828 essay on "History" and in his *History of England* (1848), declared his intention to focus on the "noiseless revolutions" of everyday life, which had been sanctioned by no treaties and recorded in no archives.[17] Thus Michelet urged historians to "make the silences of history speak"; while Augustin Thierry vowed to emphasize those parts of history about which earlier historians had been silent. It is a tradition of defining your own task by what others have failed to do which *mutatis mutandis* extends down to those present-day historians who continue to announce the importance and the novelty of going beyond élitist, "treaties and battle histories".[18]

Going on many of the ideas expressed in his earlier theoretical writings (which also played themselves through into his later historical works), Carlyle's historiography had much in common with that of his contemporaries. Even these earlier essays, however, include elements

---

17. Thomas Babington Macaulay, "History" (1828), in *Complete Works*, 12 vols, London, 1906, I, 304 and 307); Jules Michelet, *Journal: Texte intégral*, ed. Paul Viallaneix and Claude Digeon, 4 vols, Paris, 1959-76, I, 378; Augustin Thierry, quoted in Rulon N. Smithson, *Augustin Thierry: Social and Political Consciousness in the Evolution of a Historical Method*, Geneva, 1973, 293.

18. Most recently perhaps, Jacques Rancière's *Les Noms de l'histoire*, Paris, 1992, offers a renewed call for attention to be paid to the "nameless" in history. For a more extensive discussion of the points raised here, see my "De stiltes van de geschiedenis: De grenzen van de historische kennis als romantisch erfdeel", in *Romantiek and historische cultuur*, eds Jo Tollebeek, Frank Ankersmit, Wessel Krul, Groningen, 1996, 129-46.

which later become more foregrounded in his work, and which ultimately meant that his work fell out of the mainstream of the history of historical writing. I mean specifically, the sheer extent to which he insists on the *difficulties* of writing history. For what is most striking about Carlyle's work, and what distinguishes it both in the short and the long term from contemporaries like Michelet and Thierry, is the way he *dwells* on the inevitable limits of historical knowledge and historical understanding. Karl Kroeber's description of Romantic historicism as "founded upon the impossibility of any definitive, that is, rationally unchanging, representation of historical phenomena" seems above all applicable to Carlyle.[19]

If his famous statement on the importance of biography is scrutinized from this perspective, then the emphasis on unknowability becomes striking: "But if one Biography ... remains in so many points unintelligible to us, how much more must these million, the very facts of which ... we know not, and cannot know!" Or to recall another example: Carlyle's eulogy on the nameless inventor of the spade turns into a series of reflections on the radical disjunction between the importance of certain events and their subsequent knowableness. It would seem that, for Carlyle, the more worthy an event is of being known, the more difficult it is to know it:

> Well may we say that of our History the more important part is lost without recovery; and, — as thanksgivings were once wont to be offered "for unrecognised mercies", — look with reverence into the dark untenanted places of the Past, where, in formless oblivion, our chief benefactors, with all their sedulous endeavours, but not with the fruit of these, lie entombed.[20]

Seen in the light of this repeated concern with unknowability and unintelligibility, Carlyle's presentation of the nameless peasant and his hobnail shoes as something only briefly glimpsed before "the blanket of the night" closes over it "forever" becomes symptomatic not just of his awareness of the otherness of the past, but of his sense of its *radical* alterity. The revelatory detail of the boots lifts "the blanket of the Night" just long enough for us to become aware of our ignorance

---

19. Karl Kroeber, "Romantic Historicism: The Temporal Sublime", in *Images of Romanticism: Verbal and Visual Affinities*, eds Karl Kroeber and William Walling, New Haven, 1978, 161.

20. "On History", in *The Works of Thomas Carlyle*, XXVII: *Critical and Miscellaneous Essays*, II, 87.

regarding the past. As it is described here, the brief encounter with the nameless peasant stimulates us to imagine the innumerable other peasants ("the million million") about whom we know absolutely nothing — except perhaps that they probably wore shoes. Like Milton's Satan, the anecdote serves to make the surrounding darkness visible; to indicate the existence of a vast historical residue about which we are ignorant.

This sort of emphasis on the vast domains of the unknowable is the principal source, I would argue, of the aesthetic power of Carlyle's writing (witness, for example, some extraordinary scenes in *Past and Present* where we are given fragmentary glimpses of daily life in the monastery). Precisely because the past is vast, unintelligible, and real (and Carlyle insists on these qualities), it both attracts and terrifies. As Burke had written in his analysis of the sublime, the imagination is most strongly affected by those objects which are but fleetingly glimpsed and of which we have only a very "obscure and imperfect Idea".[21]

It may produce great aesthetic effect. But Carlyle's emphasis on the unknowability and unintelligibility of the past is scarcely a recipe for historiographical progress. If the most important part of the past is simply unrecoverable, it becomes hard to keep up the struggle for long. Carlyle's near contemporary Jules Michelet also wrote of the unrecoverability of parts of the past, but saw this as a restricted phenomenon and a product of social injustice, rather than something inherent to the whole enterprise. Besides, he never seemed to doubt his own Orphic powers to cross back into the land of the dead and to sort through the mess.[22] Not so Carlyle. As commentators like Trela and Rosenberg have argued, "making sense" of the past became more and more a burden for Carlyle.

Like the angry customer who complained that the food was bad and the portions too small, Carlyle complained of a lack of historical information (the most interesting part of history was never recorded)

21. Edmund Burke, *A Philosophical Enquiry into the Origin of our Ideas of the Sublime and the Beautiful* (1757), ed. Adam Philipps, Oxford, 1990, 55.

22. In the opening sections of his history of the French Revolution, for example, Michelet invoked the example of the Albigensians to illustrate the principle that barbarous acts often involve destroying all evidence relating to the violence committed; and that, as a result, past injustice may be perpetuated in the fact that the victims' story can never be fully told: *Histoire de la Révolution Française* (1847-53), ed. G. Walter, 2 vols, Paris, 1952, I, 35. On Michelet's self-representation as Prometheus and Orpheus, see his *Journal*, I, 378; *Oeuvres complètes*, ed. Paul Viallaneix, Paris, 1971-, V, 27.

and, at the same time, of an excess of information (how do you find the purport of all the information available and how do you write it all down?). Thus his edition of Cromwell's letters begins with a lurid description of the "shoreless Chaos"[23] of the archival material available to him. In the persona of Anti-Dryasdust, he laments the excess of what he considers insignificant information in the as yet largely unorganized archive. How was he to reconstruct the mind-set of a former age given the mental and temporal distance separating him from the Puritans?

> Confusion piled on confusion to your utmost horizon's edge: obscure, in lurid twilight as of the shadow of Death; trackless, without index, without finger-post, or mark of any human foregoer; — where your human footstep, if you are still human, echoes bodeful through the gaunt solitude .... There, all vanquished, overwhelmed under such waste lumber-mountains, the wreck and dead ashes of some six unbelieving generations, does the Age of Cromwell and his Puritans lie hidden from us.[24]

Carlyle's horror here at the mountains upon mountains of mouldy documents is based more on his idea of the archive than on his actual experiences there (though by all accounts, his picture of mouldy documents was not all that far off the mark).[25] On this score, Carlyle remained an old-fashioned man of letters who disliked working in libraries and used an assistant and printed sources wherever he could (in his *Past and Present*, for example, he made extensive, and very innovative, use of the Camden Society's publications of medieval source texts). Given the fact that he worked mainly from printed sources, however, his wonderstruck declaration that he was perhaps the first person in more than two centuries to read certain speeches of Cromwell is more indicative of his historical imagination rather than of his actual

23. *The Works of Thomas Carlyle*, VI-IX: *Oliver Cromwell's Letters and Speeches; With Elucidations*, I, 3.

24. *Ibid.*, I, 2.

25. For a contemporary account of the state of the archive, see Nicholas Harris Nicolas, *Observations on the State of Historical Literature and on the Society of Antiquaries, and other Institutions for its Advancement in England*, London, 1830. On the attempts made in this period to make research materials available, see Philippa Levine, *The Amateur and the Professional: Antiquarians, Historians and Archaeologists in Victorian England, 1838-1886*, Cambridge, 1986, 101-34.

labours in the field.[26]

Underlying this horror at the amount of work involved in sifting through the records was a fundamentally ironic view of history — ironic in Schlegel's sense of a clear awareness of chaos (his "klares Bewußtsein der ewigen Agilität, des unendlichen, vollen Chaos").[27] If a lack of information is a constant reminder of our own ignorance, an increase in the amount of information brings with it the difficulties of imposing a coherent shape on the past. The more detail you have, the more the contours of the particular subject you are dealing with may be obscured. For information does not lend itself automatically to narration since, as Carlyle had put it in "On History", narrative is one-dimensional and linear, whereas action is "solid".[28] A narrative can only be, as he described his "story" of the French Revolution, a "faint ineffectual Emblem of that grand Miraculous Tissue, and Living Tapestry ... which did weave itself then in very fact".[29]

In order to make an intelligible history, then, the historian has to impose order on his "amorphous" subject (one of the adjectives he repeatedly used to describe Cromwell).[30] Indeed, one might argue that Carlyle's later interest in "Great Men" came, among other things, from his search for some principle whereby he could order what he saw as the inherent *disorder* of history and so overcome the irony of knowing too much (if the "great man" imposes order at the political level, in

26. On Carlyle's research methods, see especially D.J. Trela, *A History of Carlyle's "Oliver Cromwell's Letters and Speeches"*, Lampeter, 1992, 178-79. See also G.P. Gooch's comment that when Carlyle began his historiographical career, "the study of the archives had not begun, and it never occurred to him that he ought to begin it": G.P. Gooch, *History and Historians in the Nineteenth Century* (1913), rev., with a new Introduction, London, 1952, 303. Carlyle's dislike of archival spadework should not blind us to the extent to which he did actually try to gather as much information as possible from printed sources, particularly in *The French Revolution* (1837) and the *History of Friedrich II of Prussia called Frederick the Great* (1858-65); nor should it be forgotten that he was also interested in non-textual evidence, making a point of visiting the relevant battle fields while working on his history of Frederick: see Fred Kaplan, *Thomas Carlyle: A Biography*, Cambridge, 1983, 416-19.

27. On Carlyle's irony, see also Hayden White, *Metahistory: The Historical Imagination in Nineteenth-Century Europe*, Baltimore: MD., 1973, 148-49.

28. *The Works of Thomas Carlyle*, XXVII: *Critical and Miscellaneous Essays*, II, 89.

29. *The Works of Thomas Carlyle*, II-IV: *The French Revolution*, II, 185.

30. See Trela, 14.

other words, he may also provide the historian with some sort of ordering principle at the epistemological level). As Carlyle wrote in 1841, hero-worship is "the living rock amid all rushings-down whatsoever; — the one fixed point in modern revolutionary history, otherwise as if bottomless and shoreless".[31]

But as if to confirm the truth of his earlier statements on the difficulties of writing biography, Carlyle's work exemplified the principle that it is easier to imagine writing the history of a great man than to write such a biography in practice. The practical and intellectual difficulties involved in making "a life" intelligible are reflected among other things in the many changes of plan which occurred in Carlyle's treatment of Cromwell (as well as in the protracted writing of the monstrously long biography of Frederick the Great, described by Gooch as too long for the writer and too long for the reader[32]). As Trela has shown in his detailed account of the genesis of *Cromwell*, Carlyle took a long time and many revisions before deciding what form was most suited to his material (at one point groaning in a letter that his thoughts lay around him "inarticulate, sour, fermenting, bottomless ... of use to no one"[33]), a complaint which was to be reiterated in more or less the same terms throughout the writing of his life of Frederick.

These "inarticulate, sour, fermenting" thoughts from 1845 can be seen as the outcome of his optimistic essays of fifteen years earlier when he drew attention to the exciting and as-yet-to-be-explored underworld of history. It was in this sour fermentation that Carlyle himself ended up as a historian. Things might have gone differently. If Carlyle, for example, had been willing to do the spadework in getting the archives organized, if he had been ready to plough through original documents, if he'd been ready to pool resources with others, above all, if he'd believed there was a shape to history which could be uncovered through dedicated research, if he had trusted in the possibility — however much in the long term — of an intelligible Universal history.

But then he would have been a member of the budding historical profession and not Carlyle: the man-of-letters and social commentator

31. *The Works of Thomas Carlyle*, V: *On Heroes, Hero-Worship, and the Heroic in History*, 15.

32. On the laborious and protracted writing of the biography of Frederick, see John D. Rosenberg, *Carlyle and the Burden of History*, Oxford, 1985, 159-63. A work of some 4,000 pages, Gooch described it as "too long for its readers, as it was too long for its author": *History and Historians*, 309.

33. Quoted in Trela, 18.

with such an urgent need to address contemporary problems and impose intellectual order on what seemed to be chaos. As Philippa Levine has written, however, Carlyle effectively wrote himself out of the history of historical writing[34] and it was ultimately as a "prophet" and not among the historians that he was immortalized in the national portrait gallery. But if Carlyle literally wrote himself out of the history of historical writing in the short term, he is now being written back in. The sheer extent to which he emphasized the marginal, the unknowable, and the unintelligible in history, and indeed the extent to which he thereby invested historical representations with sublimity, has meant that there has been a growing interest in the postmodernist implications of his work or, to put this slightly differently, in the place of Romantic historicism in the pre-history of postmodernism.

The fact that it is thus possible to reconsider Carlyle in the light of our current preoccupations with the limits of historical knowledge illustrates what is arguably one of the distinctive features of cultural history as distinct from political history. Where political and economic events are once-off affairs, it is in the nature of some cultural events to persist at later periods in time in the form of texts. As part of a cultural legacy defining our relationship to the past, they may be re-read in new contexts and thus remain open to re-interpretation as part of a different history.

---

34. Levine, 3.

CARLYLE'S CELTIC CONGREGATION: REVIVING THE IRISH HERO

GERALDINE HIGGINS

> *Before all else, the Phase of the Hero, of the man who overcomes himself, and so no longer needs the submission of others or conviction of others to prove his victory.*[1]

For W.B. Yeats and his contemporaries in the Irish Literary Revival, the concept of heroism is absolutely central. In the context of Ireland at the turn of the century, the heroic ideal provided a metaphor of political hope. The fall and death in 1890 of Parnell, Ireland's "uncrowned king", meant not so much a political vacuum as a scramble to find a suitable successor in both the political and cultural realms. Searching assiduously in both we find W.B. Yeats and his friends Standish O'Grady, George Russell (AE), Lady Gregory and Edward Martyn. Heroism as an ideology proved to be irresistibly attractive to those members of a declining class, the Anglo-Irish Ascendancy.[2] Hence, Seamus Deane asserts, "The literature of the Irish Revival is in essence an heroic literature; or more precisely perhaps, it is a literature which draws heavily on the idea that the revival of heroism is a necessary and practicable ambition in Irish circumstances".[3]

In examining aspects of heroic Irish literature, the brooding presence of Carlyle becomes manifest in a surprising way. Yeats rarely

---

1. W.B. Yeats, *A Vision*, London, 1962, 127.

2. Anthony Malcomson states, "The Anglo-Irish Ascendancy could be defined as comprising those who sat in the Irish Parliament or who exercised significant influence over the return of the 300 members of the House of Commons", in *John Foster: The Politics of the Anglo-Irish Ascendancy*, Belfast and Oxford, 1978, xvii-xix.

3. Seamus Deane, *Celtic Revivals: Essays in Modern Irish Literature, 1880-1980*, London, 1985, 63.

mentioned Carlyle except to disparage his prose style. Nonetheless, Carlyle's works appeared on the shelves of Lady Gregory, Edward Martyn, George Moore and John O'Leary and he was an acknowledged influence on the Pre-Raphaelites and the French Symbolists. Moreover, the principle conduit of the heroic message to Ireland, Standish O'Grady, named by Yeats "father of the Irish Literary Revival", was Carlyle's most fervent Irish disciple. I intend to show that Carlyle's ideas on heroes and hero-worship are observable in Ireland through O'Grady and, by outlining these ideas, to indicate the shape of the Revival's heroic aesthetic, particularly as it appears in the work of W.B. Yeats.[4]

Carlyle's prophetic thunderings on the theme of heroes and hero-worship may seem to belong to the Old Testament of English history, a Calvinist version of the new gospel preached by Nietzsche at the century's end. That it is Carlyle rather than Nietzsche to whom this paper now turns is due to the striking parallels between his heroic aesthetic and that of Standish O'Grady, an influence often overlooked in the clamouring to find the *Übermensch* lurking in Yeats's prose. Yeats did not read Nietzsche until 1902, and, from that date onward, the influence of *The Birth of Tragedy* and Thomas Common's anthology of Nietzsche's writings has been amply illustrated. By 1902, however, Yeats had already imbibed many of Carlyle's ideas about heroism through the writings of O'Grady.

It is now a critical commonplace to view Carlyle as the voice of his Age, borne out by Froude's analysis of his paternal and pedagogical role:

> Amidst the controversies, the arguments, the doubts, the crowding uncertainties of forty years ago, Carlyle's voice was to the young generation of Englishmen like the sound of "five hundred trumpets" in their ears ....[5]

In fact, the trumpets sounded just as emphatically in the Anglo-Irish ears of Standish O'Grady who was the first to apply Carlyle's ideas on the heroic principle to his own work. O'Grady was a Classics scholar

---

4. I am indebted to John Kelly's "The Fifth Bell: Race and Class in Yeats's Political Thought", in *Irish Writers and Politics*, eds Okifumi Komesu and Masaru Sekine, Gerrard's Cross, 1990, 109-75.

5. James Anthony Froude, *Thomas Carlyle: A History of His Life in London* (1884), 2 Vols, new imp., London, 1919, I, 313. W.B. Yeats also referred to Carlyle in *Autobiographies* as "the chief inspirer of self-educated men in the 'eighties and early 'nineties" (214).

from Cork whose *Early Bardic Literature* (1878) and *History of Ireland* (1880) excavated Ireland's heroic past into the vivid prose of his Romantic imagination. The earliest expressions of the heroic in Yeats are borrowed from the "Turin shroud" of Irish History — O'Grady's *History of Ireland: The Heroic Period*. It was this "History" which, according to Yeats, "started us all",[6] and he later described it as one of the best sources on "the most imaginative of all our periods ... the heroic age".[7]

O'Grady was an avid reader of Carlyle, shared his deeply religious background and inherited his fear of revolution and hatred of the Mechanical Age. In fact, in the notes for his unpublished autobiography, O'Grady claims that the seminal influences on his life and work were his father's "devotion to the prophetical and apocalyptic scriptures on which he loved to enlarge" and "Carlyle's notion that the Bible of any nation must be its history".[8] Most importantly, the social contract which is upheld in all of Carlyle's writings — the need for a strong heroic leader and the desire of the masses to be led by him — is embraced by O'Grady as the rationale for upholding the Irish landlord class.

Walter Houghton has ably demonstrated how the mid-Victorians, "at once destitute of faith and terrified at scepticism",[9] compensated for the terror of unbelief by an uncompromising dogmatism and intellectual earnestness of which Carlyle is the chief exponent. The Puritan temper demanded a seriousness of purpose which had as its goal truth, morality and a stable society, recreating God's kingdom on earth.[10] Carlyle is the historian of an age of uncertainty which he hopes will be the harbinger of an age of heroism. He is the antagonist of Liberalism and

---

6. W.B. Yeats, ed., *Samhain*, Dublin, October 1902, 12. See also *Autobiographies*: "O'Grady was the first, and we had read him in our teens" (221).

7. W.B. Yeats, *Letters to the New Island*, Oxford, 1934, rpt. 1970, 107.

8. Standish O'Grady, unpublished MS., P.S. O'Hegarty Collection, Kenneth Spencer Research Library, University of Kansas. Quoted in Peter Kuch, *A Critical Edition of AE's Writings on Literature and Art*, unpublished MS.D.Phil c.7236, Oxford, 1988, 130. See also George Russell, "A Tribute to Standish O'Grady", *ibid.*, 131-39.

9. For the source of this phrase, see "Sir Walter Scott", in *The Works of Thomas Carlyle*, ed. H.D. Traill, Centenary Edition, 30 vols, London, 1896-99, XXIX: *Critical and Miscellaneous Essays*, IV, 49.

10. Walter Houghton, *The Victorian Frame of Mind 1830-1870*, London and New Haven, 1957, 97.

Democracy because neither force will enthrone the greatest man, but will usher in the age when, in Arnold's words, "littleness united is become invincible".[11] In Carlyle we see the problem of the balance of power between the few and the many writ large. He is the true forerunner of Yeats in his anti-rational rejection of the Industrial Age and the compensatory belief in a society of heroes and hero-worshippers which marries mythology with fledgling racial theories.

Moreover, in his search for a replacement for the religion of his youth, Carlyle prefigures Yeats in his rejection of the rationalist thinkers who had deprived him of faith and certainty.[12] Instead, he finds in German idealism the salvation offered to Yeats by Celticism and occultism and in Goethe, a literary father figure to depose the Calvinist James Carlyle. Yet, while Carlyle seizes upon the Imagination as the new power which shapes the world, he retains a dark despair which lurks, doubting, beneath his most fervent exhortations. He attributes this doubt to the change from a time when "action ... was easy, was voluntary, for the divine worth of human things lay acknowledged" to his own age where "doubt storms-in ... through every avenue; inquiries of the deepest painfulest sort must be engaged with".[13] Carlyle sees the hero as the transmitter of cultural certainties which are not mechanistic but moral, and can only be released through decisive and conscious action. Like O'Grady, his writings have a feverish edge attempting to transmit his own sense of crisis to an indifferent audience which appears to him passive, when only action will save the day:

> Intellect is not speaking and logicising; it is seeing and ascertaining. Virtue, *Vir-tus*, manhood, *hero*-hood ... it is first of all, what the Germans well name it, *Tugend*, Courage and the faculty to *do*.[14]

---

11. Matthew Arnold, "Empedocles on Etna", Act II, ll. 90-94.

12. See W.B. Yeats, *Autobiographies*: "I am very religious, and deprived by Huxley and Tyndall, whom I detested, of the simple-minded religion of my childhood, I had made a new religion, almost an infallible Church of poetic tradition, of a fardel of stories, and of personages, and of emotions, inseparable from their first expression, passed on from generation to generation by poets and painters with some help from philosophers and theologians" (115-16).

13. "Characteristics", in *The Works of Thomas Carlyle*, XXVIII: *Critical and Miscellaneous Essays*, III, 30.

14. *The Works of Thomas Carlyle*, V: *On Heroes, Hero-Worship, and the Heroic in History*, 218.

Carlyle remains bound to the idea of social contract between the hero and his society — his greatness is defined through actions in history, whether the revelation of divine truth, the destruction of false demagogues or the promotion of social progress. Like O'Grady, Carlyle believed that examples of heroic action could establish an ideal of natural courage and that a history of great deeds would be an antidote to the despair which stalked his contemporaries and himself. The questions which exercised Carlyle, Arnold, Ruskin and Morris are in response to an Age of Progress which saw the end of feudalism, the beginning of urbanization and demands for the democratization of society. It is interesting to note that similar economic and social trends are observable in Ireland fifty years later, and that in Standish O'Grady, these anxieties are revoiced in an Anglo-Irish timbre.

Desired history

In his recovery of the Irish heroic legends and rehabilitation of those legends for the English-speaking palate, O'Grady informed the style, attitude and audience of the Irish Revival. His own discovery of Celtic mythology is significantly described as a conversion experience familiar in mission-hall rhetoric. With the deceptively offhand title, "A Wet Day", O'Grady leads the reader through his tale of discovery — a secluded house in the West of Ireland where the young O'Grady finds the first History of Ireland into which he has ever looked. This discovery, he claims "has since then governed the general trend of my life, and through me that of others".[15] O'Grady's metaphor of conversion highlights his pose as an evangelical preacher of the doctrine of heroism. His most significant bequest to the Revival is the assertion that:

> A nation's history is made for it by circumstances, and the irresistible progress of events; but their legends they make for themselves. The legends represent the imagination of the country; they are that kind of history which a nation desires to possess.[16]

This legendary loophole is of vital importance to the imagination of the Revival writers. It offers an escape route from the historical

15. Standish O'Grady, "A Wet Day" in the Introduction to *Selected Essays and Passages*, ed. Ernest Boyd, Dublin, n.d., 3.

16. Standish O'Grady, *History of Ireland: The Heroic Period*, Dublin, 1878, I, 22.

determinism which had dogged Carlyle into a realm of collective wish-fulfilment where Ireland's heroic hour is at hand. Indeed, if the history of Ireland could be reinvented to include the perceptions of the imagination as well as the prescriptions of fact, then the story of the nation would have a very different outline.

Yeats shows his willingness to cast himself as "prophet and guardian" in the vatic function of disseminating heroic values: "The arts are, I believe, about to take upon their shoulders the burdens that have fallen from the shoulders of priests."[17] This burden was at first informed by missionary zeal as Yeats led a crusade against encroaching modernism and materialism replicating Carlyle's journey from Calvinism to German Romanticism. Bearing Celtic legend as "a new intoxication for the imagination of the world", he preaches to his audience with all the fervour of the convert. Yeats's priesthood of the imagination finds its genesis in Romantic thought but is then driven by a desire to generate a specifically Irish sect of that ancient religion. Yeats learned from O'Grady to value the past created and contained in legends as a country's "desired history", ultimately more important than actual events, something set apart from "the cracked tune that Chronos sings".

In Carlyle's *On Heroes and Hero-Worship*, the identification of epochs with Great Men is the apotheosis of an historical tradition which is teleological and élitist. The nineteenth-century view of history which Carlyle had come to reject invoked the principle of progression from barbarism to civilization, the fixed nature of historical truths and the value of cause and effect analysis. Carlyle dismisses this objective, scientific school of thought as "dryasdust" historians who dig up "mountains of dead ashes, wreck and burnt bones ... and name it History ... till the Past Time seems all one infinite incredible grey void, without sun, stars, hearth-fires, or candle-light".[18] Carlyle's answer is to overthrow Utilitarian history. He intends to re-mystify history, to read it as an inscrutable "Book of Nature" rather than a "Merchant's Ledger". The German Romantic emphasis on the experience of the individual legitimizes his concentration on biography[19] as the key to

17. W.B. Yeats, "The Autumn of the Body", in *Essays and Introductions*, London, 1961, 193.

18. *The Works of Thomas Carlyle*, X: *Past and Present*, 47.

19. See *The Works of Thomas Carlyle*, I: *Sartor Resartus*: "Man is properly the *only* object that interests 'man' .... Biography is by nature the most universally profitable, universally pleasant of all things: especially Biography of distinguished individuals" (60).

historical processes as does his conception of the lectures as sermons on the "inspired (speaking and acting) texts" of Great Men. For Carlyle himself, this philosophy of history is Calvinism without God, and there is a religious sense of mission attached to his words echoed in the evangelical voice of O'Grady.

Aristotle's definition of history as "what was" and poetry as "what ought to be" grants a solidity and permanence to the former and releases the latter into the higher realm of philosophy. With Carlyle and O'Grady, the undercurrent of the poetic "ought to be" is directed as a moral counterpart to the unfolding of historical events in a way which allows "desired history" to intrude into the actual. Like Carlyle, O'Grady interacts with the Past in the spirit of a participator rather than an exegete — in rejecting the Utilitarian practice of concentrating on History's educational role, they each open up the imaginative possibilities of empathetic historicism.

Carlyle cites his historical ideal as "stern accuracy in inquiring, bold Imagination in expounding and filling-up; these are the two pinions on which History soars".[20] O'Grady's flights of fancy in his *Early Bardic Literature* and *History of Ireland: The Heroic Period* are a resurrection of the heroic spirit employing the "bold imagination in expounding and filling-up" at the expense of the "stern accuracy in inquiring" recommended by Carlyle. According to O'Grady, the historian must re-vivify his material and send his heroes abroad in a living imagination:

> I desire to make this heroic period once again a portion of the imagination of the country, and its chief characters as familiar in the minds of our people as they once were. As mere history, and treated in the method in which history is generally written at the present day, a work dealing with the early Irish kings and heroes would certainly not secure an audience.[21]

O'Grady's consciousness of the need to create the audience he intends to address informs his style, tone and "mixed-metaphor" method of combining history and myth. Not only will O'Grady instinctively home in on the "essential" elements of the legends, he will also address a

---

20. "On History", in *The Works of Thomas Carlyle*, XXVII: *Critical and Miscellaneous Essays*, II, 80. Carlyle introduces the idea that History is a palimpsest, a "real prophetic manuscript" which can never be fully deciphered since the "weightiest causes may be most silent" (*ibid.*, 88-90).

21. Standish O'Grady, *Early Bardic Literature*, Dublin, 1878, 17.

readership which he expects to share exactly his own interest in the material. That interest was in fact slow to ignite — O'Grady's Histories were published in the 1870s and 1880s but effectively lay dormant until the 1890s when the desire for an alternative heroic history was at its height. It was only after the fall of Parnell that O'Grady was lauded for his recovery of heroic literature in the galvanizing mood of the new century. His readership was almost entirely composed of those Anglo-Irish Protestants who, like himself, had bathed in the waters of Celticism and converted to its tenets with religious zeal. His treatment of myth, like that of Yeats, grows from a belief in legend as a national "collective unconscious" which could be tapped at will by the writer of vision to forge a cultural unity which had eluded the political sphere.

The heroic tradition in which Yeats places himself and on which he calls, relies upon "a new religion"[22] authenticating his role as bard. Yeats sees the bards as occupying an influential cultural space adjacent to political centres of power and from O'Grady he learns that:

> The bards were not the people, but a class. They were not so much a class as an organization and fraternity acknowledging the authority of one elected chief. They were not loose wanderers, but a power in the State, having duties and privileges.[23]

Yeats's readiness to adopt the bardic role and his acceptance of O'Grady's desired history is not merely a matter of anti-realist preference but a belief that personal interaction with the bardic past can generate a heroic myth which is archetypal rather than arbitrary. Here too, he owes an unacknowledged debt to Carlyle.

O'Grady saw his task as the archaeological recovery of heroic legends followed by the political dissemination of their feudal message. He, like Yeats, attempts to bypass the emerging and powerful middle classes by a version of the "dream of the noble and the beggar-man" which has as its central tenet Carlyle's division of society into heroes and hero-worshippers: "the modern Irishman, in spite of all his political rodomontade, does very deeply respect rank and birth."[24] O'Grady's politics never gravitated far from the Tory nook which had nourished him and which had fed the deep nationalist suspicion of his aims and

22. *Autobiographies*, 115-16 (for the full quotation, see n.12 above).

23. *Early Bardic Literature*, 50.

24. Standish O'Grady, *Toryism and the Tory Democracy*, Dublin, 1886, 271-72.

early writings. He intends to furnish Ireland with an alternative history of vigorous heroes who will be archetypes for the race that is to come.

The chosen race: heroic bloodlines

The guiding premises of *On Heroes and Hero-Worship* — the inequality of man and the natural emergence of superior leadership — typify the Victorian shift from Christianity to heterodoxy and the intellectual valorization of race and cultural continuity as compensation. The lectures deal with the two central aspects of Carlyle's secular religion, defining the essence of the hero as the saviour of English society and outlining the function of hero-worship as a stabilizing social force.

In the first instance, Carlyle uses a series of heroic specialists as variations on the theme of heroic sincerity. While his earlier essay "On History" had argued that "social life is the aggregate of all the individual men's lives who constitute society",[25] these lectures are strictly hierarchical, reflecting Carlyle's need for a secular religion and a church of heroes. He then delivers his sermons on the text that reverence is good for public order and spiritual well-being, demonstrating how hero-worship will save society from the threat of democratic anarchy:

> The confused wreck of things crumbling and even crashing and tumbling all round us in these revolutionary ages, will get down so far; *no* farther. It is an eternal corner-stone, from which they can begin to build themselves up again. That man ... worships Heroes; that we all of us reverence and must ever reverence Great Men: this is to me, the living rock amid all rushings-down whatsoever; — the one fixed point in modern revolutionary history, otherwise as if bottomless and shoreless.[26]

As O'Grady will turn to the Celts for his heroic prototypes, Carlyle finds a Teutonic parallel in Scandinavian legend, seeking there the robustness and simplicity so lacking in his own hero-less age. Both he and O'Grady claim a biological line of descent from these legendary figures to their chosen vessels in the present day — "Is it not as the half-dumb stifled voice of the long-buried generations of our Fathers, calling out of the depths of ages to us, in whose veins their blood still

---

25. *The Works of Thomas Carlyle*, XXVII: *Critical and Miscellaneous Essays*, II, 86.

26. *The Works of Thomas Carlyle*, V: *On Heroes, Hero-Worship, and the Heroic in History*, 15.

runs."[27] Carlyle is seeking not only what he calls a "consecration of valour" but also racial justification for the supremacy of heroic individuals. The question raised is whether the exceptional individual interacts with or imposes upon historical processes and furthermore, whether his heroic greatness is a genetic quality transmittable to another era.

Certainty, however dogmatic, was the order of the day, and the evolutionary theories of Darwin and Spencer were seized upon to provide pseudo-scientific backing for the necessity of a master/servant society. When Tennyson eulogized Hallam as "a closer link/Betwixt us and the crowning race",[28] he fused the Romantic belief in the progress of the species with these new evolutionary theories. For Carlyle, the idea of progress was tainted by its association with the political and economic policies of Benthamism, but he did subscribe to the belief that the race could attain a higher rung on the evolutionary ladder: "The wisdom, the heroic worth of our forefathers, which we have lost, we can recover ... man may again be all that he has been, and more than he has been."[29]

Carlyle anticipates natural selection in his belief in the biological inequality of man, yet he insists that the final purpose of evolution is a rational world obeying moral law. Starting from the same Romantic premise as Tennyson, that the hero is more God than man, different in kind, not just degree, Carlyle finds both scientific and religious validation for heroes and hero-worship. In effect, fledgling evolutionary theories meet Puritanism in these lectures to produce a campaign on behalf of a secular elect controlling and guiding the subservient many.

Similarly, O'Grady's mythological histories can be read as an attempt to distill a racial essence from the legends of the past as the justification for a self-perpetuating Irish aristocracy or "rule of the best". He claims that the best work of the bards "is probably hidden in the blood and brain of the race to this day"[30] and that "it is the same sky that bent over them, which shines or darkens over us. The same human heart beat in their breasts as beats amongst us today. All the great permanent

---

27. *Ibid.*, 30.

28. Alfred Lord Tennyson, *In Memoriam*, ll. 127-28 (cited in Walter Houghton, *The Victorian Frame of Mind*, 36-37).

29. "Signs of the Times", in *Works*, XXVII: *Critical and Miscellaneous Essays*, II, 81.

30. *Selected Essays and Passages*, 46-47.

relations of life are the same."[31]

This insistence on the continuity of the heroic past with the present day would become the chief inspiration of the Revival writers. Racial continuities and blood ties were to obsess Yeats throughout his life but in the 1880s, it is the fathering of a race of Celtic titans in verse which motivates him. Indeed as George Russell (AE), claimed:

> When I read O'Grady I was as such a man who suddenly feels ancient memories rushing at him, and knows he was born in a royal house. It was the memory of race which rose up within me as I read, and I felt exalted as one who learns he is among the children of kings.[32]

The Celtic race in which AE exalts had been rediscovered in the 1850s by Ernest Renan, whose ideas had been popularized by Matthew Arnold in his 1865 Oxford lectures, "On the Study of Celtic Literature". Arnold's recovery of the Celt for ideological purposes has been well documented and cited,[33] but it is worth tracing the "ethnic nationalism" of the Revival to Arnold's insistence on the racial distinctiveness of the Celt. Indeed, Arnold's backhanded compliment to the Celts institutionalizes the terminology of opposition or difference — the rational Saxon versus the irrational Celt, materialism versus spirituality and masculinity versus femininity. Renan had also noted the purity of the Celtic race, free "from all admixture of alien blood", but he believes himself to be recording the last notes of a primitive society before it disappears, whereas Arnold intends to use "the Celtic element" as a vaccination against the English middle classes.

Nonetheless, Arnold's reading of the Celtic race as "essentially feminine", the perfect partner to its masterful and masculine Teutonic neighbour, is overthrown in O'Grady's work. Those critics of the Revival who accepted D.P. Moran's accusation that the Celts were "secretly content to be a conquered race", that their masculinity was

---

31. *History of Ireland: The Heroic Period*, I, xii.

32. George Russell, "Standish O'Grady", in *Imaginations and Reveries*, Dublin and London, 1921, 13.

33. See John Kelleher, "Matthew Arnold and the Celtic Revival", in *Perspectives in Criticism*, ed. Harry Levin, Cambridge: Mass, 1950, 197-221. For contemporary elaborations on Kelleher's argument, see Seamus Deane, *Celtic Revivals*, London, 1985, 17-27; Terence Brown, *Ireland's Literature: Selected Essays*, Mullingar and Totowa: NJ, 1988, 3-21; David Cairns and Shaun Richards, *Writing Ireland*, Manchester, 1988, 43-51.

merely a "delirious burst of defiance on a background of sluggishness and despair",[34] overlooked the driving desire for a heroism which was decisive, masculine and painted with bold strokes. In O'Grady, it found its Old Master. As AE pointed out, he had "found the Gaelic tradition like a neglected antique dun with the doors barred ... he opened the doors and the wild riders went forth to work their will".[35]

It is this emphasis on the robust, pagan and dynamic aspects of the antiquarian recoveries that appealed to O'Grady's Anglo-Irish disciples. While Arnold's menu of natural magic, emotion and melancholy is certainly visible in Yeats's work in the 1890s, the stress is rather on that aspect of Celticism identified by Renan — messianism:

> Thence that dogma of the resurrection of the heroes, which appears to have been one of those that Christianity found most difficulty in rooting out .... The hand that rose from the mere, when the sword of Arthur fell therein, that seized it and brandished it thrice, is the hope of the Celtic races. It is thus that little peoples dowered with imagination revenge themselves on their conquerors.[36]

Where Carlyle invokes Odin as "no adjective, but a real Hero of flesh and blood! ... the Type Norseman; the finest Teuton whom that race had yet produced",[37] O'Grady rediscovers Cuchulain as the archetypal heroic Celt. Irish, mythic, and brandishing a torch of leadership to Ireland's lost aristocracy, Cuchulain provides O'Grady with the ultimate archetype and icon.

O'Grady wrote of the heroic age, "everywhere it was the custom that the weak should accept the protection of the strong and themselves

---

34. D.P. Moran, *The Philosophy of Irish Ireland*, Dublin, 1905, 6.

35. George Russell, "The Dramatic Treatment of Heroic Literature", in *The All Ireland Review*, III/35 (November 1902), 576. O'Grady later attempted to bar the door after the horses had bolted, berating Yeats and George Moore for raiding Irish mythology for dramatic material and urging them not to bring the heroic legends down to the crowd.

36. Ernest Renan, "The Poetry of the Celtic Races" (1859, trans., 1896), in *Poetry and Ireland since 1800: A Source Book*, ed. Mark Storey, London, 1988, 59.

37. *The Works of Thomas Carlyle*, V: *On Heroes, Hero-Worship, and the Heroic in History*, 24-28.

to their command".[38] His stories of the boy-deeds of Cuchulain are the Irish equivalent of Victorian tales of the Empire, salutary and inspiring in equal measure, and in Cuchulain the Irish boy finds his native hero.[39] The Red Branch are reinvented as the Irish "Knights of the Round Table" who live by a chivalric code of nobility, bravery and honour. O'Grady's Cuchulain is a symbol of strong leadership — it is he who will galvanize the weakened generations of Ireland into an awareness of their heroic masculinity, that quality which O'Grady, despite Arnold, identified with Ireland. Each of O'Grady's successors would call upon Cuchulain in his various guises, shaping the hero according to the dictates of factional political and cultural needs.[40]

Throughout O'Grady's "Cuchulain" novels, the society which emerges is unshakably two-tiered, imbued with Carlyle's sense that the rulers and the ruled are biologically distinct. His description of the schooling of the young heroes at Emain Macha in *The Coming of Cuchulain* shows Conchubar instilling these values:

> ... well aware of all the instructors and all the instructed, and who was doing well and exhibiting heroic traits and who was doing ill, tending downwards to the vast and slavish multitude whose office it was to labour and to serve and in no respect to bear rule, which is forever the office of the multitude in whose souls no god has kindled the divine fire by which the lamp of the sun and the glory and prosperity of nations are sustained and fed.[41]

---

38. Standish O'Grady, *The Coming of Cuchulain: A Romance of the Heroic Age in Ireland*, London, 1894, 41.

39. See John Wilson Foster, *Fictions of the Irish Literary Revival*, Syracuse and Dublin, 1987, 32-44.

40. John Wilson Foster describes Cuchulain as "a man for all seasons", a culture hero of Ulster who defends the province against the men of Ireland and the anti-colonial hero of nationalist interpretation who represents Ireland standing alone against the might of the imperial army (see "The Revival of Saga and Heroic Romance during the Irish Renaissance: The Ideology of Cultural Nationalism", in *Studies in Anglo-Irish Literature*, ed. Heinz Kosok, Bonn, 1982, 126-27). The battle for Cuchulain as mythic symbol is today played out in the murals of East and West Belfast. Once an icon of nationalist ideology, Cuchulain has now been summoned as a hero of Ulster, defending its separatist identity against the combined armies of all-Ireland, and as such, he enjoys new life as a symbol of Protestant heroism.

41. *The Coming of Cuchulain*, 43.

O'Grady learns from Carlyle that the heroic model can be transmitted to the modern age and so claims that the Irish race unknowingly carries Cuchulain's genes. With Carlyle, the salvation of society rests on the premise that "Great men" will inspire (or coerce) a reciprocal hero-worship in the remaining community. Believing this, O'Grady realizes that Ireland, blessed with extreme poverty and a feudal land system, could be saved from the evils of modernization and lead the world in inaugurating an age of heroism.

Hero-worship: submission burning and boundless

If we now turn to the political implications of Carlylean hero-worship, O'Grady again appears to have turned Carlyle's heroic imperative into an applied science. In an Irish *milieu* which he saw as anti-materialist, non-rational and semi-feudal, aristocracy came to embody an ideal of leadership analogous to Carlyle's heroism. O'Grady also sought to impose it as a pragmatic manifesto.

Hero-worship is ostensibly the applied side of the "Great Man" theory since it is presented as a principle of social reorganization. As Carlyle states, "Surely of all 'rights of man', this right of the ignorant man to be guided by the wiser, to be gently or forcibly held in the true course by him, is the indisputablest".[42] There is a direct correlation between the momentum of Carlyle's outpourings on the erosion of hierarchical structures in society and the nineteenth-century fear of the British Revolution which never happened. He calls loyalty and worship the "corner-stone of these Revolutionary times" because hero-worship represents for him a fixed point from which society can rebuild its vertical order. Matthew Arnold's fear of anarchy led to his search for "standards of perfection that are real",[43] setting the authority of culture against the anarchy of individualism. As we have seen, Carlyle's temperament demanded nothing less than a kingly messiah and a philosophy of heroism which Froude describes as "a creed which I could then accept as really true .... Then and always I looked, and have looked, to him as my master."[44] For Carlyle, the only way forward is to turn Jacobins into disciples, democracy into autocracy.

His tone becomes increasingly doctrinaire and authoritarian in *Past and Present* in preparation for the vitriolic outbursts of the *Latter Day*

---

42. "Chartism", in *The Works of Thomas Carlyle*, XXIX: *Critical and Miscellaneous Essays*, IV, 157.

43. Matthew Arnold, *Culture and Anarchy*, London, 1869, 51.

44. *Thomas Carlyle: A History of His Life in London*, I, 316.

Pamphlets. He adopts a Swiftian disgust for the populace and concentrates on the tyrannical possibilities of democratic government. Indeed, it is the dread of democracy which draws Carlyle to Abbot Samson in *Past and Present*, extolling the virtues of English feudalism, and it is here too that Carlyle and O'Grady finally converge. Carlyle champions the old "noble devout-hearted Chevalier" against the "new ignoble Godless Bucanier", pitching chivalry against the Captains of Industry in a battle which he refuses to see as already lost. O'Grady too advocates a return to feudal society in an Ireland peopled by good-hearted landlords and loyal tenants who, in the 1880s belonged as much to the pages of mythology as his beloved Cuchulain. They each turn to feudalism as a social salve or antidote to the invidious effects of modernism and mechanism.

O'Grady's doctrinaire sermons to the Anglo-Irish aristocracy are prefigured in Carlyle's admonishments to those parasitic noblemen who are guilty of an "impotent, insolent Donothingism in practice and Saynothingism in Speech".[45] He insists that they are obliged to "furnish guidance and governance to England" and offers a dire prophecy if his words are ignored: "A thinking eye discerns ghastly images of ruin, too ghastly for words; ... A High Class without duties to do is like a tree planted on precipices; from the roots of which all the earth has been crumbling."[46] If this is compared to O'Grady's 1882 essay, *The Crisis in Ireland*, the imagery and impulse are seen to be identical. O'Grady graphically depicts the landlord class as a rock uprooted by the storm of Irish Democracy:

> The stone is the landed aristocracy of Ireland, once firm-rooted on the crest of the hill; the rain and lashing wind are the unrecognized, unadmitted growth of the Irish Democracy ... gradually permeating millions of minds, steadily sapping and wearing away all that which once kept Irish landlordism firm in its high place.[47]

Here, O'Grady is the unabashed spokesman for and haranguer of the landlord class, those "hard-riding country gentlemen" who were soon merely to decorate the clubs they used to frequent. O'Grady, writing in 1886, to the dissolute and disintegrating group of Anglo-Irish

45. *The Works of Thomas Carlyle*, X: *Past and Present*, 150.

46. *Ibid.*, 178-79.

47. Standish O'Grady, *The Crisis in Ireland*, Dublin, 1882, 5.

landowners, seeks to incarnate a suitably bred landlord hero to save Ireland from the democratic evils so visible on the horizon:

> If you wish to see anarchy and civil war, brutal despotisms alternating with bloody lawlessness, or on the other side, a shabby, sordid Irish Republic, ruled by knavish, corrupt politicians and the ignoble rich, you will travel the way of Egalité.[48]

In using language associated with the French Revolution, he cuts a swathe across the bloody prospect of anarchy, raises the spectre of "a shabby, sordid Irish Republic", and comes to rest on the ominous word "Egalité". His vehemence and emphasis on chivalric codes of honour reflect his desire to infuse the "natural leaders" of Ireland with a sense of their own potential which must be realized if they are not to be wiped out of history. Indeed, in an unpublished letter to John O'Leary, he writes, "an active working, ruling and controlling aristocracy is all I care about".[49] In this sense, O'Grady is not so much the father of the literary revival as its Jeremiah, predicting the inglorious exit of a debased Irish aristocracy if it fails to shoulder the responsibilities of leadership: "If anyone should call me alarmist, I shall be pleased, for I wish to alarm."[50] So too did Carlyle, preaching the same message in England forty years earlier.

Both Carlyle's *Past and Present* (1843) and O'Grady's *Toryism and the Tory Democracy* (1886) attempt to defeat the forces of democracy by forging an alliance between the aristocracy and the peasant class. Carlyle distinguishes between the "idle Aristocracy" and the "working Aristocracy" in his bid to reinstate feudalism in England just as O'Grady will compare careless absenteeism with paternalistic landlordism in Ireland. When these warnings seem to be ignored, both screech doom from their respective pulpits:

> When a world, not yet doomed for death, is rushing down to ever-deeper Baseness and Confusion, it is a dire necessity of Nature's to bring in her ARISTOCRACIES, her BEST, even by

48. *Selected Essays and Passages*, 228.

49. Standish O'Grady, Letter to John O'Leary (dated "September") NLI MS 80001 (quoted in John Kelly, "The Political, Intellectual and Social Background to the Irish Literary Revival to 1901", Unpublished PhD (Cambridge, 1971), 153.

50. *The Crisis in Ireland*, 55.

forcible methods.[51]

O'Grady insists that Ireland's future greatness can only be guaranteed by recreating the heroic values he portrays. He reserves most of his energies for the excoriation of the landlord class who, having ignored his prophecies and warnings, now face extinction: "Your career is like some uncouth epic begun by a true poet, continued by a newspaper man and ended by a buffoon; heroic verse, followed by prose, and closed in a disgusting farce."[52]

His justification of the aristocratic right to rule draws on the caste assumptions of the age and the siege mentality of the threatened Protestant Ascendancy. In the 1880s, haunted by the anarchic Land League and outraged by successive Land Acts, O'Grady again saw the ghost of revolution, one which threatened to steal the aristocratic *raison d'être* — the land itself. Hence the note of desperation in his last words:

> Ireland and her destinies hang upon you, literally so. Either you will refashion her, moulding us anew after some human and heroic pattern, or we plunge downwards into roaring revolutionary anarchies, where no road or path is any longer visible at all. And, dear friend, a word at parting: Make Haste.[53]

The Anglo-Irish landlords did not "Make Haste" and by the end of the 1890s, the possibility of firm-handed rule by a landed aristocracy had greatly receded. His resurrecting call ignored, O'Grady retired in disillusionment to the Isle of Wight, contributing occasional articles to the socialist journals, *The Irish Peasant* and *The New Age*. By 1901, he recognizes that the Anglo-Irish aristocracy "is rotting from the land in the most dismal farce-tragedy of all time, without one brave deed, one brave word".[54] It will be to W.B. Yeats that the bardic task of commemorating the ruined Ascendancy in brave words falls, and is lovingly executed.

At the time of Yeats's writing, O'Grady's audience had been successfully created — Ireland's bardic history was in the hands of an intellectual coterie anxious to assert a national voice which was volubly

51. *The Works of Thomas Carlyle*, X: *Past and Present*, 215.

52. *Toryism and the Tory Democracy*, 239.

53. *Ibid.*, 290.

54. *Selected Essays and Passages*, 180.

non-English and yet not quite native-Irish. The dominant chords of O'Grady's heroic aesthetic resonated throughout the Revival and provided its major themes. Common to all his writings, political, historical and fictional, is the Carlylean belief that strong leadership is the key to an heroic and noble society. He excavates the Gaelic past for evidence that this society is native to Ireland and that the "fecundity and force" of heroic energy still courses through Irish veins. In his desire to provide the Irish landlords with a legitimizing biological precedent for their right to rule, he uses legend and myth as a form of evidence superior to the history of political failure which had produced Arnold's ineffectual dwindling Celt. Such a line of enquiry proved irresistible to the next generation of Anglo-Irish writers seeking to attain hegemony through culture. Carlyle, the high Victorian moralist had proved himself to be a Romantic prophet whose message was heard by an unlikely Celtic congregation.

CARLYLE AND RUSKIN: WORK AND ART

PHILLIP MALLETT

Men and women have always worked, but it was not until the nineteenth century and the full impact of the Industrial Revolution that they demanded a theory of work, or rather a set of theories. Not all of these were new. Thomas Carlyle closed his chapter on "The Everlasting Yea" with an allusion to the Gospel of St John: "Work while it is called Today; for the Night cometh, wherein no man can work." Lockwood Kipling carved the same text on his son's chimney piece; John Ruskin took the word TODAY as his motto (it appears, three times, on the cover of all thirty-nine volumes of the Library Edition). But as R.H. Tawney and Max Weber showed long ago, the belief that work is God's plan for man, that it is a holy duty or calling, and idleness therefore a sin, had provided a meeting ground for the ascetic virtues of Protestant and capitalist societies at least since the sixteenth century.[1] For John Stuart Mill, however, there was a right to work as well as a duty, and this was an emphasis directed explicitly to the new age; in a liberal society, where conduct and conduct alone offered an entitlement to respect, it was a moral imperative to open up to every citizen a route to that respect. The emerging feminist movement of the 1850s based much of its campaign for women's right to work on the conflation of new liberal and traditional Christian arguments: women must have work, wrote Barbara Bodichon, "if they are to stand as dignified rational beings before God".[2] Karl Marx argued that work allowed man to define himself as a "species-being": that is, not like an animal, which seeks merely to maintain its existence and to reproduce itself, but as part of mankind, with the desire and capacity to create even when free from the

---

1. See R.H. Tawney, *Religion and the Rise of Capitalism*, London, 1926. Tawney quotes Max Weber, in Carlylean vein: "Christians should earn their living by the sweat of their brow ... the honest smith or shoemaker is a priest" (92).

2. Barbara Leigh Smith Bodichon, *Women and Work*, New York, 1959, 30. For Mill's arguments, see his essay *On Liberty*, *passim*.

physical need to do so. Because work implies agency, the conscious pursuit of an aim, it becomes in effect the first moral category.[3] Freud too developed a theory of work. In his account, work is important first as an anchor, a technique for binding the individual into a shared reality — "work gives [us] a secure place in a portion of reality, the human community" — and second as a therapy, a means of displacing those libidinal energies, narcissistic, aggressive or erotic, which might otherwise invade and damage our emotional and social lives.[4] And to any number of writers, from William Wordsworth to Morris to Tolstoy, work provided a counter to the prevailing intellectualism of the age, and a means of rooting oneself in the good green earth.

Carlyle has a key place in the development of a theory of work. Anticipations or echoes of all these ideas could readily be found in his writings. He was the first to name "industrialism", and he coined the word "environment"; in "Signs of the Times", an important early essay, he argued that the new industrial world not only environed the nineteenth century worker but entered into his very being: "Men are grown mechanical in head and heart, as well as in hand .... Our true Deity is Mechanism."[5] But Carlyle was not a simple hater of the machine, as William Morris was to be; Richard Arkwright too "will have his monument, a thousand years hence", as much as those who built the pyramids. "All work", he writes in *Past and Present*, "even cotton-spinning, is noble; work is alone noble".[6] Carlyle sees labour as first and foremost a duty; it is "the one unhappiness of a man, that he cannot work; that he cannot get his destiny as a man fulfilled".[7] Work is not a means to an end for Carlyle, but itself the end for which man

---

3. See Karl Marx, *Economic and Philosophic Manuscripts of 1844*, trans. Martin Milligan, London, 1961, 105-109, for this argument.

4. Sigmund Freud, *Civilisation and Its Discontents*, in *The Complete Psychological Works*, London, 1935-71, XXI, 8.

5. "Signs of the Times" (1829), in *The Works of Thomas Carlyle*, ed. H.D. Traill, Centenary Edition, 30 vols, London, 1896-99, XXVII: *Critical and Miscellaneous Essays*, II, 63, 74. Raymond Williams points to the significance of this essay in his *Culture and Society 1780-1950*, Penguin edn, 1963, 85-89.

6. *The Works of Thomas Carlyle*, X: *Past and Present*, 57 and 153. For the response of Carlyle and his contemporaries to the machine, see Herbert Sussman, *Victorians and the Machine: the Literary Response to Technology*, Cambridge: Mass., 1968.

7. *Ibid.*, 156.

was made:[8] "Man is created to fight .... A Battlefield ... is a kind of Quintessence of Labour; Labour distilled into its utmost concentration."[9] Few writers have taken more seriously God's terrible words to Adam and Eve in the third chapter of Genesis: "cursed is the ground for thy sake; in toil shalt thou eat of it all the days of thy life." At times it seems that work is the only destiny Carlyle can imagine for mankind. The end of human life is not pleasure, nor contemplation, but action: "Conviction ... is worthless till it convert itself into Conduct."[10] What matters is not the "Speakable", which is merely "a superficial film, or outer skin", but the "Doable", which "reaches down to the World's centre".[11] Work underwrites our very existence: a man "who cannot work in this Universe cannot get existed in it".[12]

The work a man does provides the only "true verdict" on his worth. It follows that work is not merely a duty, but a means of knowledge, of ourselves and of others: "Our Works are the mirror wherein the spirit first sees its natural lineaments".[13] We create ourselves by bending ourselves to our work: the "blessed glow of Labour" is a "purifying fire" consuming the poison and sour smoke of our hope and sorrow, desire and doubt.[14] In *On Heroes and Hero-Worship*, Carlyle characteristically defines belief not as a mental or moral state but as an act: "Belief I define to be the healthy act of man's mind." We have our minds given us not to debate many things but to see into some one thing, "whereon we are then to proceed to act". Scepticism, hesitation even, are forms of sickness, "a chronic atrophy and disease of the whole soul". Action, the performance of that duty which lies nearest, is both the end and the ground of our being.[15]

8. In "The Negro Question", J.S. Mill complains that Carlyle "revolves in an eternal circle around the idea of work, as if turning up the earth, or driving a shuttle or a quill, were ends in themselves" (see *Fraser's Magazine*, XLI (January 1850), 27).

9. *The Works of Thomas Carlyle*, X: *Past and Present*, 190-91.

10. *The Works of Thomas Carlyle*, I: *Sartor Resartus*, 156.

11. *The Works of Thomas Carlyle*, X: *Past and Present*, 159.

12. *Ibid.*, 173.

13. *The Works of Thomas Carlyle*, I: *Sartor Resartus*, 132.

14. *The Works of Thomas Carlyle*, X: *Past and Present*, 196.

15. "The Hero as Man of Letters", in *The Works of Thomas Carlyle*, V: *On Heroes, Hero-Worship, and the Heroic in History*, 176 (cf. I: *Sartor Resartus*, 156: "Doubt of any sort cannot be removed except by Action").

The imagery of battle, purification, disease, reflects the underlying dualism of Carlyle's writings, embodied in the name of his hero, Herr Diogenes Teufelsdröckh, "God-born Devil's dung".[16] Work is a war against the external and internal forces making for chaos. The clear, steadfast gaze of Abbot Samson into the confused finances of the monastery at St Edmundsbury reproduces the divine *Fiat lux*, which penetrates deep into the darkness, "and of the chaos makes a *kosmos* or ordered world".[17] But it is not only the outer world that needs to be subdued: "In every the wisest Soul lies a whole world of internal Madness, an authentic demon-Empire", on which our wisdom rests precariously, "as on its dark foundations does a habitable flowery Earth-rind".[18] Our lives, that is, are endlessly threatened by volcanic forces from within. Hence "All Works, each in their degree, are a making of Madness sane", whether the madness lies within or without.[19]

The word "endless" is deliberately chosen. In another seminal early essay, "Characteristics", Carlyle insists that the world is infinitely progressive, and there can be no point of rest — which he sees, of course, as a blessing, since without the demand for constant battle man would become "spiritually defunct" and cease to exist.[20] Our reward, like Abbot Samson's, is not "the spoil of victory, only the glorious toil of battle".[21] At the same time, however, the world is purposive; our labour is endless, but it is not in vain. Carlyle often insists on the continuity of history: Teufelsdröckh tells the reader, "Cast forth thy Act, thy Word, into the ever-living, ever-working Universe: it is a seed-grain that cannot die"; in *Past and Present* Carlyle reflects in his own voice on "the quantity of done and forgotten work that lies silent under my feet in this world".[22] Each act lives on into the future, the future is bound by organic filaments to the acts of the past: "every

---

16. This aspect of Carlyle's writing is well described by John D. Rosenberg in *Carlyle and the Burden of History*, Cambridge: Mass., 1985.

17. *The Works of Thomas Carlyle*, X: *Past and Present*, 92.

18. *The Works of Thomas Carlyle*, I: *Sartor Resartus*, 207.

19. *The Works of Thomas Carlyle*, X: *Past and Present*, 206.

20. *The Works of Thomas Carlyle*, XXVIII: *Critical and Miscellaneous Essays*, III, 38.

21. *The Works of Thomas Carlyle*, X: *Past and Present*, 99.

22. *The Works of Thomas Carlyle*, I: *Sartor Resartus*, 31; X: *Past and Present*, 133.

single event is the offspring not of one, but of all other events, prior or contemporaneous."[23] Yet this is not to present history as a seamless continuity. On the contrary, every moment is a moment of crisis, where a choice can and must be made, as by Teufelsdröckh in Rue St Thomas de l'Enfer in Paris or by Carlyle in Leith Walk in Edinburgh. If Evil is, as Carlyle suggests in "Characteristics", the true name for the "dark, disordered material" of the world, man still retains the Freewill "to create an edifice of order and Good".[24] Man can intervene to change the course of history; or heroes can.

But — Carlyle's dualism means there is always a "but" — it is also true that "*all* human work is transitory, small, in itself contemptible; only the worker thereof and the spirit that dwelt in him is significant".[25] An action may be a sham, not present at all as well as eternally present; the Thing may also be a No-Thing. Carlyle swings between two reference points: Time and Space are illusions, our physical bodies — even that of "English Johnson" — are Apparitions, and actions separated by thousands of years flow together into "the Light-sea of celestial wonder"; yet it is "here, in this poor, miserable, despicable, hampered Actual", that we have to act and "Produce! Produce!" — even if only "the pitifullest infinitesimal fraction of a product".[26] In this double awareness, we might perhaps suggest that Carlyle is both Romantic and Victorian: Romantic in his insistence on the transcendent, and his sense of the cosmos, but Victorian in his emphasis on the actual, and his sense of our immersion in history.[27]

If Carlyle seems to touch on many of the theories advanced about work, it is necessary to see what he does not consider. In the chapter on "Helotage" in *Sartor Resartus*, Carlyle addresses the "toilworn craftsmen", whose "god-created Form" was destined to remain "encrusted ... with the thick adhesions and defacements of Labour", and never to come fully into being: "Yet toil on, toil on: *thou* art in thy

23. "On History", in *The Works of Thomas Carlyle*, XXVII: *Critical and Miscellaneous Essays*, II, 88.

24. *The Works of Thomas Carlyle*, XXVIII: *Critical and Miscellaneous Essays*, III, 28.

25. Thomas Carlyle, *Reminiscences*, ed. Charles Eliot Norton, introd. Ian Campbell, Everyman edition, 1972, 3.

26. *The Works of Thomas Carlyle*, I: *Sartor Resartus*, 210 and 157.

27. Cf. Gerald L. Bruns, "The Formal Nature of Victorian Thinking", *PMLA*, 90 (1975), 904-18.

duty, be out of it who may."[28] He makes no distinction, as Marx was to do in the *Economic and Philosophic Manuscripts*, between alienated and non-alienated work, between work freely chosen, and work imposed from without. Since all work is noble, and to work is the sole guarantee of our existence, the freedom to choose when or how to work is unimportant: "true liberty" is "to learn, or be taught", to work — the freedom lies in the work itself, not in the choice of it.[29] Nor has Carlyle much to say about the creative or joyous aspects of work. He does, in "Characteristics", argue that the basis of any "right performance is a certain spontaneity, an unconsciousness", of which the work of the artist provides the highest example;[30] and in *Past and Present* he allows that "He that works, whatsoever be his work, bodies forth the form of Things Unseen; a small poet every worker is".[31] But the more usual imagery of battle against the threat of chaos suggests that Carlyle sees work as a means to repress rather than express human energies. Again in "Characteristics", he acknowledges that "it is in Society that man first feels what he is; first becomes what he can be", and in *Past and Present* his attack on the Cash Nexus, brought to focus in his story of the Irish widow, makes plain his belief that work is important as a means of bringing men and women into a sense of their inter-relatedness.[32] Yet this is rather a welcome side benefit than part of the ethic of work; the duty remains even if we are alone. "Blessed is he who has found his work; let him ask no other blessedness."[33]

When George Eliot reviewed Carlyle in 1855, noting that there had scarcely been a book written in the previous ten or twelve years that he had not influenced, she also contrived subtly to suggest that his time was up. Typically oblique in his reaction to the age, her exact contemporary, John Ruskin, was just coming under Carlyle's spell. What I want to do here is to consider how far Ruskin's own ideas of

28. *The Works of Thomas Carlyle*, I: *Sartor Resartus*, 181.

29. *The Works of Thomas Carlyle*, X: *Past and Present*, 212.

30. *The Works of Thomas Carlyle*, XXVIII: *Critical and Miscellaneous Essays*, III, 7.

31. *The Works of Thomas Carlyle*, X: *Past and Present*, 205.

32. "Characteristics", in *The Works of Thomas Carlyle*, XXVIII: *Critical and Miscellaneous Essays*, III, 10; see X: *Past and Present*, 149, for the story of the Irish widow.

33. *The Works of Thomas Carlyle*, X: *Past and Present*, 197.

work followed, challenged, complicated or, perhaps, capitulated to Carlyle's. The central text is Ruskin's chapter on "The Nature of Gothic", first published in *Stones of Venice II* (1853). It soon acquired its status as a major contribution to ideas about the nature of work. William Morris described it as "one of the very few necessary and inevitable utterances of the nineteenth century"; four hundred copies, with the subtitle "and herein of the True Function of the Workman in Art", were distributed free of charge at the inaugural meeting of the Working Men's College in 1854.[34] Ruskin argues that a chief distinction between Greek and Egyptian architectures on the one hand and Gothic on the other was that the former demanded absolute accuracy from the workman, while the latter invited each to work to his utmost capacity, and even to the point of exceeding his capacity. This distinction becomes the basis of Ruskin's critique of modern society. He challenges his readers to admit that they too are drawn to perfect accuracy, preferring "smooth minuteness" to "shattered majesty", and "mean victory" in the lesser endeavour to "honourable defeat" in the greater. In Ruskin's view, the demand for commodities is a demand for labour; the consumer — the reader — must choose whether to demand goods which can be produced so as to draw out in the worker "some tardy imagination, torpid capacity of emotion, tottering steps of thought", or those the manufacture of which reduces him to a machine: "You must either make a tool of the creature, or a man of him."[35] Ruskin, accordingly, unlike Carlyle, has no sympathy for the machine or machine-produced goods. The division of labour meant the division of men, "broken into small crumbs and fragments of life". Men could endure much, but "to be counted off into a heap of mechanism, numbered with its wheels, and weighed with its hammer strokes" — this was beyond enduring.[36] Work on these terms, contrary to Carlyle's teaching, was not and could not be "noble".

Behind this critique of consumer practice lies an essentially aesthetic argument, derived from Ruskin's notion of Vital Beauty — briefly, the appearance of happy and healthy energy in living things. In *The Seven Lamps of Architecture* he had extended this concept to the study of buildings: the right question to ask of a piece of ornament was, "Was it

34. See *The Works of John Ruskin*, eds E.T. Cook and Alexander Wedderburn, Library Edition, 39 volumes, London, 1903-12, X, lxvii-lxx.

35. *Ibid.*, 191-92.

36. *Ibid.*, 195.

done with enjoyment — was the carver happy while he was about it?".[37] Ornament mattered, according to Ruskin, because it was "the work of poor, clumsy, toiling man ... the record of thoughts, and intents, and trials and heartbreakings".[38] Its very inefficiency, its clumsiness as compared with machine produce, was the sign of its value. But what was true of architectural ornament was true of all work. Ruskin began to read back, as it were, into the product the labour that had gone into producing it. Carlyle had written that "Labour is Life ... the sacred celestial Life-essence breathed into [man] by Almighty God".[39] Ruskin saw that it might be far from that. Related etymologically to "lapse" or "loss", labour is "that quantity of our toil which we die in": "It is the negative quantity, or quantity of de-feat, which has to be counted against every Feat."[40] There is an element of labour in any piece of work; labour always costs. But Ruskin made a distinction between *labor* and *opera*, that is, that happy, creative element in work which we associate with childish play or artistic inspiration. It was the task of society not simply to provide work, but also to see that the work it demanded, through its acts of consumption, enhanced rather than depleted the lives of the workers. The question became, "what kinds of labour are good for men, raising them and making them happy?"[41] Ruskin, unlike Carlyle, was not afraid of the word happy.

The short answer to Ruskin's question is, the kind of work which makes men happy is that which requires thought of them. He goes on to argue that "the workman ought often to be thinking, and the thinker often to be working, and both ought to be gentlemen in the best sense". What that sense is, is a difficult question, since the idea of the gentleman is both social and moral. The gentleman's origins lay in the gentry, historically the rank just below the aristocracy; a gentleman was a man heraldically entitled to bear arms, though not a member of the nobility. But at least as early as the Tudors the term was often extended to special groups (for example, to members of the Inns of Court), and

37. *The Seven Lamps of Architecture*, in *The Works of John Ruskin*, VIII, 218.

38. *Ibid.*, 36.

39. *The Works of Thomas Carlyle*, X: *Past and Present*, 197.

40. *Munera Pulveris*, in *The Works of John Ruskin*, XVII, 183-84. For a useful discussion, see James Clark Sherburne, *John Ruskin, or the Ambiguities of Abundance* Cambridge: Mass., 1972, 280-84.

41. Ruskin, *Works*, X, 196.

even in the fourteenth century the word "gentle" could mean "mild in manner, considerate", as well as "noble, well-born". The notion of the gentleman was thus always open to modification and moralization. In the industrial era gentlemanly status was in theory at least accessible to all, but in practice, if it was to provide a satisfactory standing-ground for the aspiring middle classes, it also had to operate as a system of exclusions — excluding those who too obviously depended on trade or manual labour, and, by and large, those who had not attended the ancient universities. The moral component of the term remained, giving it an occasional critical edge (the aristocrat was not always the truest gentleman); but it was not to be interpreted without any reference to the social order. Ruskin acknowledges the moral component, but his definition is in caste terms: "the essence of a gentleman ... is that he comes from a pure gens, or is perfectly bred ... no man can make himself a gentleman who was not born one."[42] The mongrel can be a good-tempered and serviceable animal, or a vicious one, but no amount of effort can turn it into a greyhound. Ruskin took the notion of race and breeding seriously. He was certain that the new Oxford Museum should be of Gothic design, but doubted if the workmen who could carve good Gothic for it yet existed. The task would be beyond ordinary workers; it would require "men inheriting the instincts of their craft through many generations, rigidly trained ... and then classed, according to their capacities, in ordered companies, in which every man shall know his part, and take it calmly without effort or doubt".[43] This is a long step back from the claim made in "The Nature of Gothic" that the workman should be encouraged up to and beyond his limit, and the imperfection of his work accepted as the record of his humanity. Instead, he is to be limited to tasks within his known capacities, and set to express the result of rigid training carried out over many generations. Ruskin in this instance declines to be his own ideal consumer.

But Ruskin was too intelligent, and too honest, to let the matter of the relations between gentleman and worker rest there. He provides the sharpest look at his own arguments, most notably in the concluding paragraphs of his lecture "Of Kings' Treasuries", in a fierce and difficult passage:

---

42. Letter to Constance Oldham, 1876, in *The Works of John Ruskin*, XXXVII, 197. Ruskin's most extended account is in the chapter "Of Vulgarity" in the fifth volume of *Modern Painters* (*The Works of John Ruskin*, VII, 343-62). For a valuable account of the issues, see Robin Gilmour, *The Idea of the Gentleman*, London, 1981.

43. Letter to Dr Henry Acland, 1858, in *The Works of John Ruskin*, XVI, 224.

> Which of us ... is to do the hard and dirty work for the rest, and for what pay? Who is to do the pleasant and clean work, and for what pay? .... How far is it lawful to suck a portion of the soul out of a great many persons, in order to put the abstracted psychical qualities together and make one very beautiful or ideal soul? .... we live, we gentlemen, on delicatest prey, after the manner of weasels; that is to say, we keep a certain number of clowns digging and ditching, and generally stupefied, that we, being fed gratis, may have all the thinking and feeling to ourselves. Yet there is a great deal to be said for this. A highly-bred and trained English, French, Austrian or Italian gentleman (much more a lady), is a great production, — a better production than most statues; being beautifully coloured as well as shaped, and plus all the brains; a glorious thing to look at, a wonderful thing to talk to; and you cannot have it, any more than a pyramid or a church, but by sacrifice of much contributed life.[44]

Here there is no question of the thinking worker and the working thinker finding a meeting ground in the idea of the gentleman. The task of the workman is not, now, like that of the artist in calling forth the highest imaginative and intellectual powers, but "hard and dirty" work, "digging and ditching", in order to produce fine ladies and gentlemen: not workers becoming gentlemen themselves, but workers sacrificing their lives so that others may be gentlemen. And their reward is that a gentleman, like a cathedral, is "a glorious thing to look at".

In the *Economic and Philosophic Manuscripts of 1844* Marx defines "external labour" as that "in which man alienates himself":

> ... a labour of self-sacrifice, or mortification .... the external character of labour appears in the fact that it is not his own, but someone else's, that it does not belong to him, that in it he belongs, not to himself, but to another .... the worker's activity is not his spontaneous activity. It belongs to another; it is the loss of his self.[45]

Ruskin's definition in "Of Kings' Treasuries" of the relation between gentlemen and workers might be taken as the extremest example of what Marx is trying to describe. No longer cautioned on his role as a consumer of products, challenged to accept only those the production of

---

44. *Sesame and Lilies* (*The Works of John Ruskin*, XVIII, 107-108).

45. Karl Marx, *Economic and Philosophic Manuscripts of 1844*, 72-73.

which will help develop the inner life of the worker, the gentleman is asked to regard himself as a product, consuming by the very act of his creation the life-destroying labour of others. The chasm here between gentlemen and workers is as wide as that between the weasel and his prey.

That Ruskin was pained and disturbed by this is evident; he founded the Guild of St George, and gave away most of his fortune, in the vain hope of allaying his guilt. Perhaps for the same reason, he began to write of the artist as "only a beautiful development of tailor or carpenter". There was a generous aspect to this — the artist is seen as "giving brightness to life", and not only to pictures which would be seen and understood by a few — but it marks a shift of direction, a new emphasis on the utility of the artist's work. In "The Nature of Gothic" Ruskin had argued that good work is done without pain, but writing in *Fors Clavigera* in 1875 he defined the artist (in capital letters) as "A person who has submitted to a law which it was painful to obey, that he may bestow a delight which it is gracious to bestow".[46] Rather than arguing that all workers should be artists, Ruskin begins to take the less joyous and more Carlylean line that artists should recognize their role as workers. At the same time, he adopted Carlyle's view of the beneficent whip: "the essential thing for all creatures is to be made to do right; how they are made to do it ... is comparatively immaterial."[47] It is possible to emphasize the varying contexts of these remarks: in this last instance, Ruskin's wish to develop a main part of his polemic against the economists, that since money was rightly understood as a written claim on the labour of others, those of his readers who had money were in effect slave-holders, commanding the labour of British workers, and should learn to be as tender of that responsibility as they had pretended to be about the welfare of black slaves overseas. Such an emphasis would be entirely just. But it would be improper to admit the context and ignore the harsh and illiberal tone of the passage.

Ruskin remained personally generous, and there is much in all his writings which commands respect. But his passionate insistence that a just society must consider the quality of life of the worker, balancing de-feat against feat, was not, finally, proof against the idea that there were permanent, infinite and irreconcilable differences between the natures and capacities of men, that some were lordly and some were

---

46. *The Works of John Ruskin*, XXVIII, 441.

47. *Munera Pulveris*, in *The Works of John Ruskin*, XVII, 255.

servile, and that the health of the state depended first on the separation of the two and then on according the one absolute authority over the other. Reading Carlyle's *Latter-Day Pamphlets* in 1850, Karl Marx wrote sadly, "The genius has gone to the devil; only the cult remains". Still more sadly, I suggest that a part of Ruskin's genius, under Carlyle's influence, went there too.

EBENEZER ELLIOTT, THE "CORN-LAW RHYMER": POOR MEN *DO* WRITE – THE EMERGENCE OF CLASS IDENTITY WITHIN A POETRY OF TRANSITION

KAREN WOLVEN

"It used to be said that lions do not paint, that poor men do not write; but the case is altering now."[1] Thus Thomas Carlyle spoke of Ebenezer Elliott when reviewing the poet's first edition of his overtly political *Corn Law Rhymes* in 1830. The poems would gain for Elliott a national reputation which he sought but which had been denied him by the periodical press on any noticeable scale until Carlyle's review. The expanded second edition, published in 1831, would attract the attention of another eminent critic, Edward Bulwer Lytton. Part of the fascination Elliott provided such critics was his proclaimed allegiance to the northern, urban industrial working-class. He was the first poet of national reputation to declare such an allegiance and to declare a responsibility to represent what he claimed to be the interests of this class through a politically charged literature. Many of the reviews and notices Elliott received from the time of Carlyle's first review turned at least some attention towards determining his identity within literary society (as a poet) and society in general (as a working man). As middle-class critics struggled to establish Elliott's social class, they also struggled to establish terms of masculinity and education or "self" education. As the concept of a working-class culture became more apparent, debates concerning the growth of a new literature and a new type of poetry from and for the working classes gained new importance in relation to its significance not only for literary criticism, but for society in general. As a precursor to Chartist poetry and other working-class literature which followed, the debate and the issues raised in the reviews of Elliott's political poetry concerning working-class radical political poetry and its relation to existing literary culture helped to establish a style of discourse in which future political poetry from the

1. Thomas Carlyle, "Corn-Law Rhymes", *Edinburgh Review*, LV (1832), 339.

working classes could be discussed.[2]

Elliott's geographical origins were important to those critics who attempted to associate his lineage with the type of poetry he was producing. Elliott was an ironmonger who owned his own business in Sheffield for over two decades (a business which was originally financed by his wealthier sisters-in-law). References to his iron and steel business, an industry typically associated with the North of England, are made constantly by critics when referring to both his poetry and his character. These references, coupled with the same references in the biographical material, create a working-class register in which to categorize Elliott and his work. The effect is that this material creates a new working-class sphere into which Burns and Crabbe (as rural poets) and the Lake poets and other Romantics with more affluent backgrounds cannot be placed. Discussions of Elliott and his poetry were formulated in such a manner as to make them appear to be intended as a template for future discussions of poets of his class, should there be any — a seemingly deliberate attempt to define the working class and the position of literature within that class.

The tension that exists between Elliott as a labourer and Elliott as a masculine, northern, industrial poet, implicit and sometimes explicit in the language and associations made within reviews and commentaries, can be seen as a bid to define a new type of poetry which is no longer associated simply with natural sensitivity (the word "natural" here denotes "nature" rather than "inherent"). The poetry of the Romantics, especially Wordsworth, with whom Elliott was often linked by his contemporary critics, prescribed an inherent quality within the poet to recognize and articulate in imaginative and aesthetic language the virtues and philosophical properties that communing with nature could bring. Following this type of poetry was a poet who composed a poetry that demonstrated a power and strength that was becoming more closely bound with masculine attributes. Differentiation between masculine and feminine spheres was becoming more marked as family and working life changed, modifying roles and attributes associated with those roles. An intuition, sensitivity and sensibility to nature, although still desirable in a poet to a point (evident in the many references to Elliott's nature poetry which was said by some critics to be his best), was becoming more closely associated with feminine qualities and perceptions and separated from the industrial usefulness of a public, practical world.

---

2. See Martha Vicinus, *The Industrial Muse: A Study of Nineteenth-Century British Working-Class Literature*, London, 1974, 97-98, where she discusses the importance of Elliott's poetry as a precursor to Chartist poetry.

Mary Ann Stodart succinctly confirms the sphere of the female poet when in *Female Writers* she asserts that "all that is beautiful in form, delicate in sentiment, graceful in action, will form the peculiar province of the gentle powers of woman", whereas the sphere of the male poets (and she is referring specifically to Milton) is to "ascend the height of great argument".[3] Those that admired Elliott's strength carefully constructed his identity within his occupation which was itself associated with physical strength, but they also extended the metaphor to encompass associations with his masculinity as if they were attempting to establish a definition of masculinity itself. The language of these descriptions is as much about defining the concept of what the North of England represented as a new and rapidly developing industrial entity which occasioned unprecedented circumstances as it is about defining Elliott; his character is constructed around the cultural concepts associated with the North, with industrialization, and with the associations these words have with masculinity. The 1830s in particular was a decade in which attempts to negotiate gender (as much between men as between men and women) and class were taking place in the public sphere, especially within periodical literature, and this discourse continued well into the middle of the nineteenth century.[4]

The periodical press in nineteenth-century Britain was a particularly powerful force in influencing public opinion and shaping the cultural ideas of a rapidly changing and developing society. The 1830s was a significant decade of transition, for literature as well as for the society as a whole, as writers, reviewers and authors, struggled to come to terms with shifting ideas about literature, its role in society and the structure it was to take. Positioned between the Romantic movement and the emergence of a Victorian literature, Elliott's poetry is a principal example of what Joseph Bristow refers to as "the struggles of working-class identification of the 1830s and 1840s";[5] not only was Elliott trying to identify himself through his poetry and prose, but he was also being constructed by reviewers who were themselves struggling to locate new and evolving identities.

Thomas Carlyle is very direct in identifying Elliott's class in his review of Elliott's political *Corn Law Rhymes* in the *Edinburgh Review* (1832), but his assumption is that Elliott is a "poor" man. He says "he

3. From *The Victorian Poet: Poetics and Persona*, ed. Joseph Bristow, World and Word Series, Beckenham, 1987, 136.

4. Linda Shires, *Rewriting the Victorians*, London, 1992, esp. 3.

5. Bristow, 11.

is of that singular class, who have something to say" and specifies the class two paragraphs later by revealing that this review concerns work written by a "poor" man who

> is not school-learned, or even furnished with pecuniary capital is indeed, a quite unmonied, russet-coated speaker nothing or little other than a Sheffield worker in brass and iron, who describes himself as "one of the lower, little removed above the lowest class" ... from the deep Cyclopean forges, where Labour, in real soot and sweat, beats with his thousand hammers, "the red son of the furnace;" doing personal battle with Necessity, and her dark brute Powers, to make them reasonable and serviceable; an intelligible voice from the hitherto Mute and Irrational .... To which voice, in several respects significant enough, let good ear be given.[6]

Carlyle is quite blunt in his description of Elliott — he is one of the uneducated and "unmonied"; he is a working man from the lower class, by Elliott's own admission in his autobiography, which Carlyle quotes here. Carlyle elaborates further about Elliott's trade specifically, using an allusion to the mythological Cyclops as a metaphor for the type of work Elliott undertakes. This allusion coupled with highly descriptive phrases such as "real soot and sweat", "beats with his thousand hammers", "'red son of the furnace'", evoke an imagery of hard, manual labour being conducted in extreme heat and dirt (soot). There are none of Wordsworth's daffodils or Coleridge's lime-tree bowers evident here; instead the reader is encouraged to imagine an industrial scene out of which is forged a poetry from one who is able to articulate the thoughts of the "hitherto Mute and Irrational" (Carlyle's phrase) — the industrial working classes.

Clearly, Carlyle feels that manual labour is a positive stimulation for poetry, and a good deal of his article is spent discussing Elliott's class with allusions to his trade, especially with reference to how his labour-class background has proved to be an advantage to his *Corn Law Rhymes*. Manual labour, he claims, cultivates the mind and a certain resourcefulness comes from working to survive, but "he that has done nothing knows nothing"; experience and nature are man's true teachers. The "Life of Man is a school", he says, and if a man is put behind a plough, one naturally endowed with genius, a Burns is created; put another of the same intellectual talents behind a coach-and-four and in

6. "Corn-Law Rhymes", 339-40.

universities, and a Byron is created. In Elliott's case at least, Carlyle believes that although his "hard social environment ... brought so many other retardations with it, [it] may have forwarded and accelerated him". He was fortunate "to be a workman born". His message is simple: "A boundless significance lies in work: whereby the humblest craftsman comes to attain much, which is of indispensable use, but which he who is of no craft, were he so very high, runs the risk of missing."[7]

Reviews of Elliott's poetry are replete with references to his masculinity, usually composed within a language that in some manner refers to his trade. Contained within this language, too, are connotations which simultaneously link his trade with notions of masculinity. Carlyle's article serves as a good example when he states Elliott "can handle both pen and hammer like a man", he "can beat out a toilsome but a manful living" and fronts adversity "like a man". Manhood, he says, is a bearing "worthy of himself, and of the order he belongs to ..." and Elliott uses a "manful tone of reason and determination", and quits himself "like a man".[8] He admired and respected Elliott's

> singular audacity of believing what he knows, and acting on it, or writing on it, or thinking on it, without leave asked of any one: there shall he stand, and work, with head and with hand, for himself and the world; blown about by no wind of doctrine; frightened at no Reviewer's shadow ....[9]

To be a man, in Carlyle's view, is to support and protect one's own convictions with no regard to the opinions of others, and it is particularly notable that this fearlessness extends to include the reviewers. Elliott writes what he believes rather than what he thinks someone else will approve, even if that individual has the power to ruin his reputation.

After bestowing much praise on Elliott's accomplishments and originality, the critical comments which follow are puzzling. Carlyle says that

> there is a certain remainder of imitation in him; a tang of the Circulating Libraries .... To be reminded of Crabbe, with his

---

7. *Ibid.*, 345 and 343.

8. *Ibid.*, 340, 344, 347, 352 and 356.

9. *Ibid.*, 344.

> severity of style ... we cannot object; but what if there were a slight bravura dash of the fair tuneful Hemans?[10]

To suggest that Elliott's style has hints of the type found in the popular, more prolific literature of the circulating libraries is to imply it does not participate in an élite literary culture, just as his suggestion that there is a similarity to the popular literature of Felicia Hemans is to suggest his poetry contains a certain feminine sensibility or sentimentality.[11] The latter notion is especially paradoxical since Carlyle constantly refers to the masculinity of Elliott's style. It is as if he is suggesting that the powerful indignation Elliott's poetry displays when talking of the oppression of the poor is offset by the pathos of some of his representations.

William J. Fox credits Burns with the representation of the Scottish peasant in his poetry, but it is Elliott whose originality created a "new thing in poetry, and in literature generally .... here were the feelings of the class, embodied by the power of the individual".[12] The numerous notices and reviews Elliott's popular poetry received can be attributed to, as Fox and others suggested, the overtly political content of his verse and the dedication of most of his poetry to one subject (the Corn Laws), a new phenomenon in literature. A reviewer in the October 1831 edition of the *Monthly Review* hints that there was a new attitude emerging within society, a "tide in the affairs of poets as well as other people" which the "Author of the 'Corn-Law Rhymes' may make the best of that which is now setting in to his advantage", namely, that literature is turning towards the representation of "undisguised truth" and "general utility".[13] Elliott, by producing a new type of political poetry at a time when society was turning increasingly to an interest in politics and therefore developing a taste for such poetry, was in a very good position. A reviewer for *Eliza Cook's Journal* states that this "new era in the world's history, and in the history of poetry" has enabled politics, but especially free trade, to become appropriate subject matter

---

10. *Ibid.*, 351.

11. Hemans' most popular poetry is replete with scenes of domestic contentment and sentimentality. Carlyle reviewed the *Corn-Law Rhymes*, *Love* and *The Village Patriarch*, and the latter two in particular contain some highly sentimentalized, even melodramatic, scenes. See especially *The Village Patriarch*, Book III, Sect. V and Book VIII, Sect. II.

12. William J. Fox, "Poetry of the Poor", *London Review*, I (1835), 189.

13. *The New Monthly Review*, 1 October 1831, 444-46.

for poetry to the extent that it made Elliott popular, at least for a time. It is significant that this reviewer was writing this article in 1850, a time when England was beginning to enjoy its place as the most powerful industrial nation in the world and a period when the experiments in poetry conducted by poets such as Tennyson and Robert Browning had successfully brought on an age of a new type of poetry distinguished from the "Romantic" poets. It was Elliott's political poetry advocating free trade, when free trade was an important concern for the nation's economy, which earned him the "high" and "extensive" notoriety he enjoyed. Had it not been for the "prominence into which the struggle lifted him"[14] and his unique position as a "poor" poet at a time when this too was of interest to many, he would not have experienced such success. The literary quality of Elliott's poetry was a matter for continuous debate among his critics, many of whom believed that the work of this working-class man was not of sufficient quality to merit notice and praise from eminent critics of national reputation.

Carlyle says he does not object to Elliott's use of politics as a subject for poetry (although Fox, in his 1845 *Lectures*, accuses Carlyle of doing just that); instead he acknowledges it is a topic for "all thinkers up to a very high and rare order", but his description of Elliott and his political poetry is ambiguous, since it is not clear that he approves of the way in which Elliott expresses his politics in his poetry. He calls him a "Reformer, at least a stern Complainer, Radical to the heart" whose "poetic melody takes an elegiaco-tragical character; much of him is converted into Hostility, and grim, hardly-suppressed Indignation, such as Right long denied, Hope long deferred, may awaken in the kindliest heart".[15] It seems Carlyle does not like the hostility in the poetry, or the indignation, but this description ends on a sympathetic (although condescending) note, indicating that this type of expression is "expected" even in the "kindliest heart" when terrible circumstances are inflicted. He dismisses Elliott's politics in the next paragraph of the article, claiming that no great importance can be attached to his political philosophy since there is no novelty in what he has to say, but he credits his political feeling and poetry with originality.

Claims that Elliott's poetry lacked originality stem from the influence on his poetry by such poets as Crabbe, Cowper, Wordsworth,

---

14. "Ebenezer Elliott, The Corn Law Rhymer", *Eliza Cook's Journal*, 40 (2 February 1850), 310.

15. "Corn-Law Rhymes", 347.

and Byron. The radical political poetry of Byron, Elliott's favourite poet, was used extensively by Elliott and subsequent working-class poets to discuss political issues in such a way as to manipulate the precedent already set by him and other Romantic poets, as well as that set by Shakespeare and Milton, for their own political expression and purpose. Carl Woodring accentuates this point when he ends a chapter in *Politics in English Romantic Poetry* by briefly speaking of Elliott's poetry as evidence of the "movement from the travails of *basic political thought* to proclamations on *specific issues*".[16] However, Robert Southey and Carlyle found it difficult to accept overt political opinion expressed in poetry, and many other critics agreed with their view that politics was better left out of poetry. The political content of Elliott's poetry would have been truly objectionable and unacceptable to the wider reading public had it not been found useful as propaganda for reform by better-off reform supporters such as Bulwer-Lytton and John Bowring.

Brian Maidment states that the industrial system (and working-class politics) was a muse for poetry, but the "tutelary spirit of romantic lyric poetry" was also a muse for working-class poets. He also points out that the "dominant mode of Victorian working-class self-expression was a highly mediated and derivative version of the modes and forms of Augustan and Romantic verse",[17] and this can be seen in Elliott's work. Elliott is continually compared with Thomson, Cowper, Crabbe, and Wordsworth in reviews in the late 1820s and 1830s, but his perceived lack of originality by his contemporary reviewers should be understood within the context of his time. His motives for keeping with the traditional and conventional forms of British literature for which Thomson, Cowper, and Crabbe were often praised allowed him to participate in an established literary tradition which was already well received. By adhering in some manner to the recent precedents for new forms of poetry set by the Romantics, Elliott was attempting to participate in the cultural and literary discourse concerning new types of poetry occurring in his own time. Had Elliott completely severed ties with both the traditional and the new (but largely successful) unconventional forms tested by the Romantics, and had he attempted to create a completely new structure of poetry while simultaneously

16. Carl Woodring, *Politics in English Romantic Poetry*, Cambridge: Mass., 1970, 84.

17. Brian Maidment, "Prose and Artisan Discourse in Early Victorian Britain", *Prose Studies*, X/1 (May 1987), 31.

creating a new political genre for poetry, he would have marginalized his work by taking it away from the centre of literary culture. He would have alienated himself from the very discourse of which he was trying to become a part.

The British novels of social protest published in the years between 1845 and 1855 such as Disraeli's *Sybil* (1845), Kingsley's *Yeast* (1848) and *Alton Locke* (1850), Dickens's *Hard Times* (1854) and Elizabeth Gaskell's *Mary Barton* (1848) and *North and South* (1855) bear witness to the social turmoil of the middle years of the century. The effects of industrialization and urbanization on a rapidly changing society were the impetus for these "novels with a purpose" in the same way that the Corn Laws were an impetus for Elliott's poetry with a purpose. Martha Vicinus points out that poetry expressing the personal experiences of the working classes had its origins in the poems and songs dating from the sixteenth century that were eventually replaced by factory songs as the nature of labour evolved within a working environment becoming more and more industrialized.[18] The purpose of such poetry was to challenge the rich, the employers and the Establishment, to be seen as representative of the oppressed working-classes, and to demand the implementation of improvements on a quicker scale than those in power believed possible or desired. Elliott's more popular poetry including the *Corn Law Rhymes* (many of which are set to popular tunes) subscribes to the form and content of working-class songs, yet they were collected together as poems in 1833-35, not as songs, and were sold and distributed with other poetry that conformed to traditions of élite literary culture (such as *The Splendid Village* written in heroic couplets). In this way, Elliott was part of a working-class tradition yet he was also adhering to some extent to élite literary traditions. With the combination of the two, he appealed to a wider audience in one collection. "In some sense", Isobel Armstrong points out, "he represents the dilemmas of the consciously literary working-class writer", that is, realistically representing working-class suffering without alienating middle-class sympathy. If poets asserted a strong working-class identity, they risked criticizing the very structures that caused and maintained the economic conditions as they existed which would work to dissolve "the common bond of understanding and outrage between classes ... as middle-class

18. Martha Vicinus, "The Study of Nineteenth-Century British Working-Class Poetry", in *The Politics of Literature: Dissenting Essays on the Teaching of English*, eds Louis Kampf and Paul Lauter, New York, 1972, 325.

interests were threatened".[19]

"For verse", wrote Elliott to a friend and fellow poet in May 1849 just a few months before his death, "there is no hope. The public everywhere, as with one voice exclaim, 'Away with thy Wasteful Trick.'"[20] He goes on to complain that if Wordsworth were to produce a volume in the current climate of literary demands and taste, even he would have difficulty in finding a publisher who would "risk" it. The only living poet having any success at the time was Tennyson, but even he was experiencing low sales with his latest volume of poetry. According to Bristow, Elliott's complaint is a legitimate one since poets writing in what is loosely described as the "Victorian Era" struggled with a critical niche for their poetry,

> trying to find a place for it in their culture, and, indeed, attempting to reformulate its purpose .... Poetry, as an art, was visibly breaking up in Victorian Britain, just as the nation seemed to be polarized (both in terms of class and gender) in the face of industrialization.[21]

Elliott, as a poet living during a period of tremendous transformation, was caught in a transitory state between what had been and what was on the verge of coming to be, and the chasm was extreme. The role of the poet and poetry within society was undergoing close scrutiny and redefinition by numerous writers, as was the definition of poetry itself, what it should contain and how it should relate its message to the reading public. This is demonstrated by Bristow in the sheer number of essays and lectures dedicated to these subjects.[22] This concern was demonstrated, too, by the reviews and commentaries Elliott's poetry was receiving from the time he first became popular in 1831 until his death in 1849, as a new type of poetry representing an urban, industrial working-class point of view.

Elliott was forgotten almost immediately upon the repeal of the Corn Laws and remains forgotten, appearing only occasionally in literary history or anthologies or history books as an example of the

---

19. Isobel Armstrong, *Victorian Poetry: Poetry, Poetics and Politics*, London, 1993, 159.

20. Elliott to Abraham Weldman, 9 May 1849, Rotherham Archives, MS 258/z2/8.

21. Bristow, 1-2.

22. See Bristow, Part 1: "What is Poetry", 1-116.

marginalized genre of working-class radicalism. Most evidence for this points to the finite nature of the subject matter of his most popular poetry, yet as Jerome McGann says, this is not the only reason his reputation has not survived. "Also important", he writes, "is the emergence of the New Critical view of 'lyrical' writing", a movement which "culminated the long cultural effort to disestablish certain kinds of writing, especially writing that was thought to be either too closely tied to immediate historical events/concerns ... like satire; or too nakedly emotional". Poets such as Byron, whose poetry was extremely popular in the early nineteenth century and was published in several editions, suffered from the movement away from poetic representations of the immediately historical, as did Elliott, Thomas Moore and Felicia Hemans, to name only a few. Their poetry is lost to twentieth-century audiences who are part of a culture that has, in McGann's view, "all but lost the ability to read a great many writers and writing styles, lost touch with the conventions on which they are based".[23]

Taking into consideration this view of modern literary culture, it is not the fleeting significance of Elliott's subject matter, nor the single-mindedness with which he treated it, but the ability, or the inability of audiences to read and appreciate his poetry within the context of its creation. Elliott's political poetry in particular needs to be appreciated and understood as a precursor to other working-class, radical poetic self-expressionism such as that found in the poetry of the Chartists who immediately followed him. It also needs to be considered for its position in literary history, a position of transition not only for literature and poetry itself, but for society in general. Elliott belongs to the age of emerging industrialization and class identities; he exemplifies the type of expression Louis James refers to as a "confused fascination with the world of knowledge and of writing". This confusion, James explains, was brought on by the transitory nature of the literary world at that time, motivated by a "deep spiritual dissatisfaction with the results of the industrial revolution".[24] He was the first poet to present an urban, working-class view of the effects of industrialization combined with what he considered to be deleterious legislation from the perspective of a Northerner and one who claimed he had experienced poverty and hard labour himself, either first-hand or through observation of his

---

23. I am grateful to Jerome McGann for these comments in a letter to me of 3 August 1993.

24. Louis James, *Fiction for the Working Man 1830-1850*, Penguin edition, 1974, 177.

surroundings. He attempted to take poetry to a level of political activism and pragmatic realism never before reached, forging a new genre of political-specific poetry that aimed to influence its audience and raise greater awareness to the problems he believed were caused by deficient government. For these reasons, Elliott is worthy of notice, and for his contribution to our understanding of one perspective of the spirit of his age.

UNLIKELY BEDFELLOWS: THOMAS CARLYLE AND MARGARET OLIPHANT AS VULNERABLE AUTOBIOGRAPHERS

JUDITH VAN OOSTEROM

On 10 October 1843, Thomas Carlyle wrote in his Journal:

> The world has no business with my life; the world will never know my life, if it should write and read a hundred biographies of me. The main facts of it even are known, and are likely to be known, to myself alone of created men ....[1]

From this the anxiety Carlyle felt about sharing his "life" with a reading public, either through biography or even autobiography, is clear. It was a view he loudly and frequently expounded; an attitude, as it was to prove, oddly at variance with the acts of the man in later life. Furthermore, when placed against two of his own works *Sartor Resartus* (1836) and the memoir of his father James in *Reminiscences* (1881), both largely autobiographical documents, it illustrates that Carlyle clearly held ambivalent attitudes towards biography and autobiography. Almost inadvertently he seems to have strayed into the medium but a persistent refusal to face squarely the consequences and responsibilities such writing entails was to place him in a position of vulnerability which left him wide open to editorial mismanagement and ensuing public reprehension. It was an area he appears to have studiously avoided, a literary genre extraneous to his being and an affront to what he saw as his own inalienable right to privacy. When largely unforeseeable circumstances, created by a chain of painful losses, manœuvered him into a position where a fissure was struck in this determined resistance, he was forced to conclude that writing one's own version of events in the form of a memoir remained the only viable route to take.

---

1. James Anthony Froude, *Thomas Carlyle: A History of His Life in London* (1884), new imp., 2 vols, London, 1919, I, 1.

The memoir as a thinly disguised form of autobiography was more commonly seen in women writers of the period, at pains to hide a more direct and self-revelatory style of writing about themselves. By straying in essential ways from the conventional Victorian mould the memoir achieved an acceptable form of compromise but one rife with pitfalls. It proved a potentially dangerous medium in its appeal to vanity. Even when masquerading as biography, the form is pliable and the temptation to vent emotive and personal issues far removed from the subject can override the strongest of principles. But once Carlyle had relinquished an initial distaste for the idea of any kind of autobiography at all, even in the disguise of a memoir, he seems to have embraced it gladly and the scope it provided, with a vitality characteristic of the man. Under pressure from widely inaccurate biographers and the well meaning advice of associates, he ventured little by little, almost imperceptibly into a loosely autobiographical form of prose — autobiographical only in a limited sense and far removed from the conventional male apologetic mode of the period.

By loosely adhering to what he viewed was an alternative approach, for Carlyle, autobiography became a novel experience to see how a document could emerge which could satisfy many different purposes and objects. Although the primary aim was to establish a true version of the past by dwelling on particular events, at the same time Carlyle's *Reminiscences* enabled him to forge a link with the past and to one person in particular, his wife of almost forty years, Jane Welsh Carlyle; and afforded a fitting framework in which to relate his own history, and even more importantly, on his own terms. Carlyle's initial reluctance to embark on what he regarded as "a frightful enterprise" was common knowledge. Writing to John Aitken Carlyle in March 1870 he expressed the increasing aversion he was developing towards the genre.[2] His hesitation to commit more than rough memoirs to paper before age increasingly impaired his judgement if not his intellect, turned out to be justified, since what finally emerged in his name, was destined to cause an inordinate amount of grief to friends and enemies alike.

As we have already intimated, in the nineteenth century autobiography was a predominantly male area, women's names rarely figure in a genre where structure and content were largely defined by male experience. Very few women attempted works that fell into that narrow field, circumscribed by convention. As Linda Peterson says,

---

2. See Fred Kaplan, *Thomas Carlyle: A Biography*, Cambridge and Ithaca: NY, 1983, 511.

"women possessed neither experience nor authority" to write as men.[3] Consequently, they opted for the thinly veiled autobiographical novel, the diary or the memoir, which provided singularly lean routes of access to self-expression in the autobiographical sense. Harriet Martineau had set a notable precedent but women autobiographers were to remain thin on the ground until well into the late nineteenth century. Writers like Charlotte Brontë and George Eliot favoured the autobiographical novel, using it with great ability but significantly leaving the factual accounts of their own lives to others. Other talented women like Jane Welsh Carlyle channelled their private lives solely into letter writing. Other works of a more personal note were regarded as unwomanly and to place oneself outside the female range of experience would display a lack of decorum and emphasize the inability of women to write with a "male" voice, a requisite element in either the conventional spiritual or the secular form. This perpetuating of the myth that autobiography is a male province seems to have been highly effective and resulted in a drying up of the productive flow of many an aspirant women writer.

Margaret Oliphant is a less well-known younger contemporary of Carlyle's — like Carlyle, a Scot, she was born in 1828. In her heyday, she had a solid reputation as an essayist and novelist and she was a household name — it is only recently that her literary status has begun to revive. Like Thomas Carlyle, she displayed an abhorrence of the idea of being the subject of biography and had expressly requested that "no biography of her was to be written".[4] However, Margaret Oliphant was drawn instinctively towards a journal form. The pressure of a very heavy work load meant negotiating for and juggling with every spare moment she had left when her professional work was done. The free ranging space a diary afforded provided the most feasible method available for recording her own views of life. Her writing betrays a realistic fear that her life might not attract a worthy biographer and she felt the obligation remained with her to give it form on paper.

The diary she left behind was not a well-ordered chronological record of a professional writing woman but rather a hectic, breathless flow of fractured narrative. The reader is witness to a whole range of episodes delivered in a seemingly random order, events influenced by

---

3. Linda H. Peterson, *Victorian Autobiography: The Tradition of Self-Interpretation*, New Haven: Conn. and London, 1986, 130.

4. *The Autobiography and Letters of Mrs Margaret Oliphant* (1899), ed. Mrs Harry Coghill, rpt., Leicester, 1974, Preface, ix.

heightened moods of optimism, alternating with plunges into the depths of dejection and depression. Interspersed by passages of gossip and anecdote it comes together as an often surprising and moving picture.

Whether leaving her autobiography the way she did was intended as a conscious attempt to subvert a genre, or whether it indicates a reluctance to edit her own work into a form she knew to be nearer the norm, one can only surmise. Her action suggests, however, that she had sought and discovered a means, whatever her motive, of opting out of final responsibility. Clues drawn from her own writing make it tempting to presume a certain retaliation on her part against an imposed order, but she was also known to be notoriously bad at correcting anything she had written for publication. By leaving it in the hands of her barely competent relatives she indirectly contributed much as Carlyle had done, to the undermining of her own literary reputation.

In their autobiographies, Carlyle and Oliphant share a departure from most aspects of what can be termed the traditional or conventional. These moves away from the genres they habitually cultivated in their writing resulted in exposures of a highly personal nature. The writing denuded for once of its professional writer's cover strikes a different tone, but the "voice", quintessentially the author's, loses none of its intrinsically familiar strains. By taking on a new stance, the writer has been lulled into a confessional mood. Emotion is allowed to surface and full vent given to those issues that have rankled for a lifetime. This is audible from every page as the story takes its shape from the past events, and shifts back and forth from the descriptive to the polemical. Due to its autobiographical character, the writing is necessarily influenced by weightier issues of life and death and their own inevitable, looming mortality. The temptation to submit to the mood has not been resisted and results in oddly conflicting and erratic leaps in the subject matter. Both Carlyle's *Reminiscences* and Margaret Oliphant's *Autobiography* are seen at times veering wildly from deeply subjective reflections on a grand scale to more factual accounts of mundane trivialities and a wide measure of freedom is permitted in the process. Works which could be said to be "out of character" and rife with introspection were probably better confined within four walls than exposed to public eye. But in their published form they had assumed a style and a shape which were guaranteed to spread confusion amongst an unprepared public, conditioned to anticipate an entirely different product. Both Margaret Oliphant and Thomas Carlyle crossed conventional boundaries in their autobiographical writings. The one transgressed in form, the other in content, and in both cases the unenviable task fell to their editors to prepare these unconventional texts for publication.

Reminiscences, published after Carlyle's death in 1881, is anomalous in form and controversial in content. It is a curious blend of biography, spiked with barbed criticism and nostalgic memory, and anecdotal heightened prose harking back to a bygone age. Arguably, it was a document better retained as the private unpublished exercise it was originally intended to be. Initially Carlyle intended at least one part to be committed to flames: in 1866, as a postscript to Jane Welsh Carlyle's memoir, he writes:

> I still mainly mean to *burn* this Book before my own departure; but feel that I shall always have a kind of grudge to do it, and an indolent excuse, "Not *yet*; wait, any day that can be done!" — and it *is* possible the thing *may* be left behind me, legible to interested survivors, ...[5]

This kind of ambiguity was just one of many instances of conflicting instructions Carlyle inflicted on his literary executors.

Thomas Carlyle's well-intentioned editor, James Anthony Froude, acting in good faith and left to bear sole responsibility after the untimely demise of his executors, John Forster and John Carlyle, his younger brother, released this document with other highly revealing ones on an unsuspecting reading public. A public, unequipped in every respect to deal with them, turned its back on an author whose reputation was already wavering. Froude had not done this recklessly, and certainly not before attempting first to rectify some "irregularities" through "improvements" of his own. Fred Kaplan relates in detail the complexities around Froude's ambiguous position as friend, biographer and editor of the deceased Carlyle.[6] Froude's subsequent editing, debatably insufficient, was to leave him in a lamentable position — unable to redeem his former honourable name and save himself from bearing full responsibility for the ensuing controversy. Neither his reputation and nor that of Thomas Carlyle's could be rescued from adverse public opinion and excoriating reviews.

The root of Thomas Carlyle's precipitous fall from grace in the years following his death lies in a complexity of events ranging far wider and deeper than the controversy over the publication of a collection of seemingly harmless anecdotal memoirs. *Reminiscences* is

---

5. Thomas Carlyle, *Reminiscences*, ed. Charles Eliot Norton, introd. Ian Campbell, Everyman edition, 1972, 169.

6. Kaplan, ch. 17, "A Monument of Mercy", 543-47.

merely a small but essential link in the chain triggering a storm of events, primed to ignite. Carlyle's reputation was already in a state of flux and was not aided by this glimpse into his personal life which for years he had carefully kept private. By appointing Froude as his biographer in 1871 Carlyle thought he made a clear and well-judged move towards putting his future in safe hands. Vindication of Froude's behaviour is not an issue here, since any failure in consistency of behaviour must lie squarely on the shoulders of Thomas Carlyle whether one deems his indecisiveness responsible or not. Among the papers he handed over was a highly personal and emotive document he had written in 1866 on the death of the woman who had been his wife for four decades, Jane Welsh Carlyle. Carlyle's express instructions were that it should not be published along with his other papers. As we have seen, he could never bring himself to dispose of it, although he had no desire to have it put into print. It was a conscious decision at the time, but one which became eroded over the years. What motives drove Froude to publish material he had long had in his possession and which one can only surmise he knew could be damaging, are best indicated by quoting his own words. In his bid to defend and absolve himself he writes:

> The arguments on either side were weighty, and ten years of consideration had not made it more easy to choose between them. My final conclusion may have been right or wrong, but the influence which turned the balance was Carlyle's apparently persevering wish, and my own conviction that it was a wish supremely honourable to him.[7]

When it came to a last coherent discussion they had had on the matter Carlyle had brought forth no objections, so the memoir finally came to be bundled together with other memoirs of varying length and quality to be published under the general, rather nebulous title, of *Reminiscences*. When read in conjunction with the extracts of diaries quoted by Froude and the vast inheritance of letters which rapidly followed in publication, a distinctly different private Carlyle emerges compared to the public image.

Reminiscences is a comparatively modest volume of some four hundred pages and contains not only his memoir of his wife but also of his father, written already in 1832, plus a seemingly random selection of portraits of those who had figured significantly in his life, or those,

---

7. *Thomas Carlyle: A History of His Life in London*, II, 499.

as Carlyle put it, "more or less superior to the common man ...".[8] Carlyle, once writing in this vein, had clearly warmed to his task — a task designed to occupy and distract him, urged on him initially by both Emerson and Ruskin, concerned at his passive inactivity on his wife's death. However, it was to be provocation from other quarters, from ill-informed "authorities" that goaded him into action. Whatever the impetus, by resorting to writing it meant that the most familiar creative process at his disposal, one he had been neglecting, was returned to him once more.

For one who had not distinguished himself in the past as a natural or fluent writer, in these autobiographical writings words came rapidly and easily to him. Written in the conviction he was free in a private document to say anything that came into his thoughts, his style is vital and energetic, and his memory of people and events lucid. By transforming speech into print, it served its purpose admirably by releasing Carlyle from the paralysing state of grief he had been locked in, writing it, as it were, out of his system. In his self-imposed isolation it worked to soothe a grieving, ageing and increasingly intolerant man whose greatest works had long since been written. Unfortunately the exercise is taken a step too far. Even when confining himself to accounts of people whom he admired and who had been close to him, the temptation to add little criticisms could not be resisted. The ill-judged addition of personal notes are slipped in and musings aloud put into print which serve to distort meaning. The serious nature of the subject matter tended to be lost in levity and the elevated brought down to a level of the commonplace. Jibes at Harriet Martineau's literary genius, insinuations that Southey's marital tangles were linked with his encroaching dementia and his questioning Wordsworth's intellectual capacities are just a few instances of how and where Carlyle's memoirs provoke unease in the reader. As his censure outweighs his frugal praise he slips into a casual gossipy mode.

The need to pay tribute to his father, written in the five days following his receipt of the news of James Carlyle's death, was the original stimulus for his choice of the memoir as a mode, the vehicle he evolved to salute the man who had shaped his whole character.[9] The prose used in this essay is elaborate, antiquated and Wordsworthian in

8. *Reminiscences*, 343.

9. In his first sentence Carlyle tells us that he "received tidings" of his father's death "on Tuesday, January 24th, 1832"; the memoir is dated "Sunday night, 29th January 1832" (*Reminiscences*, 1 and 34).

tone, reminiscent of a bygone age. Steeped in nostalgia, it points backwards to a simple homely world before the encroachment of an era of earnestness and rigidity: Carlyle writes here as a Romantic far removed from his habitual acerbic style. He sees himself again as the child in a world still firmly rooted in the Romantic age. Added later to this memoir were other portraits, but by then the style had perceptibly shifted in tone, with an increase of critical comment and boundaries are overstepped. Carlyle notes only that he is inclined "to include too much self", something of which he is indeed frequently guilty. Always an observant man, he is adept in depicting the shortcomings and defects he noted in others but had previously confined to his letter writing. The seemingly harmless musings and ramblings which form the major body of the text reflex a man happily reliving "reminiscences of days that are no more". Written as they were in an abject state of misery, these uncoordinated lunges into the past distorts his judgement. In a decided attempt to order his thoughts, objectivity is lost in favour of sentimentality.

The highly lyrical portrait of Jane Welsh Carlyle, suffers particularly from a heavily subjective approach and is at times cloyingly sentimental, bordering on hagiography, which tends to tell us more about the author than his subject. Carlyle had started on what might be regarded as this therapeutic labour of love by first taking on the mammoth and often painful task of editing his wife's private correspondence. Inspired by what he considered to be Geraldine Jewsbury's inaccurate account of events from Jane Welsh Carlyle's life, he felt obliged to issue his own version. This led to his picking up the threads of autobiography he had dropped in 1832, after completing his tribute to his father. Carlyle's seemingly infallible and retentive memory for place and event stood him in good stead, at least from his point of view. While editing the letters, Carlyle attempted to tidy up any inaccuracies he believed had inadvertently crept into his wife's writing. Had he applied the same approach to his own memoirs, it might have been less detrimental to both his own reputation and Froude's. There he writes without caution, as though he were speaking still to an audience of admiring and uncritical intimates who had collected regularly at 5 Cheyne Row in the past. It is the voice of a man who is happily engaged in an habitual monologue and most of this Froude unwisely retained for publication. However, in addition, the corrections that were made, which superficially appear not to be serious, and such additions and omissions as Froude judged fitting, apparently altered and distorted small shades of meaning. To those who still believed in Carlyle's long established reputation, on the day of its publication, the book must have seemed an incredible error of judgement.

Despite the book's defects, real or imagined, and the fact that the directness of some passages are close to the bone, the level of aggressive reaction it provoked would appear, more than a century on, somewhat unaccountable. One is inclined to believe that the hostile intensity of the response thinly veils far deeper disputes.

The responsibility, which lay heavily on Froude to make amends for more than Carlyle's errors of judgement, was one he shrank from. His enthusiasm for publishing outweighed his attention to the inaccuracies in his transcription of the original text and his slipshod editorial skills meant that it fell short of public expectation. These transgressions served to focus more attention on the work and to increase the reading public's hostility. Carlyle's name and Froude's bore the brunt alike. To override Carlyle's request of 1866, still evident in the text, not to publish, must have looked like gross editorial mismanagement. His warning voice still echoed off the page:

> I solemnly forbid them, each and all, to *publish* this Bit of Writing *as it stands here;* and warn them that *without fit editing no part* of it should be printed (nor so far as I can order, *shall* ever be); — and that the "*fit* editing" of perhaps nine-tenths of it will, after I am gone, have become *impossible*.[10]

"A Bit of Writing", would seem an odd turn of phrase to apply to such a work. A comparable expression Mrs Oliphant uses also, to refer to her own efforts as "a few autobiographical bits": "I wonder if I will ever have time to put a few autobiographical bits down before I die".[11] Such expressions suggest attempts to display modesty at work wherever typical Victorian reticence is expected or required. Even less conforming members of a literary élite feel at times obliged to adhere to such conventions of constraint, but neither Carlyle or Mrs Oliphant seem at ease with this exercise in understating their self esteem as writers and it is not sustained.

The revised second edition of *Reminiscences*, printed in 1887, while more faithful to the original text, also was not without flaws and did no more to vindicate Carlyle's reputation and even succeeded in damaging Froude's even further by emphasizing his failure. It served only as a source of satisfaction to Carlyle's niece Mary, who, as the legal owner

10. *Ibid.*, 169 (Carlyle's own emphases).

11. *Autobiography and Letters*, 7.

of the text, feeling Froude had mismanaged the task he had been entrusted with, had intervened after the publication of Froude's version and engineered the second one. Carlyle's public still showed little desire to be acquainted with petty remarks on people, some of whom were still living and even less patience with his morbid, introspective revelations. Carlyle's conflicting selves, the one projected here rather than the accepted one were only too evident. It exposed him as an anomalous figure, widely divergent from the public image. The desired aim to retain him on the pedestal he had occupied so long, was not served by either version of *Reminiscences*. While Carlyle might have chosen wisely with Froude and recent scholarship has done much to redeem Froude's reputation, what he had not reckoned with was his own failing powers of judgement as old age overtook him.

Juxtaposing Margaret Oliphant with Thomas Carlyle, on the face of it an unlikely literary pairing, reveals an interesting area of comparison. Like Thomas Carlyle's *Reminiscences* Margaret Oliphant's *Autobiography* only took shape after the author's death and was equally the outcome of diverse notes and memoirs. From the study of both works a picture emerges that suggests the frequent editorial mismanagement of autobiographical texts. In Margaret Oliphant's case it could be said to have had an equally far reaching if not more devastating effect. Compared to other female contemporaries she broached areas previously untouched.[12] She went further than most in indulging the need to foreground the unhappier and more insecure stages in life, resulting in a work at variance with the mainly male mode of autobiography in the nineteenth century, both in shape and content. That which evolved, despite the serious editing done on it, belongs to an age yet to come. These elements were to be observed in a reappraisal of her work by critics like Virginia Woolf and Q.D. Leavis. This innovative piece, anchored by its publication date firmly in the late Victorian period, exudes rather the air and mood of the twentieth century.

At the time of Carlyle's death, Mrs Oliphant was at the peak of her career, enjoying a wide literary fame. A prolific mid-Victorian realist writer, with a range that is as impressive as it is varied, at her death she left behind her nearly a hundred novels, fifty or more short stories, more than four hundred articles and a varied selection of diverse works on subjects including biography, literary criticism and travel. It was to be her misfortune to follow Carlyle in a fall from grace after her death

12. See Valerie Sanders, *The Private Lives of Victorian Women*, Hemel Hempstead, 1989, 86-91.

in 1897, though with somewhat less notoriety. The obscuring of Margaret Oliphant's name from literary annals was a quieter but none the less pervasive act.

Though they inhabited different literary spheres, Margaret Oliphant's and Thomas Carlyle's orbits did touch, but the links were mainly of a social rather than a professional character. They both sprung from similar roots, from sober religious Scottish stock where the work ethic held sway. Their lives followed similar paths to fame, shifting from Edinburgh to London as their literary activity expanded, to enjoy fame if not fortune of the highest order after years of consistent labour with the pen. So hard had Mrs Oliphant laboured, in 1896 in a letter to her publisher, Blackwood's, she writes that she had worn away a hole in her right fore-finger.

Mrs Oliphant's friendship with the Carlyles had arisen from their common interest in Edward Irving, the renowned Scottish churchman, who had died in 1834 when Margaret Oliphant was only six. But she grew up well acquainted with his story. Edward Irving was one of the pivotal figures in both Carlyle and his wife Jane's early years, and he features as one of the portraits in *Reminiscences* — a portrait Carlyle was not convinced he had executed well, since it seemed "to be more about myself than him". As he goes on to say in his characteristic self-communing fashion:

> Ought probably to be *burnt* when done (and possibly enough shall); but in the meanwhile the writing of it *clears* my own insight into those past days; has *branches* and sections still dearer to me than Irving; — and calms and soothes me as I go on.[13]

Commissioned to write a biography of Irving, Margaret Oliphant took on the task with some reservations. She was introduced to the Great Man, Carlyle "bearded the lion in his den",[14] and came initially to earn his approval for the work she was rightly hesitant to embark on. Carlyle, who had little good to say about most women writers, praised Oliphant's work, including, even more surprisingly, her novels. Jane Welsh Carlyle, a close friend of Margaret Oliphant's, wrote to her "I never heard him praise a *woman's* book, hardly any man's, as cordially as he praises this of yours! You are 'worth cartloads of Mulochs, and

13. *Reminiscences*, 307.

14. *Autobiography and Letters*, 77.

Brontës and *things* of that sort.'"[15] Despite this, it has been suggested that Carlyle was responsible for many writers like Margaret Oliphant being excluded from the literary canon, since he was to set the tone for the next generation who effectively removed many a worthy writer from library shelves.

In regard to Oliphant's biography of Irving, though initially polite, he was more ambiguous about its success and less expansive. One gets a glimpse of Carlyle's acerbic pen as he pinpoints what he considered to be its weaknesses:

> Mrs Oliphant's Narrative is nowhere so true and touching to me as in that last portion, where it is drawn almost wholly from his own *Letters* to his Wife. All there is true to the life, and recognisable to me as perfect *portraiture;* what I cannot quite say of any other portion of the Book. All Mrs Oliphant's delineation shows excellent diligence, loyalty, desire to be faithful, and indeed is full of beautiful sympathy and ingenuity; but nowhere else are the features of Irving or of his Environment and Life recognisably hit, and the pretty Picture, to one who knows, looks throughout more or less romantic, *pictorial*, and "*not* like," — till we arrive here at the grand close of all; which to me was of almost *Apocalyptic* impressiveness, when I first read it, some years ago.[16]

Such criticism of "Good Mrs Oliphant", as he somewhat patronizingly referred to her elsewhere in the memoir, could be regarded as a perceptive analysis and a flash of honesty refreshing in a world of conventional bland compliments, or as a judgment influenced by petty jealousy on a subject Carlyle regarded dear and as his own. Whatever, the barb found its mark and scored with accuracy. The effect was long lasting on her confidence. A decided lack of editing at moments like these not only served to emphasize the lonely position the woman writer held in the face of such eminent male opposition, but at the same time illustrates how it undermined Carlyle's credibility as critic. Yet she remained doggedly loyal to the Carlyles, especially during the period when Thomas Carlyle's memory was under the fiercest assault. This loyalty led in some instances to an inflexibility of stance that did nothing to enhance her own name in some circles. Mrs Oliphant in an article "The Ethics of Biography" makes plain her views on where she

---

15. *Ibid.*, 186.

16. *Reminiscences*, 305.

stood regarding Froude's damaging handling of Carlyle's memoirs.[17] In her own writing, she had always been highly laudatory of Carlyle's achievements, but he was less inclined to return her compliments for a work that received much appreciation from others.

In Margaret Oliphant's *Autobiography* most criticism is aimed at herself although she could be quite venomous towards others. This was partly remedied, judiciously or not, by the editing out of relevant passages by others in a bid to enhance her reputation on that score. Although she had been widowed after only seven years of marriage, and therefore had not developed the habit of depending on a partner to curb incautious remarks, Mrs Oliphant had at least learned to be tactful in general company. Not so, the widower Carlyle. Jane Welsh Carlyle had tempered and intercepted many a sour remark of her husband's by her own quick witted comments, but once beyond his wife's sheltering arm, Carlyle was on his own and clearly lost his sense of what was permissible.

Nevertheless Margaret Oliphant had few reservations about having the varied aspects of her life committed to print. She was prepared to tell her audience all; to some it was embarrassingly too much. And undoubtedly this frankness helped in the downward spiral of her reputation. She regarded it as a duty to leave her own voice behind her, fully aware of all this implied. Oliphant was on familiar ground when it came to autobiographies. She tackled the subject willingly and with enthusiasm. In 1881, for example, she had written five separate articles under the heading "Autobiographies" for *Blackwood's Edinburgh Magazine*, and another three followed between 1882 and 1884.[18] Her experience with the subject matter was rich and varied. As is evident

---

17. *Contemporary Review*, July 1883, 76-93; for instance: "If a man, on the eve of so important an undertaking, finds that the idea he has formed of the person whose good name is in his hands is an unfavourable one, and that all he can do by telling the story of his life is to lessen or destroy that good name — not indeed by revealing any system of hypocrisy or concealed vice, which might be the benefit of public morals to expose, but an exhibition of personal idiosyncrasies repulsive to the ordinary mind and contradictory of the veneration with which the world has hitherto regarded a man of genius — is it in such a case his duty to speak at all?" (90)

18. The eight *Blackwood's* articles are: "Benvenuto Cellini" (January 1881), "Lord Herbert of Cherbury" (March 1881), "Margaret, Duchess of Newcastle" (May 1881), "Edward Gibbon" (August 1881), "Carlo Goldini" (October 1881), "In the Time of the Commonwealth: Lucy Hutchinson — Alice Thornton" (July 1883), "Madame Roland" (April 1883) and "An Artist's Autobiography" (November 1884).

from what she wrote on herself and in her reviews on others, Margaret Oliphant was also well acquainted with the responsibilities the writing of biography and autobiography entailed, and she had clearly given much thought to the contents of these kinds of works. In her strongly worded *Blackwood's* article on Harriet Martineau's *Autobiography*, she states in no uncertain terms that "It is a dangerous thing to have your life written when you are dead and helpless, and can do nothing to protest against the judgement". But she goes on to say:

> But if biography is thus dangerous, there is a still more fatal art, more radical in its operation, and infinitely more murderous, against which nothing can defend the predestined victim. This terrible instrument of self murder is called autobiography and no kind interpreter, no gentle critic, ... can diminish its damning power.[19]

Therefore fully aware as she was of the likely consequences of such an action, it remains an intriguing question as to why she embarked at all on a journal so easily construed as an autobiography in the manner she did.

Like Carlyle, Mrs Oliphant had started writing her life in her middle years, prompted too by a death. Her only daughter Margaret was taken from her with an abruptness with which she found it almost impossible to cope. The document, written in a rush of despair, provided her with an outlet. It is a startling tale, reminiscent of fiction rather than fact. It was set down in the space of a few weeks — "it relieved me and exhausted me and exhaustion is a great blessing when trouble is great" — and retains its original urgency through the manner it is told. Her shifts from subjective reflection to more traditional narrative appear on first sight unconnected and even repetitive in character but it is no chance order. Blocks of text, which disregard the restrictions of grammar, fill the page. Like Carlyle's work it appears to be written at high speed, an attempt to catch volatile memories on paper. The self-questioning, also seen in Carlyle's writing and that of his contemporaries, abounds in Oliphant's work but always with a specific goal in mind. It is on closer reading that a method behind this self-questioning emerges. Through the context of her own feminine experience, caught between the roles of mother and provider, there is a consistent move towards a more coherent grasp of wider issues beyond domesticity. However, little of this bleak avowal to grief and despair is

19. *Blackwood's Edinburgh Magazine*, 121 (April 1877), 472.

left intact in the final version of her *Autobiography*. The two slim volumes which surfaced on her death, recording a seemingly incoherent narrative, were not deemed suitable for publication as they stood. This distorted perception of the intention behind Margaret Oliphant's writing led rapidly to effecting what amounts to a second and alternative version of her life. It was reasoned that the work was an aberration demanding correction, and the author needed to be saved from herself. Therefore the tone needed to be softened and the contents adulterated. The background to these events I will come to shortly.

It is abundantly evident from Oliphant's narrative that her personal life was closely bound up with her professional life. While Trollope, as she saw it, found it necessary in his *Autobiography*, published posthumously in 1883, to shelter behind and comment at length on his fictional characters, Margaret Oliphant is seen to be occupied by the realities of her life rather than by her fictional work. Her references to her literary life are purely functional, name-dropping is an exercise performed only to illustrate her own perceived subordinate position, which, however, she is clear to add is not to be construed as an inferior one. She strove always to be in control and it is the frank admission of deep frustrations she felt, her powerless to hold onto those closest to her, which reverberates throughout the text in a quite unconventional manner. The evidently defensive, sometimes apologetic tone, is not to be misconstrued as a defect but to be understood as an attempt to equate her needs with the reality of her situation, while adhering to the spirit of that same work ethic Carlyle propagated and at the same time noting all those around you profiting from your labours. She writes at length about her own insecurity, her fear of having outlived her own fame and how ill at ease she feels in contemporary literary society. It is a highly revealing and finely observed picture of an era. Her reference to the ease of George Eliot's existence compared to her own continual struggle to cope between balancing advances from Blackwood's with deadlines to deliver her work, is telling. In the shadow of larger names the temptation to descend into self pity, is carefully controlled. A concerted effort is continually made to swing back to the more mundane details of her life. The fact that one is left with a somewhat lopsided image of the women is due in part to bits that were later discovered to be missing or incomplete.

Margaret Oliphant's story is not unique in the extent of the losses she sustained; her lot was an all too common one in the Victorian era. Unique is the way she assimilated her experiences into a creative process. She was a woman who was often misread in the past by those who were inclined to presume that she capitalized on her troubles by using her *Autobiography* to catalogue her woes. Unfortunately, it is largely in this vein that Mrs Oliphant's work was originally greeted by her reading public — a public no more eager than Carlyle's to become acquainted with details of the fraught existence that the writer had led in order to achieve a pinnacle of literary fame.

With probably misplaced confidence, Margaret Oliphant had assumed that her son, Cecco, would edit her work. Using his discretion as to what should be published, she envisaged he would make his own contribution by saying the complimentary things about her that she would not be able to say about herself. As practical as ever she reasoned he would provide her memoirs with a safe passage and, at the same time, create a nest egg for himself. With the same unpredictability of events that her whole life had shown, this was not to be the case. When her son died before herself, she was obliged to place in the hands of those she deemed most suitable, a document that on the face of it bore little resemblance to a finished product. Her two executors were Annie Coghill, a second cousin and her secretary in the last years, who had once had literary aspirations herself, and her devoted niece Denny, who most of her life had been indebted to Margaret Oliphant. As it turned out, this was hardly a propitious choice, for they set about editing Mrs Oliphant's autobiography with even less compunction that Froude had approached Carlyle's work. The happy expectation that they would encounter a well-ordered chronological account, spanning a professional writer's career of over fifty years was shattered by their discovery of a document that, in any conventional sense, had neither a coherent beginning nor an end. In their own words it was with "great disappointment" they viewed the material, a seemingly chaotic jumble of introspective reflections punctured by thinly veiled anger and frustration.[20] This they had hoped to fashion into a glowing testament to Margaret Oliphant's life, but as it stood they saw it as an insult to her memory, so flatteringly portrayed in recent obituaries. It was decided to prune the text and shift the contents about in a bid to provide a more presentable finished form. No greater disservice could have been done. Over zealous editing rather than its lack caused significant damage to what was to be seen many decades later as an intriguing document, which needed no reshaping. However, this is to see the case from a late twentieth-century perspective, and in the context of feminist criticism.

The extent of the editing to which the autobiography was subject

20. Preface to *Autobiography and Letters*, ix.

only became evident a few years ago when Elisabeth Jay returned to the original manuscript preserved in the Scottish National Library and discovered that almost a quarter of the text had been erased. Not only marginal comments or less flattering descriptions had been surreptitiously spirited away but a major assault made on the structure. In her article on the editing of Oliphant's *Autobiography*[21] and more recently in her book *Mrs Oliphant: "A Fiction to Herself"* (Oxford, 1995), Jay goes into great detail as to how this was effected to the detriment of the text. The original fragmented text, moving backward and forward in time, traced the uneven route Margaret Oliphant's life had taken — altering the continuity of the flow is to alter the threads of an intricate pattern. Editing sections out or relocating them result in an imbalance in the tone of the text by shifting emphases. In 1880 Mrs Oliphant had written that

> Life is no definite thing with a beginning and an end, a growth and a climax; but a basket of fragments, passages that lead to nothing, curious incidents which look important at first, but which crumble and break into pieces, dropping into ruins. Here and there a scene detaches itself, perhaps a series of scenes. For a time in the monotony there occur indications as of a possible drama, but they all melt away into vapour, or are cut short in that arbitrary way, disconnected with all before and after.[22]

Such sentiments may be at home in an article in *Blackwood's*, but sombre thoughts on the transitory nature of life were painstakingly erased from the *Autobiography*. Thirteen pages relating to the death of her daughter Maggie were edited out of the opening pages of the first edition in 1899, as Elisabeth Jay discovered when she was painstakingly making her own word for word transcription of the original work. This passage had been conscientiously shifted to join the accounts of those of her brothers twenty years later.

Margaret Oliphant's *Autobiography*, either in its original or in its revised form, is clearly not easily accessible. By erasing references, the insecurities Margaret Oliphant displayed regarding her own writing, as seen for example in her work on Montalembert, and her handling of the

21. Elisabeth Jay, "Freed by Necessity, Trapped by the Market: The Editing of Oliphant's Autobiography", in *Margaret Oliphant: Critical Essays on a Gentle Subversive*, ed. D.J. Trela, Selinsgrove: Pa, 1995.

22. "The Old Saloon", *Blackwood's Edinburgh Magazine*, 146 (June 1889), 828.

increasing burden of family commitments laid at her door, one is led away from an explicit path carefully constructed, consciously or not, by Oliphant herself. Yet curiously enough, critical reference to her husband's last years, his mismanagement of his own business and short-sighted refusal to act in her best interest, her judgmental attitude towards her brother Frank and her impatience with her sons, all potentially damaging issues, were allowed to remain. This hardly suggests a coherent editing policy. Perhaps Mrs Oliphant's own remark that "it is exactly those family details that are interesting, — the human story in all its chapters"[23] led her editors astray. The image of an established and revered author, acquainted with and befriended by Queen Victoria and the associate and companion of contemporary literary giants, fell apart. Even those who could be counted on to write a worthy obituary succumbed to the temptation to slay her memory.[24] Soon to be little more than a curiosity, together with the most of her works, the *Autobiography* was to go unappreciated for decades until Virginia Woolf and Q.D. Leavis, and others, began to revalue it.

The well-meant intentions of editors bent on improving texts might be justified in cases where the author no longer has the ability or the heart to do it himself — as, indeed, one could argue in the case of Thomas Carlyle. But Margaret Oliphant was neither senile nor aged when she decided to bring her open-ended autobiography to a close. What she had had to say, was said. Left as it stood it afforded her the option of taking it up again should the need arise. Realizing that nobody would write her life for her this was her solution, as we know from the original text of her *Autobiography*:

> I am in very little danger of having my life written. No one belonging to me has energy to do it, or even to gather the fragments for some one else and that is all the better in this point of view — for what could be said of me.[25]

Uncomfortably aware of the fact that her editors were unsuited for the task, neither being known either for their optimism or for their enthusiasm, the danger of placing her private papers in such hands were

23. *Autobiography and Letters*, 122.

24. See, for example, Henry James, *Notes of Novelists*, London, 1914, 347-60.

25. *The Autobiography of Margaret Oliphant: The Complete Text*, ed. Elisabeth Jay, Oxford, 1990, 17. Only the first sentence of this quotation occurs in the *Autobiography and Letters* (page 7).

high. Mrs Oliphant had handled enough autobiography in her time — and even when writing her own she was reviewing that of others — not to be unaware of the risk she was running. She was still writing some of her best work and though anxious about her talent, there would seem little justification for running that risk. Although she still had some time to live when she put her autobiographical work aside, she chose not to alter anything and only to add the smallest of appendixes.

One of her greatest fears had been to be left to posterity in the form of a document such as John Cross's life of his wife, George Eliot:

> as curious a book as I ever saw. The personality of the great writer is as yet very confusing to me in the extreme flatness of the picture .... I don't think any one will like George Eliot better from this book, or even come nearer to her.[26]

Rather choose the "fatal art" of autobiography on her own terms, she reasoned, with the right to libel oneself, than a biography from an unknown hand. What she could not have foreseen was that so much of her text would be reshaped. Margaret Oliphant did seem to have an extraordinarily perceptive view of things, again in her review of Harriet Martineau's *Autobiography*, she comments dryly on how it is a fact one always speaks well of the dead. But by voicing a belief one might imagine Carlyle would have wholeheartedly endorsed, she adds:

> Posthumous books [she is referring to autobiographical ones] .... have not done much to keep up this good character of the dead. The sense of immunity from all reprisals — the knowledge that all ordinary bonds of affection, of gratitude, of courtesy, are, as it were abrogated for the benefit of the writer, who can smile in anticipation at the tumult he will cause, while sure of never being brought to book for what he has said, never called upon to substantiate any accusation or account for any spiteful saying — seems often to inspire a malign pleasure; and it is even possible that a distorted sense of the advantages of making known "the truth" may obscure the eyes, to all the baseness of confidence betrayed and injured reputation.[27]

On reading their autobiographical works, the reputations of neither

---

26. Letter from Margaret Oliphant to William Blackwood, written from Windsor, 29 January 1885 (*Autobiography and Letters*, 323).

27. "Hariet Martineau", *Blackwood's Edinburgh Magazine*, 121 (April 1877), 475.

Thomas Carlyle nor Margaret Oliphant emerged unscathed, as their critics and their reading public were quick to affirm. In the hands of the authors, the "truth" is subjective as can be expected in a work of this nature, and it is equally malleable in the hands of editors, left with the freedom to shape the picture it is felt should emerge. In relinquishing the final responsibility for the editing of their autobiographies, for whatever motives, Thomas Carlyle and Margaret Oliphant are brought together on a common ground where the term "victim" might be regarded as exaggerated but could be justified. Both writers display not only a lack of responsibility to a receptive outside world but actively contribute to the decline in their own reputations. In the case of both of them, there is an apparently similar aversion to endorsing or recognizing these works as their own — works which were always likely to be their final publications, destined to leave an indelible impression on their readers. This reluctance to give the final strokes to such works might have been felt by their authors as a means of keeping their options open, and of providing an opportunity or an excuse at some stage to make alterations or revisions. But in both cases this willed incompleteness, bequeathed to their heirs, had an adverse effect by leaving the field wide open to a whole range of misinterpretations and misunderstanding. However, since by adding the final word to an autobiography is to intimate that the moment has come to tell the only story left untold, of the author's own demise, and to bring it and its subject close to the very last action still to be performed, it is perhaps understandable that an author might be reluctant to close his life's work prematurely.

ROBERTSON ON CARLYLE:
A RATIONALIST STRUGGLING WITH VICTORIANISM

ODIN DEKKERS

Although Thomas Carlyle's reputation has suffered in the past century to an extent that would have seemed inconceivable in his lifetime, this is nothing compared to the well-nigh complete state of oblivion into which John Mackinnon Robertson sank soon after his death in 1933. There is no biography or autobiography to describe the seventy-seven years of Robertson's life, most of which were spent putting together an *œuvre* which few authors can match in size: over a hundred full-length books, hundreds of pamphlets and lectures, and thousands of articles for the periodical press. Robertson was one of the most prolific authors in a literary age noted for it copious productivity, but outside the relatively small circle of those who shared his convictions his works were soon gathering dust on the shelves. This may at least partly be attributed to the fact that, in a sense, he always remained an authentic Victorian, although this might seem an inappropriate epithet in Robertson's case. It is true that the stern rationalist ideology from which Robertson never wavered attacked many of what we would now call typical tenets of Victorianism, nor can it be denied that a considerable part of Robertson's work was written after the death of Queen Victoria. However, his strict adherence to the rationalist creed, which had its roots in a number of intellectual developments generally considered quintessentially Victorian, marks him as very much a part and a product of Victorian society and its cultural climate. The problems we have assigning Robertson to the right movement or period illustrates both how slippery the use of distictions like "Victorian" is, and how nearly impossible it is to refrain from using them.

In this article, after an introduction to the life and work of J.M. Robertson, I will go on to discuss what he had to say about Carlyle, the Victorian sage most antagonistic to Robertson's world of ideas. Although Carlyle was himself a redoubtable critic of Victorian society, for Robertson he represents much of what was wrong with that society.

Robertson's criticism of Carlyle spans a period of over thirty years, and may serve to demonstrate in how far Robertson in his anti-Victorianism remained a Victorian all his life.

J.M. Robertson's life and work

The early stages of Robertson's intellectual development deserve special attention, since they determined to an exceptional degree the course of his career.[1] John Mackinnon Robertson was born in 1856, at Brodick on the Scottish Isle of Arran. As a young child he moved with his parents to Stirling, where he went to school until he was thirteen years old. Since his parents could not afford to educate him further, this was all the formal schooling he ever received. For eight years, he earned his living as a clerk in various offices, but his mind was all the while set on a literary career. He educated himself to that purpose by reading widely and voraciously, and he rapidly acquired a degree of erudition far beyond his years. Much to his later embarrassment, he became an avid reader of the works of Thomas Carlyle, which may well have inspired him to study French and in particular German, so as to be able to read Carlyle's own examples in the original.[2] The spectacular plan he drew up for himself when he was fifteen shows his determination to dedicate himself fully to his studies: "The thing for me to do is to master Spanish, get into the coppertrade, make a reasonable fortune in twenty years or so, and then withdraw and devote myself to my books."[3] Robertson never did make a career in the coppertrade, but a literary future was clearly ahead.

In 1877, when Robertson was twenty-one years old and living in Edinburgh, he struck up a close friendship with William Archer, who had for two years been a leader writer for the *Edinburgh Evening News*, an advanced Radical newspaper. When in 1878 Archer decided to seek his luck as a dramatic critic in London, he recommended Robertson as

---

1. The most extensive biographical account currently available is Jim Herrick, "John Mackinnon Robertson (1856-1933): A Biographical Introduction", in *J.M. Robertson (1856-1933): Liberal, Rationalist, and Scholar. An Assessment by Several Hands*, ed. G.A. Wells, London, 1987, 11-30. The main source for Robertson's early life and career is the short account of his life by J.P. Gilmour which is prefixed, together with appreciations by Hypatia Bradlaugh Bonner, Ernest Newman, and John A. Hobson, to the 1936 edition of Robertson's *History of Freethought ... to the Period of the French Revolution*, London, 1936. Unless otherwise stated, this is the source for the biographical details given here.

2. J.M. Robertson, *Modern Humanists*, London, 1891, 42.

3. Gilmour, xvi.

his successor.[4] Now launched on a career in journalism, Robertson remained leader writer until 1884, when he too decided to leave for the capital. By that time, he had long shaken off the religious orthodoxy of his parents. In September 1878, he had been highly impressed by a lecture of the great atheist and leader of the Secularist movement, Charles Bradlaugh.[5] This was Robertson's first contact with the Radical movement of which he was eventually to become one of the leading lights. In Edinburgh, he joined the Edinburgh Secular Society, and he became the leader of a group of devoted young Secularists. Bradlaugh's daughters and faithful supporters in the Secularist cause were frequent visitors at the house of the president of the EES, John Lees, and it was there that Robertson made friends with them.[6] There is no doubt that he soon attracted their father's attention as well. By 1883, Robertson was making regular contributions to the *National Reformer*, the official organ of the National Secular Society and Bradlaugh's main mouthpiece, as well as to two other freethought ventures — *Progress*, edited by the leading Freethinker G.W. Foote, and *Our Corner*, edited and owned by Mrs Annie Besant, Bradlaugh's closest co-worker. It was she who finally arranged Robertson's removal from his beloved Scotland to London in the autumn of 1884. She convinced Robertson to become assistant-editor at the *National Reformer*, a position he held until Bradlaugh's death in 1891.[7] It was not long before Robertson became fully immersed in progressive London circles. As a close personal friend of Bernard Shaw,[8] he hovered for a while on the fringes of the Fabian Society, but he finally remained loyal to Bradlaugh's brand of radical Liberalism. In the mid-1880s, he was well on his way to becoming one of the pillars of the Secularist movement, and a loyal, though never uncritical, follower of Bradlaugh and Mrs Besant.

---

4. J.M. Robertson, ed., *William Archer as Rationalist: With a Biographical Sketch by the Rt. Hon. J.M. Robertson*, London, 1925, viii.

5. J.M. Robertson, "Charles Bradlaugh: The Man", *National Reformer*, 8 February 1891, 83-84.

6. Hypatia Bradlaugh Bonner, "John Mackinnon Robertson: A Tribute", *The Literary Guide*, July 1926, 111-12.

7. For Robertson and Mrs Besant, see Arthur H. Nethercot, *The First Five Lives of Annie Besant*, Chicago, 1960, 218-19; and Anne Taylor, *Annie Besant: A Biography*, Oxford, 1992, 170-71.

8. See Odin Dekkers, "Robertson and Shaw: An 'Unreasonable Friendship'", *Literature in Transition*, XXXIX/4 (1996), 431-49.

Since it was from Bradlaugh and the Secularist movement that Robertson inherited so much of his ideological backbone, the movement and its leader deserve a closer look.[9] When Robertson entered the scene in the early 1880s, the Secularist movement was at its peak, and Bradlaugh enjoyed unprecedented popularity as a champion of the lower classes. The actual membership of his National Secular Society was never very high, but among the members were many extremely active missionaries for the Secularist cause. Their mission was, as the present-day historian of Secularism Edward Royle has put it, "a radical restructuring of society by peaceful means".[10] Paramount to this restructuring was the removal of the influence of Christianity, which they saw as the main obstacle to social progress. This made them, in other words, open and avowed atheists in a deeply religious age. Similarly, they aimed to discredit the social institutions which depended upon Christianity, so that they were notorious for being republicans in the years of Queen Victoria's greatest popularity. If they can be said to have known a prophet themselves, it was Thomas Paine, whose works they tried assiduously to keep in print. At the height of their success in the mid-1880s, the Secularist could make use of a smoothly operated and wide-ranging propaganda machine, which ensured that a constant stream of freethought publications saw the light while a number of dedicated Secularist lecturers travelled all over the country to spread the Secularist word.

It need not surprise anyone that among the middle and upper classes the Secularists were looked upon with nothing short of horror. Their leader was widely regarded as a kind of devil incarnate. Not only was he a notorious atheist and republican, but the gentry also shuddered at his advocacy of the dangerous doctrine of birth control. There was a general outcry among respectable circles when Bradlaugh was elected to Parliament in 1880, although due to his refusal to swear the Oath of Allegiance, he was not allowed to take his rightful seat in parliament until six years later. It was, however, precisely the furore surrounding the Bradlaugh Case that gave the Secularists unprecedented popularity in

---

9. On the history of the Secularist movement, see Edward Royle, *Radicals, Secularists and Republicans: Popular Freethought in Britain, 1866-1915*, Manchester, 1980; and Shirley A. Mullen, *Organized Freethought*, New York, 1987.

10. Royle, x.

the mid-1880s.[11] Their success was not to last long. The attractions of Socialism (not to mention Bernard Shaw) lured Mrs Besant away from Bradlaugh in 1886, and she was followed by many who believed that Socialism could provide reform on more radical lines than Bradlaugh proposed. In spite of his reputation as a dangerous revolutionary, Bradlaugh always remained a radical liberal who believed in gradual reform and thought of Socialism as a Utopian creed which led the people away from genuinely practical social amelioration. When Bradlaugh died in 1891, a slow but unstoppable decline set in from which the Secularists were never to rise again. Although freethought continued to flower in intellectual circles, its Secularist incarnation had effectively been marginalized by Socialism.

In his *Autobiography*, Bertrand Russell, fellow rationalist, described Robertson as "the man on whom Bradlaugh's mantle had fallen".[12] This is certainly an apt description of the man who made it his life's mission to follow in his master's ideological footsteps. Although a man of considerable learning, Bradlaugh had been primarily a propagandist, who had published relatively little apart from a number of polemical pamphlets and lectures. Although Robertson would prove no less vigorous a freethought activist than Bradlaugh, he combined his missionary activities with immense scholarship and erudition. From the mid-1880s, he set out to compile an *œuvre* which has been matched in scholarly breadth by few authors of any age. As a historian, Robertson wrote a four-volume history of freethought through the ages, which, in its wealth of detail, has still not been superseded.[13] Among his other large-scale historical-sociological works we find such books as *The Evolution of States* and *A Short History of Morals*.[14] As an expert on the history of Christianity he wrote a great number of works on the "Jesus-myth", advocating the theory that Jesus was no less mythical a

---

11. On Bradlaugh's "parliamentary struggle", see Walter L. Arnstein, *The Bradlaugh Case: Atheism, Sex, and Politics among the Late Victorians*, Columbia, 1983.

12. Bertrand Russell, *The Autobiography of Bertrand Russell*, London, 1967, I, 167.

13. *A History of Freethought ... to the Period of the French Revolution*, 2 vols, 4th edn, London, 1936; *A History of Freethought in the Nineteenth Century*, 2 vols, London, 1929.

14. *The Evolution of States*, London, 1912; *A Short History of Morals*, London, 1920.

figure than Zeus or Apollo.[15] In the thousands of articles he wrote for the periodical press few major contemporary issues escaped his notice, whether in the field of politics, where he spoke out bravely against Imperialism and the Boer War, or economics, where he was one of the last to wholeheartedly defend the concept of free trade. It would not go too far to say, however, that literature always remained Robertson's greatest love. He was not only a sharp practical critic, but he also attempted to provide a system of scientific principles for literary criticism which is still noteworthy today.[16] Early in his career, Robertson threw himself on the question of the real authorship of Shakespeare's plays, and he became the leader of the "disintegrationists", who believed that the plays were the products of composite authorship.[17] To Shakespeare studies he finally devoted most of his time in the last years of his life.

Robertson's scholarly pursuits always went hand in hand with active propaganda. From 1906 to 1918, he was a particularly active MP for the Liberal Party. In 1911, Herbert Asquith appointed him secretary to the Board of Trade, and in 1915, he was made a Privy Councillor. In the Commons, he proved a particularly powerful debater, and as such he was both widely respected and feared.[18]

Robertson's career was in many ways a model of consistency. He never betrayed Bradlaugh's intellectual heritage, dedicating his whole life to the causes of Freethought and Rationalism, both of which, while open to different interpretations, he defined in similar anti-religionist terms. The true rationalist is for Robertson "one who rejects the claims of 'revelation', the idea of a personal God, the belief in personal immortality, and in general the conceptions logically accruing to the practices of prayer and worship".[19] Robertson's personal preference seems to have been for the somewhat more militant term "freethought", which he defined rather inelegantly as "a conscious reaction against

---

15. *A Short History of Christianity*, London, 1902 and 1913; *Pagan Christs*, London, 1903 and 1911; *The Historical Jesus*, London, 1916; *The Jesus Problem*, London, 1917; *Jesus and Judas*, London, 1927.

16. *Essays towards a Critical Method*, London, 1889; *New Essays towards a Critical Method*, London, 1897.

17. *The Shakespeare Canon*, 5 vols, London, 1922-1932.

18. On Robertson's political career, see Conrad Joseph Kaczkowski, *John Mackinnon Robertson: Freethinker and Radical*, St Louis, 1964 (unpublished Ph.D. dissertation); and Jim Herrick, "J.M. Robertson: The Politician", in Wells, 31-57.

19. J.M. Robertson, *Rationalism*, London, 1912, 16.

some phase or phases of conventional or traditional doctrine in religion—on the one hand, a claim to think freely, in the sense not of disregard for logic, but of special loyalty to it, on problems to which the past course of things has given a great intellectual and practical importance; on the other, the actual practice of such thinking".[20] As such black-and-white definitions indicate, Robertson was not so much a rationalist philosopher as a campaigner against religion, a controversialist and a polemicist. However, two books stand out among Robertson's works as attempts to provide a general account of his philosophical and ideological viewpoints: the *Letters on Reasoning* of 1902 and *Rationalism*, an 82-page pamphlet published in 1912. In these works, Robertson sketches the outlines of his rationalist system of thought. Religion is presented as the main obstacle to mankind's progress, and he attacks it with the heavy artillery of evolutionary science. Thus, Robertson clearly places himself in the English nineteenth-century tradition of positivist thought, of which Auguste Comte and John Stuart Mill may be regarded as the immediate ancestors.

Robertson's greatest philosophical debt, however, was to Henry Thomas Buckle, whose untimely death in 1862 prevented him from finishing the gigantic history of English civilization on a scientific basis he had projected. All that remains are the two volumes of the *Introduction to the History of Civilization in England*, published in 1857 and 1861 respectively. The central question Buckle asks is: "Are the actions of men, and therefore of societies, governed by fixed laws, or are they the result either of chance or of supernatural interference?"[21] In the course of many hundreds of pages Buckle attempted to prove the former, believing that it should be possible to discover the fixed laws governing human behaviour by applying the methods of the natural sciences to history. Ultimately, Buckle believed that it was the proliferation of knowledge that acted as the great uplifting factor in the advance of civilization. It is this belief that the steady diffusion of knowledge will eventually do away with all social evil — which is in large measure upheld by the conservative forces of religion — that is essential to Robertson's conception of Rationalism. One might even go so far as to say that Robertson's entire *œuvre* is a monument to the view that the gradual extension of knowledge and reason will eventually make

---

20. J.M. Robertson, *A History of Freethought Ancient and Modern*, 2 Vols, London, 1936, I, 10.

21. Henry Thomas Buckle, *History of Civilization*, London, 1871, 6.

man progress to a better world.

Robertson considered Darwin's law of evolution the most significant addition to man's knowledge of the world in which he lives. Robertson looked upon the law of evolution as the great unifying principle which at once did away with traditional religious creeds and provided scientific justification for the establishment of a naturalistic, progressionist "creed of science". In Robertson's view, Darwin had proved once and for all the "naturalness" of gradual progress on evolutionary lines. It is a process that may and must be stimulated, but can never be forced. It is in this theory that we find the essence of Robertson's life-long adherence to the liberal creed, and his rejection of the revolutionary ideologies of Socialism and Marxism. It also lies at the heart of his rejection of the Carlylean theory that civilization advances in fits and starts due to the influence of "great men".

Before discussing specifically what he had to say about Carlyle, Robertson's persistent preaching of the "gospel of consistency" needs to be mentioned. To Robertson, consistency in reasoning was the ultimate test of truth, the main law of intellectual life, and not to be faithful to it was for him to betray an unnerving lack of reasoning power. As he wrote: "There is something disturbing to the moral sense in the spectacle of transformations ill explained; something that troubles the intelligence in the sense of either apparent or felt inconsistency."[22] Not surprisingly, he considered religionists guilty of the grossest offences against the law of consistency: they tended to apply one set of rules to their religious thought, and a completely different one to their reasonings outside the religious realm. In Robertson's view, this was an unpardonable offence, and an eternal obstacle to progress in the world. Consistency was for Robertson the first and final criterion for truth. We shall see how well Carlyle could please him in this respect.

Robertson on Carlyle

The student of J.M. Robertson's work who is eager to test how far Robertson himself lives up to his rule of consistency has access to a convenient instrument in the form of two collections of essays on identical subjects, which were published thirty-six years apart. In 1891, Robertson brought out his *Modern Humanists: Sociological Studies of Carlyle, Mill, Emerson, Arnold, Ruskin, and Spencer*, which was succeeded in 1927 by *Modern Humanists Reconsidered*. This time, the subtitle was dropped, but the same assortment of Victorian worthies was

---

22. J.M. Robertson, *The Meaning of Liberalism*, London, 1912, 4.

being dealt with. Both collections open with the essay on Carlyle, and in both cases, that essay is the longest one in the collection. No reader can escape the notion that it is with Carlyle in particular that Robertson has an axe to grind.

Nor does he make any attempts to hide this. That much is apparent from the Preface to *Modern Humanists*, in which he predicts that the section on Carlyle "stands the greatest chance of exciting opposition, and so most needs to be backed by evidence and testimony".[23] The essay opens with Goethe's praise of Carlyle in his *Conversations* with Eckermann that "Carlyle is a moral force of great importance" (1). It is this contention that Robertson mainly wishes to examine here, and in order to approach the question of Carlyle's influence, he posits that "to estimate him aright, we have first to realise what kind of a society it was into which he was born, and how he stood related to it" (2-3). In his rationalist search for the causes of the phenomenon with which he is dealing, Robertson wishes to give the influence of society on the formation of the individual its full due. In this case, he sees that society as one in which "English intelligence was abnormally deadened and hidebound" due to the conservative backlash of the French Revolution (3-4). However, it was in two directions that "new light and life" was being developed, "in the new poetry of Wordsworth, Coleridge, Shelley, and Byron, and in the new politics of Bentham, James Mill, and the young Whigs" and it is these two developments which provide "the leading clues to Carlyle's position in his youth" (5). It was a period that had not had the chance to come fully to fruition yet. The poetry of the age, "mostly bad", as Robertson says, tried to find an artistic outlet for ideas which do not make the true subject-matter of poetry:

> Poetry, dealing with public or general and not private or special themes, is either a mere artistic expression of the trite and the traditional, or a vague yearning towards a something new which is not clearly or rationally conceived. A cause well represented in poetry is either dead or as yet only an aspiration (5).

But if the poets of the day could not offer a guiding light for the improvement of the social condition, nor could the radical politicians offer a complete programme of social improvement. What they provided were principles and theories rather than practical solutions. This was the volatile scene onto which the young Carlyle entered to make such a

---

23. *Modern Humanists*, v.

prodigious impact.

Moving on now in a scientific spirit from the larger influence of the social environment on the individual to the narrower hereditary strain in Carlyle's psychology, Robertson emphasizes the influence of the father, James Carlyle, on young Thomas Carlyle. James Carlyle could hope for little praise from Robertson's lips: "Antagonism, oppugnancy, negation, clearness of conviction only that other people are wrong—that is perhaps the most persistent note in his character" (8). To Robertson these are dominant psychological qualities, which the son could not help inheriting from the father. They also explain for him Carlyle's tendency to "idle morosely", and Robertson shows himself little impressed by the bulk of Carlyle's output: "his thirty or forty volumes represent no overwhelming product for such a long life" (9).

After having concentrated on the social and physical factors which contributed to the making of the man Carlyle, Robertson now launches into a full-scale attack on his ideas. The list of Carlyle's wrong-doings as presented here is nearly endless. In science, Carlyle was a failure, since his "general alacrity of negative criticism" made him unsuitable for it (10). In philosophy, he was "for the time dominated by the new German literature, and in particular fascinated, and in a degree tranquillised, by the large serenity of Goethe". However, "nothing is more clear than his entire failure to assume Goethe's attitude towards life" and in his early writing, he was really "priggishly" imitating what he could not really understand (14-15). In religion, Carlyle did not succeed in developing a consistent Pantheism, and finally ended up hopelessly confused. The conclusion must be that:

> with his revolt from calm science, his incapacity for analysis, he had come into a world where above all things these qualities were wanted in those who would be guides. Sound guidance, therefore, he could not give.

In the final summing-up, he was "a man of extraordinarily vivid imagination, who saw and felt separate pictures, scenes, situations, ideas, sentiments, convictions, with an unparalleled intensity, and was able to find burning words in abundance to express that; but who was fundamentally incapable of a connected philosophy of life" (22). Carlyle lacked any real set of principles: "The constant habit of aversion and mockery made him ultimately a mere mocker at all other men's hopes (26)." For Robertson there was a total lack of scientifically grounded positive ideals in Carlyle, such as could sustain the rationalist in his sometimes bleak quest for truth.

It is only with the greatest reluctance that Robertson can bring himself to admit that Carlyle's largely negative criticism may have had a favourable influence on the social condition of the nation, that he "must have counted for something as mere thunder and lightning to clear the air" (28). However, he was never constructive, offered no practical solutions, whereas less eloquent writers (Robertson is undoubtedly thinking of Mill) really set out to effect social change. Ultimately, "we must reckon him as a general force or stimulus, an awakener and censor, not as a teacher, though he figured as a teacher to those he stimulated" (30).

Where then do we find the secret of Carlyle's influence? Robertson's answer is — in his diction. At one point, Carlyle managed to give literary English new resonance and colour, but now his influence is over, and Robertson does not regret it: "Like Mr Browning, he made many people fancy he was profound by being, for them, in part unintelligible" (31). His nervous vehemence and sermonizing, once so attractive to the English but studded with "tritely sententious reflexion", had lost its appeal, which, to Robertson, can only be a sign of subtle progress in general British literary sensibility (33).

Even after reading this short summary of Robertson's essay on Carlyle in *Modern Humanists*, which is really one long diatribe against Carlyle's transgressions against rationalist principles, it may perhaps be clear that, for Robertson, Carlyle is the most provocative of ideological adversaries. Of the other Victorian "prophets" dealt with in the book, only Matthew Arnold is capable of provoking a similar stream of invective, but Robertson has far more respect for Arnold the man, and his admiration for Arnold the poet always remains without question. What is it in Carlyle that brings out the worst in Robertson? The answer may be found in Robertson's deep distrust of the prophet as a historical type. In the following passage, he criticizes both Arnold and Carlyle — though Carlyle is clearly the worst offender — for conforming to the type:

> A prophet, as you have him in ancient history, and more recently in Carlyle, may be defined as a person whose language is strong and whose theory is wrong; for such in the main, if you will look into the matter, were most of the prophets of Jewry, though they were canonised by a posterity which had lost the power of estimating the value of their prescriptions. Arnold, certainly, opens a new era of prophecy by his urbanity and amenity; but still he has the badge of his tribe: he is very apt to be wrong. Like Carlyle, Arnold ends in being at points, though

> not at so many points, behind the best thought of his time, after having set out with ideas and aspirations notably better than those in the ascendant (181).

Of all the types among his ideological enemies, it is that of the prophet which is for Robertson the most symptomatic of the evils of Victorian society. Although a self-appointed prophet like Carlyle may set out as a critic on sound rationalist lines, the prophet cannot avoid the risk of becoming a damaging influence since he does not obey the final law of consistency. Banking on divine or higher inspiration rather than on solid reasoning power ensures that the effect of his teachings may only just escape being detrimental to the overall good. The prophet may speak out against social injustice, and he may do so eloquently, but if he does not base his rhetoric on solid argument, rationally and consistently thought out, his efforts will fail to bear any real fruit. It would not be too much to say that in the end Robertson is not so much outraged by the exact doctrines Carlyle preaches (however much Robertson may resent them) but by the spirit in which they are preached. If there is one aspect Robertson resents more than any other in Carlyle's work, it is his negativism, his inability to see the possibilities for progress as scientifically validated by the discovery of the theory (Robertson would prefer to call it "the law") of evolution. What are needed are practical solutions, concrete plans, constructed on a sound scientific basis, which will actually bring about social amelioration within a reasonable time-frame. In his faith in the possibilities for progress, Robertson is a true positivist in the tradition of Mill and Comte. For him, the gloom and doom of Carlyle's prophecies smacks too much of orthodox religion in disguise.

It is curious that it is possible to read the essay on Carlyle in *Modern Humanists Reconsidered*, published thirty-six years after *Modern Humanists*, without any sense of having entered upon a new age. If anything, Robertson has become even more stringent in his adherence to a rational, coherent, consistent world view, and, as a consequence, even more critical of Carlyle. However, Robertson does see the theoretical need for reappraisal:

> Criticism, so to speak, is the means to the geography of our world of ideas. And as the early maps were but rude approximations to the actual shape and relative positions of the lands they delineated, till they were reduced to precision by patient use of exact instruments, so do our estimates of the historical past in general, and of the men who figure in it, come under revision, to the end of a truer notion of what was done,

> how they did it, and what they finally mean for us. And to that process there is no end.[24]

In spite of Robertson ostensible intention to redraw the map of Carlyle's ideas after thirty-six years, it soon becomes clear that he is using the same shapes and colours. Robertson notes the fact that in the intervening period, Carlyle's works have come to be markedly less read. This he links to the original cause of Carlyle's success (a cause he had already signalled in *Modern Humanists*), the emotional magnetism of his style: "it will perhaps be chiefly as a master of certain kinds of emotional effect, notably those of imaginative reverie" that Carlyle will go down into history. The impact he made was the result rather of his manner than of his matter. The literary sensation has lost its magic, so what are we left with?

Robertson now effectively repeats his earlier criticisms of *Modern Humanists*, but with additional emphasis on the lack of consistency in Carlyle's reasoning. He notes that Carlyle lacked "fundamental coherence", adding that "To this day the range of his self-contradictions has been little noted, and some of them were not revealed in his lifetime" (21). Carlyle was never interested in the systematic exposition of truth, for him truth was "a nervous experience, a something literally felt, not ideated as a result of a reasoning process" (33). In the Preface to *Modern Humanists Reconsidered*, Robertson calls "the persistence of self-contradiction in the human mind" nothing short of "the outstanding problem in culture-history, and as such worthy the scientific attention of the psycho-physiologist — as distinct from the so-called psycho-analyst" (vi). Robertson the psycho-pathologist diagnoses in Carlyle a "sheer lack of determinant thinking power, as against feeling power" which "left even the element of good feeling in him inhibited by the element of bad feeling towards those whose thinking had outgone his" (39). As the materialist he is he finally seeks the causes of Carlyle's pathological negativism (for that is what he finally makes it out to be) in his physical condition, notably his lifelong suffering from dyspepsia. In the great causal chain of the history of ideas, Carlyle may have a place, but it is mainly as an unfortunate variation.

In his final verdict on Carlyle, Robertson manages to express some generosity:

> Not truth of history, but a powerful and half-poetical stimulus to interest in history; not truth or depth of philosophy, but a

24. *Modern Humanists Reconsidered*, 3.

> rousing call to think on the problem of life; not light or guidance on the social riddle, but a passionate insistence on the need for them: these are the achievements of Carlyle — these, and the aesthetic thrills that he communicated by his best imaginative utterance (42).

It is not, as should now be obvious, the kind of generosity that comes from the heart. The question arises why Robertson should feel the need for a criticism which made few new points and was mainly even more caustic in tone. The answer may well be found in the fate of the rationalist world-view, to which Robertson clung which such unwavering tenacity. In the 1870s and 1880s, the rationalist position had been one of defiant attack, but in subsequent decades it was Rationalism itself which found itself increasingly forced into a mode of defence. The decline of Bradlaugh's type of militant Rationalism from the end of the 1880s onwards had not stood on its own. To a certain extent organized Rationalism was the victim of its own success. Unbelievers were no longer prosecuted for blasphemy, professing atheists could enter Parliament, church attendance had dropped to ever-lower rates. The pragmatic need for a conscious adherence to a rationalist philosophy of life seemed in abeyance. Philosophically, the rationalist position met with an increasing number of challenges. Frank Miller Turner, for one, has written about a group of prominent non-orthodox thinkers like Henry Sidgwick, Samuel Butler and Alfred Russel Wallace who increasingly felt a need for a particular emotional and spiritual fulfilment which went against the grain of iron-clad Rationalism.[25] Robertson himself was well aware of the threats posed to the rationalist ideology by philosophers like A.J. Balfour and William James. The Darwinism that gave scientific validation to rationalist theories of life was being challenged from various sides. The tide seemed to be turning again, and this time it was turning against Rationalism.

It is obvious that for many rationalists, the shock of the First World War proved the death-blow to any remnants of a Victorian faith in progress. For Robertson, the war only proved that the tenets of Rationalism had not been spread widely enough, and that even more strenuous efforts were needed. But in a sense Robertson's brand of Rationalism, as he so characteristically displays it in his essays on Carlyle, belonged to a different age, the age of Comte and Mill, of Darwin and Spencer, of Huxley and Tyndall, of the great faith in the

25. Frank Miller Turner, *Between Science and Religion: The Reaction to Scientific Naturalism in Late Victorian England*, New Haven: Conn., 1976.

blessings of science for social welfare. While Robertson is continuously trying to stir Victorian society out of its middle-class complacency, the angle from which he directs his attacks now strikes us as almost stereotypically Victorian. This impression is, as it were, magnified when we read Robertson's essay on Carlyle in *Modern Humanists Reconsidered*, written nearly three decades into the twentieth century, but really belonging to an earlier age. Although Robertson would have thought the opposition between Rationalism and Victorianism a perfectly valid one, his writings on Carlyle illustrate that no such delineations can be drawn. The delineations of literary and historical periods are forever slippery and unstable, and they tend to "deconstruct" themselves. In his essays on Carlyle, and frequently elsewhere, Robertson the rationalist may be perceived as engaged in a struggle with Victorianism, or rather his conception of it, which, in the end, can never be won.

FRANKENSTEIN, *THE THREE PERILS OF WOMAN*, AND *WUTHERING HEIGHTS*: ROMANTIC AND VICTORIAN PERSPECTIVES ON THE FICTION OF JAMES HOGG

DOUGLAS S. MACK

Two of the novels named in the title of this essay are well known, the third less so. James Hogg's *The Three Perils of Woman* was first published in 1823, and is perhaps best described as a collection of closely linked tales that combine into a novel. Its full title is *The Three Perils of Woman; or, Love, Leasing* [that is to say, Lying], *and Jealousy: A Series of Domestic Scottish Tales*; and it appeared a year before *The Private Memoirs and Confessions of a Justified Sinner*, the novel for which Hogg is now best known. In the months following its publication, *The Three Perils of Woman* was widely reviewed: this was to be expected, because Hogg was generally regarded as a major figure in the 1820s. The review in the *Literary Gazette* was typical:

> These tales ... display a vigour which is often very effective, and a well combined series of incidents, forming a plot rarely uninteresting: but at the same time they are disgraced by coarseness and gross vulgarities ....[1]

In this review, what is given with one hand is snatched quickly away by the other. There is in fact much in Hogg's novel to trouble reviewers likely to be disturbed by what passed for "coarseness and gross vulgarities" in the 1820s. For example, one of the main female characters is Sally Niven, a servant girl who clearly very much enjoys sexual activity. Equally, prostitutes figure among the characters of *The Three Perils of Woman*, and are not particularly condemned. Hogg's project in this novel, it would appear, was to write a pro-female book

---

1. This anonymous review appeared in the *Literary Gazette and Journal of Belles Lettres*, 30 August 1823, 546–48; and is quoted by David Groves in James Hogg, *The Three Perils of Woman*, eds David Groves, Antony Hasler, and Douglas S. Mack, Edinburgh, 1995, 409.

that would confront the actual realities of lower-class women's lives; a book that would face up to areas of experience normally regarded as off-limits for the nineteenth-century novel. As a result, reviewers tended to be interested but outraged.

No second British printing of *The Three Perils of Woman* was to appear until 1995, one hundred and seventy-two years after the first. Nevertheless, an American edition and a French translation were published during the 1820s. Reviewers might rail against its "coarseness and gross vulgarities", but nevertheless this text was in general circulation in the 1820s as a well-known piece of work by an author of substantial reputation. Its circulation was to be short-lived, however. In the increasingly prudish Victorian climate of the 1830s and thereafter, there was little welcome for this very indecorous text; and *The Three Perils of Woman* was censored out of all the various collected editions of Hogg's writings that began to be published after his death in November 1835. Indeed, it would be fair to say that, after the 1820s, *The Three Perils of Woman* sank almost completely from view until the 1980s, when David Groves began to draw attention to its great power and interest.[2] The writings of Groves and other critics helped to create the climate for the novel's republication by Edinburgh University Press in 1995 as one of the first volumes of the Stirling/South Carolina Research Edition of James Hogg; and the 1995 edition has attracted great interest from a new generation of reviewers. Thus John Barrell, in the *London Review of Books* writes as follows of the first three volumes of the new collected Hogg:

> Early 19th-century Edinburgh had a lot less time for James Hogg than for the Ettrick Shepherd, the literary persona created partly by Hogg himself, partly by the tight circle that ran *Blackwood's Magazine*. Comic, bibulous, full of naive folk-wisdom, easy to patronise, the Ettrick Shepherd was invented as a souvenir of the pastoral Lowlands, a survival whose presence among one of the Edinburgh literary élites could represent both the continuity of modern Scots culture and the impolite past it had left behind. The Ettrick Shepherd, though perhaps more pliable, certainly more reassuringly conservative than Burns had been, could not always be relied on to play this part, and had occasionally to be reminded of his place by editors, reviewers, even by himself. But he was much more comfortable to be with than James Hogg, the author of obsessive, experimental fictions which either

---

2. See, for example, David Groves, *James Hogg: The Growth of a Writer*, Edinburgh, 1988, 104–13.

> satirised or ignored the decencies of polite letters. To some degree even these could be bowdlerised and domesticated, as many of them were in the Victorian collections of Hogg's fiction published after his death, and passed off as written by "the Ettrick Shepherd". But one in particular, and for my money the best of them — *The Three Perils of Woman* — was immediately recognised as irredeemable by its first reviewers, and until last year had never been reprinted.[3]

In this present essay I will explore *The Three Perils of Woman*, first of all, from a Romantic perspective, and links will be traced between it and *Frankenstein*, one of the great novels of the Romantic period. I will then go on to consider *The Three Perils of Woman* from a Victorian perspective, and links will be explored between Hogg's text and *Wuthering Heights*, one of the great novels of the Victorian period.

Let us begin, then, with *Frankenstein*. Gary Kelly, who has examined *Frankenstein* in the contexts provided by the French Revolution and the Enlightenment, writes:

> The plot of the creature becoming the master of its creator was quickly picked up by political satirists, who liked to show the common people as a giant controlling its creator, the political reformists and liberals. More important, the relationship between Frankenstein and his creature could be seen as an analogy to the plot of the French Revolution, in which the Revolution's creators ... were swept away in the *coups d'état* of 1793–95 by their creatures, the Jacobins and their successors.[4]

Kelly suggests that in Mary Shelley's novel, Victor Frankenstein emerges as a manifestation of the Enlightenment's view of social progress; that in *Frankenstein*

> the hero's quest is not just to satisfy his personal desire for transcendental knowledge (the secret of life), but to benefit

3. Review by John Barrell in the *London Review of Books*, XVIII/4 (22 February 1996), 14–15. The Stirling/South Carolina Research Edition of James Hogg is published by Edinburgh University Press and Columbia University Press. By the spring of 1997, five volumes had appeared: *The Shepherd's Calendar*, *The Three Perils of Woman*, *A Queer Book*, *Tales of the Wars of Montrose* and *Lay Sermons*.

4. Gary Kelly, *English Fiction of the Romantic Period 1789–1830*, London, 1989, 190–91.

> society at large, in the spirit of "philantrophy" that was one of the Revolution's slogans. Furthermore, Frankenstein's passions of curiosity, desire for fame, and philanthropy are those recognized by major Enlightenment philosophers as causes of social progress.[5]

Mary Shelley's novel, it would appear from all this, undermines and questions the Enlightenment's optimism about social progress: the benevolent forces that should in theory produce social progress actually produce results that are deeply problematic. *The Three Perils of Woman*, likewise, is a novel that questions and subverts optimistic Enlightenment assumptions about progress. The immediate target of Hogg's novel is Sir Walter Scott's *Waverley*, a novel strongly influenced both by Romanticism, and by the teachings and insights of the Scottish Enlightenment.

Waverley had been published in 1814, roughly a decade before *The Three Perils of Woman*; and Scott's novel focuses on the convulsion of civil war that engulfed Scotland as a result of Prince Charles Edward's Jacobite rising of 1745–46. Influenced by the reading of history made available by the philosophers and historians of the Scottish Enlightenment, Scott's novel sees this convulsion as the decisive moment at which the old, feudal, world of the Jacobites died — the decisive moment at which the forces of social progress brought Scotland into the new, rational, modern, law-abiding, Enlightened world presided over by the Hanoverian British monarchy.

Waverley offers a striking scene which is in effect a concrete embodiment of its view of this moment of decisive change. The scene in question comes when Edward Waverley enters Highland Scotland for the first time. In Scott's text, the Highlands are presented as the source and origin of the eruption in 1745 of the old backward-looking forces of Jacobitism. As he enters the Highlands, Edward Waverley has a Highland guide, Evan Dhu, who speaks to him:

> "This," said Evan, "is the pass of Bally-Brough, which was kept in former times by ten of the clan Donnochie against a hundred of the low country carls. The graves of the slain are still to be seen in that little corri, or bottom, on the opposite side of the burn — if your eyes are good you may see the green specks among the heather. — See, there is an earn, which you southrons call an eagle — you have no such birds as that in England — he is going to fetch his supper from the laird of

5. Ibid., 188.

> Bradwardine's braes, but I'll send a slug after him."
>
> He fired his piece accordingly, but missed the superb monarch of the feathered tribes, who, without noticing the attempt to annoy him, continued his majestic flight to the southward. A thousand birds of prey, hawks, kites, carrion crows, and ravens, disturbed from the lodgings which they had just taken up for the evening, rose at the report of the gun, and mingled their hoarse and discordant notes with the echoes which replied to it, and with the roar of the mountain cataracts. Evan, a little disconcerted at having missed his mark, when he meant to have displayed peculiar dexterity, covered his confusion by whistling part of a pibroch as he reloaded his piece, and proceeded in silence up the pass.[6]

It is significant that it is a "Spanish fowling-piece" that Evan Dhu fires. This calls to mind the Spanish Armada, an attempt by a European Catholic power to overcome an English Protestant government; and it suggests a parallel between the Spanish Armada and Prince Charles's attempt in the 1740s, with the backing of Catholic France, to overthrow the Protestant government of the Hanoverian British kings. However, in Scott's novel the attempt to overthrow the Hanoverians in the 1740s is doomed to failure: the old, outmoded Spanish gun of Jacobitism will inevitably miss the "superb monarch of the feathered tribes". In Scott's novel the modern, Enlightened, rational social progress embodied by the Hanoverian monarchs is well beyond the range of the pop-gun of what is perceived as the romantically attractive, but essentially outmoded and backward-looking, Gaelic-speaking traditional society of the clans of Highland Scotland.

It appears, then, that *Waverley* promotes exactly the kind of Enlightenment-influenced ideas about social progress that are questioned in *Frankenstein*. Such ideas are likewise questioned in *The Three Perils of Woman*, thus placing Hogg alongside Mary Shelley in opposition to Scott. Like *Waverley*, *The Three Perils of Woman* has a scene involving the significant firing of a Spanish gun by a Highlander at the point at which the narrative enters the Highlands. This scene in Hogg's novel can be read as a direct intertextual reference to the corresponding scene in Scott's novel.

The firing of the Spanish gun in Hogg's novel takes place by night at the churchyard of the Highland clachan of Balmillo. The simple-minded Davie Duff, the local sexton, is engaged in the task of stabling the minister's bay horse for the night; but he is interrupted by Henning,

---

6. Sir Walter Scott, *Waverley*, ed. Claire Lamont, Oxford, 1981, 76.

a strongly-built and armed stranger from the Lowlands, who forces him to dig a grave in preparation for a clandestine burial. As a result of Henning's intervention, the minister's horse roams free; and Henning sits on a gravestone, looking into the grave that Davie is digging. Meantime Peter Gow, the local blacksmith, is returning from an unsuccessful deer-hunting expedition, hoping to have more success in a projected meeting with his girl-friend, the minister's maidservant Sally Niven. Sally is awaiting Peter's appearance with some impatience, being anxious to retire with him to the minister's hay-loft. All this is going on near Inverness, early in 1746: in other words, the lives of Sally, Peter, and Davie are about to be overwhelmed by the cataclysmic consequences of the rapidly approaching battle of Culloden.

As Peter, the unsuccessful deer-hunter, arrives back at Balmillo he sees a huge red stag; and this prompts him to delay his eagerly-anticipated encounter with Sally in the hay-loft. But everything is not quite as it seems:

> Now this tremendous red stag which Peter saw was no other than the minister's bay horse, taking a gallop at his full speed to keep himself warm that cold night. But Peter Gow did not know this, and it was a pity that he did not.
>
> As Peter went up by the corner of the garden, to reconnoitre whether the minister's maid was sleeping or waking, a thought entered Peter's head in one moment, and he stood still to consider of it. — "The churchyard lies straight in the line that this princely buck was pursuing," thinks Peter to himself — "Perhaps he may stop to take a snack as he goes through that, — the grass is very soft and green that grows out of them dead chaps. And if he should not have halted there, the doe is sure to be feeding at no great distance from him at this time of the year. — It is but a step — I'll go and see, any way."
>
> Peter went along by the south garden-wall, the very road that Davie Duff had ridden in the evening; and, peeping cautiously over at the end of the stile, his eyes were almost struck blind by the glorious object that he descried. Peter's head descended again below the cape of the dike, with an imperceptible motion, while his heart played thump, thump in his bosom, like an apprentice smith working at a stithy. "I declare," said Peter, in his heart, for his lips durst not so much as come together, for fear of making a noise, — "I declare yonder is the very monster feeding in the middle of the church-yard! Now, Patie Gow, acquit yourself like a man for once! Lord, what a prize is here!"
>
> ...
>
> The mark being near, the shot took effect, and a terrible effect it

> was! — Instead of a stag tumbling on the sward, or floundering away with a deadly wound, there sprung up a gigantic human figure at full length, and roaring out, "Murder, murder!" dived at once into the bowels of the earth, and disappeared.
>
> Peter Gow fainted! actually went away in a faint — And none of your cold water and hartshorn faints either — none of your lady faints, where everything is seen and heard all the while, but a true, genuine, blacksmith's faint. — He fell, as dead as if he had been knocked down with a forehammer, back over at his full length on the minister's glebe; and the huge Spanish Armado-gun fell backwards above him, at her full length too.[7]

After the unexpected result of the firing of Peter's Spanish gun, the secret burial-party for which Henning and Davie Duff had been preparing arrives at Balmillo churchyard. Unpleasant surprises await them.

> One of the men with the lantern went forward to the grave, and as suddenly recoiled; but these were men not to be daunted; they gathered round the grave, and astonishment giving energy to their voices, the dialogue became loud and confused, for they were all speaking at once.
>
> "It is Henning!" said one.
>
> "Yes, by — deed?"
>
> "That must be searched into," said he who appeared to be the chief. "And dearly shall the aggressor pay for his temerity!"
>
> "He *shall* pay for it," said two or three voices at once; and with that they hauled the body out of the grave, and began to examine how the wounds appeared to have been given, when one cried out that there was another. They looked into the deep grave, and there lay the most revolting sight of all. The body of their friend was a little striped with blood, but this undermost corpse was actually swathed and congealed in it. They hauled the body out, and the coagulated masses of blood came along with it, which so much disfigured the whole carcase, that it could hardly be taken for a human frame; while at the same time there were clots of gelid clay hanging at the hair, on each side of the face, nearly as big as the face itself. The whole group was manifestly much shocked at the sight; but how much more so, when this horrible figure bolted up amongst their hands, and after saying in a hurried voice — "Uasals, bithidh mi anmoch," (gentles, I shall be too late,) ran off towards the minister's house and vanished (281).

---

7. James Hogg, *The Three Perils of Woman*, 276–77. Subsequent page references are given in brackets in the text.

In this scene, as in the corresponding scene in *Waverley*, the firing of a Spanish gun by a Highlander creates an image that encapsulates the text's view of the essential nature of the events that unfolded in Scotland in 1745–46. Hogg's Spanish gun scene offers a very different image from that offered by Scott's text, however. In Hogg's alternative view of the events of the 1740s, war is presented as incompetent confusion, as a farcical mixture of the devastatingly horrific and the absurd. Hogg's fiction provides an interrogation of Scott's; and in Hogg's version of Scottish history, war is a theatre in which ignorant armies clash by night.

The Three Perils of Woman, then, can be seen as a novel of its time; a Romantic novel which, like *Frankenstein*, questions and subverts Enlightenment assumptions about social progress. Unlike *Waverley*, *The Three Perils of Woman* does not assume that the processes of history involve a movement from a barbaric past towards a civilized future; instead, Hogg's novel takes a cyclical rather than a linear view of history, and suggests that ignorant armies will go on clashing by night for as long as human life continues. A mixture of farce and horror is thus seen as our normal condition.

Having attempted to offer a Romantic perspective on *The Three Perils of Woman* by considering that novel in relation to *Waverley* and *Frankenstein*, let us turn to the Victorian perspective provided by considering Hogg's novel in its relationship to *Wuthering Heights*.

Hogg was much admired by the young Emily Brontë and her siblings. This was not, at the time, a particularly unusual or eccentric taste. The Brontës were members of a generation that grew up and did its formative reading in the 1820s and 1830s, when Hogg's original period of fame was at its height. However, the enthusiasm of the Brontës was particularly strong, even for members of that generation. As Christine Alexander and others have shown, *Blackwood's Edinburgh Magazine* had a central place in the intellectual development of the young Brontës; and Hogg, as a major figure in *Blackwood's*, was correspondingly important for them.[8] Winifred Gerin says about Emily Brontë's childhood interest in Hogg:

> The Scottish landscape, which she never saw, supplied those distinctive features of Gondal's lakes, inland creeks, and bays, that are not a part of the topography of Haworth. The contributions of James Hogg to *Blackwood's* on Scottish

8. Christine Alexander, "Readers and Writers: *Blackwood's* and the Brontës", *Gaskell Society Journal*, 8 (1994), 54–69.

> folklore, superstitions, customs, and beliefs, familiarized her to such a degree with the character of the highland landscape that she wrote of it almost as home.[9]

I will now go on to seek to identify intertextual references to *The Three Perils of Woman* in *Wuthering Heights*; and in the light of Emily Brontë's interest in Hogg, it may not seem wildly improbable that her fiction should contain intertextual references to a novel by one of her favourite writers.

Both *Wuthering Heights* and *The Three Perils of Woman* contain several scenes in which there is a copious flow of blood. We have already encountered one of these scenes, in the incident in which the blood-soaked figure of Davie Duff emerges from the grave. Hogg's novel, it will be remembered, calls itself a "series of domestic Scottish tales". The first edition appeared in three volumes, and the third volume narrates events that take place in the Highlands in 1746. The first two volumes, on the other hand, are devoted to a series of events that take place in the Lowland Scotland of Hogg's own day. There are many detailed parallels to be traced between the 1740s section of Hogg's novel and the modern section; and the modern section contains a striking scene that parallels Davie Duff's bloody emergence from the grave at the beginning of the third volume.

The central female character of the modern section of the novel is Gatty Bell, a Border farmer's daughter. Obsessed with emerging notions of propriety and genteel "delicacy" in the behaviour of young women, this Lowland girl is unable to communicate her love for the young Highlander M'Ion. Misunderstanding this, M'Ion feels himself to be rejected; and their failure to communicate, their failure to come together, seems to have brought their love to an end. In the grip of powerful self-destructive forces, Gatty becomes ill, and eventually swoons away, apparently into death. Medical help is called:

> The surgeon bound her arm and rubbed it — tightened the ligature, and rubbed again, using every common method of restoring animation, and all with the same effect; the vein would not rise, and the lancet made only a white wound. "Sir," said M'Ion, "if this is only a fainting fit, surely it is one of more than ordinary duration?" The doctor held his peace, keeping his finger close on the pulse, and his eye fixed on her face. At length, after a long and anxious pause, he said, "I fear it is all

9. Winifred Gérin, *Emily Brontë: A Biography*, Oxford, 1971, 21.

> over, and that life is indeed extinct. I must run home for some apparatus; and I beseech that you will instantly send for some farther assistance," (naming some medical men.) (52)

As a result of the flurry of activity that follows, M'Ion is left "the only efficient being beside his still adored mistress". In this situation,

> he put his arm below her head, and raised her up to a half sitting position. Having done this, he put his right arm around her breast, and, squeezing her hard to his bosom, shed a flood of tears on her neck, crying out, in stifled accents, "O God of life! restore her! restore her! restore her!" And, having prayed thus, he pressed her pale and placid lips to his. While in this affecting position, sobbing with the anguish of despair, and unseen by mortal eye, he felt her bosom give a slight convulsive throb, and shortly after heard, with inexpressible joy, intermitting and broken sounds of respiration issuing from her breast. He still continued to hold her up in his arms, calling on Mrs Johnson for assistance, who only answered him like one speaking through her sleep. At length he perceived that both his mistress and himself were involved in a torrent of blood. Her arm, which still continued bound, had burst out a-bleeding, and bled most copiously. In this state was he sitting when the doctor returned, supporting the lady in his arms, and literally covered over with her blood, while she struggled hard with him, manifesting great agony in her return to sensibility (52–53).

M'Ion's joy at Gatty's recovery is not universally shared. Her landlady Mrs M'Grinder is dismayed by the blood-soaked bed-clothes, and in addition she perceives that the "lucrative funeral expenses had all vanished from her grasp at once, and she was not able to repress her chagrin" (53).

Here, as in the startling re-animation of the apparently dead Davie Duff, we have the blending of horror and farce so characteristic of *The Three Perils of Woman*. However, there are differences between these two scenes. The blood-soaked figure of Davie Duff foreshadows the rapidly approaching carnage of Culloden; but the awakening of Gatty seems to be connected with forces of reviving life. When Gatty stirs to life in M'Ion's arms, we do not seem to be a million miles away from that world of folk-tale in which Sleeping Beauty is revived by the kiss of her lover. In *The Three Perils of Woman*, then, scenes involving a copious flow of blood can signify the presence of the forces of death and destruction, or they can signify a revival of the currents of life and hope.

Similar scenes involving a copious flow of blood abound in *Wuthering Heights*. For example, when Lockwood visits Wuthering Heights early in the novel he is forced by a snow-storm to stay overnight, in spite of a disturbing and humiliating reception from Heathcliff. Lockwood retires to an oak closet beside a window, where he is to sleep. He looks at some books, in which the names *Catherine Earnshaw*, *Catherine Heathcliff*, and *Catherine Linton* have been written. Having fallen asleep, Lockwood has a dream about a sermon preached by the Reverend Jabes Branderham, a dream from which he awakes when the wind causes the branch of a fir-tree to knock against the window. Again he falls asleep, and again he dreams:

> This time, I remembered I was lying in the oak closet, and I heard distinctly the gusty wind, and the driving of the snow; I heard, also, the fir-bough repeat its teasing sound, and ascribed it to the right cause: but it annoyed me so much, that I resolved to silence it, if possible; and, I thought, I rose and endeavoured to unhasp the casement. The hook was soldered into the staple, a circumstance observed by me when awake, but forgotten.
>
> "I must stop it, nevertheless!" I muttered, knocking my knuckles through the glass, and stretching an arm out to seize the importunate branch: instead of which, my fingers closed on the fingers of a little, ice-cold hand!
>
> The intense horror of nightmare came over me; I tried to draw back my arm, but the hand clung to it, and a most melancholy voice sobbed,
>
> "Let me in — let me in!"
>
> "Who are you?" I asked, struggling, meanwhile, to disengage myself.
>
> "Catherine Linton," it replied, shiveringly (why did I think of *Linton*? I had read *Earnshaw* twenty times for Linton). "I'm come home, I'd lost my way on the moor!"
>
> As it spoke, I discerned, obscurely, a child's face looking through the window — Terror made me cruel; and, finding it useless to attempt shaking the creature off, I pulled its wrist on to the broken pane, and rubbed it to and fro till the blood ran down and soaked the bed-clothes: still it wailed, "Let me in!" and maintained its tenacious gripe, almost maddening me with fear.[10]

This remarkable passage appears near the beginning of *Wuthering*

---

10. Emily Brontë, *Wuthering Heights*, ed. Ian Jack, Oxford, 1981, 23. Subsequent page references are given in brackets in the text.

Heights; but this novel has a complex narrative structure, and Lockwood's dream is an event that takes place towards the end of Heathcliff's life. There is a parallel passage near the end of the novel, a passage in which we learn of Heathcliff's death at the window which is the site of Lockwood's dream. Nelly Dean is the narrator here:

> The following evening was very wet, indeed it poured down, till day-dawn; and, as I took my morning walk round the house, I observed the master's window swinging open, and the rain driving straight in.
>
> He cannot be in bed, I thought, those showers would drench him through! He must be either up, or out. But I'll make no more ado, I'll go boldly, and look!
>
> Having succeeded in obtaining entrance with another key, I ran to unclose the panels, for the chamber was vacant — quickly pushing them aside, I peeped in. Mr. Heathcliff was there — laid on his back. His eyes met mine so keen and fierce, I started; and then, he seemed to smile.
>
> I could not think him dead — but his face and throat were washed with rain; the bed-clothes dripped, and he was perfectly still. The lattice, flapping to and fro, had grazed one hand that rested on the sill — no blood trickled from the broken skin, and when I put my fingers to it, I could doubt no more — he was dead and stark!
>
> I hasped the window; I combed his black long hair from his forehead; I tried to close his eyes — to extinguish, if possible, that frightful, life-like gaze of exultation, before any one else beheld it. They would not shut — they seemed to sneer at my attempts, and his parted lips and sharp, white teeth sneered too! (335)

In this incident it is with rain that "the bed-clothes dripped", and "no blood trickled from the broken skin". Nevertheless, this scene seems to refer back to the flow of blood in Lockwood's dream. In the dream, Cathy's spirit desperately seeks to be allowed to re-enter Heathcliff's world at Wuthering Heights; and in the immediate aftermath of the dream Heathcliff is aroused to a passionate desire to be reunited with Cathy. Lockwood narrates:

> I stood still, and was witness, involuntarily, to a piece of superstition on the part of [Heathcliff], which belied, oddly, his apparent sense.
>
> He got on to the bed, and wrenched open the lattice, bursting, as he pulled at it, into an uncontrollable passion of tears.

> "Come in! come in!" he sobbed. "Cathy, do come. Oh do — *once* more! Oh! my heart's darling, hear me *this* time — Catherine, at last!" (27)

It would appear that the breaking of the window in Lockwood's dream not only causes a copious flow of Cathy's blood, but also begins the process by which her spirit is brought back into contact with Heathcliff. The descriptions in the text of Heathcliff's final days suggest that, after the incident of Lockwood's dream, he believes himself to be involved in ever-deepening communion with Cathy's spirit (331–32). This throws light on the circumstances of Heathcliff's death. It would appear that, when his spirit leaves his lifeless body with a "gaze of exultation" imprinted on its features, he passes through the window to join Cathy's ghost, at last, on the moors. Blood does not flow from the wound inflicted on his body by the window, because Heathcliff's life is no longer *there*, in his body. Instead, it is on the moors with Cathy; and their union, as spirits, is confirmed by various sightings by the country people (336-37).

In Lockwood's dream, as in Gatty's revival, a flow of blood is associated with a revival of vitality, with a coming together of sundered lovers. A flow of blood is also involved at a decisive moment in the developing relationship of the younger Catherine and Hareton, towards the end of the *Wuthering Heights*. As Catherine begins to overcome her disgust at Hareton's boorishness, the progress of their friendship is advanced by an accident that forces Hareton to spend much more time in the company of Catherine and Nelly:

> Owing to an accident, at the commencement of March, [Hareton] became for some days a fixture in the kitchen. His gun burst while out on the hills by himself; a splinter cut his arm, and he lost a good deal of blood before he could reach home. The consequence was that, perforce, he was condemned to the fire-side and tranquillity, till he made it up again.
>
> It suited Catherine to have him there: at any rate, it made her hate her room upstairs more than ever; and she would compel me to find out business below, that she might accompany me (312).

In *Wuthering Heights*, both the flowing of blood and the presence of fire can suggest the presence of the forces of vitality. However, fire can be destructive as well as life-enhancing; and the flowing of blood can likewise signify the ebbing away of a life, as well as signifying the unfreezing and liberation of vitality. For example, as his death approaches, the younger Catherine's sickly and peevish first husband, Linton, quarrels with Hareton. The scene is described to Nelly Dean by the younger Catherine:

> "Linton was white and trembling. He was not pretty then, Ellen — Oh, no! he looked frightful! for his thin face and large eyes were wrought into an expression of frantic, powerless fury. ... I took hold of Linton's hands, and tried to pull him away; but he shrieked so shockingly that I dared not proceed. At last, his cries were choked by a dreadful fit of coughing; blood gushed from his mouth, and he fell to the ground ...." (251)

Hindley Earnshaw's death is likewise adumbrated when blood pours out of him as a result of his desperate attempt to kill Heathcliff, late on the day of Cathy's funeral. In this attack, Hindley is supported by Isabella; and the attack comes when Heathcliff, returning from a solitary visit to Cathy's new grave, seeks to force entry to Wuthering Heights through a window. Isabella tells Nelly about this incident:

> "The charge exploded, and the knife, in springing back, closed into its owner's wrist. Heathcliff pulled it away by main force, slitting up the flesh as it passed on, and thrust it dripping into his pocket. He then took a stone, struck down the division between two windows and sprung in. His adversary had fallen senseless with excessive pain, and the flow of blood that gushed from an artery, or a large vein." (176–77)

Again, Lockwood's dream is re-enacted. Significantly, Cathy's spirit is indirectly involved in the struggle that produces Hindley's injury. Having opened the new grave in the darkness of night, Heathcliff has felt Cathy's spirit close to him. When he eventually comes to tell Nelly about this grave-opening, Heathcliff does so in these words:

> "I got a spade from the toolhouse, and began to delve with all my might — it scraped the coffin; I fell to work with my hands; the wood commenced cracking about the screws, I was on the point of attaining my object, when it seemed that I heard a sigh from some one above, close at the edge of the grave, and bending down. — 'If I can only get this off,' I muttered, 'I wish they may shovel in the earth over us both!' and I wrenched at it more desperately still. There was another sigh, close at my ear. I appeared to feel the warm breath of it displacing the sleet-laden wind. I knew no living thing in flesh and blood was by — but as certainly as you perceive the approach to some substantial body

> in the dark, though it cannot be discerned, so certainly I felt that Cathy was there, not under me, but on the earth." (289–90)

"Unspeakably consoled", Heathcliff re-fills the grave and is led home by Cathy's spirit. His account to Nelly continues as follows:

> "Having reached the Heights, I rushed eagerly to the door. It was fastened; and, I remember, that accursed Earnshaw and my wife opposed my entrance. I remember stopping to kick the breath out of him, and then hurrying upstairs, to my room, and hers — I looked round impatiently — I felt her by me — I could *almost* see her, and yet I *could not*! I ought to have sweat blood then, from the anguish of my yearning, from the fervour of my supplications to have but one glimpse! ..." (290)

Clearly, the night of Lockwood's dream and the night of the flow of blood from Hindley's wrist both mark significant stages in Heathcliff's journey towards union with Cathy's spirit. Hindley's failed attack on Heathcliff is also the trigger for Isabella's departure from Wuthering Heights. Nelly tells of Isabella's arrival at Thrushcross Grange, after a headlong flight:

> ... she was dressed in the girlish dress she commonly wore, befitting her age more than her position; a low frock, with short sleeves, and nothing on either head or neck. The frock was of light silk, and clung to her with wet, and her feet were protected merely by thin slippers; add to this a deep cut under one ear, which only the cold prevented from bleeding profusely, a white face scratched and bruised, and a frame hardly able to support itself through fatigue, and you may fancy my first fright was not much allayed when I had leisure to examine her.
>
> "My dear young lady," I exclaimed, "I'll stir nowhere, and hear nothing, till you have removed every article of your clothes, and put on dry things; and certainly you shall not go to Gimmerton to-night; so it is needless to order the carriage."
>
> "Certainly, I shall," she said; "walking or riding — yet I've no objection to dress myself decently; and — ah, see how it flows down my neck now! The fire does make it smart!" (170)

Just as Gatty's "white wound" begins to bleed at the embrace of M'Ion, so blood begins to flow from Isabella's wound when the life-giving fire restores her vitality.

In *Wuthering Heights*, then, there is a pattern of significant scenes involving a copious flow of blood; and these scenes seem to involve an intertextual reference to similar scenes in *The Three Perils of Woman*. It is possible to trace other intertextual references to *The Three Perils of Woman* in Emily Brontë's novel. For example, both novels end with a triple grave, where a young woman lies with the bodies of her husband and her lover: an ending sufficiently unconventional in the nineteenth-century novel to suggest that readings of *Wuthering Heights* might profitably take account of that text's relationship to Hogg's earlier novel.

The present essay has attempted to trace the relationship between *The Three Perils of Woman* and two major novels of the Romantic period, *Waverley* and *Frankenstein*. It has also attempted to trace the relationship between *The Three Perils of Woman* and *Wuthering Heights*, one of the major novels of the Victorian period. Other little-known fictions by Hogg will follow *The Three Perils of Woman* into the Stirling/South Carolina Research Edition of James Hogg; and I suggest that some re-drawing of the map of nineteenth-century British fiction will be required as a result of the re-emergence of these powerful and seminal texts.

TENNYSON'S GOTHIC: IDYLLIC, UNROMANTIC ARTHUR

BART VELDHOEN

In this article I want to demonstrate that interpretations of *Idylls of the King* based on "Romantic" assumptions make use of models of interpretation that yield readings which an unbiased, sensitive reader recognizes as unacceptable, or at least as other than good or helpful evaluations. Secondly, I will argue that Tennyson's use of Gothic material is markedly different from Wordsworth's, Coleridge's, Keats's or Byron's. This is not exactly a new point of view, but it will enable me to contribute one new point, which has to do with the precise role of the imagery in the *Idylls*. I will also claim that Tennyson's Gothic is more aesthetic than that of the original Romantic poets and, politically, more of a *Blut und Boden* nationalistic or imperialistic type.

Implicitly, I will be addressing myself to the question of period terms: do the terms "Romanticism" and "Victorian" have any useful literary historical and literary critical value? To which, from the point of view of Tennyson's *Idylls of the King*, the answer will be, quite tediously, yes: the old traditional distinction is perfectly reasonable, Tennyson cannot be read as a Romantic, the marks of the transition are distinctly more than an illusion, and they can be demonstrated. At least, as far as the *Idylls* are concerned. Tennyson's earlier poems, apparently, struck Arthur Hallam as connected with Keats's symbolism.[1] But the *Idylls* are distinctly not Romantic. It may be interesting to remember that Coleridge had, in fact, denied the possibility, in the same year, 1833, that Tennyson published the first "Morte d'Arthur". Coleridge claimed:

> In my judgment, an epic poem must either be national or mundane. As to Arthur, you could not by any means make a poem on him national to Englishmen. What have we to do with him? Milton saw this, and with a judgment at least equal to his

---

1. H.M. McLuhan, "Tennyson and Picturesque Poetry", in *Critical Essays on the Poetry of Tennyson*, ed. J. Killham, London, 1960, *passim*.

genius, took a mundane theme — one common to all mankind.[2]

Tennyson persisted, presumably stimulated by a different outlook. Whether the differences are typically, or even distinctly, Victorian is a moot point. The *Idylls* are akin to Ruskin's idea of non-assertive art. It seems to me, however, that "Victorian" is by far the vaguer label of the two. Swinburne's, Morris's, and Arnold's use of Gothic material is again quite distinct from Tennyson's. So, the variety of fundamental responses seems to me much greater in the latter half of the nineteenth century.

The differences among the Victorian poets in their use of the Gothic is an interesting subject in its own right, but here I must concentrate on Tennyson's *Idylls* alone. First a few, admittedly fairly random, instances of readings of the *Idylls* as if they belong in the purely Romantic vein to be analysed with approaches that have become traditional for that kind. For instance, W. David Shaw applies Kierkegaard's analysis of the paradoxes of the Idealist: but in order to make this stick, his article is full of misreadings and strained interpretations.[3] A few examples: Shaw claims, because he needs to, that Gareth's mother's love dominates the whole of the Idyll of "Gareth and Lynette". In fact, the hero (Gareth) distances himself from his mother as early as line 25 (of the 1394 lines of that Idyll), after which she tries on two more brief occasions to influence him again, but with no effect. And her attempts certainly do not shape or transform or otherwise dominate the action or the considerations of the Idyll, which is really, I think, about the lonely experiences of an untried knight. And the value-system imposed is that of Arthur's dream, not the mother's love.

I am going into such detail because I do not want to appear too high-handed, for the misreadings and strained interpretations are really so demonstrable. Shaw also claims, because he needs to, that Arthur's "silent music" is inaudible even to most of the king's own knights, a point made to support his claim for the application of Kierkegaard's paradox. As proof he mentions "the suffering of his followers, who are

---

2. *The Collected Works of Samuel Taylor Coleridge*, eds Kathleen Coburn *et al.*, 16 vols, Princeton and London, 1971 - , XIV: *Table Talk*, ed. Carl Woodring (1990), I, 441.

3. W. David Shaw, "The Idealist's Dilemma in *Idylls of the King*", *Victorian Poetry*, V (1967), 41-53.

strung up in trees by members of King Mark's Satanic counter-order".[4] This refers to a tiny incidental detail in lines 430-32 of "The Last Tournament", which is wilfully overstated in Shaw's reading — for there is only one knight strung up on a single tree. The "suffering" is taken from lines 56-88 of the same Idyll, where it applies to a churl, however, and not a knight; while the perpetrator is not King Mark, but the Red Knight of the North, a figure who is rather a parallel to Pellam and Garlon in "Balin and Balan" that to King Mark. Furthermore, the word "Satanic" is not used by Tennyson anywhere in the *Idylls*: in any case, the notion would not apply either to King Mark or to the Red Knight, but might pertain to Modred and his association with "Heathen, the brood by Hengist left" mentioned in "Guinevere" (l. 16), the Idyll immediately following "The Last Tournament". Finally, the "counter-order" turns out to consist of a drunkard who topples over by his own weight when Arthur confronts him ("The Last Tournament", ll. 441-67); and apart from being overcharged, this detail is, proportionally (except in its own place in "The Last Tournament") practically insignificant in the *Idylls* as a whole compared to the many moments when Arthur's knights are listening to their king's music, however critically and even doubtfully. The article then concludes with the predictable claim that "Arthur's idealism fails to consolidate its innocence in its confrontation with experience". This, indeed, must be about a text Tennyson never wrote. I cannot find any suggestion in the *Idylls* that this was in any way the point of Arthur's idealistic construction.

In a later article, Shaw applies the Hegelian dialectic to the *Idylls*.[5] Here he even admits that this analysis requires a regrouping of the poems for it to work. And after this tampering with the text follows the inevitable claim that the "forms", which apparently means the imagery, "are antecedent to the conflicts" — in the typical dialectical manner. That this is not so is, in fact, the next step in my argument, so I'll delay it for the moment. But it leads Shaw to the inevitable conclusion that the whole of King Arthur's idealism had been intellectually and philosophically futile from the start. Shaw's romantic poet Tennyson has, apparently, devoted a good deal of his life and poetical effort to a basically simple demonstration of the ultimate silliness of the material, which, at the same time, apparently also greatly fascinated him,

4. *Ibid.*, 42.

5. W. David Shaw, "*Idylls of the King*: A Dialectical Reading", *Victorian Poetry*, VII (1969), 75-90.

although it leaves us only a few moments of tragic grandeur in nearly 300 pages of poetry. Some of us may well share the general feeling, but this is clearly not evaluative criticism. Moreover, there are so many "recognitions" in the *Idylls* of a much more hopeful and suggestive nature, even for the reluctant reader, that Shaw's conclusion cannot be justified. His oppositions are simplified beyond recognition, postulating a formalism of a typically Romantic kind which is not there.

An article by Fred Kaplan, written about the same time, looks much more promising.[6] He makes a convincing case that, in the particular Idyll of "Merlin and Vivien", Tennyson is confronting the typical Romantic concern of the failure of the imagination to sustain creativity. That may well be true of this one Idyll, though it is not of any of the others, nor is it the only possible reading of even this one. But the reader becomes really suspicious when Kaplan claims that Vivien, like Keats's nightingale, is a "deceiving elf". This analogy is obviously strained: to any serious reader Vivien is a different, far more destructive force, certainly in the final edition of 1875. His comparison of Merlin with Kubla Khan works better, although it does not really answer any questions. Kaplan himself admits that Merlin's creations are instruments for the loss of oneself, and of one's existence as an artist. He also admits that Tennyson's dealing with the destructive aspect of the Romantic "correspondent breeze" goes beyond the Romantic doubts and fears of failure of the imagination, to concentrate on "the end of energy, the end of 'use'".

Enough pole-axing. The field is clear for more affirmative action. But Tennyson's own words to his son seem to apply here, too:

> They have taken my hobby, and ridden it too hard, and have explained some things too allegorically, although there is an allegorical, or perhaps rather a parabolic drift in the poem .... Of course Camelot for instance, a city of shadowy palaces, is everywhere symbolic of the gradual growth of human beliefs and institutions, and of the spiritual development of man. Yet there is no single fact or incident in the "Idylls", however seemingly mystical, which cannot be explained as without any mystery or allegory whatever ....[7]

---

6. Fred Kaplan, "Woven Paces and Waving Hands: Tennyson's Merlin as Fallen Artist", in the same issue of *Victorian Poetry*, 285-98.

7. Hallam Tennyson, *Alfred Lord Tennyson: A Memoir by His Son*, London, 1897, II, 126-28.

What, then, is so different between the Romantic idylls and Tennyson's *Idylls*? If one places Coleridge's "Kubla Khan" beside the description of Camelot in "Gareth and Lynette" — both "built to music" by bardic figures; or "This Lime-Tree Bower My Prison" or "The Eolian Harp" or other Dejection Odes beside "Merlin and Vivien"; or Wordsworth's "Elegiac Stanzas: Peele Castle" beside the description and role of Pellam's castle in "Balin and Balan"; or his "Solitary Reaper" or "Daffodils" beside the various fields of lilies and roses in which Sir Lancelot and Queen Guinevere are regularly observed in "The Coming of Arthur", "Balin and Balan", "Pelleas and Ettarre"; and many more notable Romantic texts, including *The Eve of St Agnes* and *Endymion*; one notices that the difference in every case is primarily one of the use of the imagery, and secondarily of the presence or absence, respectively, of a self-conscious self. In the Romantic poems one sees the images doing the work: giving shape to the thought, being observed and creating simultaneously. Experience and imagination are one.

This is not so in *Idylls of the King*. Experience is expressed in action and expressed thought. The imagery confirms, strikes warning notes, elucidates occasionally, or generally widens the scope of the particular experience. As has often been argued, it is Spenserian rather than Romantic; but not the Spenser of *The Faerie Queene*, but of the "Epithalamion", perhaps even of *The Shepheardes Calender* — in other words, not the gothic allegorist, but the classicist — with Roman imperialist tendencies, I will argue later. So the imagery of *Idylls of the King* is, in fact, anything but Romantic: it is medieval in its sense of a reality infused with meaning, vision, animation. It is decorative rather than explorative, in the neo-classical manner — Milton also comes to mind.

Obviously, it would not have taken the form it did without the Romantic experiments preceding it, but it goes beyond those, in both pre- en post-Romantic ways. It is closer to the "mask"-poetry of Browning's dramatic monologues than to the characters of *Lyrical Ballads*. This is closely connected with the other difference: the absence of a self-conscious self in the concrete scenes. *Idylls of the King* differs from its medieval source-material, strikingly, in the absence of an omniscient narrator. And it differs from Romantic Gothic in the absence of self-consciously self-explorative experiences in the manner of *The Ancient Mariner* or *Endymion*. There is no central "I", nor any self-conscious Romantic irony.

My contention is that in *Idylls of the King* the imagery fulfils the function of the omniscient narrator. The *Idylls* are constructed throughout of scenes and episodes strictly presented — "seen" — each from the point of view of an individual character, a *persona* or "centre of consciousness". There are no intrusive authorial comments (except, of course, in the "Dedication" and in the epilogue "To the Queen"). The whole exploration and debate is composed of interdependent points of view kept in suspended existence. And it is, as I have said, the imagery that ties this suspended existence to reality, and that serves as objective referent.

A concrete example: Gareth's vision of Camelot "built to music" is not a record of a "participation mystique", but shows the subjective effects of a collective or social imagination — an idealism not yet his own — on a bewildered but willing self. This seems to me to be rather more complex than the Romantic situations, in that both the individual experience and that which is experienced are in flux. Both the novice and the ideal are "suspended". This is subjectivity, not "recollected in tranquility", nor ever allowed to solidify into significance, but simply "celebrated" — "mourned" is perhaps a better word — as a complex of subjectivities juxtaposed and related, in every sense of the word.

In a sense the *Idylls* are more "realistic" than most Romantic poems, but the realism is political rather than personal: the realism of the rule of kingdoms, of empires. This probably also explains the epic — rather than romance — quality of *Idylls of the King*. It is tragic, full of recognitions, and dramatic. It does not, however, have the sacrificial element inherent in epic, those highest heroic moments of epic; there are no sacrifices in the service of the people in the *Idylls*. The epic is mutated into elegy. Nor is there the happy ending typical of the romances. Instead there is the lyricism of the imagery as the controlling consciousness of this vast panorama. Tennyson may have had Spenser and Milton and *Lyrical Ballads* in common with the Romantics, but then they go different ways.

Instead of giving more instances from the *Idylls* to illustrate my point in detail, I should like to mention a few critics who, in their own ways, unbiased by doctrinaire romantic approaches, have provided very fine readings of the *Idylls*. William Brashier, for example, gives a very insightful analysis of the tragic subjectivity of the poet in the *Idylls*, from a Nietzschean perspective.[8] He argues that the tragic subjective poet recognizes the impossibility of objective values and, hence, the necessity of heroic Apollonian illusions. These, sustained by the human will, save men from Dionysian despair. Brashier claims that all of

8. William Brashier, "Tennyson's Tragic Vitalism: *Idylls of the King*", *Victorian Poetry*, VI (1968), 29-49.

Tennyson's poetry embodies the struggle of the individual to sustain an illusion of self that can withstand the disturbing force of the Dionysian realm of consciousness. In the *Idylls* King Arthur's will sustains for a time the illusion of a civilization — Camelot — above the Dionysian chaos and delays the regression into bestiality. The evil characters, lacking faith or self-confidence, such as King Mark, Vivien, Sir Modred, do not believe in these illusions. They use the weaknesses in others (who do believe, up to a point) to break up the realm. In my view, this is very much like what the description of Camelot "built to music" reflects. William E. Buckler admits that Tennyson had the notion of "the exercise of imagination as an act of faith" (James Heffernan's term) in common with Wordsworth, but stresses that Tennyson's practices and motives are very different, in fact more lyrical and more epic.[9] He points to the Romantic German *Kunstmärchen* as a model, and explores the notion of "the Ruling Passion of the Whole Mind" and the *personae* it produces as a helpful way towards understanding. His analysis of the different characters in these terms is really revealing. And last but not least, John Dixon Hunt's is the most sensitive, honest analysis I have seen.[10] His notion of every scene being presented as *completed* speech and action, as *artefact* rather than chronicle, as scenes picturesque and complete in themselves, static, presented in a *montage*-technique, especially offers a rewarding and revealing perspective on the whole. Tennyson's iconic conception of art in the *Idylls* strikes me as pre-Romantic. Hunt's reference to Dante's *dolce stil nuovo* is telling.

Buckler stressed, quite rightly, the total fragmentation at work in the *Idylls* as a deep concern of the poet. And that brings me to my last point: such a deep concern for fragmentation and the threat it poses to society is characteristically a nationalistic concern. Combined with the fact that much of the imagery in *Idylls of the King* is of a particularly earthy kind, a suspicion arises that the *Idylls* reflect a *Blut und Boden*-type nationalistic attitude. The following lines from the epilogue "To the Queen" seem quite clear on that score. The trigger was, according to Tennyson himself, an article in *The Times* suggesting that Canada should secede:

---

9. William E. Buckler, *The Victorian Imagination: Essays in Aesthetic Exploration*, New York, 1980, 36-91.

10. John Dixon Hunt, "The Poetry of Distance: Tennyson's 'Idylls of the King'", in *Victorian Poetry*, Stratford-upon-Avon Studies 15, eds Malcolm Bradbury and David Palmer, London, 1972, 89-121.

And that true North, whereof we lately heard
A strain to shame us "keep you to yourselves;
So loyal is too costly! friends — your love
Is but a burthen: loose the bond, and go."
Is this the tone of empire? here the faith
That made us rulers? this, indeed, her voice
And meaning, whom the roar of Hougoumont
Left mightiest of all peoples under heaven?
What shock has fool'd her since, that she should speak
So feebly? wealthier — wealthier — hour by hour!
The voice of Britain, or a sinking land,
Some third-rate isle half-lost among her seas?

(ll. 14-25)[11]

Fortunately the poetic image-making poet is wiser than the thinker Tennyson. The imagery of the actual *Idylls*, with its apparent paradoxes and rich natural ambiguities, has a great deal more to say than such explicit statements suggest. Yet, I suspect that the urge to produce a kind of national epic is itself an illustration of this nationalistic attitude. Or perhaps, remembering the Spenserian experiments, imperialistic is more accurate than nationalistic. In any event, I believe that the carefully absent poet of *Idylls of the King* has, what Keats would again have had to call, had he lived longer, a "palpable design" on the reader.

---

11. Alfred, Lord Tennyson, *Idylls of the King*, ed. J.M. Gray, Penguin edition, 1983, 301.

"HEIR OF ALL THE AGES": TENNYSON BETWEEN ROMANTICISM, VICTORIANISM AND MODERNISM

WIM TIGGES

Whatever is understood by "Victorianism", one thing about it is certain: that Alfred, Lord Tennyson has always been regarded as its embodiment. At the same time, one hears about his indebtedness to Keats, a major exponent of Romanticism, and of his influence on T.S. Eliot, a prime Modernist and self-confessed anti-Romantic and anti-Victorian. In this article, which will be impressionistic rather than judicial, I will briefly investigate the validity of literary periodization, with particular regard to the poetry of Tennyson.

If it is more Romantic to be a Lord by birth (as was Byron) than a Peer by creation (as was Tennyson), is the latter a Prufrock among the Lotos-Eaters, or a Byronic Hero in a Waste Land? Or are there three Tennysons: firstly, the Romantic poser in black with his wide-awake hat, indulging in medievalism, exploring the depths of selfhood and exploiting the epiphanic trance; secondly, the bearded Victorian sage with the sentimental touch, the melodramatic patriot and Laureate who was the greatest comfort to his Queen next to the Bible; and thirdly, the Modern pessimist of the clear and sordid detail, ironically observing a world fragmented by the inroads of science and scepticism upon religion and moral seriousness? A case for all three options could certainly be argued, but I prefer to categorize Tennyson here more prosaically as a Modern Romantic Victorian, and I hope to be able to demonstrate that the greatness of Tennyson as a poet lies in the fact that he was indeed, to use that phrase from "Locksley Hall", an "heir of all the ages" — or at least of Romanticism, Victorianism and Modernism, not to mention Classicism.[1]

---

1. Alan Sinfield agrees with Edward Elton Smith that the "two voices" of Tennyson are essentially a Romantic and a Classicist one: "Tennyson cannot be fully comprehended without some understanding of the modes of thought which characterized his immediate predecessors, the Romantics; but, at the same time, there are elements in his art which derive from impulses more often associated with

Born in 1809, Tennyson was obviously influenced in his earliest poetic efforts by his older contemporaries, the Romantics proper. The anecdote of the fourteen-year old Tennyson rushing out of doors when news of Byron's death reached his parental home at Somersby in 1824, and scratching "Byron is dead" in sandstone, is well-known.[2] The major Romantic influence on the work of Tennyson, however, was not Byron but Keats. Tennyson's early poems in particular, such as "Mariana" and "The Lotos-Eaters", share the sensuousness of mood and the sensitivity to sound that are the hallmark of Keats's *oeuvre*.

An early article by Patricia Ball provides a first attempt to trace Tennyson's inheritance from his Romantic precursors beyond a facile verbal comparison of say, "Mariana" to Keats's "Ode to Autumn".[3] Following up on Robert Langbaum's *The Poetry of Experience* (1957), she characterizes the Romantic period as being marked by the "crisis of personality" and what she calls "the effort to grasp the essential qualities of 'self' as the one trustworthy point of reference for humanity", an awareness which the Victorians inherited and which they pursued by the two kinds of poetical character as distinguished by Keats: the "Wordsworthian or egotistical sublime" and "the camelion poet". "If Tennyson wrote *Maud* from his chameleon instinct", Ball continues, "he conceived *In Memoriam* in response to the Romantic egotistical line of experiment".[4] Unlike Wordsworth's ego, however, Tennyson's is a tormented one, "haunted by its responsibility for itself

---

the eighteenth century" (18) and "*In Memoriam* displays the extremes of both attitudes" (*The Language of* In Memoriam, Oxford, 1971, 18 and 22, see also 17 and 18 and n.3). Sinfield repeatedly compares Tennyson's "Classicism" to that of Pope (17, 26, 36, 76, 90, 178, 180, 198). The "neat pigeonholes" of "Enlightenment" and "Romanticism" (irrespective of periodization) are indeed in the minds of modern critics (although the distinction goes back to at least as early a "modern" critic as Matthew Arnold). In our postmodern computer age we have become so used to describe phenomena, including art and literature, in terms of binary divisions and the tensions between them, that it is mainly ourselves that "do the police" — in "two voices"! The present writer is no exception.

2. See, for example, Jerome Hamilton Buckley, *The Victorian Temper: A Study in Literary Culture*, New York, 1951, 68; also Sinfield, 17, and Michael Thorn, *Tennyson*, London, 1992, 26.

3. Patricia M. Ball, "Tennyson and the Romantics", *Victorian Poetry*, I (1963), 7-16. For a concise and perceptive survey of Tennyson's development as a poet up to *In Memoriam*, see Buckley's chapter "Tennyson — The Two Voices" (66-86).

4. Ball, 9 and 10.

and its world" (13). Inasmuch as this explains anything about Tennyson's Romanticism, it also seems to point forward to an essentially Modernist concern, one strongly reminiscent of Sartrean existentialism.

As has been noted by M.H. Abrams in his somewhat over-extended but all the same intriguing *Natural Supernaturalism* (with its Carlylean title), it was Wordsworth who discovered, or at least was the first to argue in terms of poetry, that the trivial can be of supreme importance, that, in a sense, it can be sacred.[5] The Romantic poet's task, Wordsworth felt, was to give voice precisely to this insight. If, as is held by Frank Kermode, "the concept of the self-sufficient image or symbol" is what the modern movement is based on and what links it directly to the Romantics,[6] Tennyson (who receives very scant attention in Kermode's book) is to be contrasted to the Romantics not only as a "scientific" and "moral" poet, but especially as someone continuing a tradition established by Wordsworth, albeit with a twist. For if the Romantics "invented" the notion of the literary epiphany (Wordsworth's "spots of time") as a medium for ecstatic joy, a signpost on the circular road back to the lost paradise (in terms of Abrams' major thesis in *Natural Supernaturalism*), Tennyson exploited not so much the joyful, ecstatic epiphany, "those trance-like moments which Tennyson valued so highly, in his life and in his poems",[7] but added an epiphany of sadness or despair, containing inexplicable but nonetheless epiphanic "idle tears" of regret.

In his summary section, "The Romantic Positives", Abrams notes that "The Romantic aesthetic was of art for man's sake, and for life's sake".[8] The poetic imagination of the Romantics was a moral imagination, reacting to what these poets experienced as the upheaval and dislocation of their times (namely the French Revolution and its disappointing aftermath), just as Tennyson reacted to the false sense of consolidation and the economic and scientific disruptures of 1830 and 1848, and the great economic boom that followed the latter, and just as Modernists like Pound and Eliot, Woolf and Joyce, reacted to the impact of a world literally disconnected by the first global war.

---

5. M.H. Abrams, *Natural Supernaturalism: Tradition and Revolution in Romantic Literature*, New York and London, 1973, 395.

6. *The Romantic Image*, New York, 1957, as summarized by Abrams, 427.

7. Christopher Ricks, *Tennyson*, Berkeley and Los Angeles, 2nd edn, 1989, 183. Ricks is right in calling Time "Tennyson's most impassioned subject" (281).

8. Abrams, 429.

Of course, these historicisms are by now trivial points, easily scored. Abrams's statement about the Romantics that "The burden of what they had to say was that contemporary man can redeem himself and his world, and that his only way to this end is to reclaim and to bring to realization the great positives of the Western past" is equally valid for most Victorians as it is for most Modernists.[9]

Similarly, both the joyful and the despairing or "demonic" epiphany[10] can be traced throughout the nineteenth and twentieth centuries, at least up to and including the work of T.S. Eliot, James Joyce, Virginia Woolf and Wallace Stevens, and it is not until a certain school of postmodernist writing arose that it became apparently the poet's and novelist's task to give voice to the fact that the trivial is indeed trivial — a position that perhaps finds its origin in fictional characters like Joseph Conrad's Mr Kurtz and T.S. Eliot's "Hollow Men". But even these "hollow men" can already be traced in the evasive Byronic hero and to Victorian characters such as Browning's Duke of Ferrara and Tennyson's St Simeon Stylites. So the question remains: what is essentially Romantic or Victorian or Modern about all this, and how do these "essentials" feature in the work of Tennyson?

I would like to argue that the process from Romanticism through Victorianism to Modernism is basically one of an increasing sense of what Abrams calls "the fragmentation and isolation of men in modern society",[11] voiced in an increasingly secular version of the Biblical story of Fall and Redemption. In this process, there are no clear-cut breaking-points during the nineteenth century other than convenient political dates such as 1832 (the First Reform Bill), 1848, 1873 (the beginning and end of economic *hausse*) and 1901 (the death of Queen Victoria), and, perhaps, the publication dates of seminal works such as Pater's *Studies in the History of the Renaissance* of 1873. Tennyson's *In Memoriam*, published in the same year (1850) as the definitive version of Wordsworth's very Romantic *The Prelude*, is perhaps the prime example of that "Circuitous Journey" that forms the main theme of Abrams's book; what else is that "great circle" of fallen man back to

9. Abrams, 430. Cf. for instance recent attempts to fit the arch-Romantic Modernist James Joyce into the tradition of post-colonialism by scholars like Vincent Cheng.

10. The latter term was introduced by Northrop Frye; see Ashton Nichols, *The Poetry of Epiphany: Nineteenth-Century Origins of the Modern Literary Moment*, Tuscaloosa and London, 1987, 2.

11. Abrams, 314.

the paradise lost and then regained in self-realization which Abrams discusses at such great and erudite length, but the possibility "That men may rise on stepping stones/Of their dead selves to higher things" with which Tennyson opens the first lyric of his great elegy?[12] It is on this poem that the rest of this essay will be focused.[13]

The very title, *In Memoriam A.H.H.*, takes the poem beyond the tradition of the great personal elegies such as Milton's "Lycidas" or Shelley's *Adonais*. As from Wordsworth's notion of "spots of time", memory itself became a major literary theme, representing the possibility of individual redemption not only to the dead subject mourned but to the mourning poet himself, in what Wordsworth called the wedding of "the discerning intellect of Man" to "this goodly universe/In love and holy passion" ("Prospectus" to *The Excursion*, ll. 52-54). At the same time, Wordsworth's Romantic notion of "solitary anguish" (*ibid.*, l. 77) pervades the work of Tennyson from the Kraken to King Arthur — if any character suffers from it, it is St Simeon Stylites or Ulysses or Tithonus or the narrator of *Maud* or Enoch Arden, to mention only a few.[14] This same Romantic anguish,

---

12. All references to and quotations from *In Memoriam* are as in *In Memoriam: An Authoritative Text*, ed. Robert H. Ross, New York and London, 1973.

13. See Sinfield, 146 ff., for an extensive account of circle imagery in *In Memoriam*. On page 150, Sinfield comments in general terms on Tennyson's technique of creating symbols by the use of the recurring image: "one of the most remarkable facts in the history of criticism is that commentators did not notice it until the twentieth century — that is, until it became common in modern literature." For the connections between Victorianism and Modernism, see in particular Carol T. Christ, *Victorian and Modern Poets*, Chicago and London, 1984, esp. ch. 5 on the problems of periodization. "Despite their anti-Victorianism, Modernist poets explore ways of objectifying poetry that show striking continuities with Victorian poetics" (3). The dramatic monologue, extensively used by T.S. Eliot and other Modernist poets, has "clearly acknowledged Victorian roots" (15). And Langbaum argues that "The dramatic monologue ... originates when the Victorian poet writes a Romantic lyric of experience in the voice of a character separate from his own" (16). The relationship of the dramatic monologue to Modernist constructs of mask and persona is explored in ch. 2 of Christ's book, and will therefore not be further investigated in this paper. Instead, I will concentrate here on *In Memoriam*, a poem in which the "persona" and the "poet" can be said to be to all intents and purposes *un*divided — even if Tennyson contradicts this in his comments on the poem (see, for example, Sinfield, 31).

14. Cf. Christ, 26-28. She repeatedly uses the term "the burden of personality" (48, 49, 52).

elaborated by Tennyson and Arnold (Browning in this respect was more of an optimist, coupling Keats's "Negative Capability" to Shelley's enthusiasm as well as to Byron's flair in his dramatic monologues), is still the hallmark of Stephen Dedalus's and Leopold Bloom's anguish, to which it points forward, in Joyce's Modernist "epic" *Ulysses*, also to be understood as an "elegy" for the dead (Stephen's mother, Bloom's son). Such Romantic anguish also finds its niche among the "fragments", "shored against" the narrator's "ruins" in Eliot's *The Waste Land* (l. 430).[15] The "key" that each of "us" thinks of in his "prison" (l. 413) can in retrospect, so to speak, be fitted into one of the many recurrent "self-sufficient symbols" (in Kermode's terms) of *In Memoriam*, the door. It is in fact, to use a Chaucerian phrase, the "key of remembrance".[16]

We see, then, how a concern with memory and with the subjective experience of time, a concern which it is difficult to label in terms of periodization, pervades English poetry from *The Prelude* through *In Memoriam* to *The Waste Land* and *Four Quartets*, in which it becomes the dominant existentialist motif.[17] My concern will be to illustrate how Tennyson's great poem incorporates notions that can be derived from and classified as Romanticism, Victorianism, and Modernism at

---

15. T.S. Eliot, *Collected Poems 1909-1962*, London, 1963, 79.

16. For an extensive discussion of the image and the symbol in Victorianism and Modernism, see Christ, 53-100: "Both Victorian and Modernist poetics contain theories of the image which claim objective validation for the connection between image and emotion" (54). Arthur J. Carr, who in 1950 described Tennyson as "our true precursor", notes that "He shows and hides, as if in embryo, a master theme of Joyce's *Ulysses* — the accentuated and moody self-consciousness and the sense of loss that mark Stephen Dedalus". He also, less convincingly, regards *Maud* as preparing the way for the verse of Eliot's "Preludes" and "Prufrock". Moreover, "The question of 'objective foundations' permeates Tennyson's career and binds his poetry to the crisis of the arts in our century" ("Tennyson as a Modern Poet", in *Critical Essays on the Poetry of Tennyson*, ed. John Killham, London, 1960, 42-43).

17. "Tennyson's divided attitude is not without parallel. It may be found for instance in *Four Quartets*, where it is resolved in a not altogether dissimilar way" (J.C.C. Mays, "An Aspect of Form" [1965], repr. in *Tennyson:* In Memoriam: *A Casebook*, ed. John Dixon Hunt, London, 1970, 262-63). Cf. "There is a great deal in common between the *Four Quartets* and *In Memoriam*" (285). With reference to a short essay by A. Walton Litz, Christ notes that Eliot's 1936 essay on *In Memoriam* "has been related to the composition of *The* [*sic*] *Four Quartets*" .... But *In Memoriam* has much in common with *The Waste Land* as well" (131: for references, see 172 nn.43 and 44). See also Sinfield, 207-10.

the same time. If any distinction between these labels is to be at all meaningful, we must give them a useful hermeneutic sense by relating them to a pervading theme or rather a set of themes — of memory (remembrance), time, and the timeless moment or epiphany. In passing, other motifs will be commented upon as well.

T.S. Eliot, who mainly praised Tennyson for possessing "the finest ear of any English poet since Milton" (an indirect gibe, if you like, at the Romantics), and for "turning his limitations to good purpose", said of *In Memoriam* that this was where Tennyson "finds full expression".[18] However, he places it firmly in what for him is, in every respect, a generation very different from his own (except, as he notes, for the comparable shallowness of the times), a bygone age. Noting that "That strange abstraction, 'Nature', becomes a real god or goddess, perhaps more real, at moments, to Tennyson than God", and that the poet seems to compromise "between the religious attitude and ... the belief in human perfectibility", Eliot appears to discern a humanistic quality in *In Memoriam* that compares narrowly to what Abrams appreciates in *The Prelude*. Eliot's major premise that *In Memoriam* is a poem that is "not religious because of the quality of its faith, but because of the quality of its doubt",[19] valid as it is, is not in itself enough to qualify *In Memoriam* for the claim of being considered "the quintessential poem of the mid-Victorian period".[20] For that, we need a little more evidence.

First of all, there is nothing fanciful or wildly imaginative in *In Memoriam*, in comparison, for instance, with Shelley's *Adonais*. Tennyson was a stickler for factual detail, which Buckley describes as typical of the Victorians.[21] It is important to keep this in mind from the start, because the poem is framed by a decidedly positivist outlook: "For knowledge is of things we *see*" (Prologue 22; italics added); the future Man, foreshadowed (almost literally, by the secondary moonlight in the Epilogue) in the offspring of the poet's newly-wedded sister, will

18. T.S. Eliot, "*In Memoriam*", in *Selected Essays*, 3rd enlarged edn, London, 1956, 328, 332 and 333.

19. *Ibid.*, 335 and 336.

20. Thorn, 245.

21. Buckley, 133 ff. Buckley refers to the "elaborate background" of factual detail which obscures the hero in *Enoch Arden* (136). In this sense, the Pre-Raphaelites were typical Victorians as well (137). It can be argued that the factual detail contributes to the effect of "objective validation" in Tennyson's *oeuvre*: cf. n.15 above.

be "the crowning race" which "shall *look*/On knowledge" (Epilogue, 128-30). In one of the first sections written after Arthur Hallam's death on 15 September 1833, Tennyson voices the major dilemma of the whole poem, namely that he "shall not *see*" his dead friend again "Till all my widow'd race be run" (IX 17-18). The repetition of the possessive "my" ("my lost Arthur", "My friend", "My Arthur") obviously emphasizes the closeness of the relationship, which is almost that of a marriage dissolved by death — the poet is "widow'd". Of the "Strong Son of God, immortal Love" addressed in the Prologue, the poet also states that "we ... have not *seen*" His face; He can therefore only be "embrace[d]" "By faith, and faith alone". The echoing of words like "love", "see" and "light" between the Prologue (composed in 1849, sixteen years after the event now memorized) and the early section IX, suggests a clear relationship between Arthur Hallam and Christ. The difference is that Arthur can be resurrected in the poem that follows, as is indicated in its final sections; the "Dear heavenly friend that [can]not die,/Mine, mine, for ever, ever mine" (CXXIX 7-8) is in the previous lines called "human, divine", and in what follows "strange friend, past, present, and to be", which, interestingly, equates him with time rather than with timeless eternity. Increasingly as the poem unfolds, there is a curious intimation that although the Son of God is "strong" and embodies "immortal Love", the memory of the dead friend who was once "seen" is ultimately stronger than the "Believing where we cannot prove" in the Prologue suggests about religious faith. Following the main argument of Timothy Peltason[22] that in *In Memoriam* Tennyson proceeds from moment to moment in coping with the death of a loved friend, and taking it to its extreme, it can be argued that the whole poem is basically a defence of the idea that "faith" is ultimately a matter of accepting ("feeling", in Tennyson's own terms, as in section LXXXV 40 ff.) the spiritual value of the epiphany or "trance"; the only "point" of the existence of God, of life after death, of a continuation of one's own identity, is that from time to time we have precisely such "flashes" of knowledge or insight as the poet for instance obtains in XCV to which I will later return.

In section I, Tennyson expresses the desire embodied by the whole of *In Memoriam* in terms of "reach[ing] a hand thro' time" (I 7). In a strikingly succinct phrase, the poet here sums up not only the attempt to bridge the time that must elapse before his "widow'd race be run" (IX

---

22. Timothy Peltason, *Reading* In Memoriam, Princeton: NJ, 1985.

18) and he will reach "the good that grows for us out of grief",[23] but also the gap between the present time and the memories of the past, a gap which is closed in CXIX: "I take the pressure of thine hand" (12), and in CXXIV: "And out of darkness came the hands/That reach thro' nature, moulding men" (23-24).

If the epiphanic memory is spontaneous, like a sudden blow, most of *In Memoriam* is concerned with wilfully evoked memory, as is in fact very much the case in *The Prelude*, no matter the "spots of time". Thus, in the often quoted VII (to which CXIX is the complement), the poet wilfully evokes a memory of his dead friend by revisiting the latter's house at Number 67, Wimpole Street:

> Dark house, by which once more I stand
> Here in the long unlovely street,
> Doors, where my heart was used to beat
> So quickly, waiting for a hand,
>
> A hand that can be clasp'd no more -
> Behold me, for I cannot sleep,
> And like a guilty thing I creep
> At earliest morning to the door.
>
> He is not here; but far away
> The noise of life begins again,
> And ghastly thro' the drizzling rain
> On the bald street breaks the blank day.

The poet "cannot sleep", "as he [Hallam] sleeps now" (IX 15). He asks the "dark house", which compactly forms what Eliot would no doubt have recognized as an "objective correlative"[24] for the loss of the friend, and which simultaneously symbolizes the body bereft of its illuminating soul, to "behold" him, as if begging the friend who can no longer be "seen" and touched to take notice of his own almost ghostly existence, pared down to that of a "guilty thing" (the reference, of

23. Tennyson's annotation: see Ross, 4 n.2.

24. "I take it that this use of natural description to convey the poet's feeling [in LXVIII] is what Eliot meant in his familiar remark about an 'objective correlative'. The sensory experience communicated by the description of external objects evokes in the reader an emotion appropriate to the poet's feelings" (Sinfield, 124). Surely, this is not only valid for the natural imagery that Sinfield is discussing here (for instance with regard to the final stanza of VII on page 126), but also to the "townscape", if only by way of contrast.

course, is to *Hamlet* as much as to Wordsworth's "Immortality Ode").[25] "He is not here" implies "but *I* am here", whereas "far away" (which Tennyson once recorded was an enchanting phrase to him)[26] "The noise of life" (ironically counterpoised against the dead Hallam) "begins again,/And ghastly thro' the drizzling rain/On the bald street breaks the blank day". Not only is the moment-in-time of day-break "far away" (it will be there for the poet in the epiphanic XCV), but this image of the callously "blank" universe in its very modern town setting is more than an instance of Romantic "pathetic fallacy" or Victorian sentimentalism. It looks forward to the trivial memories recorded in Eliot's "Rhapsody on a Windy Night", to the oyster shells and coffee spoons that mark the passing of time in "Prufrock", and to the opening lines of *The Waste Land*. In fact, many of the images in those lines by Eliot, "mixing/Memory and desire" (ll. 2-3), such as: "feeding/A little life with dried tubers" (ll. 6-7), "a shower of rain" (l. 9), "the roots that clutch" (l. 19), all this "heap of broken images" (l. 22), seem to point back directly to *In Memoriam* — to lines like "Old yew, which graspest at the stones" and "the clock/Beats out the little lives of men" (II 1, 7-8).[27] The difference is that whereas *The Waste Land* reflects boredom and indecision ("what shall I do now?", l. 131),

---

25. See the excellent reading of *In Memoriam* by Elaine Jordan (*Alfred Tennyson*, Cambridge, 1988, 109-37). The allusions to the ghost of Hamlet's father (*Hamlet*, I.i.153) and to ll. 148-51 of the "Immortality Ode" are to be found on page 129. Jordan here also comments on the sentence "He is not here" (VII 9) as an allusion to "the words of the angel on Christ being risen from the tomb", which confirms my reading elsewhere of an identity between Hallam and Christ. Cf. Sinfield, 109-11, who expresses puzzlement at this comparison. Elsewhere, Jordan discusses the pervading "hand" image: "Holding and touching are important: the hand which writes and weaves together becomes a metonymy ... for *In Memoriam*'s major concern, relatedness" (111; cf. 117 ff.). According to Jordan, the "Romantic violence and exhilaration" of discarded verses "remain possibilities even into the Epilogue" (113).

26. See Robert Bernard Martin, *Tennyson: The Unquiet Heart*, Oxford, 1983: "... the words 'far, far away' had always a strange charm for me" (21). For the source of this quotation, see Hallam Tennyson, *Alfred Lord Tennyson: A Memoir*, 2 vols, London, 1897, I, 11.

27. See also Buckley, 97-105, on the "death by water" motif in Victorian literature (*the* Victorian "waste land" poem is, of course, Browning's "Childe Roland to the Dark Tower Came" of 1855). In *In Memoriam*, the "death-by-water" motif pervades sections IX-XIX in particular. In XIX 11-12, the poet's "tears that cannot fall" identify the mourning narrator with an emotionally as well as elocutionary waste land.

In Memoriam is informed by a very different sense of the superfluity of time.

Sinfield compares *In Memoriam* to a novel without the narrative that links individual events: the 131 numbered sections being like the expressions (or even impressions) of so many "moments", moments "in the continuum of the poet's changing attitudes, with other parts of his life neatly cut away".[28] Sinfield regards this as one of the poem's Romantic sides. I would add that it is also very Modern.

As in Eliot's *Waste Land*, in *In Memoriam* memory is transmitted in sensual images relating to concrete objects, places and events: "Old yew, which *graspest* at the stones" (II 1); "I hear the noise about thy keel;/I hear the bell struck in the night:/I see the cabin-window bright;/I see the sailor at the wheel" (X 1-4); "The chestnut *pattering* to the ground" (XI 4), and so on. These memories are drawn into the present consciousness by the predominant use of the present tense. As Jordan rightly puts it, "*In Memoriam* is a poem which tracks the experience of memory in time".[29] As a major philosophical theme, memory is introduced in sections XLIV and XLV, the previous sections being primarily elegiac:

XLIV

How fares it with the happy dead?
  For here the man is more and more;
  But he forgets the days before
God shut the doorways of his head.

The days have vanish'd, tone and tint,
  And yet perhaps the hoarding sense
  Gives out at times (he knows not whence)
A little flash, a mystic hint;

And in the long harmonious years
  (If Death so taste Lethean springs),
  May some dim touch of earthly things
Surprise thee ranging with thy peers.

---

28. Sinfield, 27.

29. Jordan, 110. Timothy Peltason remarks on the fact that in *In Memoriam*, as generally elsewhere, Tennyson's poetry "scrupulously holds itself to the moment that the poet looks back from .... Tennyson writes about the past as a felt impingement upon the present and not as another scene to which the reader and the poet can imaginatively remove themselves. His natural subject is the experience and not the content of memory" (56-57). Elsewhere, he notes that nearly all the lyrics of *In Memoriam* are narrated in the present tense (119).

If such a dreamy touch should fall,
O turn thee round, resolve the doubt;
My guardian angel will speak out
In that high place, and tell thee all.

XLV

The baby new to earth and sky,
What time his tender palm is prest
Against the circle of the breast,
Has never thought that "this is I:"

But as he grows he gathers much,
And learns the use of "I," and "me,"
And finds "I am not what I see,
And other than the things I touch."

So rounds he to a separate mind
From whence clear memory may begin,
As thro' the frame that binds him in
His isolation grows defined.

This use may lie in blood and breath,
Which else were fruitless of their due,
Had man to learn himself anew
Beyond the second birth of Death.

XLV in particular strikes at once a Romantic note (the child as father of the man), a Victorian one (the domestic and almost sentimental image of the baby pressing its mother's breast) and a Modern one (its existentialist line of argument, with the sense of separation between "I" and "other"). Note again the references to sight and touch in lines 7 and 8.

After these sections, the words "memory" and "remember", not literally used earlier in the poem, recur twelve times more.[30] Note how the time scale in the poem has by now expanded from the moment, the here-and-now of section VII, to the human life-span. As section XLV reflects on the meaning of the single, isolated human life from birth to

30. Arthur E. Baker, *A Concordance to the Poetical and Dramatic Works of Alfred, Lord Tennyson*, London, 1914. Although somewhat primitive, this concordance is very useful in tracing verbal cross-connections.

death, in sections LV and LVI the span is further extended to include geological time, forcing the poet to "stretch lame hands of faith" (LV 17) — no pressing the breast of Mother Earth! It is in the epiphanic section XCV, which is too long to quote in its entirety, that the "dreamy touch" of which we have had a premonition in XLIV occurs. "Reading" as it were in the prematurely fallen summer leaves[31] in the garden of Somersby Rectory (the parental home!) "The noble letters of the dead" (XCV 24), the narrator hears "love's dumb cry" (27) and has an epiphanic experience:

> So word by word, and line by line,
> The dead man touch'd me from the past,
> And all at once it seem'd at last
> The living soul was flash'd on mine, ... (33-36)

until "At length my trance/Was cancell'd, stricken thro' with doubt" (43-44). Much more forceful than Tennyson's later explanation of these lines ("The trance came to an end in a moment of critical doubt, but the doubt was dispelled by the glory of the dawn of the 'boundless day', line 64")[32] is the poetical statement in XCVI: "There lives more faith in honest doubt,/Believe me, than in half the creeds" (11-12). The irony in "Believe me" (to *which* "half" does this "creed" which Tennyson

---

31. And not Hallam's letters, as erroneously assumed by most earlier commentators, including Jordan (124, 136). If the purblind Tennyson literally were reading letters, which seems highly unlikely, since it is clearly indicated that night has fallen (1), and that "in the house light after light/Went out" (19-20), the dead man's "touch" would not have the force of an epiphany, as it would detract from its unpremeditated nature. I think ll. 23-24 can be related, for instance, to LXXV 13: "Thy leaf has perish'd in the green" and to the elegiac nostalgia for those pastoral "lands where not a leaf was dumb" (XXIII 10). The leaf is a recurrent image in *In Memoriam* (see Baker), another "objective correlative" for mutability and random loss. At the same time, there is only one other reference to letters, namely in X 7, and these are not from or even about Hallam. On *In Memoriam* XCV as an epiphany, see Ashton Nichols, *The Poetry of Epiphany*, 157-61, and, in more detail, see the same author's "The Epiphanic Trance Poem: Why Tennyson Is Not a Mystic", *Victorian Poetry*, XXIV (1986), 131-48. Nichols misreads the image of the fallen leaves as well (*The Poetry of Epiphany*, 162; "The Epiphanic Trance Poem ...", 140, 142, 145). For a correct reading, see Richard J. Dunn, "Vision and Revision: *In Memoriam* XCV", *Victorian Poetry*, XVIII (1980), 135-46. See also my "Leaves or Letters? A Crux in Tennyson's *In Memoriam*", *Victorian Poetry*, XXXIV (1996), 279-82.

32. Ross, 61 n.8.

suggests the reader share with him belong?), and that "half" of "half the creeds", again, strikes a remarkably modern note — although, at the same time, I would not have been surprised to encounter such lines in Byron's *Don Juan* either. The "perhaps" is reminiscent of the opening lines of "Burnt Norton" (*Four Quartets*): "Time present and time past/Are both perhaps present in time future ...." A Victorian analogue can be found in Christina Rossetti's "Haply I may remember,/And haply may forget" ("Song: When I am dead, my dearest", ll. 15-16).[33]

In the first section to reflect on the writing of *In Memoriam*,[34] section V, we find a similar type of irony: "I sometimes hold it *half* a sin/To put in words the grief I feel" (1-2, italics added). In the same section, Tennyson announces, in what sounds almost like an "Ablaut": "In words, like weeds, I'll wrap me o'er" (9). Compare this to Eliot's "My words echo/Thus, in your mind" ("Burnt Norton", I 14-15). The bird that sends the narrator of *Four Quartets* off to the rose-garden is reminiscent of the "Short swallow-flights of song", a more Romantic metaphor which Tennyson uses in XLVIII 15, to define his "brief lays". In the first stanza of that section Tennyson is quite explicit about the limited nature of his elegy:

> If these brief lays, of Sorrow born,
> Were taken to be such as closed
> Grave doubts and answers here proposed,
> Then these were such as men might scorn: ... (1-4)

In other words, no final answers are to be expected in *In Memoriam*, whose poet, like Sorrow, "holds it sin and shame to draw/The deepest measure from the chords" (11-12).[35] Eliot draws a more modern conclusion: "human kind/Cannot bear very much reality" ("Burnt Norton", I 44-45). In the second section of "Burnt Norton", which opens with that surprising juxtaposition of "Garlic and sapphires in the mud", Eliot repeats a phrase from *In Memoriam*, XLIII: "the figured leaf". The first part of this section is written in the iambic tetrameter

33. Eliot, *Collected Poems 1909-1962*, 189; *The Complete Poems of Christina Rossetti*, ed. R.W. Crump, 3 Vols, Baton Rouge and London, 1990, I, 58.

34. There are altogether 23 sections in which the poet's writing of poetry becomes a subject of the poem (Richard Gill, In Memoriam *by Alfred Tennyson*, London, 1987, 53). Self-reflexiveness is a major Romantic and Modernist motif.

35. I fail to see why this disclaimer goes "beyond the prudently modest and become[s] disingenuously disarming" (Ricks, 210-11).

which Tennyson uses throughout, and which is like the steady tick-tock of a timepiece.

What is perhaps ultimately most Victorian about *In Memoriam*, besides the formality of the metre and the restrained archaism of some of the diction, is the perfect balance Tennyson maintains between the opposing forces of the private and the public, of life and death, faith and doubt, joy and despair, a balance reflected by the poem's high formality, which is restrained from becoming over-formal by the use of four- instead of five-foot lines, which could easily have led to more ornamental and descriptive adjectives and a less tense syntax. This restraint makes *In Memoriam* less discursive than either *The Prelude* or *Four Quartets*, and more emotionally controlled as well; there is a perfect balance between sense perception and intuition (or imagination), between thought and feeling.[36] Buckley quotes Charles Kingsley's character Alton Locke about "democratic art", which is "the revelation of the poetry which lies in common things".[37] It seems to me that this notion of "democratic art" is a very apt definition of *In Memoriam*, and may serve to explain its great popularity with Tennyson's contemporaries from Queen Victoria downward.

In Memoriam, then, offers precisely the "restraint" of feeling and the "discipline" of form that were demanded of the "new" poet as early as the late 1820s, and also the "plainness of speech" advocated a few decades later by Matthew Arnold, a restraint and a plainness that are lacking almost entirely in Shelley's *Adonais*, the prototypical Romantic elegy.[38] However, it retained the self-consciousness and

---

36. This tallies with a point made by Alan Sinfield about the imagery of *In Memoriam*, namely that it "falls into four main groupings — religious, domestic, scientific and natural" (108). These four groupings respectively correspond with Carl Jung's categories of character types: intuition, feeling, thinking and sensation.

37. Buckley, 31. Kingsley's novel *Alton Locke* also appeared in 1850.

38. *Ibid.*, 25, 26. *Adonais* (as in P.B. Shelley, *Poetical Works*, 2nd edn, Oxford, 1970, 432-44) in spite of its Neoclassical garb, is direct, emotional, affirmative, a fiery lament: "I weep for Adonais — he is dead!" (1); "He will awake no more, oh, never more!" (64). That "He is made one with Nature ..." (370) and is now "a portion of the loveliness/Which once he made more lovely" (378-79), Tennyson surely could not have believed about Arthur Hallam; although we might find his repeated suggestion that Arthur is now performing his duties in "those great offices that suit/The full-grown energies of heaven" (XL 19-20) a bit ridiculous, because so very Victorian. Shelley's certainty, his "faith" ("The soul of Adonais, like a star,/Beacons from the abode where the Eternal are", 494-95) may be a mere poetic stance rather than a rational expression of comfort, and in any

introspectiveness that had been the hallmark of the great Romantics. In addition, it provided a clarity and originality of diction ("I seem to fail from out my blood", II 15) as well as a premonition of the loss of order and integration, both in general and in concrete terms ("Time, a maniac scattering dust", L 7; "The red fool-fury of the Seine", CXXVII 7) that looks forward to Modernism. This is not to say that *In Memoriam*, like *Maud* and *Enoch Arden*, and like the discursive and nostalgic *Idylls of the King*, is not in the outcome essentially Victorian. Tennyson (who in any case cannot be seen as *the* mouthpiece of poetic Victorianism, as witness the numerous adverse critiques of his poems by eminent Victorians such as Carlyle, Arnold, George Eliot and Swinburne) is neither a sensuous, ecstatic and imaginative Romantic, nor is he a Modern avant-gardist or even an experimentalist. But in his own time he was at least as much "a man speaking to men" as was Wordsworth, and a poet "occupied with frontiers of consciousness beyond which words fail"[39] as was Eliot. Tennyson, indeed, "sang to the Victorians, as Pope to the Augustans, what oft was thought but ne'er so well expressed".[40] The greatness of the "canonical" poets and writers is that they are at once men and women of their time and heirs of all the ages. Tennyson is surely one of these.

---

case hardly sincere from an atheist. This poem, with its elevated, vatic tone and bravura of imagery strikes me as essentially Romantic, just as Eliot's irony and the banality of domestic and industrial detail in *The Waste Land* surpasses anything that Tennyson would have considered suitable material for poetic treatment. On Tennyson as an early admirer of Shelley, including *Adonais*, which was reprinted in 1829 by the Cambridge Apostles of which Tennyson was a member, see Margaret A. Lourie, "Tennyson as Romantic Revisionist", *Studies in Romanticism*, XVIII (1979), 3-27.

39. T.S. Eliot, "The Music of Poetry", in *Selected Prose*, Penguin edition, 1953, 57.

40. Buckley, 67-68. Elsewhere, Buckley called *In Memoriam* "a kind of Victorian *Essay on Man*" (as quoted by Robert H. Ross, "The Three Faces of *In Memoriam*", in Ross's *In Memoriam: An Authoritative Text*, 95). In so far as *In Memoriam* has "its most important analogue" in Shakespeare's Sonnets (Ricks, 204), Tennyson is also an heir to the Renaissance.

ATHEISM AND BELIEF IN SHELLEY, SWINBURNE AND CHRISTINA ROSSETTI

VALERIA TINKLER-VILLANI

The topic of this volume — the fusion and confusion of literary periods — forms the most general framework of my present study, in which I want to consider this topic in terms of the concepts of atheism and belief and their role in the work of one Romantic and two Victorian poets. The words "atheism" and "belief" are very complex and vague clusters of ideas — atheism, for instance, could support a basically progressive view of human life, as it does, in some ways, in Shelley, or a non-progressive view, as in Swinburne. But in this short article I can do no more than open a field of enquiry into the matter of atheism and belief in Shelley, Swinburne and Christina Rossetti.

Any consideration of atheism in the context of Romantic and Victorian poetry must begin with Shelley. From early on, for Shelley atheism was not just a destructive stance, a call for the dismantling of a system, but an active source of thought, action, and poetry. Indeed Shelley is one of the first to avowedly assert his own atheism and argue logically in its support, in *The Necessity of Atheism*, "A Refutation of Deism" and other writings on the subject. Until Shelley, atheism had been used as an accusation to discredit an opponent, and, paradoxically, in philosophical discussions in order to prove the absolute impossibility of anyone believing in speculative atheism; only practical atheism was believed to exist — as immoral behaviour. For example, the 1771 edition of the *Encyclopaedia Britannica* states:

> Many people, ancient and modern, have pretended to atheism, or have been reckoned atheists by the world; but it is justly questioned whether any man seriously adopted such a principle. These pretensions, therefore, must be grounded on pride or affectation.

Or grounded on youthful spirits, or an iconoclastic attitude, one might add in the case of Shelley. Baron D'Holbach's *Systeme de la nature*, printed in Amsterdam in 1770, was a revolutionary publication, marking the culmination of centuries of thought. D'Holbach argues in defence of atheism and refutes the arguments used by theists, but, more than that, he codifies a complete system based on nature. D'Holbach was then living in Paris where he met twice a week with other *savants* for dinner and discussions, repeating a habit developed in his student days in Leiden. Shelley knew the work, and quoted it in one of his notes to *Queen Mab*.[1] Although the philosophy of the *Systeme de la nature* was materialistic and mechanistic, much in the system could well have contributed to Shelley's views, and this is an area which deserves further study. Without going into the precise nature of Shelley's atheism, it is important to stress the earnestness of his studies on this subject, for he had read and referred to Bailly, Cabanis, Hobbes, Hume, D'Holbach, Laplace, Locke, and many others; and he was aware of the seriousness of his own position. In the "Essay on the Devil and Devils", dating from 1820, with reference to Milton, but in terms which could be applied to his own position, he stated:

> It is difficult to determine, in a country where the most enormous sanctions of opinion and law are attached to a direct avowal of certain speculative notions, whether Milton was a Christian or not at the period of the composition of Paradise Lost.[2]

Shelley's defence of atheism in his early pamphlets and in the introductions and notes of his early works, is speculative and is based on an empirical approach. The arguments are structured in terms of logic and reason, and based on proofs, evidence, and experience. Poetry makes use of different tools, in particular the feelings and sensibility of the reader. In the Preface to *The Revolt of Islam*, Shelley says:

> I have made no attempt to recommend the motives which I would substitute for those at present governing mankind, by methodical and systematic argument. I would only awaken the

1. "*If God has spoken, why is the universe not convinced?*", Note VII, "I will beget a son", in *Shelley's Prose*, ed. David Lee Clarck, London, 1954, rpt. 1988, 105. D'Holbach's work and William Hammon's *Answer to Priestley*, the first English work avowedly to argue for atheism in 1782, were published anonymously, as were Shelley's *The Necessity of Atheism* and *A Refutation of Deism*; however, *Queen Mab* was not.

2. *Shelley's Prose*, 267.

> feelings, so that the reader should see the beauty of true virtue, and be incited to those inquiries which have led to my moral and political creed, and that of some of the sublimest intellects of the world.[3]

Feelings are certainly as important as reason in the poetry; his aims, as stated in the same Preface, are "the bloodless dethronement of ... oppressors and the unveiling of the religious frauds"; and he adds that "if the lofty Passions by which it has been my scope to distinguish this story do not excite in the reader a generous impulse, an ardent thirst for excellence ... let not the failure be imputed to a natural unfitness for human sympathy in these themes".[4]

Already from these early texts various ideas can be inferred. To begin with, religious, political, social, moral values are inextricably merged;[5] the unveiling of religious fraud or the dethronement of tyranny cannot and should not be distinguished from each other or from moral or social values — each stands for the rest. Atheist and Republican are synonyms, and have further connotations. It is a limitation in the state of criticism that a certain compartmentalization must of necessity take place, producing reduction by dissection. Further, Shelley's major argument in *The Necessity of Atheism* and in other texts is his view that belief is an involuntary passion. Therefore there is a strong stress both on reason, and on passion. Finally, the purpose of subverting "all the oppressions under the sun" is the creation of a public context suitable for the total reformation of man's intellectual and moral life. Shelley, that is, seems interested in systems but is more interested in man. This also probably begins to explains how it is that Shelley's interest in science, philosophy, and political and social activities so easily goes hand in hand with an interest in horror, in abnormally acute sense perceptions, and the world of demons.

David Berman says that Shelley's argument in "A Refutation of Deism" is "somewhat dulled by irony".[6] That irony reduces the

---

3. *The Poetical Works of Percy Bysshe Shelley*, ed. Edward Dowden, London, 1930, 95.

4. *Ibid.*, 95-96.

5. In the Preface to *The Revolt of Islam*, for example, one finds in the same footnote references to Malthus's *Essay on Population* and Godwin's *Political Justice*.

6. David Berman, *A History of Atheism in Britain: From Hobbes to Russell*, London, 1988, 146.

effectiveness of an argument is probably true in the case of a pure philosopher, but surely not in the case of a poet. In Shelley's prose, irony is added to argument. In his "Essay on the Devil" Shelley writes:

> I am afraid there is much laxity among the orthodox of the present day respecting a belief in the Devil .... Depend upon it, that when a person once begins to think that perhaps there is no devil, he is in a dangerous way.[7]

Here, we see atheism explored in prose not only through speculative argument, but also by moving the feelings of the reader. For this, humour and irony are important, and so is a medium which relies on the language of belief to express atheism; here, we would expect the sentence to refer to God, but God is replaced by the opposite, the Devil. In this way, a system is subverted on its own terms; profane language reveals the absurdity of its original basis.

To remain with the "Essay on the Devil" — Shelley there discusses other important ideas about the kind of poetry produced by religion, and particularly Christianity:

> Misery and injustice contrive to produce very poetical effect, because the excellence of poetry consists in its awakening the sympathy of men which among persons influenced by an abject and gloomy superstition is much more easily done by images of horror than of beauty. It requires a higher degree of skill in a poet to make beauty, virtue and harmony poetical, that is, to give them an idealized and rhythmical analogy with the predominating emotions of his readers, than to make injustice, deformity, and discord or horror poetical.[8]

In general, therefore, atheism, considered as the absence of any fixed system imposed from outside on the mind of man, is the necessary public framework without which the best poetry cannot be created. Consequently, Christian mythology must be transformed. In the "Essay on the Devil", Shelley compares the Greek god Pan with the Christian representations of the devil, and the Greek serpent with the Christian serpent: in Greek mythology, Pan and the sylvan gods are connected to "all that could delight and enliven" and the serpent was "an auspicious and favourable being", but "The Christians contrived to turn the wrecks

---

7. *Shelley's Prose*, 268.

8. *Ibid.*, 273.

of the Greek mythology, to purposes of deformity and falsehood".[9]

Any system of belief imposed from the outside is a straitjacket on the mind of man, and Christianity in particular distorts and corrupts. Far from being an iconoclastic gesture of radical passion, atheism in Shelley is a passion based on a knowledge of philosophy and of science, on evidence from personal experience and from history, and on a strong belief in the role of poetry. The poet is the most powerful reformer of human life. The language of poetry, and its music, can create multiple images, combining ideas of freedom, Nature and human love and thus reshape man's mind.

To consider Swinburne after Shelley is to look at "Romantic" and "Victorian" as purely period terms, since Swinburne is clearly part of the revolutionary movement we have come to know, in Mario Praz's phrase, as "Romantic Agony". In fact, a contemporary critic referred to Swinburne as "The second Shelley",[10] in the context of political and revolutionary poetry. Atheism is one of the many aspects Swinburne shares with Shelley, and also — as the critic saw — in terms inextricably merged with politics. When Swinburne writes about Republican Rome at the time when large numbers of Italians were struggling to take Rome away from Papal control and make it the capital of a unified Italy, the phrase expresses much more than the political hope involved with Italian unification — it is a call for the subversion of theocratical tyranny, for the marriage of heaven and hell. When Swinburne mentions in a letter that one of King Lear's speeches is "the first and greatest of all republican poems", he is talking neither of theology nor of politics, but of man's independence from any mental and spiritual constriction — a use of language derived from Shelley.[11]

Swinburne knew the work of Shelley very well; his "Notes to the text of Shelley" are knowledgeable, professional and sensitive. He also displays clear awareness of important views of Shelley, which he shared — for example, Shelley's views on Christianity and on Christ:

> That he did to the last regard it [Christianity] as by all historical evidence the invariable accomplice of tyranny — as at once the

---

9. *Ibid.*, 274.

10. In *The Contemporary Review*, 1869; quoted by Swinburne in his letter to W.M. Rossetti dated 31 March 1869 (see *The Swinburne Letters*, ed. Cecil Y. Lang, 6 vols, New Haven, 1959, II, 10).

11. Letter to William Michael Rossetti, 25 January 1904 (*Letters*, VI, 176-77).

> constant shield and the ready spear of force and of fraud — his latest letters show as clearly as that he did no injustice to "the sublime human character" of its founder.[12]

In terms of Swinburne's own atheism, his rejection of Christianity on the basis of reason is very clear in his letters, where, for example, he said that "God is the absurdest figment of the imagination" and added:

> I might call myself ... a kind of Christian* (of the church of Blake and Shelley). (* That is, taking the semi-legendary Christ as a type of human aspiration and perfection, and supposing ... that Jesus may have been the highest and purest sample of man on record).[13]

This is an acute observation, for the recognition of Blake as the antecedent both of Shelley and Swinburne himself is valid and revealing. There are three points which help us to read and understand Swinburne's poetry in terms of his atheism, which become clearer when considered in the light of Blake and Shelley. In Blake, heaven and hell were contrary states, the existence of both of which is necessary to life; Shelley, too, saw destruction and creation in similar terms. In the case of Swinburne, this goes perhaps a step further. Good and evil, pleasure and pain are not just elements of a dialectic, but are co-existent; good is part of the total experience of life and evil contributes to create good. Therefore, for this reason the Christian system which separates good from evil distorts and corrupts. In order to liberate life, poetry and language from the oppression of Christian tyranny, a new mythology has to be found. Swinburne notes that in Shelley's *Laon and Cythna* "Persian and Indian, Christian and Mahometan mythologies are massed together for attack".[14] Like Shelley, Swinburne did not believe that the best way to do this was the creation of a totally new mythology, which is what Blake to a large extent had done. But, although, like Shelley, Swinburne turns mainly to Hellenic figures, he in fact merges them with figures from other mythologies, and also he uses his figures in a way that is very similar to Blake's. The names of Sappho and Apollo, for example, are supposed to call up various ideas and different stories

12. *Essays and Studies*, London, 1875, 191. But Swinburne also recognized that Shelley could write beautiful religious poetry, as for example in the chorus in *Hellas*.

13. Letter to E.C. Stedman, 20 February 1875 (*Letters* III, 13, 14).

14. *Essays and Studies*, 194.

which accompany them. To read Swinburne's poetry without realizing this is to run the risk of missing much of its richness.

We see all this very clearly, for example, in "Mater Triumphalis":

> Mother of man's time-travelling generations,
> Breath of his nostrils, heartbeat of his heart,
> God above all Gods
> ....
> Sinned hast thou sometime, therefore art thou sinless;
> Stained hast thou been, who art therefore without stain;[15]

Addressed in the traditional terms of the Mother of God, this god who is man can only be pure by having sinned, because god can only be perfect by being perfectly human. The stress placed on the clear, causal relation ("therefore") is a stress on reason within the paradox of language. The mother figure recurs in other poems, such as "Hertha", or in *Atalanta in Calydon*, where Atalanta's mother, Althea, is also described with religious formulae associated with the Mother of God, "Mater triumphalis"; but here, in the drama, the mother is associated to other figures, such as Aphrodite (in a combination common in Pre-Raphaelite poetry) and Earth. As with Blake's Urizen, Orc and other characters, the reader of Swinburne must be aware of these various levels.

Not only mythology, but language, too, has to be reshaped. Swinburne, like Shelley, does this partly by using the language of religion, and then subverting it. The briefest, clearest example is the last line of Swinburne's "Hymn of Man": "Glory to Man in the highest, for man is the master of things."[16] Similarly, many titles of Swinburne's poems — and therefore the context in which his own utterance is placed — are derived from traditional religion: "Genesis", "Cor Cordium", "Ex Voto", "Mater Triumphalis".

In fact, Swinburne's prose and in particular certain poems are filled with almost obsessive, repeated references to God; in addition, like Shelley, he uses words such as "godlike" and "divine" continually as general terms of description. Of Shelley, for example, Swinburne says

15. *The Poems of Algernon Charles Swinburne*, 6 vols, London, 1904, II, 144, 148.

16. *Ibid.*, 93. Or see "Genesis" (117): "And death, the shadow cast by life's wide wings,/And God, the shade cast by the soul of man."

that he alone was "the perfect singing-god";[17] in lyric poetry, "he is god and lord" — "in one word, and the only proper word — divine".[18] This last quotation makes clear the dynamics behind this use of religious words: if man is god, then among men the poet is closest to the type of human perfection; indeed, he is a God. This is literally what Swinburne says about Dante. In the Prelude to *Tristram of Lyonesse*, there is a passage about Dante in Hell, who sees the eyes of a woman (unnamed by Swinburne, but to be understood as Paolo's Francesca),

> ... who made as God's own eyes to shine
> The eyes that met them of the Florentine,
> Wherein the godhead thence transfigured lit
> All time for all men ....

Dante, witnessing love, even sinful love, becomes godlike and a transfigured god; the passage continues, referring to Tristram and Iseult whom Dante also sees in Hell:

> Ah, and these too felt on them as God's grace
> The pity and glory of this man's breathing face;
> For these, too, these my lovers, these my twain,
> Saw Dante, saw God visible by pain,
> With lips that thundered and with feet that trod
> Before men's eyes incognisable God;[19]

The syntax here, as often in Swinburne, is ambivalent. We could read the third and fourth lines of the passage as meaning that the lovers saw Dante (that is, God come to Hell). But since we have read that Dante saw Helen and saw Francesca ("the woman"), so now, alternatively, we could understand that Dante sees Tristram and Iseult also, shown to him in Hell (that is to say, "For Dante saw these, too, these my lovers"), in which case "God visible by pain" refers to the lovers. And indeed, this different reading, in which the lovers are god, is also true, for love is the strongest force in life and is real divinity. Together the two interpretations tell us that Dante is God as man and poet, and the Lovers are God, for Love is the strongest force. Syntax must be twisted in order to accommodate the complex ideas involving the roles of

---

17. *Essays and Studies*, 215.

18. *Ibid.*, 224.

19. "Prelude: Tristram and Iseult" to *Tristram of Lyonesse*, in *The Poems of Algernon Charles Swinburne*, 10-11.

lovers, man, poet and god, for these ideas also include the importance of evil and pain, and the revelation which evil and pain can bring. But one should also note that, though ambivalent, the syntax is correct and totally under the poet's control, as always in Swinburne. It is a new order, but it is order, not chaos. In Christianity, the gift of prophecy and the gift of language were granted by the Holy Ghost, a light from on high, represented as flames; Swinburne's atheism requires a new prophetic wind, a profane alternative to the Holy Spirit;[20] hence also a profane version of language. Two words Swinburne uses constantly to indicate the prophetic power of the poet are "fire" and "light" — Shelleyan images which become more abstract in Swinburne.

Both the first and the second Shelley could believe strongly in human life and in prophetic poetry precisely because of their atheism. In the case of Swinburne it is not just a question of atheism, but of very strong anti-theism. How then do we account for the strange rapport between Swinburne, who was strongly attacked also on moral grounds for the alleged lasciviousness, pain and cruelty of his poetry, with Christina Rossetti, the severely religious, retiring poet? Christina Rossetti was not just a religious poet. She belonged to the High Church wing of Anglicanism which, though it rejected Roman Catholicism, was very close to it — confession, for example, being normal practice. In her poetry, she was practically haunted and consumed by the figure of Christ.

Swinburne met Christina Rossetti occasionally at her brother's, Gabriel's, house. He sent her a copy of four of his works on their publication, and, in 1893, he dedicated his *Century of Roundels* to her, after first ensuring that the dedication would be acceptable. In 1894, shortly before her death, he published a *Ballad of Appeal to Christina Rossetti*, in which he urged her to produce more work, and soon after she died, he wrote an elegy — at midnight on New Year's Eve, or, as he put it in a letter to his mother, in the last hour of the last day of the year. On the basis of this letter one could speculate that, since she was also a poet, Christina Rossetti was the only woman who could represent to Swinburne a personal, real incarnation of the Virgin Mary, Aphrodite, Sappho figure. For Christina's part, it was her brother William Michael who always assured Swinburne of his sister's high regard for him. There must be some truth in this, or William Michael surely would not have dedicated *New Poems* (1896), published soon

---

20. See Jerome McGann, *Swinburne*, Chicago, 1972, 100.

after Christina's death, to Swinburne. Christina Rossetti herself wrote a few letters to Swinburne in a friendly but not affectionate manner. There is no direct record of Rossetti's specific reaction to Swinburne's books, except for polite expressions of pleasure. William Michael Rossetti informs us that his sister pasted bits of paper on two lines of *Atlanta in Calydon*, where atheism was too strongly expressed, and criticism has repeated this detail *ad infinitum*. Consequently, Rossetti's latest biographer, Jan Marsh, for example, assumes that "Alerted by the controversy, Christina probably did not read far into them [Poems and Ballads]".[21] But this is speculation, and the biographer also notes that Rossetti was not as prudish as it is sometimes thought. Nor did Christina attempt to proselytize Swinburne, except for sending him, after having already received four books of his, her work entitled *Called to be Saints*.[22]

However, leaving biographical speculation aside, what could there be in the poetry of Swinburne and Christina Rossetti to bridge the gap between their religious views? Swinburne had the highest regard for Rossetti's poetry. In a footnote to an essay on Arnold, in which he mentions Rossetti, he describes:

> … the great new-year hymn of Miss Rossetti:
>
> "Passing away, saith the world, passing away,"
>
> so much the noblest of sacred poems in our language that there is none which comes near it enough to stand second; a hymn touched as with the fire and bathed as in the light of sunbeams, tuned as to chords and cadences of refluent sea-music beyond

---

21. Jan Marsh, *Christina Rossetti: A Literary Biography*, London, 1994, 357.

22. In fact, Swinburne was not against religious poetry; in his essay on Arnold he states that "The joy of worship, the delight or admiration is in itself so excellent and noble a thing that even error cannot make it unvenerable or unprofitable; no one need repent of reverence …; it has done him good to worship, though there were no godhead behind the shrine" (*Essays and Studies*, 148). He is probably also thinking of Christina Rossetti, to whose poetry he refers in the same article. In the course of criticizing Arnold's praise of Mademoiselle de Gerin, Swinburne turns to good women poets: "they never would come forward … as genius or as saint. The immortal women in either kind — St Theresa, St Catherine, Vittoria Colonna, Mrs Browning, Miss Christina Rossetti — belong to a different world and scheme of things. With one verse or one word of theirs any one of these could have absorbed and consumed her [Mlle. de Gerin] as a sunbeam of the fiery heaven a dewdrop of the dawning earth."

> reach of harp and organ, large echoes of the serene and sonorous tides of heaven ....[23]

Jan Marsh finds this compliment excessive.[24] But the habitual reader of Swinburne would recognize in the compliment two main points: firstly, that to Swinburne, Rossetti was a fellow poet-prophet, as indicated by his use of the words "fire" and "light" with reference to Rossetti's poetry; secondly, that the sacredness of this hymn is sustained particularly by the music of the lines. Rather than being the curse of Victorian poetry, as some have considered the stress on sound and rhythm to be, this musicality, in poets such as Swinburne and Christina Rossetti, should be seen as the attempt to take poetry not only closer to painting, but also close to music, moving it, that is to say, away from reality and imitation, and taking it out of time and place — into a religious dimension, inherent in Aestheticism's fundamental belief that "all art constantly aspires towards the condition of music".[25]

There is no doubt that Rossetti's later work is strongly and strictly Christian; but this does not always make her poetry more narrow and limited, and neither should our reading of her work be restricted within the confines of one belief, as Swinburne's reading was not. In the collection *Monna Innominata*, Sonnet 6 closes on these lines:

> Yea, as I apprehend it, love is such
> I cannot love you if I love not Him,
> I cannot love Him if I love not you.[26]

Divine love is here the basis for human love, but it is with the human that the poem leaves us. The distinction between the human "you" and the divine "Him" is clear, but the lines create a very strange pattern, with the action of the "I" remaining firm, fixed in the two lines, while the other personal pronouns shift across the lines. A full reading of Rossetti's poems reveals how the personal pronoun "you", or "him", often switches from referring to the lover to referring to Christ, and even to the speaker's own heart, in a total fusion of the three figures, so

---

23. *Essays and Studies*, 175.

24. Marsh, 357.

25. Walter Pater, "The School of Giorgione" (1877), in *The Renaissance*, London, 1925, 135.

26. *The Complete Poems of Christina Rossetti*, ed. R.W. Crump, 3 vols, Baton Rouge and London, 1979-1990, II, 89.

that we have a kind of less than Holy Trinity: Christ, the speaker, and the lover, all united in the speech of the speaker.[27]

Of course, religious poetry has always used the language of human and even erotic love. But the opposite is also true: love poetry makes use of sacred imagery. Rossetti was, indeed, probably using seventeenth-century religious imagery, and perhaps this is also true of "The Heart Knoweth Its Own Bitterness", in which Christ, or the lover, is accused of loving superficially:

> You scratch my surface with your pin;
> You stroke me smooth with hushing breath:-
> Nay, pierce, nay, probe, nay dig within ....

The poem concludes with fulfilment in Paradise:

> There, God shall join and no man part,
> I full of Christ and Christ of me.[28]

Even admitting to a whole tradition of religious poetry expressed in erotic terms, this remains very physical. I would say that these examples are a profane use of the name of Christ; other religious images are equally profane. Paradise, for example, as in the penultimate line, becomes a place where the unhappiness caused by unrequited love is finally satisfied, and the lovers reunited. That line describes Paradise using part of the formula for the celebration of marriage; is it then so shocking to read the last line as the consummation of the marriage?

In Christina Rossetti's poems faith is not generally presented in terms of triumphant achievement:

> Lord, I believe, help Thou my unbelief:
> Lord, I repent, help mine impenitence:
> Hide not Thy Face from me, nor spurn me hence,
> Nor utterly despise me in my grief;
> ....
> Say, "Come", say not "Depart," tho' Thou art just:
> Yea, Lord, be mindful how out of the dust

---

27. See my "The Italian Poems of Christina Rossetti", in *Beauty and the Beast, Christina Rossetti, Walter Pater, R.L. Stevenson and Their Contemporaries*, eds Peter Liebregts and Wim Tigges, Amsterdam & Atlanta: GA, 1996, 31-42.

28. *The Complete Poems of Christina Rossetti*, III, 265.

> I look to Thee while Thou dost look on me,
> Thou Face to face with me and Eye to eye.[29]

This can be read as a prayer, as Katherine Mayberry does: "The conclusion of the poem reminds us of the difference between God and the speaker and demonstrates how much distance has been bridged by the speaking of the poem."[30] But in the light of what I said earlier about the ambiguity in the use of personal pronouns, with the images of Lord and Christ as powerful solvers of problems, the poem can also be read as a secular poem making use of the figures and language of religion. In such a reading, the poem would describe how an insecure self mirrors itself into an elevated, powerful self; in fact, here the speaker has not, like Dante in the *Paradiso*, travelled upwards and, finally, after a long struggle, mirrored himself as man and poet into the face of Christ; here, it is the Lord who seems to have come down into the dust. In addition, "Say 'Come'" is a prayer, but could also be read as a command, particularly when followed by "be mindful ...". It is "me" that assumes the dominating position in the penultimate line, which it opens and closes, and the central position in the last line.

This is a first sonnet of two, and the second is a much more orthodox prayer which finds a solution to tensions in the idea of the church. "I" becomes "We", and "Thee" assumes the central position in the last line: "We hand in hand with Thee and heart in heart". But a secular reading of the first sonnet can continue into the second. More importantly, the sonnets do not just tell a story and establish a final achievement; each reading of the two sonnets will enact a repeated movement from unbelief to belief, from uncertainty to self-abandonment in the church and God. The tension between the abject submission and feelings of unworthiness in the first sonnet, and the feelings of safety and release from selfhood in the second finds no final solution, but becomes cyclical. Also, the solution has nothing to do with conviction or reason, but only faith, and truly in Rossetti belief is, in Shelley's words, an involuntary passion. Consider the paradox of "belief" and "unbelief" in the first line of the first sonnet: how similar, and how different, these are from Swinburne's even, reasoned statements in "Mater Triumphalis".

In Christina Rossetti's poetry, love is the strongest force, and, even

---

29. *Ibid.*, II, 185.

30. Katherine J. Mayberry, *Christina Rossetti and the Poetry of Discovery*, Baton Rouge: LA, 1986, 121.

if here it is divine love, it is enacted in terms of passionate love, and Christ becomes a figure of the lover. The speaker, too, adopts an exemplary role, a prophetic role. Perhaps, in the Victorian period a woman poet could achieve a prophetic role only by remaining within religion. In religion, Rossetti has found a system which allows her poetry to remain conventionally religious and yet explore passions and states of mind. Of course, in other senses, too, the limitations imposed by Victorian customs and values on a woman poet are central to Rossetti's position. In that sense the historical values contained in the word "Victorian" are invaluable in connection with Rossetti. But all the uses of "Romantic" I have seen recently have been the occasion of obfuscation rather than clarification. Jan Marsh quotes Theodore Watts's memories of Rossetti's reaction to beautiful scenery (she started murmuring words to herself) and adds that Rossetti's "'ever present apprehension of the noumenon underlying the phenomenon'" is "a high-Romantic approach, espoused by Shelley and eloquently articulated by Ruskin", though later this turned into a generalized nature-worship which frequently compensated for the loss of transcendental religion.[31]

Did Shelley espouse this High Romantic approach? Not according to Algernon Swinburne. Swinburne has a great deal to say about the famous incident when Shelley signed himself on more than one visitor's book in Switzerland as "philanthropist, democrat and atheist". Swinburne notes that the provocation for this was that

> … on the same leaf there appears just above his signature an entry by some one who saw fit here to give vent to an outbreak of overflowing foolery, flagrant and fervid with the godly grease and rancid religion of a conventicle; some folly about the Alps, God, glory, beneficence, witness of nature to this or that divine thing or person and such-like matter.[32]

If we agree with Swinburne's reading, then it would seem that — with her passion, tensions and response to nature — the only Romantic of my trio of poets is Rossetti, who is, in addition, also Victorian.

Maybe all critics should agree to do with Romanticism what has been done with Postmodernism, where we have a number of specific subdivisions; we could then, for example, use the term "Romanticism" exclusively for the kind of meditative self-involvement of Wordsworth, Coleridge, Keats and Arnold, whereas we could refer to most of the

31. Marsh, 446.

32. *Essays and Studies*, 192.

work of Blake, Shelley, Swinburne, Yeats or even Carlyle as "Prophetic Romanticism", and coin other terms for other varieties of "Romanticisms". There is another possibility. Swinburne said "I write not as a disciple of the dishevelled school, 'romantique à tous crins;' all such false and foolish catchwords as the names of classic and romantic I repudiate as senseless".[33] Maybe we should do the same.

33. *Ibid.*, 180.

NOTES ON CONTRIBUTORS

C.C. Barfoot, English Department, Leiden University, published *The Thread of Connection: Aspects of Fate in the Novels of Jane Austen and Others* (1982); and in the last five years has edited, alone or with others, *In Black and Gold: Contiguous Traditions in Post-War British and Irish Poetry* and *"Een Beytie Hollansche": James Boswell's Dutch Compositions* (1994), *Ritual Remembering: History, Myth and Politics in Anglo-Irish Drama* (1995), *Beyond Pug's Tour: National and Ethnic Stereotyping in Theory and Literary Practice* (1996), and *Oriental Prospects: Western Literature and the Lure of the East* (1998). His most recent articles are on Geoffrey Grigson, Shaw's *St Joan*, newspaper reports of the 1798 Maidstone treason trials, Southey's *Joan of Arc*, oriental influences on English eighteenth-century and Romantic literature, and William Blake's *Milton*.

Allan C. Christensen, English Department, John Cabot University, Rome, has published *Edward Bulwer-Lytton: The Fiction of New Regions* (1976), *A European Version of Victorian Fiction: The Novels of Giovanni Ruffini* (1996) and many articles on Victorian subjects (Dickens, Carlyle, Hardy) and other areas that derive from an interest in the connection between literature and music; co-editor of *The Challenge of Keats* (1999).

Odin Dekkers, formerly of the English Department, Nijmegen University, is the editor of John Donne, *Gedichten* (1993), and the author of *J.M. Robertson: Rationalist and Literary Critic* (1998), as well as of various articles on Victorian literature and ideas. His main interest continues to be in late nineteenth-century English literature. He is currently responsible as acquisitions editor and project manager for the *English Studies* list of Swets & Zeitlinger Publishers.

Geraldine Higgins, English Department, Emory University, received her D.Phil from Oxford on "The Concept of Heroism in Yeats, Synge and AE: 1880-1916". She has written on the heroic tradition in the Irish Literary Revival and is currently working on a study of the contemporary Irish playwright, Brian Friel.

Helga Hushahn is working on the early reception of Schiller in Britain, and of Kotzebue in the Netherlands; she has published articles on "The Anti-Jacobins and German Drama" and on how Schiller's *Die Jungfrau von Orleans* was received both in Germany and England.

Ralph Jessop, until 1997 lecturer in English Literature and Philosophy at the University of Glasgow, is now company director of The Cusp: Art, Craft & Design (Scotland). He is the author of *Carlyle and Scottish Thought* (1997) and has published several articles on Thomas Carlyle and Scottish Philosophy. He maintains academic interest specifically in Carlyle, Burns, David Hume, Thomas Reid, Sir William Hamilton and, more generally, eighteenth- and nineteenth-century English and Scottish literature.

Douglas S. Mack, English Department, Stirling University, is General Editor of the Stirling/South Carolina Research Edition of the Collected Works of James Hogg, and his publications include various editions of texts by Hogg and Scott. Most recently, he has edited Hogg's epic poem *Queen Hynde* with Suzanne Gilbert (1998), and his edition for Penguin of Scott's *Old Mortality* appeared early in 1999.

Phillip Mallett, School of English, University of St Andrews, has published essays and articles on writers from William Shakespeare to Primo Levi in various books and journals, and he is the editor of a number of volumes, including *Rudyard Kipling: Limits and Renewals*; *Kipling Considered*; *A Spacious Vision: Essays on Thomas Hardy*; *Satire* (special issue of FORUM for Modern Languages); and the forthcoming Norton edition of Thomas Hardy's *The Mayor of Casterbridge*. He is currently working on a literary life of Rudyard Kipling.

Jane Mallinson, English Department, Leiden University, has published a number of articles on the relationship between philosophy and literature, and is currently investigating the influence of Anglo-American Idealism on literary Modernism.

Judith van Oosterom is currently working on a thesis on the later life and works of Margaret Oliphant, novelist and woman of letters.

Ralph Pite, Department of English, Liverpool University, is the author of *The Circle of Our Vision: Dante's Presence in English Romantic*

Poetry (1994) and editor of *Lives of the Great Romantics*, II, *Coleridge* (1997). At present he is researching the lives and biographies of the Romantic poets and regionalism in the late nineteenth-century English novel. An earlier version of the essay in this volume was published in *Romanticism*, II/1 (1996), 68-80.

Ann Rigney, Department of Comparative Literature, Utrecht University, has published extensively on nineteenth-century historiography and on theoretical issues relating to historical representation and fictionality. She is the author of *The Rhetoric of Historical Representation: Three Narrative Histories of the French Revolution* (1990), is co-editor of *Cultural Participation: Trends since the Middle Ages* (1993), and has just completed a study entitled *Imperfect Histories*.

Margaret Rundle, English Department, University of Hartford, has published "Perhaps the Greatest Paradox of All: Carlyle's Greater Success as Prophet in the 1820s and 1830s" in *Carlyle Studies Annual* (Special Issue, 1997). She also has ten entries in the *Carlyle Encyclopedia* to appear in 1999-2000 and has presented conference papers internationally on Carlyle and Dickens. At present she is writing a book with the working title *Promethean Fire: Carlyle as Revolutionizing Prophet*.

Jacqueline Schoemaker, formerly of the English Department, Amsterdam University, is researching various aspects of Keats — his relationship to the Aesthetic Movement and his relationship to women and women writers.

Aveek Sen, St Hilda's College, Oxford, is researching and has published articles on Keats in relation to early nineteenth-century periodical writing and aesthetic philosophy.

Wim Tigges, English Department, Leiden University, is the author of *An Anatomy of Literary Nonsense* (1988), and is co-editor (with Peter Liebregts) of *Beauty and the Beast: Christina Rossetti, Walter Pater, R.L. Stevenson and Their Contemporaries* and editor of *Moments of Vision: Aspects of the Literary Epiphany* (1999). He has recently published a Dutch translation of Tennyson's *In Memoriam*.

Valeria Tinkler-Villani, English Department, Leiden University, is the author of *Vision of Dante in English Poetry* (1988), has co-edited *Exhibited by Candlelight: Sources and Developments in the Gothic*

Tradition (1995), and is now editing *Babylon of New Jerusalem: Perceptions of the City in Literature*. She has published widely on literary and historical relations between Italy and England, including recent articles on Christina Rossetti and Algernon Swinburne.

Bart Veldhoen, English Department, Leiden University, edited the *Companion to Early Middle English Literature* (1988, 2nd enlarged edition, 1995), and has published articles on Chaucer's "Franklin's Tale", on a variety of aspects of Middle English romances, on the Middle Dutch *Roman van Walewein*, and on Layamon's nationalism. He is currently working on Tennyson's transformation of medieval source-material.

Keith D. White, English Department, University of South Florida, is the author of *John Keats and the Loss of Romantic Innocence* (1996). He has also published on Lord Byron, William Dean Howells, Wallace Stevens, and various topics of linguistics and literary criticism. His short stories have appeared in various American literary magazines.

Karen Wolven, formerly of the School of English and American Studies, Exeter University, until accepting a position as Technical Writing Specialist and Consultant for a computer software development company based in New York. Her contribution in this book is based on research she did for her Ph.D thesis on Ebenezer Elliott of Sheffield, which explores English poetry of the early to mid-nineteenth century and Elliott's contribution to the development of an industrial working-class culture from the 1830s to the 1850s.

INDEX

This index includes personal names to be found in the main text of the book, but not the names of fictional characters, who, when they are discussed in the main text, are represented under the author and title of the works in which they appear. Titles themselves are included when they are those of works of imaginative fiction, poetry or drama, or of texts published before 1920. Modern critics are only included if they are mentioned in the main text.

DQR Studies in Literature

lume 1: **LINGUISTICS AND THE STUDY OF LITERATURE.** Ed. Theo D'haen. Amsterdam 1986. 287pp.
3N: 90-6203-717-8
Paper Hfl. 40,-/US-$ 22.-/Bound Hfl. 90,-/US-$ 50.-

lume 2: BETWEEN DREAM AND NATURE: ESSAYS ON TOPIA AND DYSTOPIA. Ed. by Dominic Baker-Smith and C.C. rfoot. Amsterdam 1987. 234 pp.
3N: 90-6203-959-6
Paper Hfl. 35,-/US-$ 19.-/Bound Hfl. 75,-/US-$ 41.50

lume 3: **EXPLORATIONS IN THE FIELD OF NONSENSE.** Ed. by m Tigges. Amsterdam 1987. 262 pp.
BN: 90-6203-699-6
Paper Hfl. 35,-/US-$ 19.-/Bound Hfl. 80,-/US-$ 44.-

lume 4: **THE CLASH OF IRELAND: LITERARY CONTRASTS ND CONNECTIONS.** Ed. by C.C. Barfoot and Theo D'haen. nsterdam/Atlanta, GA 1989. 288 pp.
BN: 90-5183-086-X Paper Hfl. 39,50/US-$ 22.-
BN: 90-5183-084-X Bound Hfl. 120,-/US-$ 66.50

lume 5: **SOMETHING UNDERSTOOD: STUDIES IN NGLO-DUTCH LITERARY TRANSLATION**. Ed. by Bart Westerweel d Theo D'haen. Amsterdam/Atlanta, GA 1990. 335 pp.
BN: 90-5183-186-2 Paper Hfl. 49.50/US-$ 27.50
BN: 90-5183-152-8 Bound Hfl. 140.-/US-$ 77.50

lume 6: **FABRICS AND FABRICATIONS: THE MYTH AND AKING OF WILLIAM AND MARY.** Ed. by Paul Hoftijzer and C.C. rfoot. Amsterdam/Atlanta, GA 1990. 314 pp. ISSN: 0921-2507
BN: 90-5183-182-X Paper Hfl. 49,50/US-$ 27.50
BN: 90-6203-990-1 Bound Hfl. 140,-/US-$ 77.50

olume 7: THEATRE WEST: IMAGE AND IMPACT. Ed. by Dunbar Ogden, with Douglas McDermott and Robert K. Sarlós. nsterdam/Atlanta, GA 1990. 254 pp.
BN: 90-5183-126-9 Paper Hfl. 37,50/US-$ 18.-
BN: 90-5183-125-0 Bound Hfl. 125,-/US-$ 69.-

olume 8: **CENTENNIAL HAUNTINGS: POPE, BYRON AND ELIOT THE YEAR 88**. Ed. by C.C. Barfoot and Theo D'haen. nsterdam/Atlanta GA 1990. 366 pp. with ill.
BN: 90-5183-171-4 Paper Hfl. 49,50/US-$ 27.50
BN: 90-5183-170-6 Bound Hfl. 160.-/US-$ 88.50

olume 9: TROPES OF REVOLUTION: WRITERS' REACTIONS O REAL AND IMAGINED REVOLUTIONS 1789-1989. Ed. by C.C. arfoot and Theo D'haen. Amsterdam/Atlanta, GA 1991. 401 pp.
BN: 90-5183-292-3 Bound Hfl. 180,-/US-$ 100.-
BN: 90-5183-293-1 Paper Hfl. 60,-/US-$ 33.-

olume 10: **THE GREAT EMPORIUM.** The Low Countries as a cultural ossroads in the Renaissance and the eighteenth century. Edited by C.C. arfoot and Richard Todd. Amsterdam/Atlanta, GA 1992. 258 pp.
BN: 90-5183-362-8 Bound Hfl. 120,-/US-$ 66.50
BN: 90-5183-363-6 Paper Hfl. 40,-/US-$ 22.-

olume 11: SHADES OF EMPIRE IN COLONIAL AND POST-OLONIAL LITERATURES. Ed. by C.C. Barfoot and Theo D'haen. msterdam/Atlanta, GA 1993. 320 pp.
BN: 90-5183-365-2 Paper Hfl. 50,-/US-$ 27.50
BN: 90-5183-364-4 Bound Hfl. 130,-/US-$ 72.-

olume 12: JAMES FENIMORE COOPER. New Historical and iterary Contexts. Ed. by W.M. Verhoeven. 217 pp. Amsterdam/Atlanta, A 1993. ISBN: 90-5183-333-4 Bound Hfl. 90,-/US-$ 50.-
BN: 90-5183-360-1 Paper Hfl. 40,-/US-$ 22.-

olume 13: IN BLACK AND GOLD: CONTIGUOUS TRADITIONS N POST-WAR BRITISH AND IRISH POETRY. Ed. by C.C. Barfoot msterdam/Atlanta, GA 1994. 331 pp.
SBN: 90-5183-675-9 Bound Hfl. 160,-/US-$ 88.50
SBN: 90-5183-660-0 Paper Hfl. 50,-/US-$ 27.50

olume 14: LITERATURE AND THE NEW INTER-DISCIPLINARITY: POETICS, LINGUISTICS, HISTORY. Ed. by oger D. Sell and Peter Verdonk Amsterdam/Atlanta, GA 1994. 245 pp.
SBN: 90-5183-597-3 Bound Hfl. 125,-/US-$ 69.-
SBN: 90-5183-609-0 Paper Hfl. 50,-/US-$ 27.50

olume 15: RECLAMATIONS OF SHAKESPEARE. Ed. by A.J. Ioenselaars. Amsterdam/Atlanta, GA 1994. 318 pp.
SBN: 90-5183-606-6 Bound Hfl. 160,-/US-$ 88.50
SBN: 90-5183-639-2 Paper Hfl. 50,-/US-$ 27.50

Volume 16: EXHIBITED BY CANDLELIGHT: SOURCES AND DEVELOPMENTS IN THE GOTHIC TRADITION. Editors: Valeria Tinkler-Villani and Peter Davidson, with Jane Stevenson Amsterdam/Atlanta, GA 1995. IX,298 pp.
ISBN: 90-5183-832-8 Bound Hfl. 140,-/US-$ 77.50
ISBN: 90-5183-828-X Paper Hfl. 45,-/US-$ 25.-

Volume 17: SONS OF EZRA: BRITISH POETS AND EZRA POUND. Ed. by Michael Alexander and James McGonigal. Amsterdam/Atlanta, GA 1995. VI,183 pp.
ISBN: 90-5183-855-7 Bound Hfl. 100,-/US-$ 61.-
ISBN: 90-5183-840-9 Paper Hfl. 35,-/US-$ 19.-

Volume 18: MAKING AMERICA/MAKING AMERICAN LITERATURE FRANKLIN TO COOPER. Ed. by Robert Lee and W.M. Verhoeven. Amsterdam/Atlanta, GA 1995. 360 pp.
ISBN: 90-5183-906-5 Bound Hfl. 160,-/US-$ 88.50
ISBN: 90-5183-909-X Paper Hfl. 50,-/US-$ 27.50

Volume 19: BEAUTY AND THE BEAST: Christina Rossetti, Walter Pater, R.L. Stevenson and Their Contemporaries. Ed. by Pieter Liebregts and Wim Tigges. Amsterdam/Atlanta, GA 1995. 280 pp.
ISBN: 90-5183-902-2 Bound Hfl. 125,-/US-$ 69.-
ISBN: 90-5183-896-4 Paper Hfl. 45,-/US-$ 25.-

Volume 20: **BEYOND PUG'S TOUR: NATIONAL AND ETHNIC STEREOTYPING IN THEORY AND LITERARY PRACTICE.** Ed. by C.C. Barfoot. Amsterdam/Atlanta, GA 1997. 594 pp.
ISBN: 90-420-0155-0 Bound Hfl. 240,-/US-$ 133.-
ISBN: 90-420-0168-2 Paper Hfl. 60,-/US-$ 33.-

Volume 21: **FRANCISCUS JUNIUS F.F. AND HIS CIRCLE.** Ed. by Rolf H. Bremmer Jr. Amsterdam/Atlanta, GA 1998. XII,265 pp. with Ill. ISBN: 90-5183-585-X Bound Hfl. 120,-/US-$ 66.50

Volume 22: **ORIENTAL PROSPECTS: WESTERN LITERATURE AND THE LURE OF THE EAST.** Ed. by C.C. Barfoot and Theo D'haen. Amsterdam/Atlanta, GA 1998. VII, 283 pp.
ISBN: 90-420-0582-3 Bound Hfl. 150,-/US-$ 83.-
ISBN: 90-420-0572-6 Paper Hfl. 45,-/US-$ 25.-

Volume 23: **MODELLING THE INDIVIDUAL: BIOGRAPHY AND PORTRAIT IN THE RENAISSANCE.** With a Critical Edition of Petrarch's *Letter to Posterity*. Ed. by Karl Enenkel, Betsy de Jong-Crane and Peter Liebregts. Amsterdam/Atlanta, GA 1998. 301,VIII pp. 43 Ill.
ISBN: 90-420-0792-3 Bound Hfl. 150,-/US-$ 78.50
ISBN: 90-420-0782-6 Paper Hfl. 45,-/US-$ 23.50